Org. Mgmt. J. Marentette.

Irene Naested
Mount Royal College

Bernie Potvin
University of Calgary

Peter Waldron
Mount Royal College

Understanding the Landscape of Teaching

Toronto

National Library Cataloguing in Publication Data

Naested, Irene Mae
Understanding the landscape of teaching / Irene Naested, Bernie Potvin, Peter Waldron.

Includes bibliographical references and index.
ISBN 0-13-061919-1

1. Teaching. I. Potvin, Bernie L. (Bernie Lawrence), 1950– II. Waldron, Peter, 1939– III. Title.

LB1025.3.N23 2003 371.102 C2003-902533-0

ISBN 0-13-061919-1

Vice President, Editorial Director: Michael J. Young
Acquisitions Editor: Christine Cozens
Marketing Manager: Ryan St. Peters
Signing Representative: Rick Matthews
Developmental Editor: Martina van de Velde
Production Editor: Avivah Wargon
Copy Editor: Audrey Dorsch
Production Coordinator: Patricia Ciardullo
Page Layout: Carolyn E. Sebestyen
Art Director: Mary Opper
Interior Design: Anthony Leung
Cover Design: Anthony Leung
Cover Image: Getty Images

4 5 08 07 06 05

Printed and bound in Canada.

Contents

Part 6—Society, Culture, and Schooling

Preface

> Somehow, we who are teachers and inquirers, we who love children, have to try—with their help—to read the world as it presents itself to them. We realize that, for us as well as for the children, to live is to experience a situation in terms of its meanings; and the best we can do is try to uncover, to come clear.... No longer taking the stance of outside observer, or anatomist, or quantifier, we can engage with children in a quest for what is possible. We can beckon; we can urge; we can sustain them when they *break from anchorage*, so long as we are willing to break from anchorage ourselves. (Greene, 1986, p. 783, italics added)

Understanding the Landscape of Teaching is intended to help pre-service teachers begin to understand the educational universe. In this book, we provide opportunities for pre-service teachers to engage in conversation that is informed by current knowledge and professional wisdom. We invite them to challenge and question assumptions about learning, teaching, and schooling—to deepen their understanding as they embark on a journey toward becoming members of the teaching profession.

We understand teaching as a complex series of professionally defensible intentions enacted to facilitate learning. Teaching intentions are embodied in design and planning processes that translate theories, beliefs, and schemata about learning and teaching into practical strategies to engage and motivate learners.

Teaching is a flexible process that respects the uniqueness of learners and deliberately responds to individual learning needs

We understand schooling as a collective endeavour that moves beyond classroom-based learning and teaching. The central purpose of school is learning. It is appropriate to ask: What do young people learn from the ways a school responds to them as they go about life in a school? Hallways, school offices, lunchrooms, and playgrounds, for example, are learning environments. How does a school's approach to moral and ethical behaviour, democracy, recognition, and humanness, find a place in policy, organization, and use of time? What will young people learn from the years they spend attending school? It is the old axiom at work: the whole is considerably more than the sum of its parts. So too is a school considerably more than the sum of its classrooms, administrative spaces, and curriculum prescribed by governing authorities.

Six interconnected dimensions of this book work together to provide a foundation from which to engage in learning about learning, teaching, and schooling:

1) Assumptions: Clarifying the Old and Exposing the New
2) Case Studies and Stories: Vignettes of Life in School
3) Teaching Qualities: Fundamental Considerations for Learning and Teaching
4) Research and Practice: Information for Thought and Action
5) Knowledge: Essential Information for Professional Competence
6) Theory to Practice: Strategies and Ideas for Course or Group Facilitators

1) Assumptions: Clarifying the Old and Exposing the New

Our world is becoming an increasingly complex place. Teachers must keep up with the rapid pace of change and must understand this complexity in ways that will help young learners make sense of the world.

Those who answer the call to teach are faced with the task of guiding young learners towards becoming who they will become. This process of becoming is a "breaking from anchorage": a journey toward self-reliance and community, a journey on which teachers should invite, inspire, and accompany young learners.

Practising and pre-service teachers must also contend, however, with the restrictions of anchorage. Most pre-service teachers have already experienced twelve or thirteen years of "preparation" before they set foot in a post-secondary institution, and have accumulated many assumptions about how learning and teaching are "done" that significantly influence their worldviews, or perspectives. The worldviews of many practising teachers, too, have been influenced by long-established patterns in schooling, and teachers often accept their own worldviews without questioning them in any serious way. Such unquestioned assumptions about and approaches to learning and teaching might pose difficulties for those teachers, however, when they have to contend with challenges from current knowledge and research.

The difficulty is clear: practice is often driven by tacit assumptions—assumptions that are not questioned. These assumptions must be uncovered and made explicit. The challenge, then, is to create and nurture conditions of thoughtfulness in teachers, so that openness, ownership, trust, and risk-taking permeate conversations and debates about learning, teaching, and schooling. *Understanding the Landscape of Teaching* meets this challenge by helping the pre-service teacher to make informed, practical, and wise judgments about learning and teaching, to develop a predisposition toward thoughtfulness and reflection in the journey toward becoming a practising teacher.

2) Case Studies and Stories: Vignettes of Life in School

> Story...is an ancient and altogether human method. The human being alone among the creatures of the earth is a storytelling animal: sees the present rising out of the past, heading into a future; perceives reality in narrative form. (Novak, 1975, p. 175)

Human beings are storytellers. Whenever we are together, we combine stories and anecdotes to make conversation. On the basis of stories and events recounted, social occasions are enriched, emotions shared, plans made, misconceptions generated or clarified, and truth earned. Above all, understanding is achieved when the attendant conversations are informed and open. Stories and case studies can also be engaging. We tend to be interested in events from the lives of others, especially when those "others" are our peers, those with whom we share a common interest.

Stories and case studies drawn from the professional landscapes of practising teachers are used throughout this book. Discussion flows through the stories and case studies in ways that will engage and inform the reader. We use a process of narrative inquiry to help pre-service teachers clarify their assumptions and weave new understanding into their own worldview of learning, teaching, and schooling.

3) Teaching Qualities: Fundamental Considerations for Learning and Teaching

This book presents six qualities that we believe are useful as threads to bind the chapters together: relationships, thoughtfulness, diversity, integrity, authenticity, and knowledge. Using these six qualities, we promote an integrated view of knowledge, giving the pre-service teacher a non-prescriptive framework within which to think about and make meaning of learning, teaching, and schooling. This framework is not intended to be limiting; rather, it is a learning tool, designed to nurture an expansive and integrated worldview.

Chapter 1 provides details about each teaching quality in a way that is intended to be useful for pre-service teachers.

4) Research and Practice: Information for Thought and Action

All teachers have a professional and moral obligation to engage young people in learning that is grounded in the most current professional knowledge. This book presents research from empirical sources, in-action research expressed in case studies, and narrative research within the stories of practising teachers. We have included a variety of approaches throughout each chapter.

Learning theories are also modelled throughout the book. We place particular emphasis on "constructivist" approaches to learning, and encourage pre-service teachers to use their prior knowledge as a basis from which to challenge assumptions and explore new knowledge. We hope this approach will lead to an increased understanding of the art and science of learning, teaching, and schooling.

5) Knowledge: Essential Information for Professional Competence

"What knowledge is essential for teaching?" is a question frequently asked when we consider teacher preparation. Typically, this knowledge could include subject matter, pedagogical knowledge related to subjects, practice, the workings of local and provincial bureaucracies and school organizations, learning theories, teaching strategies, curriculum, child development, politics of education at all levels, conflict resolution, current professional research, and wisdom. Where does the list end?

The search for a comprehensive answer would entail broad strokes through many disciplines, but to help a person starting on the journey, we visit five commonplaces (Schwab, 1973) of professional knowledge. The commonplaces—

learners and learning; teachers and teaching; schools and classrooms; curriculum and subject matter; and culture, society, and history—serve as a framework for the book's chapters.

In Chapter 1 we provide substantive knowledge that encourages readers to understand what it means to be a teacher and facilitates their working with the processes of learning. Chapters 2 through 12 are intended to help readers to clarify their worldviews about learning, teaching, and schooling in light of prior and new knowledge and assumptions; current issues, theories, and research; and case studies and stories; as well as to make sense of field experience through theory and practice.

6) Theory to Practice: Strategies and Ideas for Course or Group Facilitators

The process of moving from theory and research to practice is ongoing. Scholars and practitioners are constantly presenting new theories and new research, so that the professional knowledge landscape—the interface between research and theory, and the classroom—must find teachers as permanent inhabitants. Most teachers struggle with theory-to-practice implementation, for various reasons. The pragmatism that is demanded of teachers often acts as an impediment. Teachers' daily lives in school are so full of immediate tasks and decisions that often it becomes difficult to find the time needed for reflection and contemplation. However, the transfer of theory and research into practice requires reflection and contemplation, especially in today's rapidly changing world. There is no magical solution. A disposition toward thoughtfulness is a prerequisite for any theory-and-research-into-practice process. The other requirement is that a teacher's day needs to include time for conversation, for sharing stories, and for exploring the teacher's professional knowledge landscape.

Understanding the Landscape of Teaching nurtures a predisposition toward thoughtfulness for pre-service teachers that we hope will become second nature when they finally enter the classroom. Toward this goal, the book uses a number of strategies and ideas that course or group facilitators should find useful: constructivist learning activities, questioning strategies, narrative inquiry ideas, symbolic interactionist techniques, case study analyses, debate topics, arts-related learning tools, and many other engaging ways of learning. Through these pedagogical practices, we hope pre-service teachers will be encouraged to challenge and clarify assumptions, work with new knowledge, and generally gain meaning, understanding, and insight into learning, teaching, and schooling during their journey toward becoming teachers.

Acknowledgments

We would like to thank Calgary Christian School, Milton Williams Creative Arts School, Ann Potvin, Judith Waldron, Jesper Naested, Martina van de Velde, and Avivah Wargon for their contributions to this project, as well as freelance editor and indexer Audrey Dorsch and proofreader Susan Adlam.

We also acknowledge the valuable feedback provided by the following reviewers: Lorraine Beaudin, University of Lethbridge; Deborah Berrill, Trent University; Mark Danby, Trent University; Benedicta Egbo, University of Windsor; Ruth Forsythe, University of New Brunswick; Bill Gadsby, University of Winnipeg; Joi Freed Garrod, University College of the Cariboo; Margaret McNay, University of Western Ontario; Kathy Sanford, University of Alberta; Lynn Thomas, Bishop's University; John Vaillancourt, Acadia University; and Patrick Walton, University College of the Cariboo.

Chapter 1

Becoming a Teacher

Never trust an experimental result until it has been proven by a theory.

—Sir Arthur Eddington

Chapter Focus

This chapter will help you understand what it means to be a teacher. You will be guided toward integrating ideas about teaching into your worldview. In inviting you to view teaching in an integrated way, we are asking you to recognize teaching for what it is, a complex, often ambiguous, and almost always thought-provoking activity. We invite you to understand teaching in a way that does not leave out anything important, a way in which all the significant aspects of teaching are included. It might be helpful to compare integrating ideas to putting together a jigsaw puzzle. All the pieces of the teaching puzzle are scattered out there in schools, books about teaching, teacher experiences, and, of course, in your personal experience. There are idea pieces about what constitutes good classrooms and schools, how to design and teach subject matter, what is the best and worst in society, who children really are, how they learn, and what the activity of teaching is really like. Your task in this chapter is to begin to put the pieces together in your mind, to integrate ideas into your worldview. Teaching is a complex activity. Despite this complexity, when there is integrity in your thinking about teaching, and when you think about teaching from a worldview perspective, we believe you can be an effective teacher.

Learning With Others

We will give you suggestions regarding **shared praxis** (Groome, 1981), which is a particular, but important, way of integrating knowledge about what teaching and learning mean and about how to be a teacher who can help people learn. Shared praxis means systematic, careful, and deliberate reflecting on the experiences that you and others have regarding teaching and learning. Only then, we believe, can you draw integrated conclusions about how to be a teacher that reflect wise, practical, and soundly ethical and moral decisions.

Integrating Pieces of the Puzzle

In this chapter we intend to help you identify and make sense of the major professional and personal influences on a teacher. These influences are learners and learning; teachers and teaching; schools and classrooms; curriculum and subject matter; and culture, society and history. Probably you already have a number of important, well-earned assumptions about these influences. We invite you to begin deepening and broadening your understanding of teaching by reconsidering many of your assumptions. We will pour meaning into all your assumptions, asking you to consider research, stories, and the experiences of others, and how they call into question or affirm or disaffirm your assumptions.

In this chapter you will begin systematic, careful, and deliberate reflection on your own experiences. In each chapter we will present some relevant ideas, stories, and experiences of experienced educators intended to guide you toward an integrated view of teaching and toward choosing a wise, practical, ethical, and moral way of being a teacher.

This chapter introduces the way the entire book is organized. It introduces focus questions, teaching illustrations from the real world of classrooms, theory, research findings, key terms, and tasks called "For Your Consideration," all intended to guide you to develop an integrated worldview that understands teaching.

Focus Questions

1. What is a worldview and what does a worldview mean for a teacher's effectiveness? What is the importance of a worldview approach to understanding teaching, learning, and schooling?
2. What are the roles of integration, schemata, and praxis in developing one's world-view?
3. How would a shared praxis approach influence teaching, learning, and schooling?
4. Why does a teacher's worldview need to be integrated?
5. How does a teacher make decisions regarding teaching? What are the influences of the five commonplaces of teaching on teacher decision making?
6. What does it mean to integrate your philosophy of teaching by combining insights drawn from each of the five commonplaces of teaching?
7. How might teachers approach the development of their worldviews through a shared-praxis approach to coming to insight regarding teaching and learning?

Integrating and Understanding Teaching

It is a story that has been told many times (Curtis, 1996). Four blind men chance upon an elephant. One man finds the trunk and, after touching it, concludes that elephants are like water hoses. A second man finds the tail and concludes that elephants are like brooms. A third man touches one of the elephant's legs and concludes that elephants are like telephone poles. The fourth man touches the elephant's side and concludes that elephants are like walls. Each man comes to a logical conclusion from his experience. Yet each man is wrong because he does not combine his experience with those of the other blind men. They do not integrate their conclusions. As a result, they do not have a complete and accurate picture of an elephant.

Recognizing the Influence of a Teacher's Worldview

> I've had a lot of bad experiences in my life, and some of them actually happened.
>
> —Mark Twain

The problem was not with the elephant. The problem was with the assumptions the men initially held and continued to hold despite their experience with the elephant. Perhaps in the same way, the problems that teachers encounter in teaching may not result from teaching, children, subject matter, schools, or society. The problem may be with the teacher's **worldview,** that mental model, that inner representation of the outer world, which is composed of the theories, beliefs, and assumptions about the big issues of life. A worldview is most influential in what teachers understand when they see children (brats or human beings), teaching (job or profession; work or calling), curriculum and subject matter (to be covered or to be constructed and discovered), and society (going to hell in a hurry or a beautiful place).

Teachers who are like the blind men might benefit from talking with the stakeholders in education—parents, teachers, school boards, professional associations, departments of education, and learners—people who have a legitimate interest in teaching, teachers, and public schools. These stakeholders would be able to warn them about what happens when people do not integrate their views of things. Unfortunately, the blind men were left to their own fragmented and partial view of elephants. Their initial assumptions, left unchallenged and unchanged, became the fences in the worldview that kept new and truthful ideas out.

Using a Worldview Approach to Understand Teaching

To understand the concept of worldview and how one's worldview influences one's teaching, we first need to understand three related concepts: integrated knowledge, schemata and shared praxis.

Integrated Knowledge

To **integrate** means to combine different ideas into one whole, non-fragmented, and coherent idea. It means that a person draws together all the facts about something, such as teaching, into an idea that makes sense. When ideas are integrated, a person can choose a deliberate, reflective, ethical response regarding a phenomenon such as teaching. **Integrated knowledge,** the combined knowledge from more than one source, is the key to understanding teaching. To have integrated knowledge about teaching means to weave into your worldview the needs and interests of teachers, learners, curriculum and subject matter, schools, classrooms, society, culture and history. Developing an integrated view of teaching will help you put together the puzzle of what it means to be an effective teacher. An integrated set of ideas about teaching will help you recognize more accurately what is really happening in classrooms with children. Integrated ideas will assist you when working with parents, administrators, and colleagues because you will have considered ahead of time, and woven into your own worldview, their interests, needs, and ideas.

Schemata

An integrated view of teaching means that you have schemata that are thoughtful and truthful. That word **schemata** (plural) can be thought of as self-organized clusters of particular information, attitudes, and possible behaviours about a concept. Your teaching schema (singular) is that cluster of information, attitudes, and possible behaviours related to teaching, organized in the mental file folder marked "teaching." We hope that after you read this book, when someone says "teaching," you will open that mental file folder and find that what is in there is integrated. The information about teachers will be sensibly integrated with schemata about learners, teachers, schools and classrooms, curriculum, and subject matter. Your teaching schema will have been threaded together by your understanding of the shared place of each stakeholder in education and in your teaching. You will know their respective vested interests in teaching and how their

1.1 FOR YOUR CONSIDERATION

People acquire knowledge in five main ways: intuition, logic, experience, empirical/research, and revealed truth. How a person thinks about learners, teachers, schools, curriculum and subject matter, and society and culture depends on one's preferred way of acquiring the knowledge on which one's thinking is based.

1. Do you agree? Does it matter how a person comes to know about teaching?
2. Why is it preferable to think about children, let's say, using all five ways of knowing combined rather than just one way?

interests can be aligned with your interests. Your schema will have been formed through deliberate consideration to developing **teaching qualities** for effective teaching—qualities such as knowledge, thoughtfulness, diversity, authenticity, integrity, and relationships. Finally, your schema will have been put together as you examine, deliberately and intentionally, the commonplaces of teaching that influence the teacher's role.

Shared Praxis

The third concept to understand, as you develop a "worldview understanding" of teaching, is **shared praxis** (Groome, 1981). As you deliberately think about the specific interests of each commonplace, and integrate their interests into your teaching practice, you are engaging in praxis. When you share your reflections with practising teachers, principals, and professors, that praxis is shared reflection. This book helps you develop, through shared praxis, an integrated view of teaching, a thoughtful and truthful schemata that will make up your worldview.

To develop an integrated worldview, you will need to think in ways we believe are rarely asked of teachers in pre-service education. We hope that you will uncover the assumptions you already have regarding teaching and the five commonplaces, and will be prepared to engage in a *shared praxis* with your professor, your classmates, and your partner teachers and principals in the schools where you do your field experience. We invite you to identify, with your colleagues, what it is you actually do and why, regarding each aspect of teaching: what you do and why when you teach at your summer camp class or coach your community basketball team, and how you care for those with whom you work in your part-time job.

Be prepared to go even deeper than identifying your behaviours. We will guide you to uncover the theories, assumptions, and beliefs that give rise to that behaviour. Once both your assumptions and behaviours have been identified, we invite you to let the stories, research, assumptions, and experiences of others inform and, if necessary, call into question your behaviour and its assumptions. You should also be prepared to let your behaviours and assumptions affirm and, if necessary, disaffirm the research, assumptions, stories, and beliefs of others.

As you hear others' stories and others' hopes of the way they would like teaching to be, you will be invited to ask questions, inquiring into each story as to what insights are there. **Narrative inquiry** means reading and inquiring into a story for what insight it provides. Narrative inquiry characterizes this book. We believe that narrative inquiry may become for you a main way of deepening and broadening your understanding of teaching.

Finally, by the end of this book, we hope you will begin to choose a deliberate, reflective way of being a teacher. This choice begins with choosing a personally relevant worldview and a practice that will take you on to the next learning experience of what it means to be a teacher. This is a shared praxis way of becoming a teacher.

Narrative inquiry is used to deepen and broaden understanding.

First Steps Toward Integrated Knowledge about Teaching

The first steps toward integrated knowledge about teaching include identifying and challenging your assumptions about teaching. Your worldview is made up of your assumptions and understandings about the essential nature of the world, which directly affect the degree to which you are able to make sense of your world. When they are left too long unchallenged, they are like walls a previous owner put up around a property. You might accept the wall but are not sure why it was put up in the first place. At the same time, if you take down a wall, before doing so it is good to ask why the wall was put up in the first place. We invite you to uncover old assumptions and understandings and then develop new ones. In the next section, we guide you on your first steps toward integrating your knowledge about teaching. We begin by examining the different ways teachers organize their knowledge about teaching.

Propositional Statements

How a person acquires knowledge affects a person's understanding of things. Eat all your meals at McDonalds, and you might understand fine dining to necessarily include Big Macs. If you teach only younger children, you might be hard pressed to understand how older children typically think and behave. People's knowledge of things ranges from simple to complex. It might be helpful for you to think about this range of **declarative knowledge** (an idea or concept that corresponds to the real thing) as a "food chain" of knowledge representations. People internally represent the external world in an increasingly complex, integrated way.

Propositional knowledge is the simplest knowledge representation. A proposition is a simple noun-verb relationship, such as "People eat food." In their language and behaviour, people present these forms of knowledge as "gists," or the essence of the thing. Teachers might comment that "teaching is hard work," or that "children are all different." Propositional knowledge can result in fairly simple and sweeping ways of behaving. Sometimes, this type of knowledge is called **macro-propositional** (Pressley, 1995). It would be simple and easy to behave toward the world of teaching in macropropositional ways. Have you ever heard someone say, "All children love to play?" That is an easy and quick way to represent the complexity of the external world of young people. Have you ever heard anyone say, "Teenagers are all sexually active?" That again, is an easy and quick way to represent the complexity of the world of adolescents and could lead to a simple and sweeping way of responding. Teaching, however, is more complex than what any proposition can handle.

Scripts

Scripts are a more complex knowledge representation in the food chain of knowledge representations (Pressley, 1995). These sequentially specify the steps to take in particular situations, such as ordering food from McDonalds. The script is clear and well-known. Stand in line, wait your turn, approach the till, place your order, pay, wait for your food, and so on. You might be tempted to want to learn a "script" for being teacher. Unfortunately, teaching is far more complex than what a script might be able to handle.

Concepts

Concepts are more complex knowledge representations than scripts. A concept is like a set of rules that a person uses to determine what something means and where it fits in a person's understanding (Pressley, 1995). For example, if something has four legs, is furry, and meows, it is a cat. If a place that sells food looks like a McDonalds, it is likely that ordering food takes place in a certain way. If someone is physically smaller than an adult, enjoys games, and needs adult care, that someone is a child. Accurate concepts are helpful for teachers. However, conceptual knowledge alone is not sufficient for teachers to have integrated knowledge and to become effective teachers.

Schemata

A more complex and integrated form of knowledge is a schema. A **schema** is a cluster of knowledge, attitudes, and proposed behaviour around a concept. (*Schemata* is the plural of *schema*.) For example, within one's "eating schema" are the eating behaviours, eating attitudes, and knowledge about food that characterize that person. Do you know any health-food zealots? That particular way of thinking about eating includes that person's attitude toward both junk food and good food, and that person's attitude and behaviour toward people who eat those foods. Teaching schema are helpful to teachers because they include concepts, scripts, and propositions, but also include attitudes and behaviours that ensure effective teaching.

Before we discuss the more complex knowledge representation, worldviews, we need to consider the profound ways that schemata, the building blocks of worldviews, affect our ability to think about teaching, learning, and schools.

1.2 FOR YOUR CONSIDERATION

1. Draw a picture of a clock face. Put the numbers on the clock face, using roman numerals. Did you put IV for four o'clock? If you did, you were resorting to your "Roman numeral" schema. In fact, if you were to look at a clock face that uses roman numerals, you would see that all clocks use IIII and not IV. Your ability to think about clocks accurately was impaired, influenced more by your schema than by what Roman numeral clocks actually look like.
2. Think back a few years to your earlier school experience. Put a face and name together, if you can, as you do this activity. Think of a boy or girl in your elementary school who caused problems for teachers and students. Do you think that child turned out okay? If your first response was no, were you influenced to conclude that by your "what happens to bad kids" schema, or by another, more hopeful schema? For example, "There is hope for everyone," "People can be late bloomers," "If a child is loved, anything good can happen."

Worldviews

By far the most complex knowledge representation is worldview. We believe that teaching should be considered from the perspective of worldview because teaching is a complex activity, an ethical and moral way of being, one in which human beings and their well-being are at stake. Teaching deserves to be considered in the broadest and most profound ways possible. When worldviews are fragmented, and knowledge about the commonplaces of teaching is not integrated, teaching will be ineffective. When teaching is thought about only in terms of propositions, scripts, concepts, and schema, teaching is not well understood.

The Implications of Integrated Knowledge

A non-education professor once remarked that he couldn't understand why it took four or more years to prepare elementary school teachers because after all, he said, elementary school teaching isn't rocket science. He was right, of course. Elementary school teaching is far more complex and perhaps more demanding. The professor was speaking from a single perspective, the small, teaching worldview of a post-secondary professor, one whose teaching has consisted only of lecturing. He understands only one aspect of teaching. He does not have an integrated worldview of teaching. He is like the fisherman in an often-told story who fished in the ocean for fifty years with a net that had two-by-two-centimetre mesh. At his retirement party he stood up in front of the crowd, and with the certainty of fifty years of successful fishing behind him, stated emphatically that he knew, beyond a shadow of a doubt, that there were no fish in the ocean smaller than two by two centimetres. The net of our worldview can let all kinds of important and true ideas about teaching slip through.

A worldview provides a person with an inner representation of the world, one that spells out the answers to the big questions of life. What is most important? What is the role of human beings in history? What is most worth knowing? It is worldview that ultimately gives rise to, and most profoundly influences, a person's procedural knowledge—how to treat diversity in a classroom, for example, or how to engage in thoughtful reflection about a teaching problem. It is worldview that most profoundly influences a teacher's most important knowledge: knowledge about who children "really" are or what kind of relationship a teacher should develop with a child.

When a worldview is not integrated, when it consists of one or two perspectives only, it is like the fisherman's net. It is the premise of this book that to become an effective educator, one must have a view of teaching that is integrated.

1.3 FOR YOUR CONSIDERATION

Think of a teacher whose worldview consists of the following outlooks:

Life is hard; then you die.

When it comes to life, no one gets out of it alive, so eat, drink and be merry.

1. How might those influence the teacher's relationship with learners?
2. Is hope necessary to be a good teacher?

Five Commonplaces of Teaching

To develop an integrated worldview regarding teaching, learning, and schooling, you will need to understand the five greatest influences in a teacher's work: learners and learning; teachers and teaching; schools and classrooms; curriculum and subject matter; and culture, society and history. It is toward an understanding of the five **commonplaces** and how you can integrate these into your understanding of teaching that we now go.

The notion of teaching "commonplaces" was introduced into the teaching field nearly twenty years ago and was evident in the writing of curriculum theorists like Joseph Schwab (1973). We believe it is a useful way for you to deepen and broaden your understanding of teachers, teaching, and schools, because the notion of commonplaces reminds us all that teaching is a practical, social, and complex activity. Theory alone, we believe, is of limited value in helping us understand teaching.

Theory, the plausible explanation for the way things work, might be helpful in understanding black holes in the universe or why birds migrate, but theory alone is not helpful in understanding teaching. A theory is a concept, and, as we discussed earlier, concepts can be limited in helping you become an effective teacher. Shared praxis is more helpful than theory.

It is also helpful to know **domain-specific procedural knowledge** (Pressley and McCormick, 1995), which is particular teaching skills wisely applied through judgments made about particular situations. Procedural knowledge develops over time, through reflecting with others, deliberately and systematically, on experiences. These experiences are often revealed in teachers' stories, in the language teachers use to tell their stories. We encourage you to listen closely to what teachers tell you about teaching.

Teachers do not work outside a social setting. You will hear teachers tell you this in their stories. Teacher's judgments about particular situations are influenced by principals, departments of learning, school boards, professional associations, parents, and by societal and cultural phenomenon such as media, violence, and family breakdown. Two very important issues to consider as you move toward developing an integrated worldview of teaching are

1. What influences do the commonplaces have on what it is like to be a teacher?
2. How might a teacher deliberately and reflectively make decisions regarding teaching through integrating the interests of each of the five commonplaces of education? How might a teacher make wise judgments about particular situations without compromising his or her own teaching worldview?

Learners and Learning

Learning is a profoundly complex activity. To understand learning and to teach with integrity means that you will need to understand the needs of children and youth, their developmental, psychological, and spiritual needs. You might not have expected that you will need to facilitate learning, guiding young people to be thoughtful, self-reliant, and self-directing, to be able to take risks, ask questions, and have real ownership over their learning. This is easier to write about than to do. Understanding learners and learning will be central to this book. We hope to convince you that understanding learning is central to your integrated understanding of what it means to be a teacher.

Teachers and Teaching

A lot more learning happens in a classroom than children learning to read, write, and do arithmetic. A look into classrooms may not reveal that right away. Reflection on your life and what teachers meant to you might be a better source of information regarding what else happens as a result of teachers and teaching.

Who has made an impact in your life? If you were to list ten people who were influential in your life, we suspect that a teacher would make the list. Why? What was it about that teacher that made a difference? We will look closely at your teachers who made a difference, the characteristics of great teachers, what those great teachers knew and did in order to be effective. For a hint of what is to come in Chapter 7, we invite you to look at For Your Consideration 1.4, below.

1.4 FOR YOUR CONSIDERATION

When you think of great teachers, even good teachers, what picture comes to mind? What does that great or good teacher look like? Make a list of these characteristics.

1. Did the list you create have more skills in it than attributes?
2. Did great teachers do something better than less great teachers, or were they better people than less great teachers? What was it about them that made a difference?

We suspect that your list contained words such as caring, enthusiasm, interesting, and respectful more than terms such as scholar, great teaching technique, or knowledge of physics. Not that we think a teacher shouldn't be these things too. It is evident that teachers who make a difference have some characteristics that are special.

You will not be a nobody when you become a teacher. Before you dismiss too quickly the significance you might one day have as a teacher, consider the following. Who taught today's great world leaders such as Nelson Mandela (South Africa) and Vaclav Havel (Czech Republic), and inspired their courage and motivated them to a life of public service and creative expression? Who influenced Mother Teresa at a particular point in her life to think about a life of service to the poor? Who was influential in creating the passion for music that drove the great musicians, the love of art to lift us up out of the daily drudgery. Who were those "nameless, anonymous people"? We might never know, but there were teachers in every life.

We believe that you can be a shaper of hopes and dreams, that you can ignite passion and insight. You can build or defeat a young person's hope in a better world. You can fill minds and hearts with love for what is best in the human situation, practices of love, hope, and justice.

Schools and Classrooms

We invite you to see schools and classrooms from the perspective of other stakeholders, from the point of view of teachers, parents, society, and administrators. It might surprise you when we suggest that it is a myth that schools are just for learners and learning. Schools are for teachers, too. They are places where teaching careers are built, relationships are formed, skills are developed, and personal growth is experienced.

We will explore a number of other myths. We will look carefully at how schools are organized and governed, and how important it is that individuals who govern schools use leadership styles that are moral, civil, participatory, and empowering. You might have assumed otherwise. If you did, you are not alone. Many young teachers are surprised to learn that leadership and governance in schools involve more than just setting timetables and holding assemblies.

We invite you to look at classrooms from a different perspective, as well. We will pose some important and thought-provoking questions. For example, we will ask you to consider whether other settings than a classroom might be preferable for learning. We will ask you to consider how classrooms could be better connected to the school culture and the goals of the school.

1.5 FOR YOUR CONSIDERATION

What was your favourite school subject? Consider the reasons you chose that subject. If you said gym class, why did you call it "gym class" and not "physical education"? If you said science class, was science taught primarily in a classroom? Outside?

Curriculum and Subject Matter

Curriculum is about all that a learner learns in school. It includes programs of study, subject guides, and school-specific policy decisions that affect the ways of working and general conduct of a school. Curriculum includes the goals of schooling, the outcomes intended or unintended, and all the experiences a learner has in school. The word *curriculum* comes from the Latin word *currere*, which means to run a course. Curriculum is very complex.

Many educators have raised the question, What do children really learn in school? When children come home from school and are asked what they learned, they may reply, "Nothing." Perhaps they should really be saying that they learned how to give teachers the answers they want rather than what they think is true. They learned how to be safe and quiet. They learned that other people can be mean if they want to, and they learned how to camouflage feelings of rejection and pain. They learned how easy it is to be bored, but learned how to hide boredom.

The **planned curriculum** is about what is intended that children learn in schools, the courses of study, the intended learning outcomes, and the teacher strategies.

The curriculum of a school includes the **null curriculum.** The null curriculum concerns what is not taught, perhaps about important issues such as death, sex, and love. The null curriculum is learned through what is not intentionally presented to learners.

1.6 FOR YOUR CONSIDERATION

1. What were the most important lessons you learned at school? How did you learn those lessons?
2. What did schools not teach you that you now are convinced they needed to?

We will look closely at the topic of curriculum later in this book. We will analyze what we mean by curriculum, how curriculum is developed, implemented, and assessed. We will look at various approaches for implementing curriculum, including on-line learning and other forms of distance education delivery.

The other piece of this commonplace is subject matter. Subject matter in schools is organized according to the logic inherent in the subject matter and to what learners may be developmentally able to handle. Science, for example, lends itself to inquiry, therefore the subject matter of science in modern schools is inquiry-based and often hands-on. Learners in elementary schools can understand scientific concepts in very concrete terms. Learners in high school may be able to understand scientific concepts in more abstract terms. Your choice of subjects to teach may depend on your passion for a subject and your expertise developed in the subject matter. Physical education teachers, for example, often have a great deal of sport experience before attending teacher education programs.

Assessment, evaluation, measurement, and reporting are vast fields of study in education and are critical components to your profession.

Culture, Society, and History

We invite you to think about another commonplace, Canadian culture—the values, ideologies, and competing worldviews evident in Canadian history and society—that influence what it means to be a teacher in Canada. For now, we will give you a small illustration. The following are two debates that teachers can find themselves drawn into. We present these for you to initiate discussion with your classmates, professors, and partner teachers. Embedded in both stories are many cultural and ideological assumptions and understandings about what is most important to learn, whose interests are being served by education, and what is the role and place of religion in schools.

> Students at Lakeview Elementary School won't be dressing up as witches or ghosts this year. In fact, they won't be dressing up at all. Paper witches on broomsticks no longer adorn classroom bulletin boards and windows. Complaints from various religious groups say the holiday is linked with the devil and several school violence situations have led many schools to tone down the Halloween celebration and replace them with neutral "fall festivals." The contemporary celebration of Halloween has its roots in Samhain, the Celtic harvest festival and New Year. On this day, the Celts believed the souls of those who died would wander and enter the land of the dead. ("U.S. Schools," 2000)

Students at Upper Gulch school will not celebrate Christmas this year. As a result of special interest groups, any reference to Jesus, Mary, and Joseph or to the traditional Christmas story will be removed from the school's December program. This decision was made despite the fact that most parents in the school either wanted the Christmas story told, primarily because it is a traditional part of their culture, or could not care less what happens at Christmas. The argument of the interest-group members was that public school should be neutral and should not be a place where people's beliefs are presented.

1.7 FOR YOUR CONSIDERATION

1. What do the stories reveal regarding contemporary culture? Is a resolution possible in each story?
2. What assumptions, beliefs, and theories does each story reveal?
3. How can a teacher be neutral?
4. Is there a way to be a value-filled teacher and not offend religiously?

There are many other important issues to consider, including poverty, gender, race, and the media and their influence in schools and children's lives. The issues of society are not simple. Someone once remarked that the more complex the issue, the more people settle for simple answers. We will try not to do that in these chapters. Instead, whether we are discussing parenting, the rise in alternative schools, the social and economic struggles of cities, or the politicization of schooling, we will try to help you develop an integrated view, a worldview that will help you become the professional educator you want to become.

Creating Conditions for Insight

The one activity that most characterizes a teacher's role is creating conditions that promote learning. The more effective you become in creating conditions that promote learning, the more joyful and fulfilling will be your work as a teacher.

Stuart and Thurlow (2000) claim that pre-service teachers tend to be relatively passive in their student roles. They are reluctant to challenge the status quo after twelve or so years in classrooms as a student. "They have internalized, through an apprenticeship of observation, many of the values, beliefs, and practices of their teachers" (p. 114). Although pre-service teachers' beliefs and assumptions about teaching and learning are well-established, they are frequently simplified as well as unarticulated. If pre-service teachers do not uncover their beliefs and assumptions, examine them, and consider new understandings, "they will perpetuate current practices and the status quo will be maintained. This is unacceptable given that the student population has dramatically changed and many of the beliefs teachers and children hold are counterproductive to the teaching/learning process. As pre-service teachers begin their careers, they will be in a position to break this cycle" (p. 119).

According to Finders and Rose (1999), "to best prepare the prospective teacher, a teacher education program must provide teaching experiences and tools for reflection on that experience. In order not to reinforce simplistic views of teaching, we must also provide opportunities to help students gain understandings of the complexities of classroom contexts" (p. 205).

Following are descriptions of some of methods we recommend that you engage in to uncover and articulate your assumptions of learning, school, and schooling. We hope that through the various processes you will affirm or disaffirm previous thoughts, beliefs, and assumptions on the topic under consideration and connect new theories of teaching, learning, and schooling.

Critical Reflection

The beliefs one holds about schooling are formed early; they tend to reflect traditional educational experiences, and they continue until they are reflected on critically which, according to Yost, Sentner, and Forlenza-Bailey (2000) is the highest level of reflectivity. Dewey (1916) felt that the "vision of teacher education postulated the development of future teachers empowered to improve upon the conditions of schools. The teacher quality Dewey believed most important is critical reflection" (Yost et al., 2000).

Reflection is an active, persistent, and careful consideration of any belief or supposed form of knowledge in light of the grounds supporting it. Reflection implies that something is believed or disbelieved because of evidence, proof, or grounds for that belief. The higher thought process involved in critical reflection involves "reflection on the assumptions underlying a decision or act and on the broader ethical, moral, political, and historical implications behind the decision or act" (Yost et al., 2000, p. 41). A reflective teacher is one who makes decisions on the basis of a conscious awareness and careful consideration of the assumptions on which the decisions are based, and the technical, educational, and ethical consequences of those decisions. We hope that you will practice critical reflection on your journey into the professional landscape of teaching. When you encounter a For Your Consideration section, please take time to consider the questions, discussions, reflections, surveys, or other tasks. This process is intended to assist you in developing your understanding of the teaching qualities and commonplaces.

Situated Performances

Finders and Rose (1999) wanted to teach reflective practice to pre-service teachers who had much experience as students and little experience as teachers. They conceived situated performance as a postmodern version of role-play.

Situated performances are role-playing activities in which the learners participate by assuming specific subject positions, where the performed actions, motives, and circumstances are subject to critical reflection. Vignettes contextualize teaching that freezes a moment in time in order to examine the options.

Situated performances view the classroom as a scene from a play where the participants are assigned roles. The scene is not highly scripted. Roles are given, and improvisation becomes the key. These performances enable pre-service teachers to imagine a variety of ways to respond to particular learning, teaching and classroom situations, define a problem, explore, examine and apply (Finders & Rose, 1999).

Co-operative and Collaborative Learning

Social constructionists such as Vygotsky (1987) assume that knowledge is socially constructed, that learning occurs among persons rather than between a person and a thing. The issues facing education today hinge on social relations, not cognitive ones, and knowledge involves people's assimilation into communities of knowledgeable peers. "Liberal education today must be regarded as a process of leaving one community of knowledgeable peers and joining another" (Bruffee, Palmer, Gullette, and Gillespie, 1994, p. 40). Therefore according to the social constructionists, the more a pre-service teacher discusses issues and observations, the better prepared he or she will be to enter the professional landscape of teaching.

Co-operative learning is a learner-centred instructional process in which small, selected groups of three to five individuals work together on a well-defined learning task for the purpose of increasing mastery and or understanding of course content (Karre, 1994). According to Graves (1991), "academic controversy can be constructive and useful when the parties involved conduct a dialogue with the goal of understanding each other and arriving at a synthesis that takes all points of view into consideration" (p. 77). To be meaningful, co-operative learning requires listening carefully to each member in the group. Co-operative learning groups provide an immediate forum to talk through ideas and promote understanding through consultation. Members gain a diversity of perspectives and assist in the building of reflection, ownership, and relevance of information and ideas. Co-operative groups can be formed and used many ways. They include informal groups, brainstorming groups, response discussion groups, representative groups, master-learning groups, jigsaw strategies, and fishbowls. Guidelines for each must be followed for group learning to work. This includes both accountability as an individual and as a group. We hope you will collaborate with your peers and discuss the issues, stories, vignettes, and research found in this text.

Discussion and Debate

Brookfield and Preskill (1999) describe discussion as being more serious than conversation. Discussion requires participants to be mutually responsive to different views expressed and is primarily concerned with the development of knowledge, understanding, or judgment among those taking part. The purpose of the discussion should be to help participants reach a more critically informed understanding about the topic under consideration, to enhance participants' self-awareness and capacity for self-critique, to foster an appreciation among participants for the diversity of opinion that invariably emerges when viewpoints are exchanged openly and honestly, and to act as a catalyst to help people take informed action in the world (pp. 6–7). However, the main prerequisite for good discussion is that the participants be fully informed on the topic under consideration (p. 43). Therefore, the discussion participants need to have read or have access to relevant materials.

Materials presenting alternative perspectives need to be reviewed in advance. "Participating in discussion involves exposing oneself to a variety of alternative ideas and perspectives" (Brookfield & Preskill 1999, p. 47). We will provide relevant, topical information from alternative philosophies and pose questions for discussion and debate.

Jigsaw Strategy

In a jigsaw strategy, or representative groups of co-operative learning, participants are assigned to groups. Each group must have the same number of members. Each member of the group is assigned a subtopic to represent, investigate, or read about. They then meet with the members who explored the same subtopics in the other groups. They become a new group to discuss their subtopic. Following this discussion the team members go back to their original groups and share what they have discussed or learned in their subtopic groups.

Master-Learning

Master-learning, or expert, groups are similar to the jigsaw strategy. Here participants are given a topic or sub-topic to research and study. They then share their research and understanding with the members of their co-operative group.

Fishbowl

In a fishbowl discussion participants are divided into two groups that sit in a circle. The inner-circle group members are the observed and the outer-circle group members are the observers. The inner-circle members are assigned a topic to discuss while the outer-circle members observe and later give positive feedback or else feedback that is supported by concrete descriptors. The groups then change places and roles. This form of co-operative learning is helpful in enhancing individual and group observational and discussion skills (Barlow, Blythe, & Edmonds, 1999).

Brainstorming

Brainstorming is a useful way of generating a large number of alternative ideas for discussion and evaluation. It begins with the posing of an open-ended question. Members in a group work to generate and record a list of alternative ideas. Guidelines for brainstorming include the following: do no evaluation of ideas until after the brainstorming; consider the quantity of ideas as more important than quality; expand on others' ideas; and record all ideas. We will present various topics and issues that will require you to use this brainstorming technique to gain greater understanding or expose assumptions.

Mind-Mapping and Concept Mapping

"Inspiration is profoundly linked to memory" (Grudin 1990, p. 19). **Mind-mapping,** or concept mapping, is a technique to "link memory" for the learners by representing thoughts with pictures and colours. Mind, concept, or "knowledge maps are two-dimensional node-link networks that interrelate important concepts" (O'Donnell, 1994, p. 9). Mapping can be done by an individual or in small groups. The map is generally started in the centre of a page and is created as the learner reads, listens to a presentation, or watches a video. The act forces the learner to organize ideas and consider relationships between the ideas presented. Mapping can also be used to plan a lesson, presentation or story. The use of colour and symbols helps one to organize and make meaning of the idea under investigation and serves as an aid to memory. According to Margulies (1995), one does not have to be a great artist to draw symbols for mind-maps. It requires the creator to become a "visual thinker," and the more one creates mind-maps the better one will be at it. We invite you to use mind-maps while reading the chapters. Develop your own symbols and choose your own colours for the teaching qualities that are presented in Chapter 2.

Questioning

Students and teachers ask questions; it is traditionally their stock in trade. Professional journals and textbooks tend to assume that questioning is a popular means of instruction, but few people believe that the questions teachers ask are the best questions—questions that go beyond simple recall or rote memory. Only thought-provoking questions can elicit thoughtful responses. The ability to ask this type of question is not inborn but can be learned. Bloom (1982) developed a taxonomy of higher-order questioning from recall of knowledge to application, analysis, synthesis, and evaluation. These five levels of questions have key verbs and can initiate learning processes and products. It is our intention to assist the pre-service teachers in a study of questioning patterns, practice in composing questions, and analysis of the responses the questions evoke.

How would you describe the learning taking place in each of these classrooms?

Narrative Inquiry, Case Studies, and Autobiographies

"Telling and writing stories have been identified as powerful ways for helping pre-service teachers understand how their world works." (Hunter & Hatton, 1998, p. 235) Narrative is sometimes called "poetic social science," the integration of anthropology and literature, which is one form of ethnography. Narrative inquiry in education, primarily used for research and professional development, has become a vehicle for pre-service teacher development (Conle, 2000). The purpose of self-narratives, according to Bochner (2000), "is to extract meaning from experience rather than to depict experience exactly as it was lived ... to grasp or seize the possibilities of meaning" (p. 268).

Cases are narrative accounts and the field of teaching is essentially about a body of cases. Hunter and Hatton (1998) consider case writing to be an invaluable methodology that will help pre-service teachers and educators capture the complexity of practice and reflect on practice. Actual stories from pre-service teachers are seen as essential ingredients for professional preparation—serious learning and reflective tools (p. 236) that can focus attention on "the pedagogical moment," exposing its complexity, uncertainty, success, and failure, and provide a context for making meaning of school situations.

We suggest that during field experiences you capture a specific pedagogical moment related to a specific commonplace or teaching quality. Autobiographies are different from case studies in that they are stories written by individuals regarding their impressions of themselves as learners and teachers (D. Brown, 1999) and reflections on personal knowledge and history.

There is a human need for story as fundamental as the need for food and water. "Storytelling (including narrative song) was the principle medium for passing on a culture's knowledge and traditions" (Carroll, 1997, p. 1). Stories can create an emotional environment resulting in deeper meaning and understanding of an idea or issue. We hope our stories create "emotional environments" for you.

Reflection and Perspective on the Chapter

Teaching is a profoundly complex yet ethical and moral activity. Teaching involves decision making of the highest order, decisions that must be made with consideration to the influences that are common to teaching.

The task you will face as a teacher is indeed challenging. Your role will include creating conditions that promote learning, while aligning your teaching to the requirements and needs of others who have an interest in what happens in your classroom. The more knowledgeable and competent you become about creating those conditions, the more effective and joyful your teaching will become.

Key Terms

cases 19
commonplaces of teaching 9
concept 7
co-operative learning 16
curriculum 12
declarative knowledge 6
domain-specific procedural knowledge 10
integrate 4
integrated knowledge 4
macro-propositional (knowledge) 7
mind-mapping 18
narrative inquiry 5
null curriculum 12
planned curriculum 12
propositional knowledge 6
reflection 15
schemata 4
scripts 7
shared praxis 5
situated performance 16
teaching qualities 5
worldview 3

Suggested Further Reading

Groome, Thomas. (1981). Some philosophical roots for praxis as a way of knowing are found in Chapter 8 of *Christian Religious Education*. San Francisco: Harper and Row. Providing a brief overview of the historical source of the word *praxis*, this chapter is a good introduction to a term that has been misused yet remains important and applicable in the Canadian classroom.

Chapter 2

Teaching Qualities

Chapter Focus

Teachers live in a complex universe. The professional teacher must visit many disciplines daily as the profession is practised. This complex array of knowledge may be vexing for those who are commencing professional studies. As one begins to engage in learning about the teaching profession there is, perhaps, a need for some frameworks, some benign structures, to provide guidance, reassurance, and utility, a need for something on which to "hang your hat" that will help make sense of this professional universe. Six teaching qualities serve in this capacity throughout the book. You will find that teachers consider and apply these qualities in the course of their practice. Figure 2.1 presents the six qualities in visual format to illustrate how they are interconnected, providing a framework for a complex matter.

The qualities are not exclusive, but they are considered to be fundamental to reflection and action in teaching. We invite you to consider the teaching qualities when responding to questions in the text and learning opportunities presented as considerations throughout the book.

A teaching qualities symbol will appear in page margins throughout the book to draw your attention to particular teaching qualities addressed in the text.

Focus Questions

1. Of what value are teaching qualities to a practising teacher?
2. How could a teacher's strong relationships with young people contribute to successful learning?
3. In what ways do successful teachers understand the concept of diversity?
4. To what extent is authenticity in teaching and learning a prerequisite to success for teachers and students?

Figure 2.1
Teaching qualities for decision-making and praxis

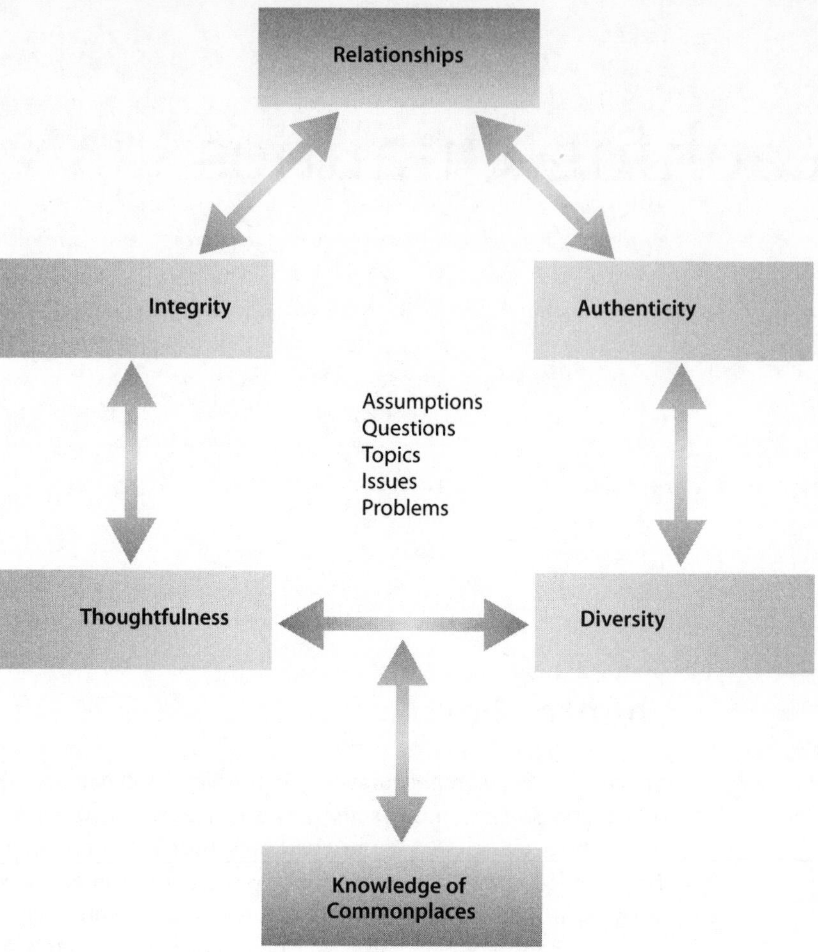

5. Why is it essential that thoughtfulness permeate all aspects of teaching and learning environments?
6. What dimensions of integrity contribute not only to success in learning and teaching, but also to feelings of personal efficacy and well-being?

The Teaching Qualities

This chapter discusses each quality in some detail, but the discussion is not intended to present a definition or prescription. You will provide meaning and understanding to the teaching qualities, based on your conversations about them, your use of them, and insights you gain as you embrace new knowledge. The meaning and understanding you gain will be constantly changing. And this is how it must be. Thoughtful teachers constantly understand theory and practice differently as they are exposed to new knowledge, concepts, and ideas. Thoughtfulness is the hallmark of a good teacher.

Knowledge

Knowledge of commonplaces is given a position of prominence as a teaching quality in Figure 2.1 because it is clearly the foundation for all the other qualities. As assumptions, questions, topics, and issues arise, we visit teaching qualities within the commonplaces of knowledge so that you can enrich your perspective and general worldview of learning, teaching, and schooling. These qualities are not discrete; they are not offered as an all-inclusive panacea for creating a "rose garden" in teaching. Rather, you should use them as fundamental areas for thought and reflection in decision making and praxis related to learning, teaching, and schooling. The qualities are not exclusive. Pre-service teachers may consider these teaching qualities as a useful foundation upon which to engage in reflection and contemplation about assumptions, questions, topics, issues, and problems related to learning, teaching, and schooling.

2.1 FOR YOUR CONSIDERATION

Create your own symbol for the Teaching Qualities Model.

1. What colours would best describe each quality in this figure?
2. For each quality, visualize a symbol that taps into your understanding of that quality.

Substitute your own symbols and colours for the teaching qualities as they are introduced in the book.

Relationships

> Whether it is a relationship to one's own self, to others, or to the world, the experience of deep connection arises when there is a profound respect, a deep caring, and a quality of "being with" that honors the truth of each participant in the relationship.
>
> Students who feel deeply connected through at least one such relationship are more likely to survive the "lure of risk" (Elias et al., 1997) and the damage of stress; they are more likely to discover and contribute the gift they are meant to bring to the world. (Kessler, 2000, p. 18)

What does the above quotation mean to you? Think back to your grade school experience. How important were relationships? What qualities did the teachers you really liked possess? We guess that, for most people, the common thread running through the responses would be one of connection. Typically, teachers whom you liked probably showed compassion, caring, sensitivity, maybe a sense of humour, along with clear professional competence. In short, the teacher was able to "connect" with the class.

A fundamental part of our human makeup is a profound need to belong. Even seemingly hardened souls, when their shells are uncovered, need to be wanted,

A principal welcomes students as they arrive at school.

need to be accepted, and need to belong. Many of us can probably think of situations in which people (of whatever age) presented an austere exterior marked by "in" language, rebellious clothing, overt expressions indicating pseudo-confidence, and a rejection of acceptable behaviour. Many of these same individuals probably had a fragile inner self that was crying out to be wanted and included.

Secure relationships are at the heart of our human experience. Learning—all forms of learning—will prosper when it is founded on good relationships. Young people deserve to have bestowed upon them a humanness that is without degree.

> From the exalted statesman to the new-born child, we are equally human. To be human is to be competent, to have a view of the world, and to have ways of dealing with one's life. To interact with another human being is to accept the equality of humanness with humility. To know humanness is to know who a person is, to know how they see their world. (Waldron, Collie, & Davies, 1999, p. 52)

What, then, are the implications for learning, teaching, and schools? New learning very often entails taking a risk. Asking for help is easier when you know the person to whom your request is directed. Discipline takes on a different complexion when a good relationship exists between teacher and child. As you read the following story, think about how the outcome for Chris might have been different if he and Mr. Tanaka had had a good relationship.

> Chris was a lively boy who had difficulty with learning. His attention span was much shorter than one might expect for a boy of thirteen, and he couldn't apply himself very well to his work. One Friday Chris came to school in a seemingly bad mood. Even his friends were excluded from his company. Math was a particular problem for him. Even on a good day he struggled with its complexities. On this particular Friday, Chris couldn't understand what the teacher was saying. Mr. Tanaka stood at the blackboard with his piece of chalk, trying to explain the mysteries of quadratic equations. He wrote an example and demonstrated how to solve the equation when X equalled 3. Chris was completely confused, but he wouldn't think of asking for help. Mr. Tanaka looked dourly at the class, stating gruffly that he couldn't make things any clearer.

"Anybody who can't understand this simple equation shouldn't be in Grade 8," he growled. "Take out your textbooks and complete questions 1 through 10 at the end of Chapter 6."

Chris was making a nuisance of himself, bothering students around him to give him some paper, lend him a pen, or let him use a ruler. It wasn't long before Mr. Tanaka had had enough.

"Get down to the office, Chris. Maybe you'll be of some use down there."

So, after an extended visit to the bathroom, a visit to the gym, and a trip outside to waste more time, Chris arrived at the office, announcing that Mr. Tanaka had sent him.

"Well," said the principal, "what can I do for you Chris?"

How would you describe Mr. Tanaka's general manner and disposition toward young people? What particular information in the story caused you to arrive at your conclusions? Do you think Mr. Tanaka's manner and disposition in any way contributed to Chris's learning difficulty and behaviour?

Young people who experience difficulties with their learning do so for myriad reasons, but their difficulties are often exacerbated by insensitive treatment from adults. Parents may be overly critical or may simply not care. Teachers often are more concerned with their lesson plans and covering the material; consequently they teach to the whole class, making disparaging comments to those who do not conform.

Confused and bewildered students act out their frustrations in ways that inevitably land them in trouble. Chris is a classic example of a frustrated learner. How might Mr. Tanaka have conducted himself differently so that Chris could have been helped? How might Mr. Tanaka's teaching approach have been modified so that Chris could have been helped? What role do relationships play in Mr. Tanaka's class? How might a more positive relationship between Mr. Tanaka and his class have helped Chris? And, finally, how do you think the principal should respond to Chris?

It is very important that students receive encouragement when making contributions to classroom learning, especially when their responses are incorrect. Students should always be left with their dignity intact after responding to a question or offering an opinion. Learning is not easy, and to learn successfully people must feel comfortable in their learning environments. New learning often involves risk-taking and it is only in environments where people feel safe and comfortable that they will easily take risks. Clearly, when a good relationship exists between teacher and students there is a positive correlation between this relationship and its effect on learning. Mr. Tanaka's relationship with his class was such that directing and telling marked his teaching style. His style also entailed an orientation toward teaching the whole class. A young man like Chris was simply one of the group and received attention only when Mr. Tanaka ventured down the rows of desks. What happens to young people like Chris when a teacher adheres to traditional forms of direct teaching, when flexibility in learning is at a minimum, and when individual help is cursory at best?

Diversity

Diversity, in our Teaching Qualities Model, assumes a broad context. We understand **diversity** to mean variety in the backgrounds and learning abilities of people, and in approaches to learning and teaching. Teachers must be constantly aware of diversity as they respond to learning needs in social and pedagogical contexts.

Diversity in People

Transience is a common feature of society today. People emigrate with increasing frequency. Many school districts comprise multicultural populations. The cultural traditions of recently arrived families present interesting challenges for school districts and teachers. Cultural and religious practices from distant countries must merge with those of the receiving culture in a harmonious way. Teachers must reflect upon the invitations to learning they offer to ensure that newly arrived young people will interpret the learning intentions in a positive manner.

Children from recent immigrant families are welcomed into school, where they must contend with values and social conventions that often conflict with their home culture. *Culture* is the way of life common to a group of people, consisting of the values, attitudes, and beliefs that influence their traditions and behaviours. *Ethnicity* is the quality of being a member of an ethnic group. Ethnic groups are identified by distinctive patterns of family life, language, recreation, religion, and other customs that differentiate them from others. "The concept of *race* is used to distinguish among human beings on the basis of biological traits and characteristic." (Parkay, Hardcastle-Stanford, & Gougeon, 1996, p. 135)

Diversity also exists within the mainstream student population. You will often hear teachers express beliefs about diversity, using statements such as, "Children learn in different ways," "Young people learn at different rates," and "Every child is unique." You will appreciate the need to think deeply about the diverse needs of children and how you, as a teacher, must accommodate diversity in your ways of working with them.

Diversity also includes the range of ability levels, which can extend from gifted children, who are very capable of learning within the conventions of schooling, to children with diagnosed learning disabilities. Other children will have physical and mental conditions that do not fall within the learning disabilities classification. You will come across debates about "inclusion" with regard to this latter group of children. Your response to the inclusion question will be emotional and challenging.

Questions about diversity also concern teachers as a group. The majority of people entering the profession of teaching in Canada are white, middle-class females, who tend to hold middle-class values and attitudes, which they, consciously or unconsciously, impart to their students (Parkay et al., 1996; Solomon, 1997; Futrell, 1999).

Men and women tend to respond to the world differently. *Sex* refers to biological differences (Deaux, 1993), and *gender* usually refers to judgments about

2.2 FOR YOUR CONSIDERATION

Schools, more than any other institution in our society, assimilate persons from different ethnic, racial, religious, and cultural backgrounds and pass on the values and customs of the majority. (Parkay et al., 1996, p. 109)

Two concepts in that Parkay quotation may be controversial: the role of assimilation, and the passing on of values and customs of the majority. Should majority values and customs be honoured in schools? Should each student be expected to assimilate the values and customs of the majority?

masculinity and femininity that are influenced by culture and context (Woolfolk, 1998, pp. 178–81). Gender–role stereotyping begins early in a child's life, though different treatment and expectations continue throughout a lifetime. Schools often foster gender bias in many ways—through textbooks, teachers' attitudes, assignments, roles, and responsibilities. It is important that teachers be aware of possible gender bias in their teaching and teaching resources to ensure that no students are excluded.

2.3 FOR YOUR CONSIDERATION

- *Dimensions of Culture*

List some ways that you as a teacher can learn more about the different cultures and values of your students.

- *Language and Culture*

It is often said that language is culture and culture is language because the relationship between the two is so enmeshed. What implications does this statement have for school systems in terms of the teaching of more than one language?

- *Ethnicity and Race*

According to Montagu (1974), "It is impossible to make the sort of racial classifications which some anthropologists and others have attempted. The fact is that all human beings are so ... mixed with regard to origin that between different groups of individuals ... 'overlapping' of physical traits is the rule" (p. 9). Some people limit their view of ethnicity to people of colour. Why is this so?

- *Schools and Diversity*

Schools today must find ways to meet the needs of all students and parents, regardless of social class, gender, or ethnic, racial, or cultural diversity (Parkay et al., 1996, p. 112). What are the implications of this statement for you as you begin your teaching career? How can schools better address diversity?

- *Gender Discrimination in Classrooms*

"One of the best-documented findings of the past 20 years is that teachers interact more with boys than with girls. This is true from pre-school to college. Teachers ask more questions of males, give males more feedback (praise, criticism, and correction), and give more specific and valuable comments to boys. As girls move through the grades, they have less and less to say. By the time students reach college, men are twice as likely to initiate comments as women." (Woolfolk, 1998, p. 181) Why does this happen and what is the long-term effect of this pattern?

In a discussion group, have all members of your group complete the following stem anonymously:

"I appear to be ________________ but really I am ________________."

1. What is the common thread in the responses to "but really I am"?
2. What do the answers reveal about "the hardened shells" referred to at the beginning of the chapter, under "Relationships"?
3. What might you discover through this exercise about a class of grade school students?

Diversity in Learning

The essential question regarding diversity in learning is this: How do you respond to the learning needs of a group of students? To answer this question fully you must examine your beliefs and assumptions about people generally. Do you believe that young people are all different? Do you believe they have different learning styles, different abilities, different intelligence levels, and different rates of learning? What was your grade school experience like? Did your teacher teach everyone in your class the same way? Traditional teaching methods see a great amount of time spent teaching the same way to the whole class. If you believe in the kinds of differences we have just discussed, do you see any problems with a teaching methodology that spends most of the time teaching to the whole class?

Understanding this issue will be fundamental to your understanding of learning and your role as a teacher. Diversity has occasionally been conceptualized as a problem to be overcome through programs designed to reduce differences among learners. Ability grouping, in which children of differing abilities are segregated into different classes, is an example of an approach used to reduce differences among learners. This practice is also known as streaming, tracking, or banding.

Goodlad (1984) conducted on-site, longitudinal studies in many classrooms and schools, during which he surveyed secondary school teachers about their preferences and opinions about ability grouping. Just over eighty percent of those surveyed thought that ability grouping was a good thing. When asked if they would be prepared to teach the lower-ability groupings, only three percent said they would. What does this tell you? Do you think Goodlad would have obtained the same results if he had surveyed elementary school teachers? Why?

Ability grouping is not a common practice in schools, though some schools create same-ability groupings for short periods of time to meet specific student needs. Interestingly, Good and Brophy (2000) report the tendency of educators to see diversity as an asset rather than as a liability. They explain, for example, that "students with different backgrounds can interact with one another and learn how the same text material or concept can be interpreted differently by persons from different backgrounds" (p. 322). Since the days of the one-room schoolhouse, teachers with classrooms of varying ages, backgrounds, and abilities have used diversity through various forms of peer learning, in which students helped each other with their learning. The idea of students helping students may experience a renaissance in the context of today's diverse learning environments.

Diversity in Teaching

Teaching is, of course, inextricably tied to learning. One thing to remember is that your primary goal is to meet the learning needs of the students. In meeting these needs your responsibility is twofold. First, you must understand the students: their learning difficulties, their learning styles, their differing levels of skill development, and so on. Your second responsibility is to inject sufficient variety into your teaching approach to engage and motivate your students to learn. Can you see how diversity looms large in teaching? The astute connections you are able to make within these central responsibilities have much to do with your effectiveness as a teacher.

Authenticity

The word *authentic* is defined as "reliable, trustworthy, of undisputed origin, genuine" according to the Oxford Dictionary (Fowler & Fowler, 1954, p. 76). Webster's Dictionary (Woolf, 1979) is a little more expansive: "worthy of acceptance or belief as conforming to fact or reality. Not imaginary, false, or imitation. Being actually and precisely what is claimed.... Stresses fidelity to actuality and fact and may imply authority or trustworthiness in determining this relationship" (p. 75). We refer to dictionary definitions to show that our use of the term is grounded in everyday language. We use the word **authenticity** in the book to refer to professional behaviour that is genuine and sincere. In learning and teaching we understand *authentic* to apply to explicit connections between learning in school and in life beyond the classroom, and the opportunities afforded students to demonstrate their understanding of these connections.

The presence of authenticity in schooling takes many forms. A consideration of schooling uncovers five general areas where a discussion of authenticity is germane: relationships, leadership, learning and teaching, curriculum, and assessment.

Authenticity in Relationships

Relationships have already been discussed as a teaching quality on p. 23, but we invite you to revisit this discussion in the context of authenticity. Consider the following scenario:

> September had finally arrived and teachers were assembling in the staff room, sharing stories about their summer experiences. Camping, house renovation, exotic holidays, hiking, and visits to relatives were typical topics of conversation. A number of teachers new to the profession were trying to mask their nervousness as they circulated around the room, introducing themselves to the veteran staff. Reassuring comments dominated these conversations, as experienced teachers offered encouraging words and willingness to share resources. The atmosphere was positive and an aura of enthusiasm permeated the room.
>
> Dan Brock had been teaching for about twenty years, during which time he had developed a way of dealing with students that he had changed little. His classes were reasonably well disciplined. He kept control with his firm manner and intimidating presence.
>
> On this first day of his twenty-first year, Dan found himself talking to Zinta, a twenty-two-year-old teacher in her first teaching job. After sharing stories about their summers, conversation turned to the practice of teaching and the inevitable questions a first-year teacher might have about managing students.

"What do you do, Dan, when the students enter the room for the first time? What kinds of things do you say to them?" Relishing the opportunity to flaunt his experience, Dan began to impart his views on kids, discipline, and control. After a lengthy monologue, Dan concluded with the advice, "Your best bet is to jump on them right away. Don't take any nonsense, don't give them an inch, and above all, don't smile 'til Christmas." At that point the PA announced that the staff meeting was about to begin, and staff began to make their way to the library. Zinta was left with Dan's pointed advice ringing in her inexperienced ears.

If Zinta followed Dan's advice, what image would she be presenting to the class? If Dan were to sustain that approach until Christmas, what would that say about Dan's character? Darling-Hammond (1997) reports research demonstrating that students experience much greater success in school settings that are structured to create close, sustained relationships between students and teachers. Could Dan Brock have a "close, sustained relationship" with his students? Brock's attitude of controlling students, not giving them an inch, and not allowing a smile until Christmas is hardly an example of getting to know his students as people. Would Mr. Brock's attitude toward his students be consistent with the definitions of authenticity presented on page 29?

2.4 FOR YOUR CONSIDERATION

Given the definitions of authenticity presented above and the research alluded to by Darling-Hammond, to what extent could we expect Mr. Brock to meaningfully engage his students in effective learning?

Authenticity in Leadership

There was a time when leaders ruled through power and autocratic behaviour. No doubt some still do. Increasingly, leadership in schools is becoming a shared responsibility. No longer do we assign leadership solely to those in administrative positions. Leaders are considerably more effective if they work with and through people in their enterprise. Trungpa (1988, pp. 159–160) speaks about "authentic presence," of being in an almost spiritual realm where we exhibit a genuine openness and honesty in the way we present ourselves to others. When leaders exhibit an authentic presence, they exert an enormous attraction over other human beings. Literature from many disciplines increasingly acknowledges the need for the relationship between the leader and the led to become less dependent on power and authority. Sergiovanni (1992) speaks of "moral leadership." Bender (1997) believes in "leadership from within," and Percy (1997), in his discussion of life and leadership, talks about "going deep." Kouzes and Posner (1999), on a practical level, espouse the merits of encouragement: "Expressing genuine appreciation for the efforts and successes of others means we have to show our emotions. We have to talk about our feelings in public. We have to make ourselves vulnerable to others" (p. 6). Clearly, this kind of expression of our inner self demonstrates who we really are, and not any pseudo role or act we might wish to offer. In short, it is a requirement that we exhibit authenticity.

Senge, Kleiner, Roberts, Ross, Roth, and Smith (1999), speaking from a business context, offer a useful message for schooling when they equate leadership-related relationships having to do with authenticity and "walking the talk." They write that leaders "who inquire effectively into their own values and behaviors ... become more reflective and credible. In effect, they become models for the integrity and interpersonal trust needed to explore a host of organization-wide issues" (p. 564). In many of today's more enlightened schools, shared leadership is commonly understood in concept and action. Teachers are leaders in a very authentic sense.

2.5 FOR YOUR CONSIDERATION

Discuss the following scenarios:

A. Arrowsmith Junior High School has a policy against throwing snowballs. Miguel and Tinisha, two Grade 8 students, are caught bombarding a group of Grade 7 girls with snowballs as they return to school from lunch. Mrs. Antonelli, on seeing the aggressors, herds them into the office, informs the secretary of what they were doing and leaves.

B. Jack Grogan had just finished doing some work in his classroom at the end of the day when he decided to head for the staff room. On his way he came across two Grade 6 boys who were shouting at each other angrily, and one boy was roughly pushing the other around....

1. Complete the Jack Grogan scenario in the context of "authentic presence." If you were Jack, how would you deal with the altercation?
2. How did your completion of the Jack Grogan scenario differ from the action taken by Mrs. Antonelli? To what extent was Mrs. Antonelli demonstrating "authentic presence"?

Authenticity in Learning and Teaching

Schools are social institutions where teachers and young people work together with a common intention: learning. Young people attend school to learn. Learning helps them to understand their world, their life. And life for a youngster is immediate—it's now. The arrows in Figure 2.2, below, illustrate the connection between young people, their learning, and their world.

The primary intention behind all activity in a school is to effect successful learning for all people, and this is represented in the centre of Figure 2.2. As teachers work toward this central intention, fundamental considerations pertaining to the lives of people in learning contexts must influence and drive the teaching–learning process. It is very important that teachers understand the nature of the learners as they prepare to engage young people in learning. How long can six-year-olds remain still, for example? How would a class of young adolescents react to being talked to for most of a class just before lunch? What is the socio-economic background of the class?

Figure 2.2
Reflection on authentic learning

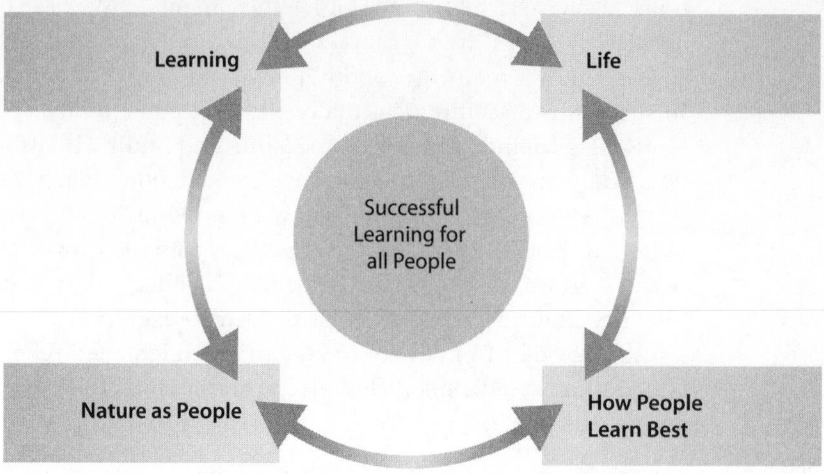

A further consideration connected to the nature of people is the general question, How do people learn best? Young children, for example, are very inquisitive. Young teenagers tend to be kinesthetic; their bodies prefer to be active. People generally have preferred ways of learning; some through hearing, some through watching, and others through touching and doing. The peer group is a very strong influence in the lives of adolescents. Chapter 5 explores some aspects of social learning, which will have implications for successful learning for adolescents.

You have probably heard of deferred gratification. Simply put, this means that you do something that you may not find particularly interesting or enjoyable because it will be good for you at some time in the future. For young people in school this is seldom a useful practice. Because life for a youngster is now, successful learning is achieved when learning is connected to life, when it is meaningful and relevant.

A final consideration in Figure 2.2 is learning, where we ask you to consider what and how students are being asked to learn. If, for example, you are asking students to learn quadratic equations, then in what ways would you take into consideration the nature of your students, how they learn best, and how quadratic equations are connected to their lives? If your intention is to effect successful learning for all students then all aspects of the illustration must be connected to thinking and praxis. Perkins (1999) says that, "...most students just plain forget most of what they have been taught. They often do not understand well what they do retain. And what they retain and understand, they often do not use actively" (p. 90). What are the implications of this for teaching?

Later chapters of this book will discuss learners, learning, and teaching, in which you should gain greater insight into the connections presented in Figure 2.2.

Chapter 8 addresses the concept of "transfer in learning," the ability of learners to apply their learning in different contexts. Life is the primary context for young people, and to the degree that is reasonable and possible, teachers should help young people to make connections between their learning and life.

2.6 FOR YOUR CONSIDERATION

Authentic Learning

1. Discuss the meaning of the schema presented in Figure 2.2 in the context of authenticity as it is defined on page 29 and of working in groups.
2. As a result of your discussion, write an explanation of your understanding of authentic learning.

Schools have a tendency to require students to learn skills and concepts for which the students see little or no purpose. Students often ask, "What do we have to do this for?" "What use is this to me?" Teachers may often struggle to provide justification for what they are teaching, and the essential message may be summed up by the term deferred gratification—in short, "You are doing it now because it will be good for you later." "Later" can mean anything from future grades to post-secondary education or some other time in life. Clearly, some things fit this justification. The question is, At what age can children understand this reasoning, and when is it appropriate?

When students perceive learning to be irrelevant to their lives, that is often a cue that the learning is not authentic; it is not real to them and they have difficulty becoming engaged in the learning. In cases such as this teachers often find themselves having to "make" students learn and "tell" them to learn. When these kinds of tactics are necessary, teaching and learning are hardly dynamic and effective. The challenge, then, for teachers, is to present learning to young people in ways that connect learning to their lives. Learning may then become real for students; it becomes authentic.

Authenticity in Curriculum

Our discussion of learning leads us to a consideration of curriculum and the need for authenticity. A detailed discussion of curriculum will take place in Chapter 11. For now, however, let us understand curriculum as the programs of study, subject guides, and school-specific policy decisions that affect the ways of working and general conduct in a school.

Curriculum should be presented in meaningful ways. New information and learning in the classroom and the ways that behaviour and conduct are guided throughout the school should all be effected in ways that are appropriate to the ages of young people in question. When new information and learning are not connected to what is real for young people, when behaviour and conduct are not guided by age-appropriate understandings, then a lack of authenticity pervades the learning environment. In circumstances such as these teachers may rely on authority and control to effect learning. These kinds of power responses will have only limited effect. Nicholls and Hazzard (1993) remind us that "teaching requires the consent of students, and discontent will not be chased away by the exercise of power" (p. 76). Authenticity in the presentation of curriculum will significantly contribute to contentment among learners.

2.7 FOR YOUR CONSIDERATION

In the discussion on authenticity in curriculum, you have read that new information and learning in the classroom and the ways that behaviour and conduct are guided throughout the school should all be effected in ways that are appropriate to the ages of young people in question.

Discuss the following questions pertaining to age-appropriateness, using your prior knowledge as the basis for your answer:

a) Why are young adolescents often restless during academic classes scheduled around 11 A.M.?

b) In elementary schools, where children tend to remain with the same teacher for most of their learning, why must recess be at the same time for all classes?

c) A characteristic of adolescence is that young people want to have some say in decisions that affect their lives. To what extent do schools respect this characteristic?

d) Is it a good idea for children in, say, Grade 3 to be sitting at desks, in rows, for much of their days in school?

Authenticity in Assessment

Assessment plays a significant role in a young person's schooling. Results from assessment activity are used as indicators of performance and progress on report cards, in communications with home, to demonstrate success at a grade level, and many other statements about students that responsible parties might have a right to know. In other words, assessment results are used to make rather profound decisions about (and for) a young person.

It is important that the methods used to assess students' performance in learning are such that students have a genuine opportunity to demonstrate or exhibit mastery of what they have learned. Assessment should be an authentic test of a stu-

Curriculum is presented in authentic ways.

dent's ability. Sizer (1984) is of the opinion that "any exhibitions of mastery should be the students' opportunity to show off what they know and are able to do, rather than a trial by question" (as reported in Brandt [ed.], 1992, p. 86). Assessment methods that rely on questions to be answered on paper, either written or computer scored, tend to limit students' opportunity to demonstrate their mastery of learning. Not all people are at their best sitting at a desk with pen or pencil in hand, trying to respond to written questions within a specific block of time.

2.8 FOR YOUR CONSIDERATION

Vignette 1: Jenny and her friend Alena sit down on June 25 to write their final exams in social studies. The exam is a fifty-question, multiple-choice instrument, covering all aspects of the program. Jenny earns a score of 24 out of 50 and Alena scores 26 out of 50. Jenny fails the exam and Alice does not.

What could you speculate, from the scores the two girls received, about the degree to which they had learned successfully in social studies?

Vignette 2: Jaroslav has to deal with a form of assessment that is different from that used for Jenny and Alena, but one from which significant judgments will be made about his performance. Jaroslav is a boisterous boy who, from time to time, gives his Grade 4 teacher some difficulties with his behaviour. He comes from a single-parent home where he is left alone for extended periods of time until his mother gets home from work. On Tuesday morning his mom had to leave in a hurry for work and Jaroslav was left to fend for himself for breakfast, not an infrequent occurrence. Later in the morning the teacher had planned a written test of largely short-answer questions that would provide a significant contribution to the upcoming report card mark. Jaroslav was restless and distracted throughout the test. On three occasions the teacher had to caution Jaroslav for turning around and generally distracting others. He did not score very well on his test.

1. What do you think Jaroslav's teacher might have said to his mother at parent–teacher interviews about his performance?
2. How might Jaroslav's life outside school affect his learning in school?

Accountability is the practice of holding people responsible for their behaviour. Provincial and territorial governments hold school systems accountable. School systems hold teachers and schools accountable for the effectiveness of learning and teaching. We're sure you agree that schools, like any other institution, must be accountable. The issue tends to be one of "how?" In what ways would accountability requirements be met such that young people are afforded opportunities to truly demonstrate their success in learning? How might young people demonstrate their learning in authentic ways? Sizer, in the quotation above, uses the term, "trial by question." What does this expression mean to you? Is he perhaps being sarcastic, even cynical? You probably know young people who are learning a sport, learning to dance, learning to act, learning to read, learning to drive a car. How do they demonstrate their success? They demonstrate success by actually doing the activity they are learning. The learning of skills could be viewed as rehearsal. They are rehearsing the parts that will eventually be put together for the ultimate goal of the learning—playing the sport, dancing, performing a role in a play, reading a book, driving a car. All these opportunities to demonstrate learning are in what we would call authentic, real, or free-form expression.

> In school our conventions determine success in learning using measures that are mostly unrelated to actual demonstrations of learning; they do not allow a young person the opportunity to demonstrate what has been learned in a real sense. Students are almost indoctrinated in the psychometric modes of learning measurement—short answer quizzes, multiple choice tests, fill-in-the-blanks, power tests, percentage-letter grades, computer-scored test sheets, and so on. (Waldron et al., 1999, p. 83)

You will hear these psychometric modes of measurement referred to as "pencil-and-paper" forms of testing. They are within what Sizer calls the "trial by question" form of testing. It is important that authentic testing, or assessment, allows students to exhibit, or demonstrate, what they have learned in authentic tests of their ability.

2.9 FOR YOUR CONSIDERATION

1. How could you have demonstrated your learning in high school math, for example, in authentic ways?
2. Do you feel that the pencil-and-paper forms of testing, when used exclusively, allowed you to earn the best grade possible?
3. To what extent do your assumptions about testing govern your thoughts about authenticity?
4. Pick a unit or topic from your most recent high school experience in any subject you choose, and think of ways the assessment could have been more authentic, more real. Share these ideas with the rest of your class.

Thoughtfulness

> If thought is awakened by a problem, not by the authoritative claims of a teacher or a text, then knowledge must be seen as the product of inquiry, as the answer to some set of pertinent questions that focuses inquiry and calls forth a search for knowledge. (Wiggins, 1987, p. 70)

Young people experience freedom of choice in their learning.

Perspective essentially governs and determines all of our beliefs about the way we behave and the way things are. *Thought* is defined as the action or process of thinking (arranging ideas, new or old, turning something over in the mind), and being *thoughtful* is being absorbed in the process of thought, showing consideration for others. **Thoughtfulness,** therefore, is engaging in thought, reflection, and research, identifying and questioning assumptions, and thinking of others. It is in an environment of reflection, research, and questioning that thoughtfulness is evident.

In this book thoughtful learning and teaching are understood as a process of examining the beliefs and assumptions that constitute one's worldview. It is the unfettered application of knowledge—new and prior—to teaching practice, the genuine listening to the stories of other teachers, reflection on and in practice, and the elevation of the voices of young people to a level of eloquence.

Why is it important that teachers be thoughtful in their learning and teaching? What are the optimal conditions for thoughtfulness? Could these include situations that force an individual to think hard about something; an atmosphere conducive to questioning and inquiry; being around curious people who also inquire and question? Would it help one in becoming a more thoughtful learner and teacher to be in an environment where one was free to make mistakes, had time to reflect, and had opportunities to read, write, and discuss?

> Thoughtfulness requires close reading and disciplined debate about what has been read. It requires substantial writing—not just narrative writing but argumentative, analytical, and evaluative writing that is then closely read, discussed and rewritten. Thoughtfulness requires a great deal of time devoted to discussion—not just any discussion, but disciplined, Socratic dialogue. (R. Brown, 1987, p. 50)

Thoughtfulness, then, though ultimately a very personal process, is nurtured in social contexts. Wiggins reminds us that thought is a "product of inquiry." Brown states that thoughtfulness is making meaning by negotiating with others through disciplined Socratic dialogue. Social contexts for learning involve important processes for gaining understanding and making meaning. We will discuss social learning and some approaches to its application that you may encounter in schools in Chapter 5.

These children are thoughtfully analyzing a story.

Integrity

To include integrity as one of our teaching qualities should intuitively make good sense to you. The word **integrity** has ethical connotations; it is typically used to refer to doing what is right and good. Teaching is like any activity that requires humans to work closely with each other. It is more effective when people are good to each other, when they do what is right. The word *integrity* also has another meaning, however, that raises a few more questions about how to be a teacher. The Oxford Dictionary (Fowler & Fowler, 1954) defines the word as "wholeness." The opposite word is fragmentation, or coming apart. A teacher who acts with integrity, then, acts in a way that corresponds to his or her thinking, beliefs, and assumptions. Let's look at this second understanding of integrity as a teaching quality for a moment.

There are some areas of teaching in which the value of teachers behaving with integrity is self-evident. Consider relationships, a teaching quality we have already discussed. From personal experience you know that when your relationships—with your parents, your spouse, or your friends—are whole, not fragmented or broken, you feel better and perform better. The same principle holds true for the staff in a school. If there is integrity on the part of the staff, then those involved feel that they are part of something bigger; they are more likely to enjoy one another; and they are better able to effectively deal with the stresses that inevitably rise when people work together in close proximity.

Your relationships with young people also require integrity. You will learn early in your teaching career that your students want to have a relationship with you, and want one that is good and healthy. You will also learn that they want this integrity on their own terms. Therefore, you will feel the fragility of this relationship, and will work hard at trying to preserve the relationships with your learners, both individually and as a class. You will want your learners to like you, and that is normal.

2.10 FOR YOUR CONSIDERATION

Students want a relationship with you that is good and healthy and characterized by integrity.

1. Should a teacher like every learner in the classroom?
2. What if a teacher does not like a student? How can he or she show integrity toward that student? Is there a solution?
3. How might a teacher learn to value and respect each learner?

The value of having the quality of integrity is not always as evident in other areas of teaching. Teachers also need personal integrity; that is, they need to feel and experience their own personal lives as being unfragmented. They need to be able to be themselves in the classroom and school. To behave in a way that is fragmented from who you really are tires you out and, sooner or later, produces stress. This expression of integrity is like the quality of authenticity that we discussed earlier.

You may also experience fragmentation with regard to curriculum. You will sometimes be concerned with integrating the goals of the curriculum with your own goals for learners. Another area concerns value systems. You may have a religious worldview and wonder how or whether you can have integrity in a public school setting in which religious views are to be treated in a purely objective, academic way. You may wonder if you are too fragmented in keeping your opinions about the key issues of life and death to yourself. Later chapters of this book will invite you to consider these ideas in more detail. Chapter 11 on curriculum and curriculum planning will provide insight and opportunity for you to gain clarity on questions relating to integration, fragmentation, and integrity in curriculum and its implementation in schools.

2.11 FOR YOUR CONSIDERATION

In a discussion group, identify the aspects of teaching in which you might have the greatest struggle with integrity.

1. Why would this aspect be a struggle for you?
2. What is the most logical approach to handling this issue?
3. Is there a common theme among members of your group in the different struggles for integrity? If so, what does this reveal to you about the nature of integrity?

Reflection and Perspective on the Chapter

We hope you will keep these six teaching qualities in mind as you read the rest of the book. The qualities, as we have discussed them, are not exclusive; nor are they cast in concrete. Your understanding of them will constantly change as you gain new knowledge and form new meaning. The qualities are offered, however, as a useful framework within which to consider the assumptions, topics, issues, and ideas that you deal with as you "break from anchorage" on this exciting journey toward becoming a teacher.

You will read many times in this book that a good teacher is a thoughtful teacher. It is imperative that teachers constantly reflect on their practice. In professional circles you may hear the phrase "reflection *on* and *in* practice." Professional discussions outside the classroom—professional development days, staff meetings, planning sessions—would be situations where the practice of teaching and ways of responding to young people exemplify reflection *on* practice. Teachers talk about their work, sharing thoughts and ideas about learning, teaching, and schooling. Reflection *in* practice is less common, but equally important, because it entails thinking about professional actions and decisions at the time they occur. In-practice reflection is most effective when two or more colleagues are working together. However, since most teaching contexts are not designed to facilitate this kind of collaborative work, teachers must rely upon self-designed techniques for reflection *in* practice.

We now move on to Chapter 3. Keep in mind the need to be reflective, to be thoughtful. The commonplaces of knowledge provide a structure for the book and each demands reflection and thoughtfulness, where new knowledge presented in the book is considered alongside your prior knowledge. During this process the assumptions that you hold will be identified, perhaps uncovered (some of them may be tacit), and professionally challenged. Various contexts for discussion, debate, and conversation are presented throughout each commonplace of knowledge and it is within these contexts, particularly, that we invite you to apply the teaching qualities to your reflective actions. Whenever you encounter the following symbol for teaching qualities, it is a cue for you to reflect on the qualities as they apply to a particular discussion within the text. We will lead your thinking a little by listing the most pertinent teaching qualities each time the teaching qualities symbol appears, but we urge you not to allow your thinking to be limited by this list.

It is our hope that you will adopt this process for reflection into your way of being so that when you enter the profession you will model the very essence of a dynamic professional who responds to new knowledge and change in ways that benefit young people.

Key Terms

accountability 35
authenticity 29
diversity 26
integrity 38
thoughtfulness 37

Suggested Further Reading

Henderson, James G. (2001). *Reflective Teaching: Professional Artistry Through Inquiry* (3rd ed.). Upper Saddle River, NJ: Prentice-Hall Inc.

Hill, Linda D. (2001). *Connecting Kids: Exploring Diversity Together.* Co-published: Gabriola Island, BC: New Society Publishers; Duncan, BC: Building Bridges Consulting.

Kilbourn, Brent. (1998). *For the Love of Teaching.* London, ON: The Althouse Press.

Pike, G. and Selby, D. (2000). *In the Global Classroom.* Toronto, ON: Pippin Publishing.

Unrau, Norman J. (1997). *Thoughtful Teachers, Thoughtful Learners: A Guide to Helping Adolescents Think Critically.* Scarborough, ON: Pippin Publishing.

Chapter 3

Assumptions about Learning

Chapter Focus

Conditions for Learning

Children attend school to learn. A teacher's responsibility is to facilitate learning and to provide conditions in which learning can occur. A condition for learning can be external or internal. An **external condition for learning** might be a classroom rule such as "no laughing at wrong answers," or a poster of reminders regarding the steps in writing a good essay, to which learners can refer during writing periods. Learners' freedom from the fear of failure would be an example of an **internal condition for learning**, where making a mistake does not lead to ridicule. An internal condition might be a learner's expectation of success before applying a strategy in completing a task; for example, the student expects that using a particular strategy for writing essays will be effective.

You may conclude that internal and external learning conditions should be related. Arguably, the teacher's main challenge is to establish the external conditions necessary for learning, such that the internal conditions—motivation to learn or freedom from the fear of failure, for example—are created. You may also conclude that learning is a complex process with many facets. This complexity, however, may be understood in meaningful ways.

Assumptions and Their Place in Learning

What assumptions do you hold about learning? What prior knowledge do you bring to your pre-service study? The best place to discover your assumptions is in your behaviours and actions. As you read this chapter think about your actions and behaviours with regard to the practice of teaching. We will help you uncover your assumptions about learning by introducing you to some assumptions commonly held by many educators and non-educators.

Throughout the chapter we will ask you to dismantle these assumptions for what actions they might imply, and to question why people tend to believe them. How might these assumptions be changed to become more accurate and learning-relevant?

We will then provide new information to help you to understand these and other assumptions that you and your professors, field experience partners, and classmates might have. We will ask you to critically consider how research, case studies, and narrative-based understandings of learning inform your understanding of teaching and learning. We ask you to be ready to have your assumptions disaffirmed, affirmed, called into question, and challenged where necessary; we also invite you to challenge the information we provide. This is how reflective teaching develops praxis that leads to wise, practical judgments about creating conditions that lead to learning. This, then, is the goal of this chapter: your greater knowledge of learning and your greater ability to design learning conditions that best promote learning.

Focus Questions

1. How do good learners learn? To what extent do good learners possess common characteristics, regardless of individual learning styles?
2. Can teaching help a young person to learn? What external conditions can teachers reasonably be expected to create that will help classrooms full of students to learn?
3. What role does prior knowledge play in learning?
4. How do learners represent the external world internally?
5. How do young people make meaning and gain understanding of new knowledge and concepts in their learning?
6. To what extent is thoughtfulness essential to effective learning?
7. In what ways do attribution, effort, and ability contribute to the affective component of learning?
8. What forms of knowledge contribute to successful learning for young people? What influences learning more—knowledge or ability?

Assumptions about Learning

What assumptions do you hold about learning? How well do you learn certain things and not others? What is the best way to help people learn? These are important questions and to answer them will require that you take a critical look at your theories, beliefs, and ideas about learning. Assumptions are often tacit; many people are not aware of the assumptions they hold. You can imagine the difficulties that arise when teachers respond to issues through assumptions of which they are not even aware.

Three Letters From Teddy

by Elizabeth Silance Ballard

Teddy's letter came today and now that I've read it I will place it in my cedar chest with the other things that are important to my life.

"I wanted you to be the first to know."

I smiled as I read the words he had written and my heart swelled with a pride that I had no right to feel.

I have not seen Teddy Stallard since he was a student in my fifth-grade class, fifteen years ago. It was early in my career, and I had only been teaching for two years.

From the first day he stepped into my classroom, I disliked Teddy. Teachers (although everyone knows differently) are not supposed to have favorites in a class, but most especially are they not to show dislike for a child, any child.

Nevertheless, every year there are one or two children that one cannot help but be attached to, for teachers are human, and it is human nature to like bright, pretty, intelligent people, whether they are ten years old or twenty-five. And sometimes, not too often fortunately, there will be one or two students to whom the teacher just can't seem to relate.

I had thought myself quite capable of handling my personal feelings along that line until Teddy walked into my life. There wasn't a child I particularly liked that year, but Teddy was most assuredly one I disliked.

He was dirty. Not just occasionally, but all the time. His hair hung low over his ears and he actually had to hold it out of his eyes as he wrote his papers in class. (And this was before it was fashionable to do so!) Too, he had a peculiar odor about him which I could never identify.

His physical faults were many, and his intellect left a lot to be desired, also. By the end of the first week I knew he was hopelessly behind the others. Not only was he behind; he was just plain slow! I began to withdraw from him immediately.

Any teacher will tell you that it's more of a pleasure to teach a bright child. It is definitely more rewarding for one's ego. But any teacher worth her credentials can channel work to the bright child, keeping him challenged and learning while she puts her major effort on the slower ones. Any teacher *can* do this. Most teachers *do* it, but I *didn't*. Not that year.

In fact, I concentrated on my best students and let the others follow along as best they could. Ashamed as I am to admit it, I took perverse pleasure in using my red pen; and each time I came to Teddy's papers, the cross-marks (and there were many) were a little larger and a little redder than necessary.

"Poor work" I would write with a flourish.

While I did not actually ridicule the boy, my attitude was obviously quite apparent to the class, for he quickly became the class "goat," the outcast—the unlovable and the unloved.

He knew I didn't like him, but he didn't know why. Nor did I know—then or now—why I felt such an intense dislike for him. All I know is that he was a little boy no one cared about, and I made no effort in his behalf.

The days rolled by and we made it through the Fall Festival, the Thanksgiving holidays, and I continued marking happily with my red pen.

As the Christmas holidays approached, I knew that Teddy would never catch up in time to be promoted to the sixth-grade level. He would be a repeater.

To justify myself, I went to his cumulative folder from time to time. He had very low grades for the first four years, but no grade failure. How he had made it, I didn't know. I closed my mind to the personal remarks:

First Grade: "Teddy shows promise by work and attitude, but has poor home situation."

Second Grade: "Teddy could do better. Mother terminally ill. He receives little help at home."

Third Grade: "Teddy is a pleasant boy. Helpful, but too serious. Slow learner. Mother passed away end of the year."

Fourth Grade: "Very slow, but well behaved. Father shows no interest."

Well they passed him four times, but he will certainly repeat fifth grade! Do him good! I said to myself.

And then the last day before the holiday arrived. Our little tree on the reading table sported paper and popcorn chains. Many gifts were heaped underneath, waiting for the big moment.

Teachers always get several gifts at Christmas, but mine that year seemed bigger and more elaborate than ever. There was not a student who had not brought me one. Each unwrapping brought squeals of delight and the proud giver would receive effusive thank-you's.

His gift wasn't the last one I picked up; in fact it was in the middle of the pile. Its wrapping was a brown paper bag and he had colored Christmas trees and red bells all over it. It was stuck together with masking tape.

"For Miss Thompson—From Teddy" it read.

The group was completely silent and for the first time I felt conspicuous, embarrassed because they all stood watching me unwrap that gift.

As I removed the last bit of masking tape, two items fell to my desk. A gaudy rhinestone bracelet with several stones missing and a small bottle of dime-store cologne—half empty.

I could hear the snickers and whispers and I wasn't sure I could look at Teddy.

"Isn't this lovely?" I asked, placing the bracelet on my wrist. "Teddy, would you help me fasten it?"

He smiled shyly as he fixed the clasp and I held up my wrist for all of them to admire.

There were a few hesitant *ooh's* and *aah's* but as I dabbed the cologne behind my ears, all the little girls lined up for a dab behind their ears.

I continued to open the gifts until I reached the bottom of the pile. We ate our refreshments and the bell rang.

The children filed out with shouts of "See you next year!" and "Merry Christmas!" but Teddy waited at his desk.

When they had all left, he walked towards me clutching his gift and books to his chest.

"You smell just like Mom," he said softly. "Her bracelet looks real pretty on you, too. I'm glad you liked it."

He left quickly and I locked the door, sat down at my desk and wept, resolving to make up to Teddy what I had deliberately deprived him of—a teacher who cared.

I stayed every afternoon with Teddy from the end of the Christmas holidays until the last day of school. Sometimes we worked together. Sometimes he worked alone while I drew up lesson plans or graded papers.

Slowly but surely he caught up with the rest of the class. Gradually there was a definite upward curve in his grades.

He did not have to repeat the fifth grade. In fact his final averages were among the highest in the class, and although I knew he would be moving out of the state when school was out, I was not worried for him. Teddy had reached a level that would stand him in good stead the following year, no matter where he went. He had enjoyed a measure of success and as we were taught in our teacher training courses: "Success builds success."

I did not hear from Teddy until seven years later, when his first letter appeared in my mailbox.

> "Dear Miss Thompson,
>
> I just wanted you to be the first to know. I will be graduating second in my class next month.
>
> Very truly yours,
> Teddy Stallard"

I sent him a card of congratulations and a small package, a pen and pencil gift set. I wondered what he would do after graduation.

Four years later, Teddy's second letter came.

> "Dear Miss Thompson,
>
> I wanted you to be the first to know. I was just informed that I'll be graduating first in my class. The university has not been easy, but I liked it.
>
> Very truly yours,
> Teddy Stallard"

I sent him a good pair of sterling silver monogrammed cuff links and a card, so proud of him I could burst!

And now—today—Teddy's third letter.

> "Dear Miss Thompson,
>
> I wanted you to be the first to know. As of today I am Theodore J. Stallard, MD. How about that!!??
>
> I'm going to be married in July, the twenty-seventh, to be exact. I wanted to ask if you could come and sit where Mom would sit if she were here. I'll have no family there as Dad died last year.
>
> Very truly yours,
> Teddy Stallard"

I'm not sure what kind of gift one sends to a doctor on completion of medical school and state boards. Maybe I'll just wait and take a wedding gift, but my note can't wait.

"Dear Ted.

Congratulations! You made it and you did it yourself! In spite of those like me and not because of us, this day has come for you.

God bless you. I'll be at that wedding with bells on!"

(Source: From "Three Letters from Teddy," by Elizabeth Silance Ballard, *Home Life*, March, 1976 (pp. 34, 35). Copyright 1976 The Sunday School Board of the Southern Baptist Convention [now LifeWay Christian Resources of the Southern Baptist Convention]. All rights reserved. Reprinted with permission of the author.)

The problem in the above story was not with Teddy. The problem was with the assumptions in the teacher's worldview, assumptions that were not entirely true.

3.1 FOR YOUR CONSIDERATION

Consider your assumptions about learning in each of the following situations:

1. Imagine that Teddy has a concerned grandmother who understands his problems and wants to help him cope. What is Teddy able to understand when his grandmother tells him to not worry, this problem will pass, and life goes by so fast? What is Teddy not able to understand? What can Teddy learn from his grandmother?
2. What does a Grade 11 learner learn when a seventeen-year-old single mother comes to class and describes what it is like to raise a child alone? Why? What is the most desired learning intended in this situation of a single mother speaking to young people? Is there a learning situation, a condition for learning that might be helpful or more meaningful in teaching young people about sexual responsibility?

Review your answers and see whether you can identify your assumptions about learning. For example, if you concluded that Teddy, in the first example, can't learn anything about the passage of time from his grandmother until he experiences the passage of time himself, your assumption may be that "people learn only from personal experience."

Consider the following ten commonly held assumptions about learning and teaching, (presented without regard for order of importance).

Assumption 1: People learn from experience.

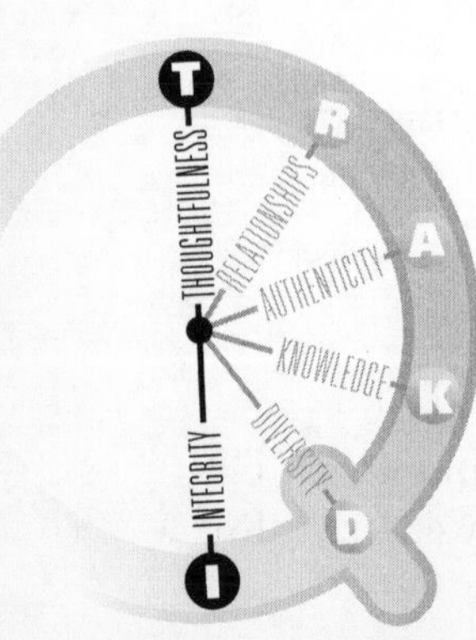

Do you believe that people learn only from experience, or is it something else that results in learning?

To begin with, we will make our own assumption: that people really learn very little from an actual experience, if what we mean by experience is a person intentionally being exposed to or consciously influenced by an event. For one thing, experiences happen too fast; we are not hard-wired cognitively to make sense of or learn immediately from an event. For another, the provider of a particular experience usually intends only one meaning (unless there is some deliberate ambiguity, as when the author of a story intends a double meaning), but the recipient of the experience may interpret it differently. Consider a statement made by a teacher, a plot in a story, a math problem given aloud in class, even a romantic look by a boyfriend or girlfriend. The statement, the story, the math problem, or the look have only one intended meaning (unless there is deliberate ambiguity or irony). When the learner thinks about the experience or event, however, he or she may construct other meanings than the one intended. Meaning-making, ultimately, resides within the learner.

Meaning is created out of one's reflection on the event, through the cognitive activity before, during, and after the event (e.g., before: predicting what might happen as a result of the event; during: identifying something familiar in one's experience to use to interpret the event; or after: inferring reasons for the event's occurrence). Learning occurs in reflecting and deliberating on the event. We are not saying that events are not in and of themselves factual, or that they do not hold any meaning or value. That would be a serious error of logic. If things have no intrinsic meaning, then learners would never find out any meaning (e.g., we cannot call something big without having some idea of what is small). Learning ultimately takes place in the learner through reflection on experience. When the lingering effects (another way of saying long-term memory) of an event, or experience, are brought up into that workroom in the mind (another way of saying short-term memory), and when a learner "goes to work" on that experience, learning occurs. Short-term memory may be considered the working memory or the attentional capacity of a person. Long-term memory is the permanent store of procedural and declarative knowledge. Ultimately, the meaning resides not in the math problem, in the story being read, or in the romantic look, but in a learner and the **construction of meaning** in that learner's mind. Learning is enhanced when a teacher deliberately directs learners to do something with the ideas that have been produced in the short-term memory. Effective teachers are able to create the conditions for personal meaning-making to occur.

Learning, then, occurs as a result of reflection in and on experience. The question for you to consider is, How can a teacher help learners reflect on experiences in ways that facilitate learning?

Reflecting and Learning in the Workroom of Your Mind

You can lead learners to do a number of reflective activities that will help them make meaning and help them learn. We will consider only a couple at this time.

People learn from experience.

Elaboration

Learners can be asked to elaborate on an experience or event. **Elaboration** means going beyond the event or experience, such as when a teacher asks "why" questions or directs children to relate new information to their prior knowledge. Elaboration strategies can be as simple as learning words in a new language by pairing each new word with a familiar word in English, or as complex as asking learners to activate hypotheses about the outcome of an experiment in science.

The evidence is quite unambiguous that elaboration strategies are very useful learning strategies (Pressley, El-Dinary, & R. Brown, 1994). Older children use them more effectively than younger children. Elementary-age children and adults often do not use elaboration strategies on their own, even when they know them (Pressley & Levin, 1977; Pressley et al. 1994). There is even evidence that university students do not use elaboration strategies when studying, writing, solving problems, or attempting to comprehend texts (Devine, 1987), even when they know them.

Abstraction

In **abstraction,** learners abstract, or extract, meaning from their experience (this is much like squeezing the lemons to get lemonade). A teacher does this by asking a learner to consider the main idea of a story, the problem to be solved in science, or the main question to ask of a social problem in social studies.

Consider Teddy's teacher in the story at the beginning of this chapter. Miss Thompson did not fully understand her initial experience with Teddy. She did not appear to understand what Teddy "meant" and how to teach him. Later, after reflecting on her experiences, she chose a more deliberate, ethical way of teaching. In a real way, the meaning of Teddy Stallard was realized after Teddy left the school. The nature of Miss Thompson's learning—the meaning that was created—came as her assumptions, theories, beliefs, and understandings were called into question and disaffirmed by new information and insights.

Consider also how Teddy's understanding of his teacher was influenced by his prior knowledge of his mother. His understanding of the events in which his teacher was a participant was very different from his teacher's understanding of the same events.

We invite you to consider another example of learning from experience.

3.2 FOR YOUR CONSIDERATION

Do you remember the first time you tried a new physical activity such as skiing, dancing, or hitting a tennis ball? What conditions needed to exist for you to learn the skill? Once you have identified those conditions, create a matrix, listing the conditions across the top of a sheet of paper. Then, down the side, write out a list of strategies that might best produce those conditions. Now, what is your conclusion about the statement "People learn from experience"?

Assumption 2: There is meaning in a fact; learn the fact and you learn the meaning of the fact.

The First Problem: Thoughtfulness in Learning

Have you ever thought about why you and your friends see different things in the same movie? Do you sometimes arrive at different conclusions regarding the same story? Maybe the meaning of movies, stories, and other objective facts of life exists not in the facts, but in the thoughtful conclusions you draw from those facts.

It is through thoughtfulness that the learning goals of teacher preparation programs are best achieved. Teacher effectiveness is developed over time, with the right opportunities, and through the consistent practice of thoughtfulness leading to wise, practical judgments. Teachers are encouraged to choose ethical, moral actions for the classroom. Let us illustrate the problems inherent in assuming that meaning resides in the fact being presented to a learner, and not in the thoughtful reflection and choosing of ethical actions.

3.3 FOR YOUR CONSIDERATION

After reading the following excerpt, take a sheet of paper and draw what is described below. (This is a description of an actual organism.)

> Size small to medium, width and length about equal. Slight or no neck; caudals in single series: scales small with width and length about equal, smooth, in rows 35–45 or more; rudimentary hind legs present, more evident in males; tail very short, blunt, rounded, and ending in large plate, not prehensile; large shield on top of head; scales on chin between lower labials small; snout short and broad; rostral large, broad; 1–2 loreals; eye small with vertical pupil; eyes rest on upper labials; maxillary and mandibular teeth in graduated series; colour above the sides of the organism is pale tan to dark brown or drab, frequently with yellowish, bluish or greenish tinges, sides yellow-brown and the belly some tone of yellow-orange. Tip of the tail may be slightly lighter brown than rest of the body but generally no pattern.
>
> (Adapted from a learning activity created by Dr. Wally Samiroden, University of Alberta.)

Compare your drawing with those of your classmates. What problems did you encounter in drawing the organism? What conclusions arereasonable to make regarding the facts you have just read and tried to use in drawing the organism? Where does the meaning reside?

The Second Problem: Transfer of Learning

Evidence is mounting that learners do not apply what they have learned (Rabinowitz, Freeman, & Cohen, 1992). For example, learners do not always apply strategies that they have learned to new situations, even when the strategy could be used profitably. Remember when you studied percentages in school? Did you apply that knowledge when you were shopping for clothes during sales with percentage discounts? What about angles and forces? Did you apply that knowledge to throwing a ball? Moving a piece of furniture?

Further, learners may not even apply a well-learned strategy to a similar situation (Gick & Holyoak, 1983; Rabinowitz et al., 1992). Far too often, learning is not transferred, even when it is obviously helpful to do so. For example, learners may have learned that "soft hands" is a necessary condition to catch a football pass, but may not use soft hands to catch a basketball pass unless specifically directed to do so. For such learning, the meaning of soft hands appears to be limited to the situation in which it is learned.

Think of subjects you studied in school. Can you think of times when you were able to transfer lessons from your school experience to everyday life? What conditions did your teacher create to facilitate this transfer?

The Third Problem: Interpretation of Facts

The assumption that there is meaning in facts alone is evident in many of the issues we face in our complex world, issues that provide learners with wonderful opportunities to learn about the nature of problems. The meaning within problems is beyond the facts presented by the problems.

Apparently the world's six billionth person was born, quite likely in India, sometime in 1999. One "fact" that is often drawn from this mathematical number is that the world is overpopulated. The overpopulation of the world is often presented as a fact and a problem. Experientially, overpopulation may appear to be a fact, particularly if you find yourself on a street in Shanghai, China, or in a marketplace in Jakarta, Indonesia. And yet, the entire population of the world could fit physically into Canada's three Prairie provinces (you can do the mathematics if you are someone who enjoys mathematical facts). Is the problem, and the meaning of the problem, then, that the world is overcrowded? Is it a matter of space? Or, is the problem and the meaning really a matter of the distribution of the world's resources? Should we have concerns about justice? Do poverty and its causes play a part? You and your classmates must decide what is a fact and what is not, how to interpret what is true and what is not.

One Final Thought Regarding Meaning and Understanding

Unless a writer, in the spirit of Shakespeare, intends some ambiguity, there can be only one intended meaning in a written statement. Many applications might be

How important is it for students to apply new learning?

possible, a lot of generalizations can be made, a number of applications can be proposed, but there can be only one intended meaning in the original statement.

Write a sentence that has more than one meaning. You can do this only if you actually try to. Otherwise, what you write and what you say has one intended meaning only. Likewise, when a physical education teacher describes a bent-arm pull in a front-crawl swimming stroke, that describes only one action of which the teacher is knowledgeable. There are, however, many different ways of applying that knowledge, and the learner needs to be free to make those applications personally relevant, meaningful, and safe. The challenge in teaching is creating the conditions for the learner to make personally relevant meaning of the facts being presented. This takes deliberate reflection, systematic thoughtfulness, and time.

For a teacher, thoughtfulness is about learners developing personal meaning, generalizations, applications, and significance from the intended meanings in books, on the Internet, and in class discussions. Learning is a cognitive journey, a learner moving through the facts of teaching and learning toward what is personal meaning, thoughtful and wise application, in each situation.

You may help this meaning-making in many ways. Let us give you one example of how to do this. Facts are best understood within a conceptual framework that assists the learner to consider what the fact(s) might mean. For example, the fact of apartheid, the formal segregation of races in South Africa, can best be understood by Canadian school children in a conceptual framework of ethnocentrism, the idea held by members of an ethnic group that their way of seeing the world is best. Children in Canada can understand ethnocentrism; perhaps many of them have experienced it. Apartheid may be understood only at a surface level if the concept of ethnocentrism is not used to provide the conceptual framework for deeper understanding of this political and social phenomenon.

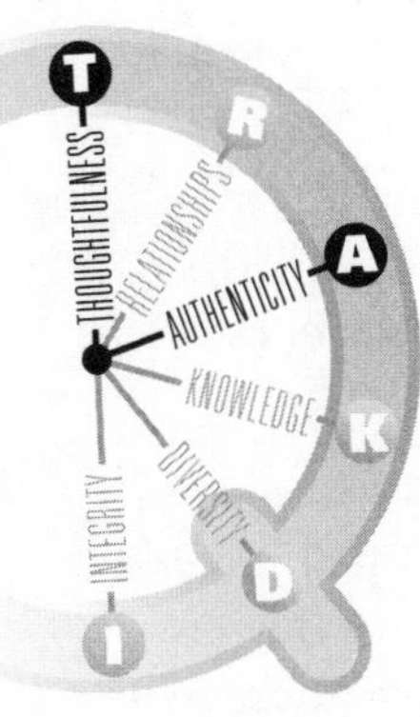

Consider Miss Thompson, Teddy's teacher in the story that began this chapter. The "meaning" of Teddy was revealed after his year with Miss Thompson. His teacher also gained a lot of meaning about learning that she might be able to transfer to other learners and other learning situations. She might have memorized in her education pre-service class the "fact" that learning needs conditions of trust, safety, and acceptance if it is to happen at all. However, she learned the "meaning" of that fact only after thoughtful consideration of her experience with Teddy. Whether this learning is transferred or not is largely dependent on the teacher's reminders to herself and the encouragement and opportunities that others might provide for her to transfer her learning to new situations.

Assumption 3: Children automatically apply their learning.

As we discussed in Assumption 2, learners often do not use what they already know to solve problems (Gick & Holyoak, 1980; Nist, Simpson, Olejnik, and Kealey, 1991). Learning a strategy for solving a math problem, designing a science experiment, accomplishing a physical skill in hockey, or negotiating your way through a social problem with your friend does not guarantee that you will use that strategy. Does this surprise you? Do you agree? We invite you to consider how teachers might teach to promote transfer of learning.

Experienced teachers often comment that they have learned that many truths about learning are, curiously enough, counterintuitive. The relationship between self-esteem and learning is one example. It might seem logical and sensible that if a learner feels good about his or her physical appearance, then physical self-esteem will be high and academic success is more likely. It turns out that this might not be true (Kohn, 1994). However, it does appear that learners' academic self-esteem—how learners feel about themselves academically—does influence academic performance (Kohn, 1994). A teacher may be most helpful to a learner by promoting a learner's academic self-esteem, by focusing lots of positive feedback and praise solely on the learner's academic work. Enhanced academic self-esteem, in turn, may further academic achievement.

Another truth about learning, this time an intuitive one, addresses the relationship between self-preoccupations and academic performance. Young people who have strong self-preoccupations tend to do more poorly academically. You probably know this to be true from reflecting on your own experience. You will need to study carefully and have integrated knowledge to avoid creating learning conditions that simply will be counterproductive (such as trying to make young people feel good about themselves physically so that they will do better academically).

Your task in helping learners learn will include going beyond just teaching strategies and then assuming that those strategies will be applied and transferred to new situations. It will be your task to create the conditions in which learners learn how to choose appropriate strategies and how to transfer them in new learning situations.

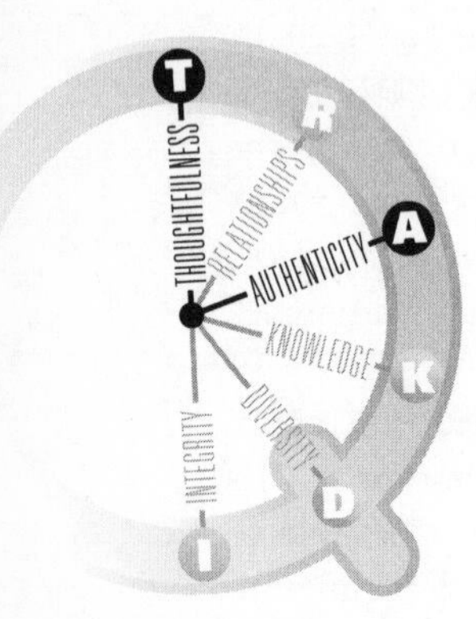

Finally, good learners know and use more strategies to accomplish tasks than do not-so-good learners. Good learners take notes, plan strategically when writing, regulate their use of time, analyze tasks more accurately, persist longer on learning tasks, and use more **metacognitive** strategies (thinking about one's thinking) than less successful learners (Zimmerman, 1990). It is a reasonable, intuitively correct assumption to conclude that your role will include not only teaching mathematics and art, for example, but teaching learners how to learn in many different ways, in all subjects.

Assumption 4: Learners who are successful in subjects like math are smarter than those who are not successful in these subjects.

The educational community you are preparing to enter owes a great deal to individuals like Howard Gardner, Robert J. Sternberg, and Anthony Gregorc, who have contributed much to our understanding that we all have individual preferences, orientations, and strengths when it comes to learning. We have our own **learning styles,** preferred ways of perceiving and processing information. We each have our own individual **intelligence,** a person's inherited and developed capacity for learning, that is unique, as is one's fingerprint or personality. Think again about Teddy Stallard. Obviously Teddy possessed strengths and individual style that were not recognized or applied until much later in his school career.

Gardner (1995a) has broadened our view of intelligence by suggesting that there are multiple intelligences—ways in which we are smart—and a number of ways to express those intelligences. There are many ways for learners to be successful if teachers provide opportunities for learners to express their learning, and their unique intelligences, in preferred ways.

R. Sternberg's (1989) approach to intelligence, the triarchic theory of intelligence, is also very important to educators. He focuses on how intelligence can be used in everyday life. His notion is that intelligence is a positive adaptation to, and selection and shaping of, real world environments relevant to one's life and abilities (p. 65). It includes experiential intelligence (coping with novelty), component intelligence (using metacognition, problem-solving, and new learning) and contextual intelligence (adaptation, selection, and shaping).

Gregorc (1982) has deepened and broadened our understanding of learning styles, suggesting that we have preferred ways of perceiving and interpreting information, which may be concrete or abstract, or preferred ways of ordering information in our long-term memory, which may be random or sequential. A learner's preference in learning is evidenced in the learner's behaviours. A concrete sequential learner will approach learning tasks in a unique way, characterized by attention to detail, a preference for facts, neatness, and order. An abstract random learner, on the other hand, will approach learning tasks with attention to talk, imagination, possibilities, and creativity.

Kenneth Dunn and Rita Dunn (1978) have reminded us that we have preferences regarding how we receive information. Some learners prefer to hear information (auditory learners). Some are visual learners, and others are **kinesthetic** (hands-on) **learners**.

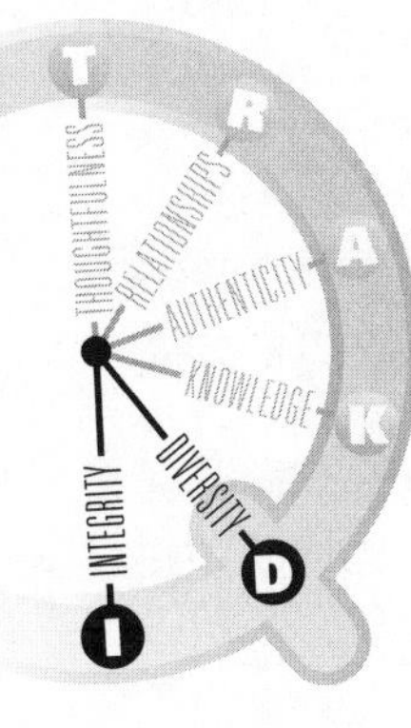

Thinking back to the Teddy Stallard story, did you consider that perhaps his teachers did not understand Teddy's learning style or his personality? Have you ever thought about your own preferences for learning and whether or not you were taught in the way you most preferred to learn?

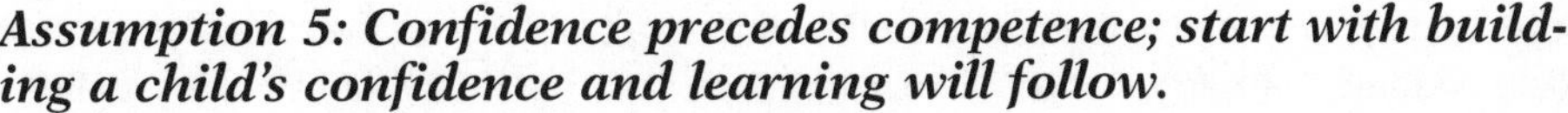

Assumption 5: Confidence precedes competence; start with building a child's confidence and learning will follow.

The problem with this assumption is best illustrated through the following example.

3.4 FOR YOUR CONSIDERATION

Imagine that you have been asked to dive off a ten-metre board into a swimming pool. You have never dived before, and you read that by the time you reach the water you will be travelling close to 45 km an hour.

What is your response to the request to dive? In considering your response, would your confidence precede your competence? Or would you need to be a competent before you would feel confident in this situation?

We invite you to consider that the opposite of this assumption is true, that competence precedes confidence. Learning does have a very real and important affective component. **Affective learning** includes a learner's feelings of confidence, fear, expectancy of rewards, desire to please someone, and many other feelings intricately connected to learning. One's affective response before and during a learning experience influences greatly how that learning will proceed and to what extent the learner will learn. Knowing that learning is under one's control, or self-efficacy, has been shown to influence learning (Bandura, 1977). **Self-efficacy** is confidence that a specific skill applied in a particular situation will produce results. Social models, the opportunity to watch people who are similar to us engage successfully in learning tasks (Schunk, 1991), and feedback from those models represent influences on a person's perceived self-efficacy. Self-efficacy, however, is highly domain-specific; that is, a learner may have high self-efficacy in physical education but may have low self-efficacy in reading.

To assist a learner in developing self-efficacy means providing learning experiences that are just a little beyond the learner's ability, to create a scaffold (Vygotsky, 1987) for the learner to learn the new skill, concept, or strategy. A **scaffold** is a piece of existing knowledge, similar to the new information and familiar to the learner, on which the learner can make personal meaning. An example of a scaffold would be teaching the concept of racism on the scaffold of a person's individual experience of rejection. This area just beyond the learner's experience is sometimes called the **zone of proximal development** (Vygotsky, 1987). If competence can be achieved by effectively building scaffolds, teachers will be encouraging confidence.

3.5 FOR YOUR CONSIDERATION

Imagine yourself in a drama class where everyone has to perform different roles in front of an audience. What can the teacher do to provide the scaffold that would reduce anxiety and improve performance? In your imagination, did you consider looking at the back wall above the audience during your performance to help your confidence? Perhaps avoiding eye contact with your audience would increase your confidence. This is one example of a scaffolding technique that may help you to move into the zone of proximal development. What other techniques might build your competence, resulting in greater confidence?

Another important affective component in learning concerns the role of attributions in motivating learning. It is likely that you attribute your success either to skill or to effort. Perhaps, from time to time, you might attribute your good performance to luck or task difficulty, and your poor performance to lack of effort.

"Confidence precedes competence." Does this statement apply to the student shown in this photo?

Generally, you have an attributional makeup, a persisting and fairly consistent approach to attributing your success to luck, effort, task difficulty, or skill. There is good news and bad news for you in your journey toward helping learners become competent. The bad news is that attributional makeup—that is, how learners explain their success and failures in school—is developed early on in schooling and is difficult to change (Weiner, 1990).

3.6 FOR YOUR CONSIDERATION

If you were to ask a Grade 5 learning-disabled student why he or she is having problems in school, what answer do you think you would you get?

Chances are, the Grade 5 student would say, "Becausel am dumb." What does this tell you about the attributional makeup of that student?

Once a learner's attributional makeup is set, there are a number of difficult obstacles for a teacher to overcome. These include **learned helplessness,** when people come to believe that events and circumstances in their lives are uncontrollable (Woolfolk, 1998, p. 368), a persistent passivity in approaching learning tasks, and generally low academic self-esteem.

The good news is this: of the four things to which we attribute success (luck, effort, task difficulty, or skill), the one most likely to promote adaptive motivational tendencies is effort—one's success and academic fate can be influenced by one's personal effort. A learner can decide to try to be successful. Another part of the good news is that attributional makeup can be re-trained (Pressley, Borkowski, & Schneider, 1989). If students are taught strategies that are not contextually bound—that is, that the learner recognizes how the strategy can be applied across to new learning situations—there are hopeful indications that attributional makeup can be changed for the better.

Assumption 6: Knowledge is less important than general ability in learning; being intelligent is better than knowledge, when it comes to learning.

Have you ever said something like this, "If only I were as intelligent as ______, then I'd do well in school?" You might be surprised to find out that a good deal of research, as well as practical wisdom from classroom teachers, calls this assumption into question. In fact, the more you know the better you might be able to do, in school, in your work, on your sport team, and in just about every area of life. It is important to understand how knowledge is made, what knowledge is, and how knowledge is used. We invite you to think about knowledge in ways that might be new and helpful to you.

Domain-specific procedural knowledge (how to) and domain-specific declarative knowledge (what) are stored in different ways in the long-term memory (J. Anderson, 1990). They are related only in that procedural knowledge was first declarative knowledge. For example, your ability to read a page in this book (a domain-specific procedural knowledge) is due in part to your having some strategies that are well-learned and automatically applied when pulled up into that workroom called the short-term memory. Until the strategies are activated and communication occurs in the workroom with the procedural knowledge, there is no production of the strategies and no further learning.

Knowledge is very important in learning, perhaps more important than one's general intellectual ability. You will recall, from Chapter 1, that declarative knowledge is organized in a food chain of knowledge, beginning with macropropositions (the gist of things) up to the level of a worldview. The questions in this section are, How do we help learners acquire both the declarative and the procedural knowledge they need in each subject area? and, How does the knowledge they have influence further learning?

There is a growing belief that knowledge is situational, that knowing is not separable from the actions that gave rise to it or from the culture in which that knowledge is embedded (J.S. Brown, Collins, and Duguid, 1989). The most meaningful knowledge then, is constructed through real problem solving, authentic learning and assessment activities, and in social situations. In a real sense, thinking is socially constructed; knowledge is a social construction.

The following example might help you understand this point. One of the authors taught for a time in Zambia, Africa. One day, he and another teacher paid a farmer a few dollars to be transported across the river into Mozambique. On the return trip, when the boat was nearly across, a number of hippos popped up around the boat. This author recalls looking at his fellow teacher and saying, "How exciting! This is one reason I came to Africa." The hippos were so close that the author recalls calculating that he could have spat on one. This author, who had never seen a hippo before, had learned about hippos watching Walt Disney productions on television back home in Canada, sitting comfortably in a warm, safe living room. He certainly did not know that hippos are highly aggressive, very territorial, and kill more people in Africa every year than any other animal. And this author was going to spit on one of them! Clearly, the author's knowledge was situational, and an intuitive, wise judgment was not possible. The expert decision making of a well-informed person whose knowledge was constructed in an authentic social situation was obviously absent. The transfer of learning was only superficial.

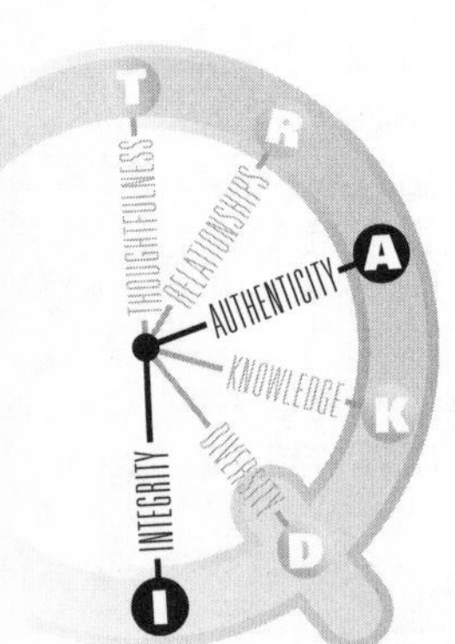

As you can see, knowledge is very important to learning, to what can be learned.

3.7 FOR YOUR CONSIDERATION

How does a learner's prior knowledge influence new learning? How might it interfere with new learning?

Working in groups, consider the topic of ethnocentrism, the notion that one's own culture is superior to another person's culture. What prior knowledge of each group member might have the greatest influence on the ability of the entire group to learn about the impact and significance of this notion? What might be the greatest interference in each individual's ability to understand ethnocentrism? How might you assist the learning of this concept in your class?

Assumption 7: Relationships are of secondary importance in learning.

Children and adults can learn from observing others. However, if learning through observation is to occur, some conditions are necessary (Bandura, 1977). First, the person observed (the model) needs to have some status with the observer. Second, the observer needs to have some cognitive abilities to anticipate similar consequences to those experienced by the model. Also, the observer needs to have the performance capabilities to perform the action being observed. However, models can be far off and unrelated to the observer. Children can observe and learn from movie stars and musicians. Sometimes what children learn is not appropriate. Because children do learn from observing others, it is important that the models children choose are worthy of being observed. Good relationships with good models can be a very important condition of learning for children.

Your great-great-grandparents quite likely believed four things about learning: 1) there was a right way to do things; 2) there was a wrong way; 3) one learned the right way by being trained in it; 4) the way to get children to learn the right way was to provide models of virtue and character for children to emulate (Kirkpatrick, 1983). There is wisdom inherent in Kirkpatrick's simple suggestion: children need to learn from observing models of respect, dignity, and care.

3.8 FOR YOUR CONSIDERATION

Name the person who has had the greatest influence in your life. Describe that person's attributes, the characteristics that were the most endearing to you. Compare your list of attributes with a classmate's, and note the similarities and differences between your lists. We suspect that, despite the differences, each of you had a very good relationship with your chosen person. What characteristics did you and a classmate identify in common? Did your list include respect? Care? Enthusiasm? Others? Drawing from the characteristics on your lists, what conclusions would you make about the kind of teacher you would like to be?

Assumption 8: Learning does not happen in randomness.

Do you think that order and quiet are absolute requirements for learning? Consider the suggestion that perhaps randomness and activity are better conditions for learning. The following few ideas call into question notions regarding quiet and order in learning.

What can be done to increase a learner's depth of processing knowledge? One way is to introduce deliberate **contextual interference**, in which new skills and concepts are introduced in the midst of practising recently learned skills and concepts. Suppose you are learning the game of basketball. Is it better to practise one skill over and over until that skill has become rather automatic before going on to the next skill? You might intuitively be led to say yes. But to what extent could boredom be a problem? What about lost opportunities to practise the real game? Loss of attention to details may be a problem with repetition. It might be a better strategy to introduce a new skill part way through the practice of a previously

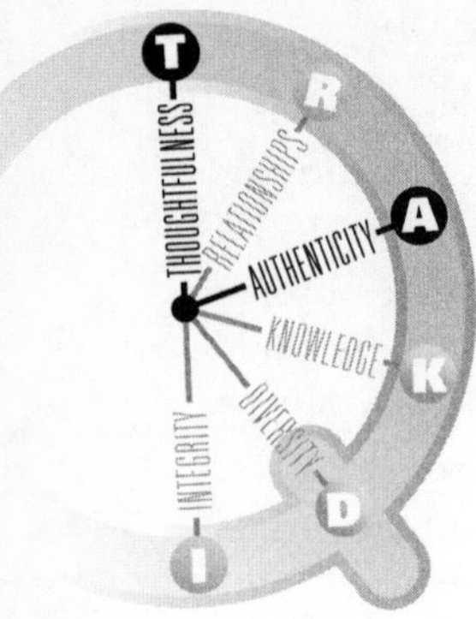

learned skill and distribute practices throughout the ongoing learning of basketball (Kintsch, 1988; Druckman & Bjork, 1991).

Random learning helps to promote depth of processing. The question you will need to address as you assume responsibility for a learning environment is how much randomness can you tolerate? Is a quiet classroom, full of order and routine, necessarily the atmosphere most conducive to learning?

Assumption 9: The brain is of limited value in learning.

The brain seems to be programmed to expect some experiences (Anastasiow, 1993). Language learning is one; walking is another. When relevant stimulation is provided, particular neurons are activated in areas corresponding to that experience, and that area of the brain develops. These expectation synapses are prepared to create permanent synaptic connections, and when they do, learning has occurred. It is clear there are biological determinants of learning that program us to learn some things, providing we receive the necessary environmental stimulation. If we do not receive the required experiences during sensitive periods, we find that these experience-expectant synapses permanently die off (Anastasiow, 1993).

The brain literally grows, develops, and changes through experiences (Diamond, 1991). This occurs through myelination, the coating of the sheaths of the synapses. It is true that there are sensitive periods in which learning is most likely to have the greatest long-term benefit. Biology predisposes; nurture, or experience, disposes. It is necessary for us to create the conditions in our classrooms through which the brain can develop to its optimum.

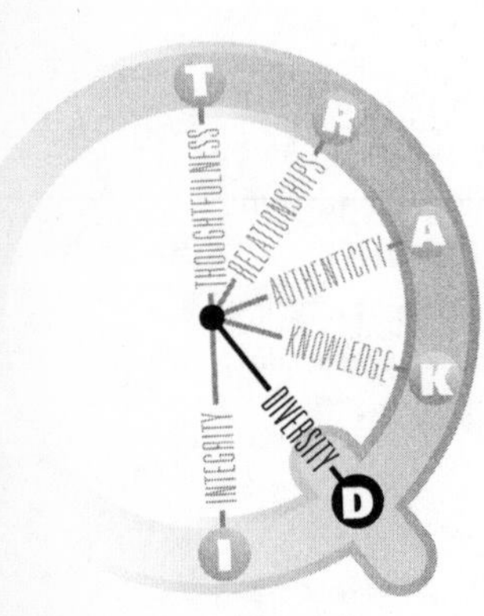

It is useful to remember that some learning is much more attributable to nurture, such as learning to type or learning to respect a teacher. We advise you to exercise caution and engage in lots of further study as you try to understand the intricate and complex relationship between the mind and learning; between nature and nurture.

Assumption 10: A change in behaviour is the only real indicator of learning; if behaviour does not change, learning has not occurred.

What exactly is learning? If you have found yourself asking this question up to this point in the book, then the first nine assumptions have been successful in encouraging you to be thoughtful about learning. You have demonstrated thoughtfulness. Most educators and psychologists agree that learning means that some form of change in knowledge and behaviour has occurred as a result of some experience. This change can be observable, as in being able to send an email or drive a car, but it can also be internal, as in a changed idea about what is right and wrong, or, a change in feelings toward a person. In these last two examples, a change in behaviour is not necessary, although it would be logical to conclude that a change in behaviour would eventually be evident. But is it always so? Does a change in behaviour always mean that learning has occurred? Conversely, can learning occur if there is no change in behaviour?

Suppose a person reads a research study that positively links eating high cholesterol foods with heart disease. If the person continues to eat potato chips, should we conclude that no learning has occurred? To reach such a conclusion would be incorrect. We may very likely hear a great deal of comment from this person, rationalizing and perhaps angrily defending his diet, and reflecting on the validity of the research. It would not surprise you that this person may even feel a little guilty when eating deep-fried food, chocolate-covered desserts, and sugar-coated snacks, particularly when a loved one who knows about the same research study is sitting nearby. We can conclude that learning has in fact occurred, even if the person carries on eating such food.

Children can learn without demonstrating it through behaviour. A child may learn that grades are important to parents and teachers, but not change behaviour to achieve good grades. Can you think of other examples?

Reflection and Perspective on the Chapter

Assumptions have a powerful influence in our reflections about learning, teaching, and schooling. In this chapter we explored a number of typical assumptions that pertain, broadly, to schooling. From these assumptions we have raised questions and presented information that is intended to expand your meaning and understanding of some important aspects of learning and teaching. Think about these matters carefully, especially those that connect facts, experience, meaning, understanding, activity, and knowledge in the context of thoughtfulness.

Of the teaching qualities presented in Chapter 2, it is the quality of thoughtfulness that is the most essential for creating dynamic and effective learning environments.

Schools are increasingly being challenged on matters such as results, morals, standards, trends, character, performance, and skills. Implicit in these accusations is the seeming reticence of schools to change. Society is changing with such rapidity that many are struggling to keep pace. Consider the following observations typical of schools, and in a thoughtful way uncover the assumptions about learning, teaching, and school management that would likely be at work. Ask yourself, If the following were the *predominant* practices of learning/teaching/management, what assumptions would be motivating behaviour?

- A whole class learning the same way
- All students working on the same text questions
- Students working in co-operative groups
- A sixty-minute examination for all children in a class
- Student desks in rows with the teacher's desk centred at the back
- Students working with the teacher to set class rules and expectations
- The whole school breaking for recess at 10:15 A.M.
- The teacher explaining the solution to a math problem on the chalkboard, followed by the class completing practice questions from the end of a chapter in a textbook

All behaviour is driven by assumptions that provide validation for that behaviour. There is nothing inherently wrong with this so long as we are constantly questioning our assumptions to ensure that we are working in ways that are consistent with current professional knowledge. Difficulties arise when this questioning, this thoughtfulness, is not practised. Newman (1987) has challenged teachers to uncover assumptions that describe practice. She posits interesting ideas about tacitness. Senge (1990) and Sergiovanni (1992) see assumptions as mental models and mindscapes, respectively, and raise similar ideas of tacitness. Assumptions influence how we respond to our world; they help shape and determine our actions, and describe our beliefs about learning, teaching, and school organization.

> If mental models [assumptions] are the ways we understand and respond to our world and are often tacit, then schooling behaviors that need to change become problematic. Any tacitly held behavior-driving mental models [assumptions] are not available for challenge. They will continue to inspire and influence attitudes, understandings, and behavior toward conventional practice, even while overt intentions may be considering change. (Waldron et al., 1999, p. 15)

The challenge for you, then, as you engage in reflection and perspective about this chapter, is to think deeply about learning, teaching, and schooling, and to question whether or not your own behaviours are driven by assumptions rooted in current professional knowledge. We encourage you to think about change: to what extent it is needed in schools. Do schools tend to operate from assumptions that are seldom questioned? Does the relative isolation in which teachers work tend to militate against change? What are the assumptions that describe the ways we "do" schooling? The following chapters describe different facets of learning against which to consider your assumptions.

Key Terms

Suggested Further Reading

National Research Council. (2000). *How People Learn: Brain, Mind, Experience and School*. Washington, DC: National Academy Press. The product of a two-year study conducted by the Committee on Development in the Science of Learning. The volume provides links from research findings to the classroom.

Chapter 4

Individual Learning

Chapter Focus

In this chapter, we will describe theoretical perspectives that represent the broad area of individual learning. **Individual learning theories** centre on individual changes in behaviour and on thinking through individual experience. In contrast, **social learning theories** centre on learning through observing other people and acts, being influenced by what is seen more than by what is said. Individual learning theories we will discuss are cognitive, behavioural, and psychomotor.

Cognitive learning theories posit that knowledge is constructed in the minds of learners, that knowledge acquisition, not a behaviour or response, is the goal of education. These theories study how behaviours are learned, how children process information and construct meaning. Cognitive theorists such as Bruner (1971) and J. Anderson (1990) believe that the goal of instruction is not just the total number of right responses a child gives in a math test, or the child's performance of five good behaviours in physical education class. Education should be concerned about *how* learners learn math, *how* they acquire, organize, and use knowledge in physical education. As cognitive theory matured, different cognitive-related frameworks emerged, from discovery learning (Bruner, 1971) and a process-based understanding of learning (R. Gagne, 1985) to an emphasis on styles of learning (Dunn, 1999) and multiple intelligence theory (Gardner, 1995), referred to later in the chapter.

Behavioural theorists argue that emitted behaviours (observable behaviours) and responses to stimuli are both important facts of classroom life for a teacher (Skinner, 1950). That is not to say that behaviourists do not account for internal, cognitive processes. They recognize, however, that what a teacher will see, day by day, is observable behaviour, and not a schema or a worldview. The goal for the teacher, then, is to shape the observable behaviours and responses of children.

The last theoretical perspective, **psychomotor learning**, studies the sequential development of understanding and skills in managing one's body and manipulating physical objects (Harrow, 1972). Some of life's most important lessons can be learned through this physical activity.

Focus Questions

1. How does the brain provide for learning? Does the brain learn some things better than others?
2. What is intellect? Are some learners smarter than others? Are there different kinds of intelligence? Can we improve our intelligence?
3. How could conditions for learning in the various subjects taught in schools (mathematics, language arts, physical education, drama, etc.) best be created? Is there a preferred way to teach each subject?
4. What implications does intelligence testing have on the way things are done in the classroom and schools and in testing?
5. What implication does the theory of multiple intelligence have on the classroom?
6. If our emotional system drives our attentional system, what should teachers consider when working with young learners?
7. Given that all people have perceptual learning preferences, do teachers tend to teach according to their own learning preference and, if so, does this make a difference to learners?
8. To what extent is it important for teachers to understand behavioural theory, classical conditioning, operant conditioning, and punishment?
9. In what ways are psychomotor learning and academic learning compatible?

4.1 FOR YOUR CONSIDERATION

In Grade 7 one of this book's authors made an incredible discovery. A teacher started a science class by placing a piece of paper over a very full cup of water and quickly and smoothly turning that cup of water over on his desk, but the water did not flow out. The author had not carefully watched how the teacher had prepared the cup, the paper, or anything else (not being accustomed to paying much attention in science class—or in any other class, for that matter). But he did pay attention for those few moments and as a result, developed an interest in science that has stayed with him to this day. He developed a very tangential interest in magic (recalling how hooked he was that day on seeing something happen that, ostensibly, shouldn't have happened). His respect for that teacher grew (though his behaviour did not change).

1. Did the author learn anything, even though his behaviour remained largely unchanged?
2. Can you recall a discovery incident like this one in your life, where learning occurred, but behaviour remained unchanged?

Cognitive Learning

We take memory for granted—until, for example, we can't recall someone's name at work or where we left our car keys. We may panic for a few seconds, feel we are losing our minds or experiencing early signs of failing memory. Memory is essential for going about the daily business of our lives. We need memory for everything we do: perceiving the world, synthesizing and analyzing information, and applying knowledge to new situations (Weiss, 2000). This is the cognitive theorist's perspective on learning.

Role of the Brain in Learning

The brain is the most mysterious organ in the human body. Scientists and educators are keen to understand how memory and learning happen, and new technologies are helping us gain understanding of how the brain works. Chemical changes are created at the neuron level. Although the brain weighs only approximately three pounds, it contains billions of neurons (cells). Without these cells there is no substance for our minds to work with (R. Sternberg, 1995).

Biologists can tell us much about brain chemistry; but for educational practice, the concept of complexity is more helpful for understanding the layers of organization within the brain that act together, apparently miraculously, to handle not only memory, but also vision, learning, emotion, and consciousness.

Right and Left Hemisphere Specialization

The concept of **hemisphere specialization** (the notion that the human brain is divided into halves, or hemispheres, each with specialized functions) was entrenched in popular culture of the 1980s. In 1981 Roger Sperry received a Nobel Peace Prize for his research into the different ways the left and right hemispheres of the brain process information. Hippocrates, the Greek founder of medicine, first noticed the idea of a divided brain in 400 BCE. He noted that soldiers struck on the left side of the head with a sword often suffered speech impairment, whereas those struck on the right side did not. He concluded that the two sides of the brain must function differently (Gross, 1991). This historical theory is not without criticism, but it has become firmly established on the educational landscape.

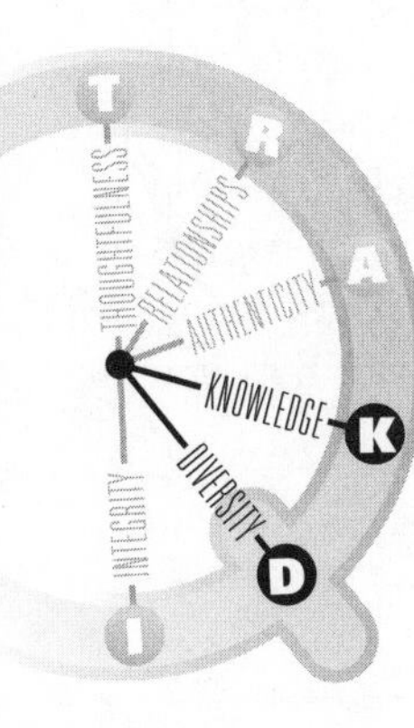

This theory of the structure and functions of the brain suggests that the two different sides, or hemispheres, of the brain control two different "modes" of thinking. In the research from experimentation (Gross, 1991) the left brain thinker was considered more logical, linear-sequential rational, analytical, objective, and more likely to look at parts rather than the whole. The right-brain thinker was considered more random, intuitive, holistic, able to synthesize, able to be more subjective, and more likely to look at the whole picture. B. Edwards (1999) discusses the strengths of both sides of the brain in her book, *Drawing on the Right Side of the Brain*. This right- and left-hemisphere brain theory has assisted teachers in their advocacy of the fine arts, practical arts, and physical education in the school system.

According to Springer (1989), neuropsychologists do not agree with "polarizers," those who support the theory of right- and left-hemisphere specialization and the link between learning styles and brain asymmetry. Educators are looking at more current brain and learning theories from psychologists and neuroscientists to assist them with more effective teaching. The career that you are about to embark on will continue to be concerned with brain and learning theories.

New Learning Theories and Brain Research

The most basic unit in the human body is the cell. The brain contains about 100 billion nerve cells, or neurons, and one trillion supporting glia cells. Together these cells make 1000 trillion synaptic connection points with each other. All neurons are composed of three basic parts: the cell body, the axon, and the dendrites (R. Sternberg, 1995). Visualize a growing plant's root system, the seed being the cell body, and the stem and its branches being the axon and dendrites. With the development of new brain imaging devices such as the magnetic resonance imaging (MRI), positron emission topography (PET), and other technologies, neuroscientists are learning more about the brain. Mountcastle (1998) stated, "[T]he use of PET has produced a basic fund of information about the functional anatomy of the brain and how it changes in different behavior states, particularly when humans execute cognitive tasks" (p. 10). "In the coming years, we can expect new and more accurate technologies to further illuminate the brain's mysteries" (Jensen, 1988, p. 2).

You may be surprised to know that you were born with all the brain cells (neurons) you will ever have. How, then, do these brain cells contribute to learning? D'Arcangelo (1998) offers an explanation: "As far as we know, neurons are the only cells that process information. With a few exceptions, you can't grow new neurons, but you can grow new connections between neurons, and these connections create learning and memory" (p. 22).

According to Jensen (1988), "learning changes the brain because it can rewire itself with each new stimulation, experience, and behavior" (p. 13). Novices who are learning something new for the first time will use more of their brain, but will use it less efficiently: "It is like trying to clear a path through a forest. The first time is a struggle because you have to fight your way through the undergrowth. The second time you travel that way will be easier because of the clearing you did on your first journey" (Buzon & Buzon, 1996, p. 29). You will get to know and understand the path better by travelling the same path in different fashions, (for example, walking, biking, and running on the same path). Learning the same information in different ways, such as reading, seeing, touching, singing, and drawing, will also contribute to understanding. The brain adapts and rewires itself quickly; therefore learning something new, doing something new, listening to new music, visiting a new place, solving a new problem, or making new friends can stimulate the brain (Jensen, 1988). Regardless of how you define intelligences, "the key to getting smarter is growing more synaptic connections between brain cells and not losing existing connections" (Jensen, 1988, p. 15).

4.2 FOR YOUR CONSIDERATION

No two brains are exactly alike. No enriched environment will completely satisfy any two learners for an extended period. Teachers need to engage learners through interaction. "Our challenge in education is to determine what makes an enriched classroom environment" (D'Arcangelo, 1998, p. 22). What are some ways teachers can engage and challenge their learners? Consider the six teaching qualities discussed in Chapter 2.

Recall Assumption 9 from Chapter 3: "The brain is of limited value in learning" (page 58). In light of this information on the brain and learning, has your understanding of this assumption changed?

Good arts programs, unlike math or language arts, are difficult to evaluate, particularly in an era concerned with measurable standards. Sylwester (1998) writes that the arts aren't about the security of a correct answer. The arts have important biological and human value, not only for muscular development, but also for the development of communication and emotional systems. Consider the following:

> Evidence from the brain sciences and evolutionary psychology increasingly suggests that the arts (along with such functions as language and math) play an important role in brain development and maintenance—so it's a serious matter for schools to deny children direct curricular access to the arts. (Sylwester, 1998, p. 32)

Emotions and Learning

What are your assumptions about emotions and learning? Most educators agree that emotion and mental attitude are both important to learning. But how important are they? Consider the story "Three Letters From Teddy" in Chapter 3. When

4.3 FOR YOUR CONSIDERATION

Think back to when you were a student in elementary school. Do you have fond memories of your involvement in the arts—art, drama, dance, singing, playing musical instruments? Did these experiences affect you emotionally, physically? Do you remember these arts experiences and the teachers who exposed you to the arts? What were they and why do you remember them with fondness?

Good arts programs are difficult to evaluate in an era of measurable standards.

did Teddy "get caught up with the rest of the class" and show "a definite upward curve in his grades"? Why did this occur? What caused Teddy's situation to change? "Researchers have demonstrated that emotional states can affect learning, memory, social judgements, and creativity" (Zimbardo & Gerrig, 1996, p. 471). Does how we feel affect the way we enter the learning environment and, ultimately, whether or not we experience success?

Think back to your student days. If you're like most adults, even cursory reflection will evoke images, vivid snapshots of what you did in class and off-campus, topics you studied, teachers, a classmate or two, and even things hanging on the walls. Along with those snapshots, you may recall feelings of joyful anticipation, a warm-hearted laugh in an environment of good humour and caring, and memories of events in your favourite classes. On the other hand, you may recall feelings of dread, an uneasy sensation in the pit of your stomach, humiliation, or anger related to classes in which you were unsuccessful (Kovalik & Olsen, 1998).

In searching your memory, you will discover what neuroscientists have stated: emotions drive attention and attention drives learning and memory

Emotional Intelligence

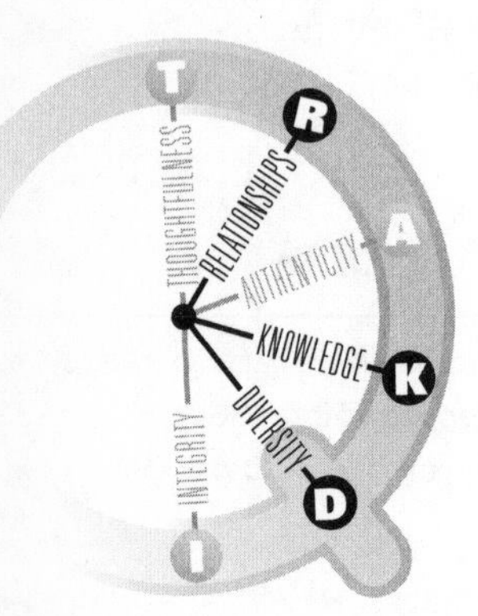

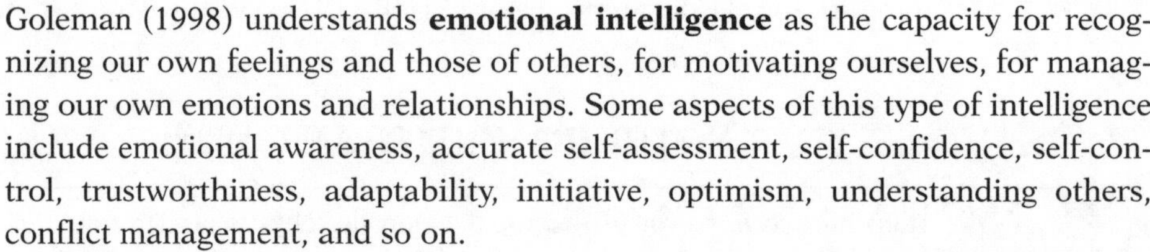

Goleman (1998) understands **emotional intelligence** as the capacity for recognizing our own feelings and those of others, for motivating ourselves, for managing our own emotions and relationships. Some aspects of this type of intelligence include emotional awareness, accurate self-assessment, self-confidence, self-control, trustworthiness, adaptability, initiative, optimism, understanding others, conflict management, and so on.

We remember little about things that have no emotional tag on them (Kovalik & Olsen, 1998). The emotional system tells us whether something is important—whether we ought to devote any energy to it. Traditionally, teachers told children that school was for learning (and memorizing), and that emotional expression was to be saved for recess and for art or drama class.

4.4 FOR YOUR CONSIDERATION

"Imagine a classroom learning session which is so powerful that many students have almost total memory of it twenty years later. When these student begin to recall this session, it becomes quite vivid, and they actually appear to be reliving it"(Bloom, 1982, p. 193). Bloom calls this a "peak learning" experience. Was there a learning situation in your elementary school that you remember with great fondness or fear?

Perceptual Learning Preferences

According to Dunn (1999) **learning style** is the way individuals concentrate, process, internalize, and remember new and different material. She conceptualizes learning styles as "perceptual strengths" or preferences, and describes four types: (1) visual learners, those who learn best by seeing; (2) auditory learners, people who learn best by listening, hearing the spoken word, and sometimes by talking; (3) kinesthetic learners, who learn best by getting their body involved through physical activity and direct involvement; (4) tactual (tactile) learners, who learn best by getting their hands involved in the learning. The last two are often grouped under one heading, tactile-kinesthetic (Filipczak, 1995).

Classroom instruction can also be based on five stimuli and twenty-one elements designed by Dunn (1999) from research on learning styles, shown in Table 4.1.

The learning style inventory analyzes the conditions under which students in Grades 3–12 prefer to learn new and different materials. It uses 100 statements that elicit self-diagnostic responses on a five-point Likert-type scale, statements such as, "When I really have a lot of studying to do, I like to work alone and I enjoy being with friends when I study" (Dunn, Dunn, & Price, 1990).

What Does It Mean to Be Intelligent?

In your family, who would you consider to be most intelligent? When you think of an intelligent person, what characteristics does he or she possess? Recall "Three Letters From Teddy" from Chapter 3. What did Teddy's teachers believe about his abilities and intelligence when they first met him? What words did Miss Thompson use to describe Teddy? Was this a fair or accurate assessment of Teddy? What circumstances led to Miss Thompson's belief about Teddy's academic potential, and what caused her to re-evaluate her first impressions?

Educators, researchers, and the lay public have held various beliefs and numerous debates about intelligence. What is it? Is it many things? Is it inherited or developed and nurtured? Does being labelled "intelligent" depend on what is valued in the culture or society? In the following sections, we will look at various theories of intelligence in an effort to understand what it means to be intelligent.

Table 4.1 Dunn's Learning Style Inventory: Twenty-one Elements

<table>
<tr><th></th><th colspan="9">Diagnosing Learning Styles</th></tr>
<tr><th>Stimuli</th><th colspan="9">Elements</th></tr>
<tr><td>Environmental</td><td colspan="2">Sound</td><td colspan="2">Light</td><td colspan="3">Temperature</td><td colspan="2">Design</td></tr>
<tr><td>Emotional</td><td colspan="2">Motivation</td><td colspan="2">Persistence</td><td colspan="3">Responsibility</td><td colspan="2">Structure</td></tr>
<tr><td>Sociological</td><td>Peers</td><td colspan="2">Self</td><td>Pair</td><td colspan="2">Team</td><td colspan="2">Adult</td><td>Varied</td></tr>
<tr><td>Physical</td><td colspan="2">Perceptual</td><td colspan="2">Intake</td><td colspan="3">Time</td><td colspan="2">Mobility</td></tr>
<tr><td>Psychological</td><td colspan="2">Analytic/Global</td><td colspan="3">Cerebral Dominance</td><td colspan="4">Impulsive/Reflective</td></tr>
</table>

(Source: Designed by Rita Dunn and Kenneth Dunn. From *Learning Styles Inventory* (p. 18). by R. Dunn, K. Dunn and G.E. Price, 1990. Lawrence, KS: Price Systems. Reprinted with permission.)

Alfred Binet and the Intelligence Quotient

A century ago psychologist Alfred Binet was given the task of developing a means for determining who would experience difficulty in school. At that time France was experiencing a great influx of provincials and immigrants "of uncertain stock," and the ministry of education wished to know which children would not advance smoothly through the system. Binet developed a series of questions that, if answered incorrectly, would indicate whether a child was likely to experience difficulty in school. Psychometricians, who at that time earned their living in England and Germany by measuring psychological variables, contributed to the conceptualization and instrumentation of intelligence testing. These came to be known as IQ tests. An IQ, or **intelligence quotient,** designates the ratio between mental age and chronological age (Gardner, 1999). By the 1920s, the intelligence test had become a regular practice in educational systems in North America. Today intelligence tests are no longer widely administered in schools. However, students are selectively administered tests that measure aptitude and achievement in specific disciplines or areas. An example would be the SAT, or Scholastic Aptitude Test (R. Sternberg, 1995).

Changes to Intelligence Testing

Although intelligence tests are no longer widely administered, interest in intelligence and scholastic measures will still be of interest. Psychometric researchers continue to investigate the predictive powers of various instruments that might correlate measured intelligence and success in life. Many are looking to neuroscientists for a biological basis of intelligence in the genes, neural structures, and brain-wave patterns.

4.5 FOR YOUR CONSIDERATION

The effect from art experiences is expressed as an intelligence, usually referred to as emotional intelligence. As in the cognitive area, emotional intelligence is measured as a quotient (EQ). What is emotional intelligence? Most of us perceive intelligence as a mental quality, and emotions as a feeling quality. We are beginning to realize, however, that true intelligence is a blend of the head and the heart. Goleman (1998) emphasizes the need for people to assess and develop their emotional savvy as though it were a unique form of intelligence. All EQ tests reflect the biases of those who created them. All tests are merely indications of potential in the moment. EQ is not an easily quantifiable measure. It pivots on such intangibles as social deftness, persistence, and empathy.

Howard Gardner and Multiple Intelligences

Howard Gardner, a professor of education at the Harvard Graduate School of Education, believed that the psychometric view of intelligence is too narrow, and that we actually possess nine forms of mental representation, or **multiple intelligences.**

> Owing to the accidents of heredity, environment, and their interactions, no two of us exhibit the same intelligences in precisely the same proportions. Our "profiles of intelligence" differ from one another. This fact poses intriguing challenges and opportunities for our education system. We can ignore these differences and pretend that we are all the same; historically, that is what most education systems have done. Or we can fashion an education system that tries to exploit these differences, individualizing instruction and assessment as much as possible. (Gardner, 1999, p. 71)

These intelligences include musical, bodily–kinesthetic, logical–mathematical, verbal–linguistic, visual–spatial, interpersonal, intrapersonal, naturalistic, and spiritual intelligences.

1. Musical intelligence is based on the recognition of tonal patterns, including various environmental sounds, and on a sensitivity to rhythm and beats.
2. Bodily–kinesthetic intelligence relates to physical movement and athletic performance.
3. Logical–mathematical intelligence, at times called "scientific thinking," deals with inductive and deductive thinking/reasoning, numbers, and the recognition of abstract patterns.
4. Verbal–linguistic intelligence relates to words and language, both written and spoken.
5. Visual–spatial intelligence relies on the sense of sight and being able to visualize an object, including the ability to create mental images and pictures.
6. Interpersonal intelligence operates primarily through person-to-person relationships and communication.
7. Intrapersonal intelligence relates to inner states of being—self-reflection and metacognition,
8. Naturalistic intelligence is based on the human ability to discriminate among living things (plants, animals) as well as sensitivity to other features of the natural world—consumer discrimination.
9. Spiritual intelligence is the most recent criteria added to the list. This intelligence includes five related competencies, or capacities: the capacity to transcend the physical and material, the ability to experience heightened states of consciousness, the ability to sanctify everyday experience, the ability to utilize spiritual resources to solve problems, and the capacity to be virtuous (K. Edwards, 2000, p. 71).

The "MI approach" to learning entails focusing on the child and planning an education program appropriate for that child. For curriculum and assessment, this means drawing on intelligence in various ways, including interdisciplinary studies and arts integration.

Gardner concludes that "only if we recognize multiple intelligences can we reach more students, and give those students the opportunity to demonstrate what they have understood" (Gardner, 1995a, p. 2).

Which kind of intelligence is being used by the children shown in each of these photos?

4.6 FOR YOUR CONSIDERATION

1. Is intelligence singular, or does it consist of various more or less independent intellectual faculties?
2. Is intelligence (or are intelligences) largely inherited?
3. Do you know what the term *culturally biased* means when applied to intelligence testing?
4. How can we account for the diversity of skills and capacities that are or have been valued in different communities around the world (Gardner, 1999)?
5. Which of the nine intelligences have been most dominant in your school experience?

Implications for Multiple Intelligences in the Classroom

Gardner's MI theory attracted the attention of the educational community, which agreed that not all students learn the same way, that not all students have the same kinds of minds. For education to work for most learners, these differences in "mentation and strengths" need to be taken into account "rather than denied or ignored" (1995, p. 206). B. Campbell (1991) implemented Gardner's theory of multiple intelligence in his Grade 3 classroom and discovered many differences compared to a more traditional classroom teaching approach. Students had an opportunity to specialize and excel in at least one area, but most excelled in three or four, and each student learned the subject matter in a variety of ways. Campbell believed this multiplied the students' chances of successfully understanding course material and increased their retention of this information. The students were challenged intellectually, and they exercised their creativity. They also met emotional needs by working with others and feeling successful. Campbell believed that teaching and learning using multiple intelligences helped to solve many common classroom problems and optimized learning for the students and the teachers.

Multiple Intelligence and Testing

How can we be sure that what we teach and how we teach it results in student learning? Does multiple intelligence theory improve test scores? Gardner feels that educators need to get away from tests and correlation among tests, to not

4.7 FOR YOUR CONSIDERATION

Assumption: Learning does not happen in randomness.

In light of the discussion on intelligence, we invite you to consider the following tasks as a way of presenting information.

Task 1. Scheduling learning experiences

Take the information of a subject, such as physical education. Instead of scheduling the content in blocks, or units of study (when learners might do three weeks of basketball, followed by three weeks of dance, and so on), schedule the content into one week, where your learners play basketball on Monday, dance on Tuesday, perform gymnastics on Wednesday and so on. Would there be benefits of scheduling the content in this way?

Task 2. Reflection

Incorporate a deliberate reflective activity, such as journal-keeping, in which learners keep both a log of activities and conclusions drawn about those activities. For example, in physical education, learners could record gymnastic sequence progress, insights gained into how to transfer learning across subjects (tennis to badminton), and learning gaps in dance (linking strong movements with light movements).

reduce human intelligence and achievements to test scores, and to develop more natural sources from which to gather information (Oliver, 1997).

If we believe that children do not all learn in the same way, then educators cannot assess all learners in a uniform fashion. Preferred assessment methods include student portfolios, independent and group projects, student journals, multiple ways of demonstrating what they know, understand, and are able to do. Documentation of student growth can include collections of significant student work, student successes, comments, photographs of presentations, plays, three-dimensional creations, and self-evaluations (Hoerr, 1992). A good assessment instrument can be a learning experience that occurs while students are working on engaging problems, projects, and products. This form of assessment may not be as easy to design as the standard multiple-choice tests, but it is more likely to capture the student's full repertoire of skills and to yield information that is useful for subsequent advice and placement (B. Campbell, 1992).

4.8 FOR YOUR CONSIDERATION

Many schools consider themselves "MI Schools," with or without Gardner's endorsement. Ideally, Gardner describes a school he would be happy to send his children to as a place where

> differences among youngsters are taken seriously, knowledge about differences is shared with children and parents, children gradually assume responsibility for their own learning, and materials that are worth knowing are presented in ways that afford each child the maximum opportunity to master those materials and to show others (and themselves) what they have learned and understood. (Gardner, 1995b, p. 206)

Can you visualize what this classroom might look like? What might it sound like? What might the students and teachers be doing?

Behavioural Learning

In the scientific community, behaviourism is psychology's success story. **Behaviourism** is about using reinforcers deliberately to control student behaviour. The effects of reinforcing observable behaviours have been well researched and well documented. Reinforcement works. **Reinforcement** is about an increase in some behaviours, often through use of reinforcers that follow behaviours. **Reinforcers** are usually stimuli that follow behaviour. When reinforcers are used and are contingent upon behaviour, they increase the likelihood that the behaviour will reoccur. Sometimes, however, a reinforcer can be removed as a consequence of a good behaviour. We call this type of reinforcement **negative reinforcement**. When you buckle your seat belt in your car (a good behaviour) to remove an aversive stimulus—perhaps the annoying buzz programmed in your car to remind you to buckle your seat belt—you are negatively reinforced. You engage in a good behaviour to remove the aversive stimulus. Can you think of examples of how teachers use negative reinforcement to bring about good behaviour?

One question we ask you to consider, however, is, If something works, does that make it good? As a teacher, you will be able to modify behaviour by using reinforcers, and will feel it necessary quite often to modify your learners' behaviour. Is the modification of behaviour, as an outcome, good and appropriate? Are there other questions to be asked before drawing a conclusion? We believe that there are, and invite you to consider the following ideas about behaviourism.

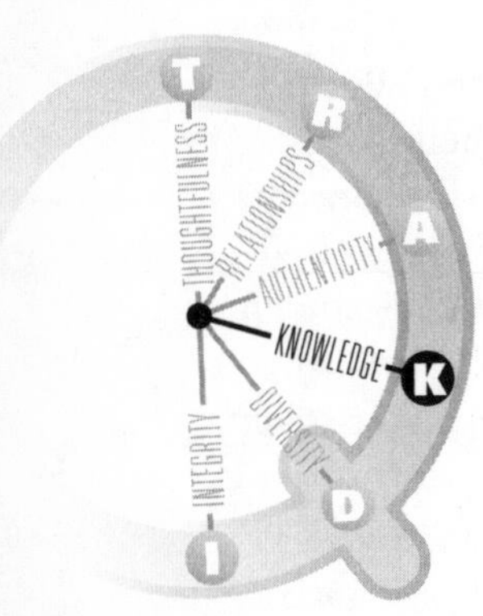

For the behaviourist, learning constitutes a change, or modification, in behaviour. If behaviour is caused to change, learning has occurred. For the behaviourist, there is little if any emphasis on schemata, worldviews, integration of concepts, or metacognition. The focus is on behaviour. Let's examine the three most prominent behavioural-oriented learning theories: classical conditioning, operant conditioning, and punishment.

Classical Conditioning

Insights regarding a phenomenon in research are often discovered by accident. The main insight about learning in **classical conditioning** is that responses, particularly physiological and emotional responses such as anxiety, fear, excitement and so on, can be drawn out of animals and people through a stimulus that would ordinarily not draw out that response. Let us try to explain by going back to the very beginning. In 1916 Ivan Pavlov, a Russian scientist, was testing the physiological responses of dogs, in particular the digestive responses to stimuli. When Pavlov's assistant brought food to the dogs while in their cages, the dogs would salivate at the sight of the meat. This, we are sure you would agree, is normal and not unusual. However, what happened next was unusual. When the assistant entered the room and accidentally clanged the feeding dish against the metal cage, the dogs salivated. In other words, a stimulus that would not ordinarily cause a dog to salivate—a dog pan and a noise—came to have the power to cause a dog's salivation. Put another way, the salivation response appeared to be caused by the clanging of the cage, and not by the sight of the meat. Being the good scientists that they were,

Pavlov and his assistant were curious. How could an originally neutral stimulus (noise from a dog pan) come to be associated with salivation? A noise and the food pan were clearly unconditioned stimuli; that is, they originally had no power to evoke a response. No learning history, normal physiological mechanism, or anything ordinary could explain this result. But the good scientists began to "put two and two" together. What happens when this unconditioned stimulus (dog pan) is presented to the dog just before the conditioned stimulus (the meat) appears, not just once but a few times? Is it possible that this might explain this unusual form of learning? Now the hunt for understanding was on.

Classrooms have been beneficiaries of what behaviourists have discovered about shaping behaviours—creating conditions for learning that reduce anxiety, for example, and paying attention to conditions that increase anticipation and promote good behaviours.

That learning could happen through an unconditioned stimulus turned out to be a fact. Present an originally neutral stimulus (an unconditioned stimulus) just preceding a conditioned stimulus a few times, and presto! New learning occurs. Are you wondering if anything here is of importance to you as a teacher, or if this is an important for your learning about learning? Consider this: One author's daughter, early in Grade 1, announced to her family that she would have her first test, a spelling test, next day. Her eyes were bright with happy anticipation. She expressed excitement and an "I can't wait to do this test" attitude. Ten years later, this same girl suffers anxiety attacks before tests, dislikes them intensely and wishes that they would go the way of the dinosaur. What do you think happened?

4.9 FOR YOUR CONSIDERATION

1. Have you ever been evaluated or assessed about what you know and understand using any of the alternative methods suggested above? Which did you prefer? How well did you feel the evaluation process demonstrated what you knew and understood about the topic?
2. After reading and discussing Gardner's MI theory, what are your thoughts on the following quotation: "If education is to give a gift to the future, then that gift must be one of wholeness—wholeness that is inherent in our design and our experience on this planet" (Samples, 1992, p. 66)?
3. Visit the Association for Supervision and Curriculum Development for more information on MI and other educational topics: **http://www.ascd.org.** (Note: This Web site requires registration and the payment of a fee).

Operant Conditioning

A far more prominent form of learning is operant conditioning. When an emitted response, or observable behaviour, is followed by a satisfying state of affairs, such as praise for work well done, **operant conditioning** maintains that learning has occurred. A particular response is learned. In this case learning is attributable to praise.

There are three important differences between operant and classical conditioning. First, operant conditioning is concerned with emitted responses and not with physiological responses. Second, when an emitted response is followed by a reinforcer, it increases the likelihood that that response will reoccur; it is not necessary to have close pairings of different stimuli. It is necessary for teachers to follow a desired response with an appropriate reinforcer. And third, it is in reinforcers that the operant conditioning "science" is applied. A learner's behaviour is somewhat less important than what happens after the behaviour, and success relates to the types, schedules, and numbers of reinforcers applied. If the reinforcer is contingent upon the learner's behaviour, learning can occur. Learning depends on reinforcement.

We will deal more with behaviourism in later chapters on teaching and schooling.

4.10 FOR YOUR CONSIDERATION

At one time, you might not have been afraid of examinations, anxious at the prospect of speaking in front of people, or nervous when a teacher came to stand by your desk. If today you are anxious about these things, what stimulus do you think led to this learning? Can you explain this learning in classical conditioning terms?

We remind you that experiencing a history of rewards has, for many students, led to industriousness. It is important to reward good behaviour. If you do not believe that rewards are important, let us ask you this question: Do you want to get a good mark in this class? Do you like to receive praise from the person you love the most? Do you like to receive money for your hard work? Do you enjoy positive feedback for a presentation given in school? Or would you prefer a failing mark, criticism, and no concrete rewards for a job well done in school? We think we know the answer.

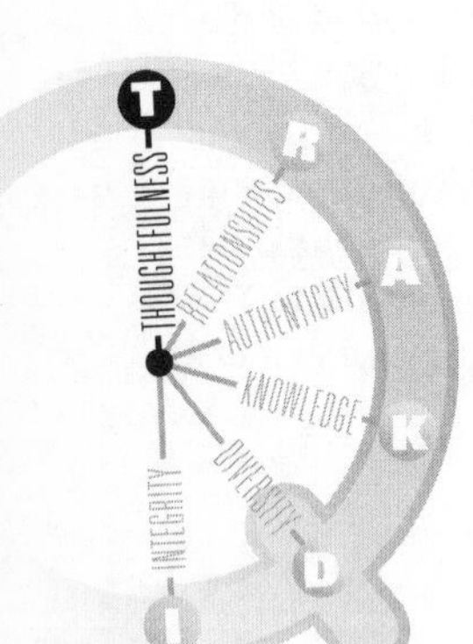

One of the arguments against behaviourism is that it creates a dependence on reward and punishment that may result in students' failure to develop personal responsibility. We caution you to listen carefully and be thoughtful regarding the criticisms often levelled against behaviourism. To be a thoughtful teacher means that you will engage in shared praxis with your colleagues, and choose ethical, informed, and deliberate teaching behaviours that are in the best interests of learners.

Punishment

The third area of behaviourism concerns punishment. In operant conditioning, the emphasis is on reinforcing good behaviour, with the goal of having that good behaviour happen again. With **punishment**, however, the goal is to apply an undesirable consequence to bad behaviour in order to diminish or even eliminate the bad behaviour.

There has been considerable debate in the educational and psychological community regarding the use of various types of punishment, the undesirable side effects of punishment, and the desirability of using other forms of intervention to diminish undesirable behaviour. We cannot examine all the questions regarding punishment here. We do, however, encourage you to think about this very important topic. Punishment exists in schools, and you will likely use some form of punishment during your teaching career. However, we advise you to be cautious and, above all, thoughtful regarding your decisions about punishment. You have no doubt read that using corporal punishment teaches children to use physical violence to solve their problems, that "might makes right." Though this sounds defensible and logical, we also invite you to look carefully at the research about punishment and draw your own conclusions. Keep in mind that aggression, violence, and physical injury to another person in any way, for any reason, are wrong, ethically and intuitively. Try to guard against decisions about punishment that do not include an ethical component.

4.11 FOR YOUR CONSIDERATION

We have put some definitions in the glossary for your convenience. Use these definitions as you and your classmates thoughtfully consider the following scenario:

Ms. Jeziak struggled with her Grade 4 class from day one in September. They would not sit still, raise their hands before answering questions, or leave other kids alone when they walked by their desks, and often they were rude to each other and to her. Someone suggested that she use behavioural modification techniques. She began by hanging a chart on which her desired behaviours were written out. When she saw an example of good behaviour, she immediately put a star next to the student's name. This worked for a while, but only for a few students. She decided to put a music centre at the back of the classroom and give the "good" students free time there when they put up their hands before answering questions. This worked for a while, but became very difficult to administer. She tried threats of forfeiting recesses; for some students this worked quite well, but again, only for a time. Students seemed to become adjusted to every technique she tried. By Christmas Ms. Jeziak had grown exhausted and decided to try punishment instead. She used time outs, detentions, and in-school suspensions, but found that students were still not presenting the "good" behaviours. She tried behavioural contracts, token economies in the form of colourful stickers, and varying the types of reinforcers, from food to praise. What should Ms. Jeziak do?

Psychomotor Learning

Psychomotor learning is the sequential development of understanding and skill in managing one's body and other physical objects. Does this aspect of learning add anything important to our understanding of teaching young people? Consider the central role that movement, play, music, art, drama, dance, sports, and physical activity play in a young person's life. Also, consider just how much learning occurs through these normal, healthy activities. Some of life's most important lessons can be learned through physical activity and play—lessons about self-control, teamwork, risk-taking in safe ways, leadership development, managing one's fears, and creativity development, for example. The development of simple and gross motor skills serves as a foundation for the development of more refined and specialized skills later in life.

Unfortunately, physical-activity classes can be taught poorly, especially when untrained teachers are involved. How often, for example, does physical education mean no more than playing murder ball, over and over? Or an art lesson simply have children colouring pre-drawn maps? How often is music cancelled as a punishment when children misbehave? We suspect that you never heard a teacher say, "If you kids do not sit still, we are going to cancel your math class." Why is it that physical education is called "gym" class, and the word "education" eliminated from the name? We acknowledge that in the past, far too much emphasis has been placed on winning, competing, and comparing in gym classes, to the extent that important learning has not always occurred. When learning has occurred, invariably important conditions and practices have been present. Let's examine these next few ideas to help you develop your understanding of learning.

Skill Development

Physical skill acquisition, perhaps more than any other type, is influenced by heredity, or nature. You may have heard the expression "You can't make a silk purse out of a sow's ear." This means that you can't make a Michael Jordan out of a Peter Waldron, one of this book's authors. Perhaps if Peter had been born to different parents, then the genetic outcome would have been more favourable to him and his currently misplaced dream to be a star basketball player. But even if Peter had had different parents and a stronger genetic predisposition for basketball skills, it would have remained just that—a predisposition and not the actual skill we see in a world-class athlete like Michael Jordan. Genetic make-up predisposes; nurture disposes. Another way of thinking about this is that your genetic predisposition, or potential, is like an elastic band. How far that elastic band of genetic potential will be stretched is dependent on environmental influences, such as good coaching opportunities, the right kind of practice, and a good diet. Positive psychological conditions, such as freedom from the fear of failure, a strong sense of self-efficacy (see Chapter 3, pp. 53–54), a good body image, and, perhaps most important, motivation, are additional environmental influences.

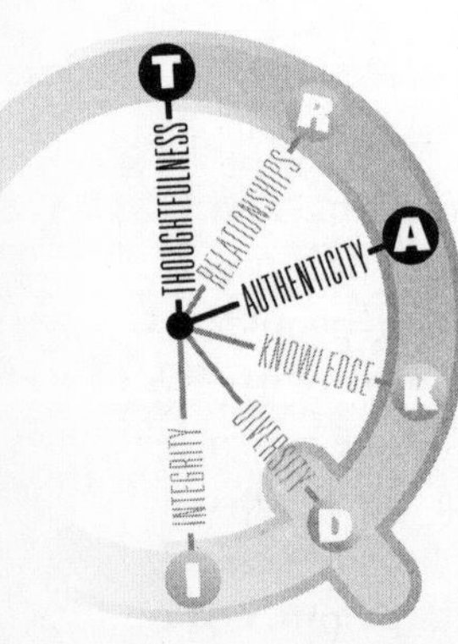

A good teacher understands this intricate relationship between nature and nurture. She or he designs learning experiences in physical education that are individualized, sequential, and developmentally appropriate. To put it another way, a good teacher tailors the activities in gym class to the child, rather than trying to fit the child into the activities. If need be, the teacher will modify the activities, not the child. She or he will shorten the courts for younger children, allow bounces in volleyball to slow down the ball, use batting tees in baseball, and change rules to promote maximum activity time, such as allowing children to run between dribbles in basketball. If you are troubled about such modifications, ask yourself why. If your learners try out for the national volleyball team and let the ball bounce before passing it, then there is a problem. But physical education is about learning skills that underlie all physical activity and sport, and that permit the lifelong pursuit of a healthy lifestyle. As long as there is minimal or non-existent negative transfer of skill development to another, more complex and related skill, then why not modify? Your goal in physical education class is the learning of physical skills, not the creation of highly competitive world-class athletes. The best teachers know this; they individualize and try to guide learners to be able to perform skills automatically, smoothly, with minimal or no conscious thought. Above all, they try to guide learners to have healthy, fun-filled learning experiences in physical education classes.

4.12 FOR YOUR CONSIDERATION

Test the following assumption in light of the information presented on skill development.

Assumption: Students automatically apply their learning.

Consideration 1. The Five Ts

For every topic in a class, give each student time (T) to write, read, speak, do, and listen. For example, in a recent education class on short-term memory, we began by

1) Doing (tying ties). The task was for each person to teach another how to tie a tie.
2) Writing. Learners were to record the learning problems encountered along the way in trying to remember the instructions, and also to record their proposed solutions to the problems they encountered.
3) Speaking/listening. The class discussed the problems and proposed solutions. We challenged the problems, offered advice regarding each other's solutions, and tried to draw some general conclusions regarding the limitations and strengths of short-term-memory-assisting strategies.
4) Writing (again). The class wrote in their notebooks three things: the main points about short-term memory, their main conclusions, and things that were still fuzzy about short-term memory.

Consideration 2. Deep Meaning

Through questioning, proceduralization activities (practice) and feedback, move learners to record (actually write out) before the end of a learning experience, the meaning they have arrived at regarding the topic.

Consideration 3. Distributed Practice

Over the next number of weeks in the education class mentioned in Consideration 1, we referred consistently to short-term memory, and we regularly practised tasks in different classes to deepen and broaden understanding short-term memory.

Teachers know that a child's perceptual system develops in a biologically determined pattern, that sight, hearing, and kinesthetic systems develop together and contribute uniquely to a child's ability to perform skills. Good teachers, then, use expressions that are word pictures, expressions like "softhands," or "punch the beat board with your feet," or "make a movement sentence with actions." They schedule skill development sessions to maximize learning; they know that learning can happen between practice sessions; and they encourage learning by guiding learners to journal their learning in writing.

Teachers know that readiness to learn skills is complex and needs particular attention. Learners need to know about their learning, sense the importance of the new learning, have an expectation of success, take some part in the planning of the learning experience, and feel that they have some ownership for the learning process. These are components of readiness to learn.

Teachers know that a lot of social learning can occur in physical, fine arts, and practical arts education, and they are careful to structure learning situations in which learners are not threatened and can indeed develop the competency that precedes confidence.

Good teachers know that skill learning helps learners to increase fine motor skills, that developing flexibility in smaller regions of the body comes after developing flexibility in large regions of the body. They also know that hitting a still ball is easier than hitting a moving ball, and that having people watch you, particularly when you learn new skills, is probably not a good idea. Good teachers make sure that every child has a ball, so that each child is free to explore, develop, refine, and apply skills in settings that are safe and free from the fear of failure.

Reflection and Perspective on the Chapter

In this chapter we discussed cognitive, behavioural, and psychomotor theories of individual learning. Central to the cognitive theories is the complex role of the brain. Theorists and researchers have, for many years, attempted to understand connections between the brain and learning. New insights are being discovered daily. Other theories that inform learning include emotional intelligence and perceptual preferences, such as visual, auditory, kinesthetic, and tactual.

We have not discussed many new and interesting developments in the field of individual learning. Action learning is one of these new developments. **Action learning** is concerned with learning through problem solving. **Informal learning** and **situational learning** are concerned with learning that occurs informally through reflection with a coach or mentor within the day-to-day events of a school.

We encourage you to be the type of teacher who is learner-centred and who seeks to improve teaching by considering how learning is influenced by proposed improvements in teaching.

Key Terms

Suggested Further Reading

Analoui, F. (1993). *Training and Transfer of Learning*. Brookfield, VM: Ashgate. A good discussion about the problems in designing teaching and learning experiences so transfer of learning can occur.

Chapter 5

Social Learning

Chapter Focus

Social learning is a relatively new arrival on the professional landscape and in its many manifestations has met with a checkered response. Some teachers have embraced it with enthusiasm; others have been skeptical.

Social learning is a fairly radical departure from conventional teaching practices, many of which were founded in behaviourism. You will remember from Chapter 4 that behaviourism tends to place a fairly heavy emphasis on individualism. However, the very term *social learning* suggests that groups of people would be learning together—the antithesis of learning based on individualism. One of the central questions in learning theory is, How do students, as they engage in learning, make meaning and gain understanding? Further questions concern the assumptions and prior knowledge that learners bring to the learning experience. The degree to which a teacher is able to help young people make explicit their prior knowledge and assumptions as they engage in learning often indicates the degree to which new learning can be effective. Think about times you have been involved in new leaning. If you had to learn on your own and your learning involved high degrees of difficulty and complexity, how did you cope? Were you frustrated? Of course, to a considerable extent the answer depends on the kind of person and the kind of learner you are, but, generally speaking, young people experience a certain amount of discomfort when dealing with difficulty and complexity on their own. Sharing learning with others often brings with it comfort and the possibility of insight and enlightenment from the thoughts and ideas expressed by others.

Leinhardt (1992) presents three core assumptions about learning gleaned from a number of modern researchers.

1. Learning is an active process of knowledge construction and sense-making by the student.
2. Knowledge is a cultural artifact of human beings; we produce it, share it, and transform it as individuals and as groups.

3. Knowledge is distributed among members of a group, and this distributed knowledge is greater than the knowledge possessed by any single member.

The larger questions are, How do we use these core assumptions about learning? What do they mean for a classroom teacher? This book looks at the professional landscape and asks, Where to begin? The particular theoretical perspective within social learning that we are choosing to discuss is social-cognitive learning. In the following section we will discuss three facets of social-cognitive learning considered to be useful for those embarking on pre-service learning: constructivism, narrative inquiry, and pro-social skills. There are also, of course, many other areas of credible knowledge that occupy the professional landscape. The ones selected here represent current research and practice, and on this basis we judge them to be a useful starting point for pre-service teachers.

A second aspect of social learning with which we will conclude the chapter is ethical and moral learning.

Focus Questions

1. What conditions would provide learners with opportunities to apply their own efforts at understanding information?
2. Why do people learn from the stories of others?
3. How might schools develop in learners the pro-social skills that are required in society?
4. What is the source of empathy in children? How could learning experiences be designed in order to promote empathy learning?
5. How might learning conditions be created to enhance a learner's internal and external motivation to learn?
6. What role do schools have in the moral and ethical development of learners?
7. How might schools contribute to a student's formation of self-concept and identity?

Social-Cognitive Learning Theory

If behaviourism is psychology's success story in the scientific community, and social learning theory is responsible for increasing that respect, then social-cognitive learning theory is most responsible for deepening that respect. Rigorous scientific studies of children (Bandura, 1965, 1989; Zimmerman, 1990) have extended our understanding and acceptance of social-cognitive learning theory's most important contribution to our knowledge of how people learn—that thinking is socially constructed, that knowledge is a social construction. Put another way, people learn new ways of thinking and behaving from each other.

Today the widely accepted branch of social learning theory is social-cognitive theory (Bandura, 1989). It is important that you understand this plausible explanation of learning, because not only does it help explain one important way that children learn, it also integrates and considers theory from cognitive and behavioural understandings of learning. Perhaps most important for you in your practice as a teacher, social-cognitive learning theory will help you be thoughtful and articulate when commenting on issues such as the effects of television; bullying and its solution; and the influence of societal role models on young people. If you know and understand the basics regarding social-cognitive learning theory, you will understand that children's learning involves a "...cognitive processing activity in which information about the structure of behavior and about environmental events is transformed into symbolic representations that serve as a guide for action" (Bandura, 1977, p. 51).

In social-cognitive learning, children do not need to be reinforced for their behaviours. They can learn by watching what happens to others. This saves time and prevents dangerous situations from being the "teachers" of children. Children can learn from reading stories, watching events, or hearing others tell of their experiences. Finally, we suspect that you already know that people learn from each other because you remember learning from others: your friends, parents, and role models you looked up to. How did that learning happen?

Social-cognitive learning theory is concerned with social behaviour and the social setting in which that behaviour occurs. Social settings are the contexts of behaviour that help create the understanding of what is meaningful in the world of young people. This social setting includes people, of course, but it also includes the media, the sub-text of messages in advertising, and the values and ideologies of the communities in which people live. Why? Because it is setting, or social context, that creates the meaning people see in things, and subsequently influences what can be learned and how it can be learned (Bronfenbrenner, 1989). Perhaps the next two illustrations will help you understand the power that context, the social setting people find themselves in, can have in helping people make meaning and learn.

5.1 FOR YOUR CONSIDERATION

Analyze the following scenario to understand how context is powerful in helping people make meaning.

In one school, Grade 12 students were asked to design their own walk-about. In a walk-about, a concept taken from Australian Aborigines, a person goes into the wilderness with very little supporting equipment, tools, clothing, or means to gather food or build shelter. The task is simple—to survive. In this particular school, students designed their own walk-about, a real life situation for the region in which they lived. One student designed a week-long experience of living on the street as a homeless person. She had to find meals, stay warm, and keep safe. Another student designed a week-long bike trip through the Rocky Mountains. All students had real problems through which they learned as they applied strategies and knowledge to their solution.

Students prepared for the problem in the best way they could; reading, discussing, and simulating situations. However, the real learning occurred when they actually encountered problems in the situations they designed and when they carefully documented how they solved those problems. Many found mentors to help them in their situation, others listened carefully to experienced problem-solvers. All students learned informally in the situation through solving the real-life problem.

In terms of learning in schools, social-cognitive learning theory presents many important and relevant practical considerations. Sitting still means something different in physical education than it does at a school assembly. Praise from

5.2 FOR YOUR CONSIDERATION

Suppose you found an unfinished Beatles song (or Nirvana, if that's your taste) in an attic. Likely, you'd want to know what the finished song would sound like, how the songwriter would have finished it. You would, wisely, get someone who knows the group—their style of music, way of thinking, and approach to writing—to help finish the score. You would trust someone who is an expert, with the background knowledge to be able to study the unfinished song and apply that knowledge to finishing the song. The expert would use the setting, the context, both his or her own context, including background, and the Beatles' context. The closeness of fit between the now-finished Beatles song and what John or Paul might have done is higher because of the expertise of those in the setting. Who might have a closer fit, you or the experts?

Keeping the above scenario in mind, how does context, or setting, influence meaning-making for young people? Consider movies, music, friends, and the community in your discussion.

a teacher in front of peers means something different than praise from a teacher when no one is watching. Young people will put meaning into things they hear, read, and see, using the social setting to do so, and their ability to symbolically represent that which they see and hear. Because they do, important behaviour and thinking happens in this social setting called school. Socialization can become normal or abnormal because of a setting's influence on a young person. Learners learn to symbolize, regulate themselves, develop a sense of confidence in their abilities, and see the future consequences of their actions. Also, they learn to imitate and figure out whether they should imitate, based on the consequences of the person's behaviour they are imitating.

Imitation alone does not explain learning. Learners also learn to regulate their behaviours by observing the effects and reinforcements that others receive for their actions. At times they determine whether a particular behaviour is a good idea or not by seeing how it turns out for the person they are watching. Learners may not even need reinforcement. They simply need to observe a high-status person repeat the behaviour a number of times and get a slap on the wrist, and they learn not try the same behaviour.

Learning is even a little more complicated in social-cognitive theory than it is in behaviourism or in other branches of social learning theory, because in social-cognitive theory young people act cognitively on their setting as much as the setting acts on them. To illustrate, consider the following question: Who socializes whom more, a young baby or the parents of that baby? Is the answer simple?

Some implications of social-cognitive learning theory are addressed in the following questions:

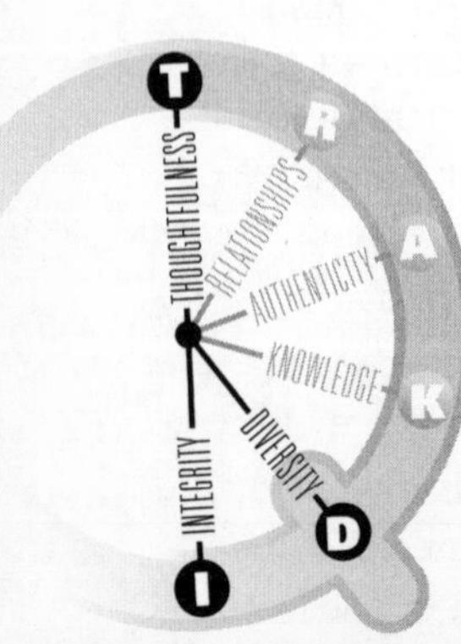

1. Is television a neutral stimulus? How might children symbolically represent violence they see in television?
2. Should teachers and parents be more involved in choosing the friends of young people in their care? How should they express their concern?
3. How should teachers call into question objectionable societal practices?
4. To what extent should teachers consider the school and the community in their moral and ethical decisions? (Refer to teaching qualities in Chapter 2.)

Above all, we encourage you to be thoughtful when addressing the settings in which the young people live.

5.3 FOR YOUR CONSIDERATION

What does *key* mean?

If you replied, "I don't know what you mean by key," you are right, of course. You don't know for sure what we mean by key, because you do not have enough context to help you make meaning. So, let's broaden the context. The key is in the first chapter of the book. Now you have a little more information to go on to help you make meaning of the word *key*. However, you would still be guessing, because you do not have enough context. Try these sentences: The key is in the first chapter of the book. Make sure that you put it back there when you return, and fill up the car with gas; and do not be late.

Are you surprised by the ambiguity in the sentences? Now you know what *key* means. But there might be more. What if the two sentences about key were in a paragraph in a story about secret agents, spies, and other mysterious things? Then key takes on even more meaning in the broader context.

Keeping the above illustration in mind, how might the various settings in which young people find themselves influence what they think about issues such as dieting and body image, money and material possessions, jobs and careers, and friends and loyalty? Why is setting important? Why is it important that young people learn as much as they can from as many points of view as possible, including ethical and moral, about important issues in life?

The point we are making is that the social setting influences meaning.

Constructivism

Teachers do not always warmly receive the word *constructivism.* Since constructivism is a relatively recent arrival on the professional landscape, its newness tends to run headlong into old assumptions. Teachers who have not been exposed to constructivism, either during their teacher education or their professional development experiences, may not embrace it as part of their worldview. It does not play a part in their assumptions, which determine how they approach learning and teaching.

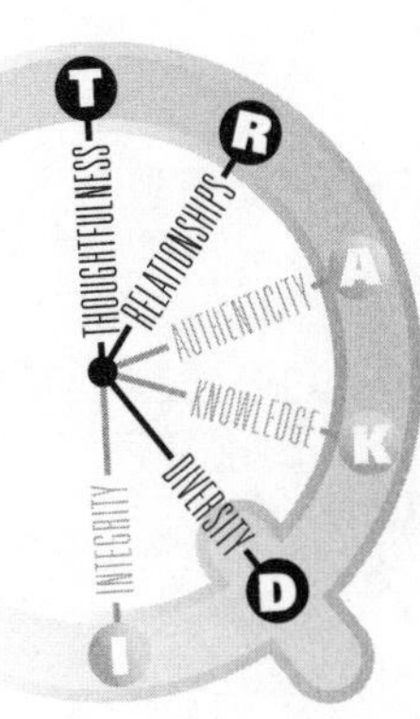

Such reluctance to accept new research and practice is not uncommon in teaching. Perhaps it is too early in your pre-professional experience for you to have experienced instances of this kind of implementation problem. However, you might find it interesting to talk about this issue with your peers. Some might have some interesting stories to tell. If you try this, you yourself are engaging in a form of social learning. You will be sharing stories, asking each other questions, perhaps challenging each other's views, and gaining clarity and understanding on issues about which you were previously unsure. In short, you will be learning.

What is constructivism? A book of this kind cannot pretend to fully answer this broad question, but we will present a working definition followed by some core understandings of the concept. We define **constructivism** as an approach to learning and teaching that encourages learners to take an active role in their learning. Central to the practice of constructivist learning is the learner's constructing new knowledge on prior knowledge, building understanding, and above all making sense and meaning out of new information. The following quotation provides a useful beginning.

> Much of traditional education breaks wholes into parts, and then focuses separately on each part. But many students are unable to build concepts and skills from parts to wholes. These students often stop trying to see the wholes before all the parts are presented to them and focus on the small, memorizable aspects of broad units without ever creating the big picture.... We need to see the "whole" before we are able to make sense of the parts. (Brooks & Brooks, 1993, p. 46)

Constructivist classrooms help young people to make sense of their world through actively acquiring, building, and understanding meaning and knowledge in social contexts. Perkins (1999) cautions that constructivism is more than one thing. He quotes Phillips (1995), who has identified three distinct roles in constructivism: the active learner, the social learner, and the creative learner. You might want to refer to the Perkins article for a discussion of the three distinct roles in constructivism.

The essence of constructivist theory is that young people experience successful learning when they are actively engaged in the following:

- building (constructing) knowledge for themselves—considering new knowledge against prior knowledge and understanding
- reflecting on their views and how they might differ in their understandings with the views of others
- arriving at new understandings that expand their worldview

What conditions should exist in a constructivist classroom? An important condition is that young people be given numerous opportunities to explore ideas, sometimes called phenomena (Vygotsky, 1987), individually, but most often in social contexts. In exploring ideas they would be encouraged to employ problem-solving skills such as hypothesizing, speculating, conjecturing, predicting, and decision making. The whole process would lead students to revise their original thinking. In short, constructivism encourages interplay between new knowledge

These photos show two situations in which students are solving problems and constructing knowledge.

about a phenomenon and prior knowledge about the same phenomenon that a young person brings to the learning experience. The social context in which the learner engages in exploration enables the learner to gain new meaning and understanding through considering the views of others against his or her own views.

The term *constructivist* may conjure up images of building and architecture. However, in this context it represents the construction of intellect, the design of learning experiences that invite students to construct knowledge and make meaning of their world. Architects who design buildings might borrow from earlier masters; so do educators. Many educational theorists believe that we actively construct knowledge based on what we already know and new information we encounter. Jean Piaget (1983), Lev Vygotsky (1987), and John Dewey (1973) are names worthy of note. Their work supports constructivist perspectives on learning and teaching, and continues to influence today's classrooms, encouraging teachers to put "students' own efforts to understand at the centre of the educational enterprise" (Prawat, 1992, p. 357).

Having considered how constructivism might look in an elementary classroom, we will now examine its application in the wider context of a university learning experience. The learning experience is designed to help first-year education students construct their own understanding of how some influences on learning, such as feedback, might be more powerful than others, such as praise.

5.4 FOR YOUR CONSIDERATION

Read the following scenario and answer the questions that follow.

Some years ago, an observer visited a Grade 3 class as the class was about to begin a reading lesson. Very quickly the children were engaged with papier-mâché, wire, toothpicks, and other assorted material from the teacher's art supplies. Working in groups of three, they were building castles. A little perplexed, the observer made his way over to the teacher and inquired about the reading lesson.

"This is it," said the teacher, in a preoccupied voice.

"But where are the books?" the observer asked.

"Give me a moment and I will be with you," said the teacher. "Let me get them all going."

A little later, the teacher stepped aside from a busy class and explained what was happening. "Before children see the printed words it is important, first of all to find out what they already know about castles. Let them have the chance to show what they look like, and if they know the names of the different parts, let them write the names and stick them on the model castles."

The observer looked over at the castles under construction and names were beginning to appear: "draw brige," "mot," "flag." The children were engrossed in their work. Industry took on a new meaning.

a) Why do you think the children were building castles as part of their reading class?

b) How would this help them to learn to read?

c) When the castles were finished, what do you think the teacher would do next?

d) In the context of teaching reading, research the meaning of terms such as *decoding*, *encoding*, *comprehension*, and *context*. How do these terms connect with the teacher's approach described above?

e) Do you think the vignette is consistent with a constructivist approach to the teaching of reading? Why? Why not?

5.5 FOR YOUR CONSIDERATION

In the first stage of a university learning experience designed to be constructivist, the task was for students to identify current practices for influencing the behaviours of loved ones.

Step 1. Naming Present Action: the "what" movement

Here the teacher/facilitator asked learners to identify their actions, or behaviours, related to a topic.

In an education class, one of the authors of this book asked students to describe their preferred way of influencing the behaviours of a loved one (boyfriend, girlfriend, husband, wife, parent). The list, written on the board, included praise, thank-you statements, affection, and others.

Step 2. Identifying Assumptions in Actions: the "why" movement

Here the teacher guided the learners to unwrap their actions to expose underlying theories, beliefs, and understandings.

In the class on influences, we questioned each other about why we chose the influences we did. The questions ranged from, Whose interests are being served by a particular choice of reinforcer? to, Is a person's dignity subverted when the person is praised for what he or she should do naturally?

Step 3. Seeing the Research: The Educational Community Story and Vision about Influences on Learning

Here, for the first time, there is a presentation of research; the story of the scientific community—the narrative-based understandings presented in oral or written form—is brought into the learning process. The goal for the students is twofold:

1. Hear the story of the larger community, the experiences of others, the research from the scientific community, the logic and insights from others. It is important that the story and the vision inherent in others' stories are heard and treated with respect in the hearing.
2. Talk about, challenge, and pose questions about the story.

The teacher can present the educational community's story in a number of ways. In the particular education class referred to here, one of the authors asked students to do a simple penny-tossing experiment in groups. All students tossed pennies toward a target, trying to come as close as possible. All tosses were measured. We called this our baseline behaviour. Next, students tossed pennies again, but this time they were blindfolded. One blind group was praised, but given no specific feedback regarding performance (i.e., closeness to the target). A second group was given feedback but no praise. A third group was allowed to take off their blindfolds after each toss to see how close the toss was to the target, before re-blindfolding themselves and trying again.

Before the penny-tossing experiment, each student was asked to predict the outcome of the three scenarios. After the experiment, they compared the results. The insight that feedback is a better influence on performance (at least on a simple task like throwing pennies) than praise was quite startling to many students. They were ready for the fourth, and arguably most instructive, movement.

Step 4. Interpreting and Synthesizing

Here the goal is for students to discuss two related questions:

1. How does the community's story and vision, the research and its understandings, call into question, affirm or disaffirm, or call upon you to change your understandings and actions?
2. How do your understanding and actions help you comprehend more fully the community's story and vision; how do your understanding and actions confirm the research and its application?

In the class in question, the limited influence of praise in a simple motor task and the very significant influence of feedback regarding performance, was very disconfirming. Most students were surprised and therefore willing to revisit the effectiveness of using praise as the main means to promote learning.

Step 5. Taking Reflective, Constructive Action

Here students make deliberate, ethical, and moral decisions regarding how they will act in the future. In the class in question, many students agreed to carefully study the research and the stories of teachers regarding the use of both feedback and praise in assisting learning.

Go back now and thoughtfully reconsider the original assumption that people learn from experience. Are you more or less convinced now that people learn from reflecting on experience more than they learn from experience itself?

(Adapted from Thomas Groome, 1981, *Christian Religious Education*, San Francisco: Harper and Row.)

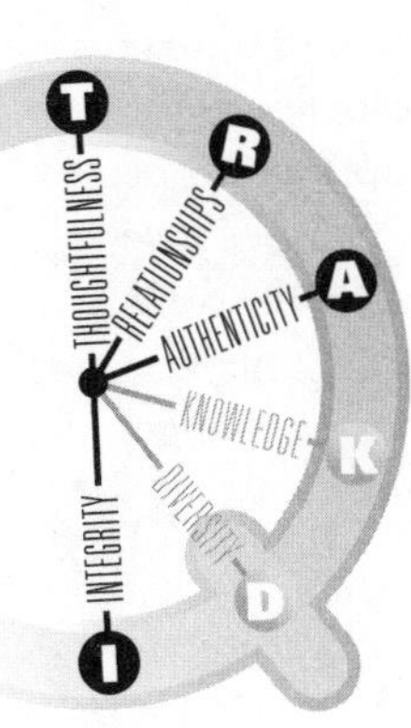

Narrative Inquiry

Human beings are storytellers. The advent of publishing, even the hand-written work of scribes, is a relatively recent occurrence in the human story. Prior to the written and printed word, knowledge, tradition, and culture were passed down from generation to generation by word of mouth, through an oral tradition. Elders taught through stories. Younger people learned from the elders' stories.

Stories still represent the way people communicate when they are together in social settings. Narrative inquiry seeks to gain clarity and understanding from the stories that people tell. Connelly and Clandinin (1988) describe narrative as "the study of how humans make meaning of experience by endlessly telling and retelling stories about themselves that both refigure the past and create purpose in the future. Thus to study narrative ... one needs to ask questions not only about the past, or the present, or the future, but about all three" (pp. 24–25). **Narrative inquiry,** then, is the purposeful attempt to capture the experiences of people through asking questions about their personal stories. Narrative inquiry seeks to explicate the past, explain the present, and anticipate the future through a respect for the knowledge contained in the storied lives of people.

How often have you listened to a speaker and noticed how your attention was captivated when the speaker began to relate a story? We all seem to be captivated by stories. Why? Is it because a story provides a snapshot of life experience, a vignette that describes how a person or group of people coped with some facet of life? Even fictitious stories, although they are the products of fantasy or imagination, can teach us about life. In the preface to this book we reminded ourselves that, "Whenever we are together, we combine stories and anecdotes to make conversation. On the basis of stories and events recounted, social occasions are enriched, emotions are shared, plans are made, misconceptions may be generated or clarified, and truth is earned. Above all, understanding is achieved when the attendant conversations are informed and open."

The important thing is that we can learn a great deal from stories if we know how to listen, how to ask questions, and how to generalize to the larger context from which the story emanates. The main claim for the use of narrative in educational research is that humans are storytelling organisms who, individually and socially, lead storied lives. The study of narrative, therefore, is the study of the ways humans experience the world. This general notion translates into the view that education is the construction and reconstruction of personal and social stories; teachers and learners are storytellers and characters in their own and others' stories (Connelly & Clandinin, 1990, p. 2).

In the context of learning, young people and teachers lead storied lives. Young people and their teachers are characters on the professional landscape. To listen to their stories is to understand this landscape. How do we tell our stories? How do we listen to stories? How do we learn from stories?

When teachers speak about teaching, when they speak about their professional landscape, in their voices you will hear their deeply held beliefs about education, teaching, and learning. It is through talk that our beliefs and assumptions are self-critically analyzed (Waldron et al., 1999).

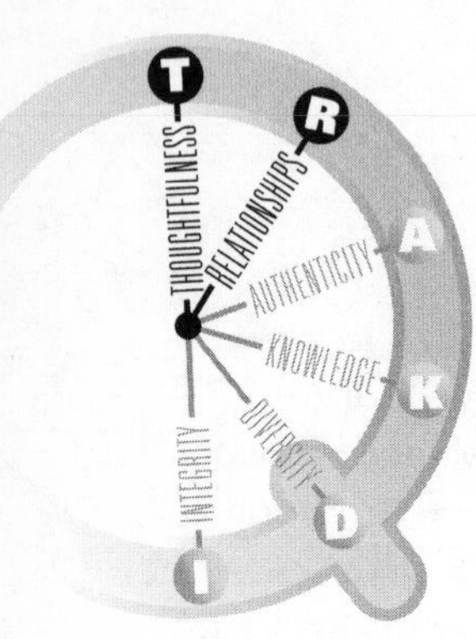

> "Talk" is essential. It is through talk that teachers (students) and administrators articulate their beliefs and values and expectations, their understandings of the context and their uncertainties, and that they come to know the beliefs and values and expectations, the understandings and uncertainties of others. (LaRoque & Downie, 1993, p. 1)

From our earlier discussion of assumptions you will recall the implications of worldview, that uniquely personal perspective that describes how people understand and present themselves to the world. Essentially a person's worldview is the accumulation of assumptions. It is not uncommon for some assumptions to be held tacitly. Occasionally, tacitly held assumptions may be troublesome because they drive a person's response to life in ways that may test the harmony of working relationships. Stories and attendant conversations can be useful for uncovering tacit assumptions so that they become available for clarification or challenge.

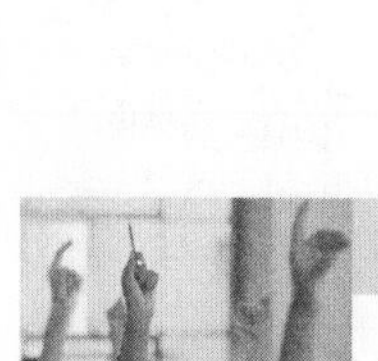

5.6 FOR YOUR CONSIDERATION

Read the following story and, in groups of four or five people, answer the questions that follow.

During a recent experience observing Grade 8 mathematics teachers, some of the teaching methods raised significant questions. Typically, a lesson would begin with a request for students to sit down and take out their textbooks. Teachers reviewed the previous night's homework and then explained the day's new learning through verbal explanations and demonstrations on the board, answering questions from the class. After the explanation of new learning, teachers distributed worksheets containing practice questions for completion within a given period of time. Teachers then assigned questions from the textbook for students to start in class and complete for homework.

At this point, in one of the classes, a student challenged the teacher.

"Mr. DeVries, I already know how to do this stuff, do I still have to do it for homework?"

"Yes," said the teacher, "because the mark you will receive makes up part of your grade for the term."

"But what's the point of doing it anyway? When will I ever use it in real life?"

The teacher was clearly uncomfortable with the question and provided an answer that alluded to benefits for further study in later grades and post secondary requirements.

1. What assumptions did the teacher hold about learning?
2. To what extent are students viewed as passive recipients of knowledge?
3. What do you think of the student who was asking the difficult questions?
4. Read the last sentence in the story again. What do you think the teacher began to think about?
5. How would you have answered the student's questions?
6. How would you teach math in a way that would not have invited those tough questions?

7. How might teachers invite learning in ways that respect the humanness of the learner?

Think about the group discussion you have just completed, in which you inquired into the lives of the two characters in the story. The questions about the assumptions the teacher held would help, in some way, to understand his worldview. As you formed opinions about the teacher's life on the professional landscape, you would likely think about what you yourself would do in this situation, and what you would say if your peers asked why you would act that way. To provide a sound reason why, you would draw upon your professional knowledge base for a response. Others might contribute responses that were different from yours, causing you to ponder their response ... and so on. Stories, or narratives, provide useful vehicles for professional conversation through which learning can occur, insights can be gained, and professional landscapes can be explored.

Pro-Social Skills

The term **pro-social skills** refers to skills that promote social and emotional growth and development in young people. Pro-Social skills include so many categories and sub-categories that we are again confronted with the question of which to select for a book such as this. Rather than present brief details on each form of pro-social skill, we will offer a few as a foundation from which, as pre-service studies progress, you can explore and add others.

The first pro-social skill we present is really a grouping of common skills aimed at developing co-operation among young people. These skills are generally grouped under the umbrella heading of co-operative learning. The second will deal with a particularly human quality called empathy, that special faculty that allows us to project ourselves into the feelings of another to truly understand that person's predicament. Finally, we will present the work of social psychologist, Erik Erikson, whose insights into social growth and development have interesting import for teachers seeking to understand children and nurture their social skills.

Co-operative Learning

Co-operative learning refers to a set of teaching methods in which young people work in small, mostly heterogeneous groups, of three to five members. Members of the groups are responsible for a number of things that typically would include engaging in the intended learning, assuming assigned responsibilities to contribute to the group's effectiveness, and contributing to the learning of the group. Co-operative groups operate with a clearly stated purpose, which, ideally, group members have had some opportunity to shape to give them a sense of ownership. One of the key aspects of co-operative group learning is the assignment of particular responsibilities to group members. Generally speaking, there are three broad types of learning within which young people benefit from these forms of pro-social skills: 1) learning that involves research to gain knowledge, meaning, and understanding, 2) conversation around particular topics, intended to gain meaning and understanding, and 3) peer teaching and learning activities aimed at consolidating learning or helping those whose learning is uncertain.

The important thing to stress is that the foundation for whatever method is chosen, for whatever reason, is the social skills that the young people need to make the co-operative learning successful. What skills do they need to get along with each other? How can they co-operate with each other so that learning can occur? It is important that the skills required are taught quite specifically so that the young people can apply them toward co-operation and successful learning in the social group context. Co-operative learning motivates students to help one another learn. Johnson and Johnson (1987) present a set of conditions necessary for students to co-ordinate efforts to achieve mutual goals:

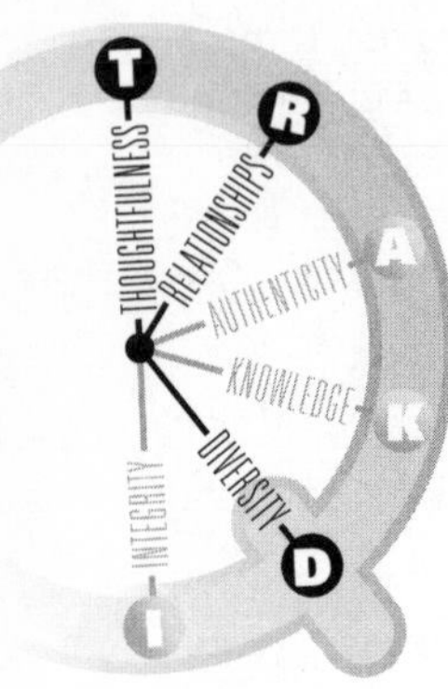

1. Get to know and trust one another.
2. Communicate accurately and unambiguously.
3. Accept and support one another.
4. Resolve conflicts constructively.

Johnson and Johnson (1990) further state that "interpersonal and small-group skills make possible the basic nexus among students; and if students are to work together productively and cope with the stresses of doing so, they must have at least a modicum of these skills" (p. 30). Slavin (1987, p. 4) provides further support for the value of social skills in motivating young people to help one another learn:

1. Students can translate the teacher's language into "kid" language. Students experiencing difficulty understanding from a teacher, often gain the understanding when explained by a peer.
2. Those students who do the explaining learn by doing, so when students have to organize their thoughts to explain ideas to other group members, they must engage in cognitive elaboration that greatly enhances their own understanding.
3. Students can provide individual attention and assistance to each other. In a co-operative group there is nowhere to hide; there is a helpful non-threatening environment in which to try out ideas and ask for assistance.

Learning Empathy

Schools are uniquely social places. Hundreds, sometimes thousands, of people congregate there each day to engage in learning, which requires being with oth-

5.7 FOR YOUR CONSIDERATION

We have suggested that for co-operative learning, young people work in small, heterogeneous groups of three to five members.

a) What does the term *heterogeneous* mean?

b) Using criteria that you glean from the information on co-operative learning, design a scenario for a co-operative group of two working in a math class in Grade 4. Share your scenario with others and discuss the criteria.

c) Apply the Teaching Qualities Model to your scenario. What new insights do you uncover?

d) How does the teaching quality of authenticity inform the discussion of your scenario?

ers, co-operating with others, and generally getting along with others. If all this is to happen effectively, then to a considerable extent, the "getting along" will benefit from the ability of people to be empathetic. **Empathy** is the ability to respond positively to personal emotions and to understand and respond to the feelings of others in compassionate ways.The more we are able to project ourselves into the feelings of others, to understand them in compassionate ways, the more harmonious and sensitive the relationships will be. Think about relationships in the teaching qualities cycle. To what extent would the ability of young people to be empathetic contribute to relationships that support successful learning? Clearly there would be much to gain. The teaching quality of thoughtfulness would also benefit from consideration in the same context.

Nurturing empathy includes three broad dimensions. Young people need to learn what empathy is and how to recognize emotion in themselves and others. Learning how to respond positively to emotions within themselves and others tends to enhance their abilities to be aware of emotions and the skills for positive response. Secondly, it is important for young people to focus on their own feelings at first. They need to be clear about how they feel in certain situations. Only through this self-understanding will they be able to understand the feelings of others. A third step is to try to have the learners see similarities between themselves and others.

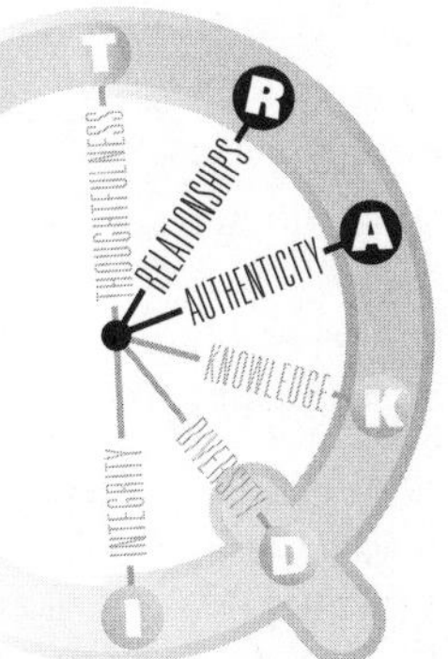

Empathy is a desirable quality at any age, but in young people it needs to be nurtured in a positive, explicit way. Occasionally you may hear teachers speak almost dismissively about concepts and qualities such as empathy. School, after all, is for learning about subjects that are important to success in life. Basic skills, discipline, hard work are the stuff of schooling! How do you feel about this kind of attitude? Think about the teaching qualities of authenticity and relationships. Learning is frequently a difficult task. As young people struggle to engage in new learning, to what extent would understandings of these two teaching qualities be useful for a teacher in knowing how to respond to a young person's struggles?

Empathetic understanding and other related qualities can contribute to academic performance. Occasionally you may hear comments suggesting that character-related matters are not the domain of schools. Families, churches, and other social institutions should be responsible for the development of these character traits. We have taken a position in support of empathy development at the beginning of this discussion, but we can also say that academic achievement is a beneficiary. There is a strong correlation between students' skills and abilities in empathetic understanding and academic achievement. Kohn (1991) reports

5.8 FOR YOUR CONSIDERATION

Design a co-operative learning situation in which peer tutoring is involved.

1. Write a short script for a two-minute situated performance. In your script demonstrate the value of empathetic understanding in the peer-tutoring situation.
2. Rewrite the same script, changing the scenario to one in which empathetic understanding is not present.
3. Discuss the two scripts. As part of your discussion, consider each teaching quality and identify its implications for students in this context.

program evaluation results on measures of higher-order reading comprehension, showing that students in schools with programs designed to increase empathy have higher scores than schools that do not. Gallo (1989) cites evidence that the teaching of empathy enhances critical thinking skills and creative thinking.

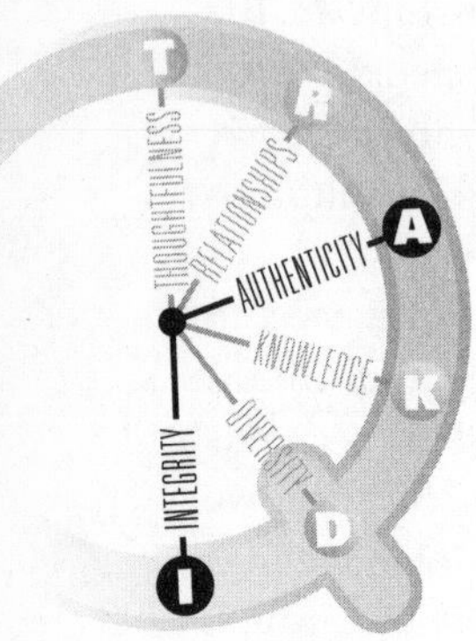

Identity Learning

Identity learning is really a person's attempt to answer the question, Who am I? It is a person's quest to achieve confidence, to feel a sense of well-being through successful lifestyle decisions. Among the theorists who have researched and considered how people form their identities, none has been more influential than Erik Erikson. Erikson studied the social development of people from birth through adulthood. Psychosocial development may be described as a passage through a series of stages, each with its particular goals, concerns, accomplishments, and dangers. The stages (shown in Table 5.1) are interdependent, with a

Table 5.1 Erikson's Eight Stages of Psychosocial Development

Stages	Approximate Age	Important Event	Description
1. Basic trust vs. basic mistrust	Birth to 12–18 months of age	Feeding	The infant must form a first loving, trusting relationship with the caregiver or develop a sense of mistrust.
2. Autonomy vs. shame/doubt	18 months to 3 years	Toilet training	The child's energies are directed toward the development of physical skills, including walking, grasping, controlling the sphincter. The child learns control but may develop shame and doubt if behaviour is not handled well.
3. Initiative vs. guilt	3–6 years	Independence	The child continues to become more assertive and to take more initiative, but may be too forceful, which can lead to guilt feelings.
4. Industry vs. inferiority	6–12 years	School	The child must deal with demands to learn new skills or risk a sense of inferiority, failure, and incompetence.
5. Identity vs. role confusion	Adolescence	Peer relationships	The teenager must achieve identity in occupation, gender roles, politics, and religion.
6. Intimacy vs. isolation	Young adulthood	Love relationships	The young adult must achieve identity in occupation, gender roles, politics, and religion.
7. Generativity vs. stagnation	Middle adulthood	Parenting/Mentoring	Each adult must find some way to satisfy and support the next generation.
8. Ego integrity vs. despair	Late adulthood	Reflection on and acceptance of one's life.	The culmination is a sense of acceptance of oneself as one is and a sense of fulfillment.

(Source: Adapted from Lester A. Lefton, *Psychology*, 5/e (p. 65), 1994, Boston, MA: Allyn and Bacon. Copyright © 1994 by Pearson Education. Adapted by permission of the publisher.)

person's success in later stages being dependent on success in earlier stages. At each stage a person faces what Erikson calls a psychosocial crisis. The way an individual resolves each crisis will have a lasting effect on the person's self-image and world view. The crises he identifies are of interest to teachers as they respond to the learning needs of young people.

You should also note the dominant virtues associated with the age-related crises. The implications of these virtues for teaching will be apparent. Reflect upon the teaching qualities cycle, with specific reference to diversity. The quality of diversity has many dimensions, and Erikson's work exemplifies one such dimension. What implications would Erikson's work have for a teacher working with any age group of young people?

5.9 FOR YOUR CONSIDERATION

You are teaching Grade 8 classes in a school of 500 students. In addition to your teaching assignment, you have an advisory responsibility for a group of fifteen students with whom you meet for twenty minutes every day. One member of your group has been ostracized by her social group of girls, who are also part of your advisory group.

Using Erikson's model and the teaching qualities cycle, determine a course of action to deal with the problem.

Motivation and Learning

To bore someone, according to Webster's dictionary is "to weary with tedious dullness." "The word boring has its roots in an Old English word meaning to drill using the same motion over and over. When faced with constant repetition, we become bored—and we become unmotivated" (Silver, Strong, & Perini, 2000, p. 45). Teachers are interested in developing ways to motivate their students. Most teachers want to go beyond corporal punishment or disapproval and ridicule as a major source of motivation. They want to positively motivate their students to learn, and to be active participants in the students' learning. They want students to be excited about learning, happy to come to school, ready for and interested in the learning experience.

5.10 FOR YOUR CONSIDERATION

Consider the story of Teddy from Chapter 3. Do you believe there was a change in the way Teddy felt about school once Miss Thompson took extra time for him? Was there something that motivated Teddy to continue his schooling even when "university was not easy"?

What is motivation? Motivation involves goal-oriented behaviour. It "is the general term for all the processes involved in starting, directing, and maintaining physical and psychological activities" (Zimbardo & Gerrig, 1996, p. 428). We define **motivation** as the disposition or willingness of a person to engage in learning through a commitment to complete the learning task. Various types of motivational theories emphasize various perspectives, such as biological or social; intrinsic and extrinsic; nature, nurture and environmental influences; and drive theories. It is perhaps unrealistic to expect a single theory to explain the variety of motives that encourage students to learn. In the following section, we present several theories that educators have considered in their attempt to understand the best ways to motivate their students. While you read these, reflect on how your understanding of each of the theories is informed by the teaching qualities introduced in Chapter 2.

Another perspective on motivation that you might find interesting and informative is found in the work of social psychologist Abraham Maslow (1962, 1970). Maslow proposed a sweeping overview of human motivation. His theory assumes that people have many needs, which he organized hierarchically (see Figure 5.1).

Intrinsic and Extrinsic Motivation Some explanations for why students are motivated to learn include internal factors, such as personal reasons, need, interest, curiosity, enjoyment, and the reward of the activity itself. These are called intrinsic motivators. We define **intrinsic motivation** as the internal pleasure, enjoyment, and satisfaction a person derives from working in an activity.

A second set of factors is called extrinsic motivators. **Extrinsic motivation** occurs when learners work on tasks for external reasons—for reward, such as a grade or material object; avoidance of punishment; or parental approval, for example. In the classroom have you witnessed these two types of motivation?

Figure 5.1 *Maslow's Hierarchy of Needs*

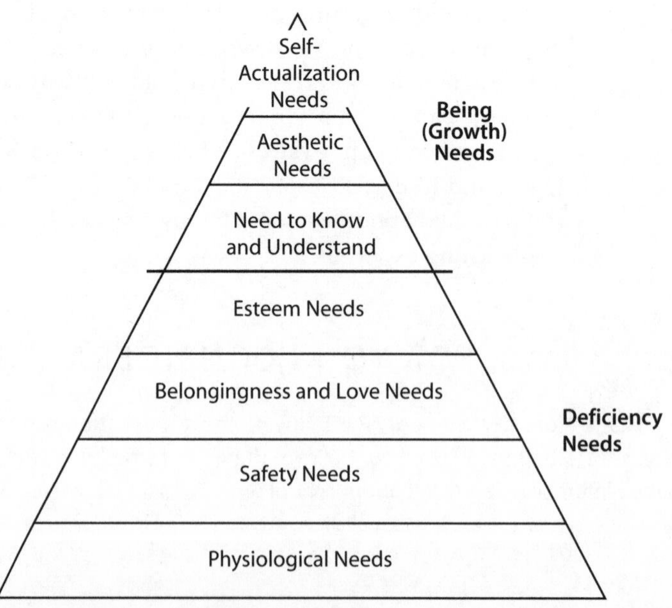

(Source: Data for diagram based on Hierarchy of Needs from *Motivation and Personality*, 2nd ed., by Abraham H. Maslow © 1970. Reprinted by permission of Pearson Education, Inc., Upper Saddle River, NJ.)

Sources for internal motivation include personal goals, intentions, expectations, and explanations for success or failure; self-concept, self-esteem, and self-confidence; self-knowledge and sense of self-efficacy. Personality factors include willingness to undertake risk, ability to manage anxieties, curiosity, and persistence in effort (McCown, Driscoll, Schwean, Kelly, & Haines, 1999). External motivation may come from the desire to please or to meet expectations of a teacher or parent; to avoid getting in trouble; to achieve a reward, prize, or other incentives. It may not surprise you that intrinsic motivation is a preferable motivational state. "The intrinsically motivated person is more likely to stay involved in and demonstrate commitment to learning than is the extrinsically motivated person" (McCown et al., 1999, p. 275).

5.11 FOR YOUR CONSIDERATION

During your field experience, observation is more meaningful when you are focused on a particular goal and have a clear purpose for this observation. During your next field experience, observe the ways students are motivated intrinsically (from within) and extrinsically (from factors outside themselves) (Parkay et al., 1996). You may find it more useful to look at the two motivations individually, one session at a time.

Intrinsic Motivation

Answer the following questions in detail:

- What topics do students talk about with enthusiasm?
- When do they appear most alert and participate most actively?
- When do they seem to be bored, confused, frustrated?

(Adapted from Parkay et al., 1996, p. 63.)

What else have you noticed with respect to intrinsic motivation in this field experience?

Extrinsic Motivation

Answer the following questions in detail:

- How do teachers show their approval to students?
- What reward programs do you notice?
- What punishments are given to students?
- What forms of peer pressure do you observe?

(Adapted from Parkay, et al., 1996, p. 63.)

What else have you noticed with respect to extrinsic motivation in this field experience?

1. Which of the teaching qualities (knowledge, relationships, authenticity, integrity, thoughtfulness, and diversity) enhance your understanding of intrinsic and extrinsic motivation?
2. Can your understanding of the motivational make-up of your students be of assistance in teaching your students?
3. How would you encourage intrinsic motivation in your students?

Ethical and Moral Learning

> Can you tell me, Socrates, whether virtue is acquired by teaching, or by practice; or if neither by teaching nor practice, then whether it comes to man by nature, or in what other way?
>
> —MENO'S QUESTION TO SOCRATES

These children are co-operating in their learning tasks. What aspect of social-cognitive learning theory might be at work here?

Moral learning has been part of the schooling debate for many years, rising and falling in popularity with the mores of society. The debate might be summed up in this question: Should schools teach morals and, if so, whose morals? Sometimes moral learning is presented as character education, but whatever its incarnation, whether as morals, ethics or character, the concern is with developing thinking and action that reflects "right," "good," and "proper" ethical conduct in ways that complement teachings and practices from family, religious, or humanistic beliefs. In short, **moral education** may be understood as a process whereby principles for action on complex societal issues are formulated and applied.

Today's society has many problems that give us cause for concern. The media presents daily reports of crime, teen pregnancy, theft, suicide, bullying, and assault, suggesting a moral crisis. Clearly, not all these examples are moral issues, but concerned citizens are increasingly looking to schools to teach morals and values. Parents who choose private schools frequently do so out of concerns related to morals and values.

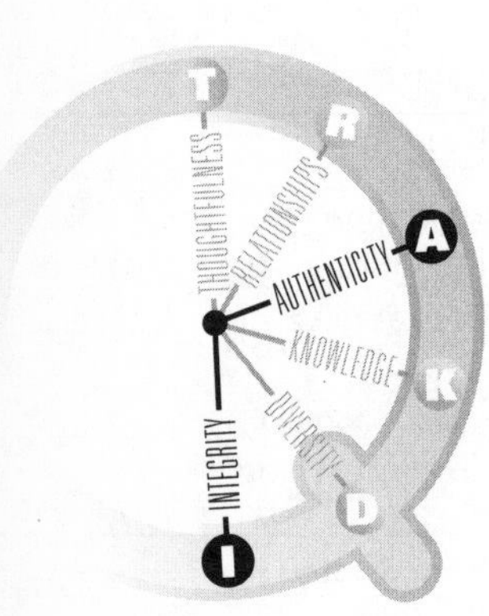

Think about your time in grade school. How many issues of a moral nature occurred that had some impact on you? There is a danger when responding to moral concerns. Should teachers be left to decide for themselves which morals and which values to deal with in their classrooms? Should teachers be left to decide, whimsically, how to teach morals and values? One could easily imagine the pitfalls inherent in such licence. In deciding not only what morals to teach, but how to teach those morals, teachers should refer to research on the topic. In later pages of this chapter, we introduce four researchers whose work provides interesting approaches to moral learning.

We believe that moral learning is essential for today's young people and that schools must pay it appropriate attention. Some would argue that moral development is the domain of church and family, and that schools should stick to the business of intellectual development within subject areas and their related skills. The argument has some merit in this time of crowded curricula. However, the issue is complex and certainly more profound than the "crowded curricula" position. Leaving aside the "dysfunctional family" and "significant decline in religious adherence" debates, consider two pertinent conditions:

1. Young people are exposed to many influences in their lives, many temptations, many pressures on their decision making, many forces attempting to

persuade and convince, many images presenting unrealistic expectations. Do you think schools therefore have an obligation to make a contribution to the moral education of young people?

2. Young people congregate in schools, where large numbers of their peers meet for hours each day in social contexts. Schools have little choice about functioning as social institutions. They do, however have choice, as to *how* they will function.

Morality and Spirituality

The current interest in spirituality is worthy of note. Human beings have always had some compelling attraction toward a greater, often unfathomable, power. People have worshipped multiple gods, spirits within inanimate objects, physical features such as mountains, and deferred to greater powers within their environments. Religions, before the relatively recent education of the masses, would project morality almost by decree. Priests, rabbis and holy people would determine the appropriateness of thought and action through their position and preaching. Philosophers and theologians would engage in debate with only limited impact on society at large. Attilla's Huns, Roman legions, Viking hordes, and knights of the Crusades, for example, perpetrated their conquests with scant regard for what is "right" in today's sense of the term, but with a firm belief in their own sense of what was "right" to them at the time.

The Renaissance period of European history, beginning in the fifteenth century, saw the advent of modernism, that period when reason became a hallmark of progress and thought. Feudalism began to wane, and all forms of dogma were challenged and questioned. It was, in short, the era of scientific thinking. Universities began to appear and scholarship blossomed. Churches were very much involved with the establishment of modernism and their hierarchies were often in opposition to secular scholars. The church would debate from beliefs grounded in faith, and academia would argue from more secular positions. Both sides valued reason. It was within this kind of climate that the Reformation took place.

During the nineteenth and twentieth centuries morality was postulated by rules and regulations imposed on society by both authority and societal self-regulation, through custom and tradition. Authority was still, by and large, imposed through church and state, and societal self-regulation through civil codes and forces of law and order. Philosophers, however, were still at work. Descartes, in exploring the essence of self, coined his now-famous logic in the expression, "I think, therefore I am." Sartre explored existentialism. Kant insisted that moral acts could be considered to be so only if they were performed out of a principled sense of duty.

Jurgen Habermas, a "critical theorist" from Germany, posited educational theories that arguably hold significant meaning for moral education and for the advent of post-modernism. He identified three distinct types of human "interest," each of which would lead to a particular way of knowing. His first human interest was *technical,* with a related way of knowing called *empirical.* A more traditional teaching style would be related to this, with an emphasis on "banking" knowledge. His second human interest was *hermeneutical,* with a related way of knowing called *interpretative.* The teacher and student make meaning from knowledge, as they look for connections in learning through conversation and discourse. Habermas's third human interest was *emancipatory*, with a related way of knowing called *liberation.* In this interest, a teacher believed that without liberation, any belief system becomes static and susceptible to control by vested interest groups. The *emancipatory* way of knowing would move students from passive, possibly submissive, receiving of knowledge, to a more thoughtful, critical reflection leading to liberation and change.

When the emancipatory interest is served, students gain a deeper understanding of knowledge and confront knowledge and reality, theory and practice, in short, engage in shared praxis. In Chapter 1, we described the concept of praxis as the deliberate integration of ethical reflections and understandings about the commonplaces of professional knowledge into teaching practice. When you share these ethical reflections and understandings with others, in the course of your practice, then you are engaging in shared praxis. This whole notion of praxis, especially shared praxis, is worthy of further reflection at this juncture. Revisit the discussion of shared praxis introduced in Chapter 1 and think about the importance of the concept to moral learning.

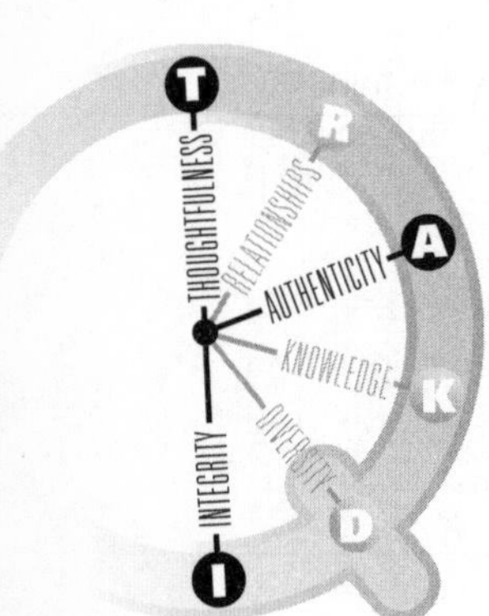

The idea of moving from thought to action is important in any learning endeavour, but think how critically important it is in the moral domain. Habermas's emancipatory interest encourages people, ultimately, to engage in critique and reflection on knowledge and behaviour, to challenge it and develop new knowledge leading to action for change. "Critical reflection, in the emancipatory way of knowing, leads to *praxis*, when 'theory' or 'handed down knowledge' is scrutinized and critiqued, and new knowledge, which changes or challenges accepted knowledge, is forged" (Engebretson, 1997). Very often we know, intellectually, what should be done in a given situation, but it may be debatable whether we actually do it. Think about the complexity of this giant leap from thought to action. Cast your mind back to, say, Grade 8. Were there instances when perhaps you knew the right thing to do, but you didn't do it? Maybe you were with a group of your friends when some of your group verbally abused a younger student. You knew it wasn't right but you said and did nothing. Maybe some of your friends used vulgar language. You did the same even though you didn't think it was a good idea. You really didn't like it and you knew your parents wouldn't approve. Could your parents, your church, your school, or any other human influence in your life have done anything differently to make a difference in this regard? Of course, it is a very complex matter. The big question is, Can we afford not to pay attention to the moral learning of learners?

5.12 FOR YOUR CONSIDERATION

Think of two ways that the emancipatory interest could be explored by a teacher in a grade three classroom. Is it reasonable or important for a Grade 3 teacher to consider this question?

It is interesting to contemplate the recent interest in spirituality. Habermas's postulation that people have an emancipatory interest would subscribe to the seeming wish people have to form their own opinions, to think for themselves. Within this interest, amid the complexity of today's world, there is an apparent search for deeper meaning to human behaviour. Leaders in the corporate and educational worlds, for example, address this meaning in works such as *Going Deep* (Percy, 1997), *Synchronicity: The Inner Path Of Leadership* (Jaworski, 1998), *Leadership from Within* (Bender, 1997), *Encouraging the Heart* (Kouzes & Posner, 1999), *Principle-Centred Leadership* (Covey, 1992), *Moral Leadership* (Sergiovanni, 1992), and *The Soul of Education* (Kessler, 2000). The commonality in these works is the search for a deeper understanding of self, of one's place in the scheme of things, and the harmonious coexistence of intrapersonal and interpersonal relationships in all facets of life. This seeking for spirituality has interesting connections to those peoples we often somewhat arrogantly call "primitive," those who have not been influenced by western civilization. Perhaps a need for morality in our lives is innate? Perhaps, in this age of an educated populace, where people enjoy liberation in thought, the emancipatory interest is emerging and the always-present need for moral codes is becoming more explicit.

Morality and Co-operation

Co-operation is a fundamental requirement in the human community. The skills and competencies of co-operation contribute to our survival. In the days of hunting and gathering, people co-operated for physical survival. Later, when societies were more settled, co-operation led to advancement in industry, arts, health, and welfare. The sense of community that co-operation inspires appeals to the inner needs that human beings have for care and compassion. It is altruism; it is concern for the welfare of others, it is other-centred; it is doing the "right thing;" it is the Golden Rule. "Co-operation is an essentially humanizing experience that predisposes participants to take a benevolent view of others. It allows them to transcend egocentric and objectifying postures and encourages trust, sensitivity, open

A co-operative group at work.

communication and pro-social activity." (Kohn, 1991) Co-operation in schools is a pre-condition for the social life, but also a powerful means of learning. Within the school, then, there are extant conditions that lend themselves to moral learning. The task for the school is to render moral learning explicit within the social learning community.

Moral Learning and Ethics

Moral learning and ethics are two terms that are often used interchangeably: **Ethics** is concerned with principles of conduct generally considered to be "good," "right," and "proper" for both the welfare of the individual and society. **Moral learning** is the process by which people acquire and practice principles of right, good, and proper ethical conduct.

Moral education seeks to understand how people learn to conduct themselves in right, proper, and good ways, to do the right thing. The fundamental question often is, What is the right thing and who decides what it is? The debate is rooted in considerations of altruism and socialization. The moral learning of children must, of course, proceed from a clear understanding of their overall development as maturing young people. The over-arching goals are to nurture altruism, empathy, and a general disposition toward concern for the welfare of self and others. The subjugation of self-centred interest to the welfare of others is a particularly admirable human quality. It is a quality based in reason, our ability to be thoughtful, and our ability to act on that thoughtfulness. It contributes to becoming fully human.

Moral Learning in Schools: The Moral Dimension of Teaching

Schools are places where children and adults congregate for the purpose of learning. Children arrive at school to be taught, in groups, by adults who are responsible for the learning and teaching that takes place, and for the orderly conduct of daily life in the school. How is daily life in school to be regulated? How are decisions made that go beyond the regulatory rules and policies of the place? Interactions between people in schools are constant. The interactions concern learning, conduct, consequences, interpersonal events, decision making, responsibility, and so on. They all involve choices. How are these choices made and on what bases do people found their decisions? "The choices embed themselves in and arise out of individual moral agency grappling with obligation to others." (Thomas, 1990) Thomas takes the position that teaching is, inherently, a moral enterprise. Using what he calls a "simple vocabulary to describe teaching" he offers three statements in an attempt to bring clarity to the morality of the schooling enterprise:

1. Parents entrust their children to school. Trust obliges teachers to be careful. Teachers are to proceed carefully with the work of empowering students.
2. Empowerment is remarkable. One human being sets out to make others strong and able. That one human being is not to exploit, coerce, or manipulate the

others.... At the outset, we can at least say that the empowering teacher must be powerful, for impotence does not call forth potency.

3. Parents entrust their children to teachers. School is mandatory.... The teacher, then, is obliged to care for children and be responsible for their empowerment. (Thomas, 1990, pp. 266–267)

Trust, care, obligation, and *responsibility,* Thomas believes, are words that carry the burden of morality. Not only teaching, but schooling also is a moral enterprise. Think, for a minute, about daily life in school. How are students spoken to in the school office? What tone and manner do teachers display when they observe a learner misbehaving? If two boys engage in a heated argument in the hallway at lunchtime, how would teachers deal with the situation? If a school has a detention room, why are students sent there and what do they do during their detention time? The larger question to ask of all these situations is, What will the students learn from their treatment? Therein lies a critical consideration as to whether teaching and schooling constitute a moral enterprise.

Moral Learning Research

Moral learning is a process through which young people acquire and practise principles of right, good, and proper ethical conduct. *Character education* is often used synonymously with *moral education.* In the design of this process schools must look to research that explores human development and demonstrates how, through the different phases of development, young people might be nurtured toward thinking, reasoning, and acting in moral ways. We now present a summary of the work of four researchers as useful references for that process.

Jean Piaget (1896–1980): Cognitive Development and Moral Judgment Piaget's research in developmental psychology attempted to understand how knowledge grows. In his pursuit of this understanding, Piaget spent a great deal of time observing children as they reacted to their environments. He presented stories to children and engaged them in discussions. He would question them about the stories. Over time, Piaget began to formulate a description of how moral judgments develop and how cognitive development occurs in young people. His premise was that children learn through actively interacting with their environments. Table 5.2 on the next page summarizes his theory of cognitive development.

Lawrence Kohlberg (1927–1987): Developmental Stages of Moral Development Kohlberg explored Piaget's work, modifying and elaborating on Piaget's conclusions to lay solid groundwork for current debates on moral education and moral learning. Like Piaget, he used stories to investigate moral reasoning for all ages. Kohlberg's stories presented **moral dilemmas** on which his subjects were asked to judge the best course of action. He concluded that young people form ways of reasoning through their experiences, which include under-

Table 5.2 Piaget's Stage Theory of Cognitive Development

Stage	Age	Characteristics
Sensorimotor	Birth to about 2 years	It "is primarily characterized by the development of sensory (simple input) and motor (simple output) functions" (R. Sternberg & Williams, 2002, p. 46). Two main accomplishments at this stage are object permanence, the understanding that objects continue to exist even when not immediately visible, and representational thought, mental ideas of external stimuli (R. Sternberg & Williams, 2002).
Preoperational	Approx. 24 months to 7 years	Children begin to communicate using words, use words as symbols for concrete objects, and are often egocentric, "centered on the self without understanding how other people perceive a situation" (R. Sternberg & Williams, 2002, p. 47).
Concrete Operational	Approx. 7–12 years	Children at this stage "not only have mental representations but also can act on and modify these representations. They can think logically as long as the logical thinking applies to these representations" (R. Sternberg & Williams, 2002 p. 48). An example of this is their development of conservation, "the recognition that even when the physical appearance of something changes, its underlying quantity (how much there is of it—number, size, or volume) remains the same—or in other words, is conserved" (R. Sternberg & Williams, 2002, p. 48). At this stage the child's thinking is reversible; he or she can see the higher level of liquid in the tall thin beaker after pouring out the same amount into a shorter wide beaker.
Formal Operational	About age 11 through adulthood	Individuals in this stage can form abstract as well as concrete mental representations, and can see second-order relations, "or relations between relations, as required by analogical reasoning" (R. Sternberg & Williams, 2002, p. 49).

(Source: From Robert J. Sternberg and Wendy M. Williams, *Educational Psychology,* 2002, Boston, MA: Allyn and Bacon. Copyright © 2002 by Pearson Education. Reprinted by permission of the publisher.)

standings of moral concepts such as justice, equality, fairness, and human welfare. The following moral dilemma is typical of those used by Kohlberg in his research:

> In Europe, a woman was near death from cancer. One drug might save her, a form of radium a druggist in the same town had recently discovered. The druggist was charging $2000, ten times what the drug cost him to make. The sick woman's husband, Heinz, went to everyone he knew to borrow the money, but he could only get together about half of what it cost. He told the druggist that his wife was dying and asked him to sell it cheaper or let him pay later, but the druggist said, "No." The hus-

band got desperate and broke into the man's store to steal the drug for his wife. Should the husband have done that? Why? (Kohlberg, 1969, p. 376)

Kohlberg classified the reasoning used by young people to respond to the dilemmas he presented. On the basis of his research he identified six stages of moral reasoning, within three levels (shown in Table 5.3)

Refer to the reasoning you used when responding to the dilemma involving the man whose wife was dying of cancer. If you accept Kohlberg's model, into which stage of moral reasoning would you fit? Do you feel you fit comfortably into one stage or does your reasoning embrace a number of stages? Kohlberg would argue that people have a dominant stage and that to develop to more advanced stages they benefit from questions that reflect the moral reasoning of the next more advanced stage.

In response to criticism, Kohlberg later modified his stages to reject Stage 6 as a logical progression from Stage 5. He considered it to be more of a theoretical endpoint that rationally follows, rather than a specific stage. Stages 1 to 5 have

Table 5.3 Kohlberg's Theory of Moral Development

Level 1—Preconventional Level of Moral Reasoning	Child is responsive to cultural rules and labels of good and bad, right or wrong, but interprets these in terms of consequences of action (punishment, rewards, exchanges of favours).
Stage 1: Punishment-and-Obedience Orientation	Physical consequences of action determine its goodness or badness. Avoidance of punishment and deference of power are valued.
Stage 2: The Instrumental–Relativist Orientation	Right action consists of that which satisfies one's own needs and occasionally the needs of others. Reciprocity is a matter of "You scratch my back and I'll scratch yours."
Level II—Conventional Level of Moral Reasoning	Maintaining the expectations of the individual's family, group, or society is perceived as valuable, regardless of consequences.
Stage 3: The Interpersonal Concordance or "Good Boy–Nice Girl" Orientation	Good behaviour is that which pleases or helps others and is approved by them.
Stage 4: The "Law and Order" Orientation	Orientation toward fixed rules and the maintenance of the social order. Right behaviour consists of doing one's duty and showing respect for authority.
Level III—Postconventional, Autonomous, or Principled Level of Moral Reasoning	Effort to define moral principles that have validity and application apart from the authority of groups.
Stage 5: The Social Contract, Legalistic Orientation	Right action is defined in terms of rights and standards that have been agreed on by the whole society
Stage 6: The Universal Ethical Principle Orientation	Right is defined by conscience in accord with self-chosen ethical principles appealing to logic and universality.

(Source: Excerpted from Lawrence Kohlberg, "The Claim to Moral Adequacy of a Highest State of Moral Judgment," *Journal of Philosophy, LXX, 18*, (Oct. 25, 1973): 631–632. Reprinted with permission.)

been empirically supported by findings from longitudinal and cross-cultural research (Power, Higgins, & Kohlberg, 1989).

Concerns about Kohlberg's Model Kohlberg's model has been criticized. His claim that young people pass through stages in "invariant sequence," that is, from one stage to the next in sequence, with the only variant being the precise age at which they might move to a higher stage, has been challenged. Holstein (1976) found that children might vary in their stage of development depending on the particular dilemma to which they were responding. He found high levels of ambiguity in Kohlberg's stage developmental theory. Kohlberg has also been challenged on the basis of gender. His research subjects were male, and notable differences were detected when his dilemmas were applied to female subjects (Holstein, 1976; Gilligan, 1982).

Further criticism concerns Kohlberg's dependence on moral reasoning, or thinking. The whole question of feeling appears to be absent from the stages. When people are confronted with a moral dilemma, feelings, emotions, and attitudes cannot be discounted. Peters (1977) argues that empathy and altruism should be high on any list of considerations when responding to moral dilemmas. Moral reasoning is not, solely, an objective, intellectual exercise.

Strengths of Kohlberg's Model Regardless of the absence of emotion, feelings, and attitudes in Kohlberg's approach, he does present useful insight into the process of moral reasoning. Moral learning is clearly a complex matter that is composed of many interconnected dimensions in which reasoning and thinking are prominent and practical. Relationships are very important and later discussion of Gilligan and Noddings will show the profound nature of positive relationships to the effectiveness of moral reasoning. Teachers, on a daily basis, deal with young people who display inappropriate behaviour. Frequently this behaviour involves other students and raises moral concerns. If a teacher has an understanding of a young person's capacity for moral reasoning, then the teacher knows that responding with comments and questions within the child's ability to comprehend will likely encourage understanding and resolution. If this kind of response is in the context of good relationships, then a successful outcome is much more likely. Kohlberg's theory represents a significant contribution to our understanding of moral development. "A good scientific theory is one that generates new research. In this regard, Kohlberg's theory has proven to be very successful" (McCown et al., 1999, p. 87).

Carol Gilligan: Gender Differences in Moral Development Gilligan (1982) noted that Kohlberg's research subjects were all males and concluded that his findings were biased against women. She conducted research in which she listened to women's stories and experiences. She concluded that it was possible to discern, from women's experiences, a morality, or **ethic of care.** This contrasts with Kohlberg, who determined that morality was based on justice and fairness. The essential equality upon which Kohlberg's theory is founded provides an interesting apposition to the compassion and empathy of Gilligan.

Gilligan's research suggests three stages of moral learning with two periods of transition. Her first stage, individual survival,would see a person with self as one's

5.13 FOR YOUR CONSIDERATION

Task 1

Shawn O'Malley is behaving badly in Ms. Harrison's Grade 4 class. He is calling Jennifer Coltroni nasty, hurtful names and threatening to spoil her nice new school bag. Jennifer was given the last piece of green construction paper in the art class, and Shawn wanted it. Ms. Harrison pulled Shawn to one side and started to speak sternly.

"Shawn, why are you being so mean to Jennifer?"

"Because she always gets what she wants," said Shawn. "She's such a goody-goody, I hate her."

"Now look here, Shawn O'Malley, there are rules in this school that we all must follow. The principal has made these very clear and if you don't follow these rules you will finish up in his office."

"Well, why does she have to get the last piece of art paper?"

"You are now being very rude to your teacher and you are breaking another rule we have in this school ..."

Complete this scenario. How do you think it will end? Why? Discuss your reasons in a group setting.

Task 2

Shawn O'Malley is behaving badly in Ms. Harrison's Grade 4 class. He is calling Jennifer Coltroni nasty, hurtful names and threatening to spoil her nice new school bag. Jennifer was given the last piece of green construction paper in the art class and Shawn wanted it. Ms. Harrison pulled Shawn to one side and ...

Now discuss this scenario in the context of moral development. How would you talk to Shawn? How would you reason with him? How would you resolve the situation?

The broad question, "Can moral reasoning be taught?" looms large. Concepts such as empathy, justice and fairness, altruism, compassion, and caring are important humanistic qualities that most would agree are necessary for a healthy society. Surely the learning of these moral qualities contributes to a complete individual; they are part of the whole person.

Kohlberg suggests that the following three conditions can help children internalize moral principles.

1) Exposure to the next higher stage of reasoning.
2) Exposure to situations posing problems and contradictions for the child's current moral structure, leading to dissatisfaction with his [or her] current level.
3) An atmosphere of interchange and dialogue combining the first two conditions, in which conflicting moral views are compared openly. (Banks, J., 1993, p. 3)

sole concern. The first transition would see a person moving from egocentrism to an emerging sense of responsibility, arriving at the second stage of goodness, self-sacrifice, and social conformity. The second stage would see the person demonstrating greater social participation and a general acceptance of social conventions and protocol. The final transition is from goodness to truth. The characteristic of this transition is a subservience of self to the interests of a morality of care. An individual at this stage wrestles with looking after one's own self-interest before the interest of others. This leads to Gilligan's final stage, morality of non-violence. In this third stage the individual engages in comfortable concern for self and others. Altruism is understood and practised. There is a reconciliation of selfishness and responsibility.

At each level, the complexity of the self–other relationship increases. During the two periods of transition, responsibility becomes more sophisticated within the self–other context.

Gilligan used cohorts of girls for her research and in this regard her work may be thought of as a theory of female moral development. Her work certainly does pertain to female moral development, but it is not confined to one gender. Other research (Walker, deVries, & Trevethan, 1987) indicates that some people value justice while others value caring, and it is not possible to link either preference to gender. Gilligan's theory respects the role of affect in the moral development of young people. Kohlberg's adherence to justice, fairness, and the rules and regulations focus is expanded to introduce those aspects of character described by caring, compassion, feelings, emotions, and attitude. Clearly there is more to moral development than cognition. The role of gender in moral development is still in need of greater clarity, but Gilligan has helped to create awareness that care is an essential dimension of moral reasoning.

Nel Noddings: An "Ethic of Care" and Moral Learning Noddings explores moral learning through caring as a moral orientation in teaching. She acknowledges that, "caring has often been characterized as feminine because it seems to arise more naturally out of woman's experience than man's" (Noddings, 1984, p. 218). She believes, however, that on reflection, the ethical orientation of caring may be understood as **relational ethics.** Such ethics are tied to experience, because all questions and considerations focus on the human beings involved in the situations being considered and their relations to each other. Noddings presents the following definition of relational ethics:

> any pairing or connection of individuals characterized by some affective awareness in each. It is an encounter or series of encounters in which the involved parties feel something toward each other. Relations may be characterized by love or hate, anger or sorrow, admiration or envy; or, of course, they may reveal mixed affects—one party feeling, say, love and the other revulsion. (Noddings, 1984, p. 218)

A relational ethic, an ethic of caring, differs significantly from the more conventional understanding of ethics in that it does not root itself in an emphasis on duty. Kohlberg and Piaget both stress the adherence to rules for the determination of right, wrong, and justice. Piaget believed that morality is defined individually through struggles to arrive at fair solutions through the consideration of rules. Kohlberg determined his stages of moral reasoning based on an individual's response to duty understood through rules and laws of social conventions. An ethic of care prefers acts done out of love and natural inclination. When acting out of an ethic of care, judgments are not grounded in conformity to rules or principles; rather they are concerned with the relation itself. The concern is two-fold: a) the physical impact on those involved in the relation, and b) the feelings and ways of responding to the actions from those involved in the relation. Responding through an ethic of care calls on a sense of obligation to stimulate natural caring. Noddings (1984) considers natural caring to be a superior state, "because it energizes the giver as well as the receiver."

Noddings' approach to moral learning is not a stage developmental approach such as Piaget's, Kohlberg's and, to a lesser extent, Gilligan's. Rather it is more of a series of conditions that need to be present for an ethic of care to be nurtured. The first relational ethic is one of modelling an ethic of care, where self-affirmation and responsibility are encouraged in young people. Noddings refers to the teacher as the one caring, and to the learner as the one cared for. "When a teacher asks a question in class and a student responds, [the one caring] receives not just the 'response' but the student ... [f]or the brief interval of dialogue that grows around the question,... indeed 'fills the firmament'." (Noddings, 1984, p. 176) Her second relational ethic is dialogue. The intention is to encourage a form of dialectic between feeling and thinking that will lead, in a continuing spiral, to the basic feeling of genuine caring and the generous thinking that develops in its service. Openness on any topic is encouraged. A third relational ethic is practice. Opportunities are created for practice in caring, with the emphasis being on how the skills developed contribute to competence in caring. A final relational ethic is that of confirmation, in which the hope is to shape an acceptable child by assisting in the construction of his or her ethical ideal. "When we attribute the best possible motive, consonant with reality, to the cared-for, we confirm him; that is, we reveal to him an attainable image of himself that is lovelier than that manifested in his present acts." (Noddings, 1988, p. 224)

We have now considered the work of four people in the area of moral development. What does this work mean for schools? What implications would it have for you as a teacher? First of all, you would have to be aware of your school's approach to moral learning. Young people of all ages benefit from consistency. It is very important that adults in a school treat young people in ways that aim to encourage the same kinds of behaviour in similar ways. To pursue this question in a little more depth, refer to Task 2 in For Your Consideration 5.13 on page 105.

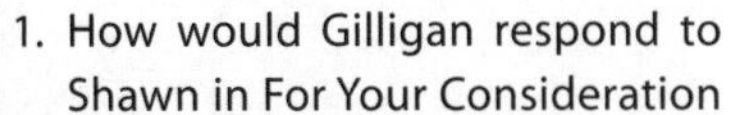

5.14 FOR YOUR CONSIDERATION

1. How would Gilligan respond to Shawn in For Your Consideration 5.13? How would you introduce the role of affect to Shawn's situation? How would compassion and empathy be employed in Shawn's situation?
2. Noddings explores moral learning through caring. Using her understanding of caring as relational ethics, how would you respond to Shawn through the relation itself?
3. Finally, think about our teaching qualities and apply them to Shawn's situation. Consider the work on moral learning, but don't confine yourself to it. Use any knowledge and experience you have in your professional repertoire as you consider and reflect upon each of the teaching qualities.

One thing to remember is that teachers should always apply professional judgment to any school situation with which they must deal. Children are unique; seldom is there a standard, single way of responding to them. When dealing with almost any matter with young people, the single important question is what will the young person learn from the way you respond to her? With Shawn, the question is particularly germane. What would he likely learn from his treatment in Task 1 in For Your Consideration 5.13?

Reflection and Perspective on the Chapter

The main goal of a teacher is to facilitate learning in students. Teachers can fail in that goal, however, if they make incorrect assumptions about learning in social settings. One goal of your education, the same goal of the lifelong learning of teachers, is to adjust your assumptions so that they are more accurate. Many seemingly evident assumptions about learning need to be reconsidered. These include the role of the setting in which young people learn.

There are a number of plausible explanations for social learning and how it occurs. All theoretical perspectives regarding social learning refer to the role that others have in learning. The core premise in each explanation is that learning is socially constructed, that knowledge is a social construction. Learning depends on others. We have identified and discussed two educational approaches to designing learning experiences so that social learning is positive. They are constructivist-oriented teaching and narrative inquiry. We have also discussed broad areas in which social learning might be considered, either as outcomes (e.g., pro-social skills), or as areas in which social learning might make a contribution to a child's development (e.g., moral learning). We believe that our choices of topics are the most influential ones for designing learning experiences in classrooms. The other areas in which social learning might be considered are co-operative learning, learning empathy, identity learning, and motivation and learning.

Social-cognitive learning theory is a branch of social learning theory in which the learner is considered to be an active-cognitive participant in learning. Learners can symbolically represent the events they see and hear, and can learn vicariously from considering the results that others experience from their actions. This saves time and prevents potentially dangerous experiential learning from having to be designed and implemented.

Throughout the chapter we have discussed the social conditions of learning, how teachers can create the external social conditions that create, in turn, the internal conditions of learning. Motivation is an example of an internal condition; keeping children free from the fear of failure by increasing the number of times they are successful is an external condition.

Key Terms

Suggested Further Reading

Bay, Theresa M., and Turner, Gwendolyn, Y. (1996). *Making School a Place of Peace*. Upper Saddle River, NJ: Prentice-Hall Inc. and Thousand Oaks, CA: Corwin Press, Inc.

Fullan, M. (2003). *The Moral Imperative of School Leadership*. Thousand Oaks, CA: Corwin Press.

Malicky, Grace, Shapiro, Bonnie, and Mazurek, Kas. Eds. (1999). *Building Foundations for Safe and Caring Schools*. Edmonton, AB: Duval House Publishing.

Simon, Katherine, G. (2001). *Moral questions in the classroom: How to get kids to think deeply about real life and their school work*. New Haven, NH: Yale University Press.

Chapter 6

Learners

> Generally, by the time you are Real, most of your hair has been loved off, and your eyes drop out and you get loose in the joints and very shabby. But these things don't matter at all, because once you are Real you can't be ugly, except to people who don't understand.
>
> —The Velveteen Rabbit

Chapter Focus

Understanding Learners

This chapter is about the nature of learners: who they are, what their real needs are, and how they develop. We will consider what is most useful for a teacher to understand about learners, the young people entrusted to a teacher's care. We will also review some important conditions necessary for learners to learn.

Our focus on learners will include an invitation for you to build a personal theory of learners. Your theory building regarding learners is an important step in your development as teacher. A **theory** is a set of "coherent statements that describe, and predict some aspects of some phenomenon" (Gormlay & Brodzinsky, 1989, p. 7). Theories are necessary because they set appropriate limits on understanding, so teachers do not expect more than they ought to regarding learners. Theories help shape teaching practices. Teachers can be most reasonable, fair, and effective when they are aware that their theories are a close match to what is true about learners. For example, consider the topic of **individualizing instruction.** If your theory of learners includes the statement that "each learner is unique in areas that should be considered in designing learning experiences," areas such as personality and learning style, your design of learning experiences will be likely to produce positive outcomes. Your theory of learners will predispose you to plan learning experiences and teach in ways that preserve the dignity of all learners as they individually struggle to understand some concept. And if your theory includes the statement that learners are similar in some important areas, such as sharing deep needs for security and significance, you will plan learning experiences and teach confidently in ways that embraces all learners and their shared human needs. All learners need some encouragement at some time. This theory building is good and important. Your theory will influence you to avoid designing "one-size-fits-all" type of learning experiences, or lesson plans, to help each learner learn.

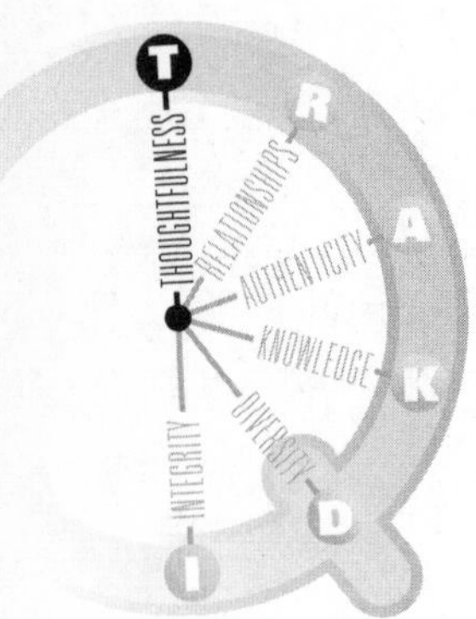

Theories of Learners

This chapter will ask you to consider thoughtfully some contemporary and traditional theories of learners. The intended outcome is for you to consider how each theory confirms or disconfirms your own emerging theory of learning. In addition, we hope that you use your emerging theory of learners to affirm and, where necessary, disaffirm theories you encounter in this chapter. This approach of mutually considering different theories of learners is particularly important and helpful in becoming a thoughtful, integrated teacher.

Relational Stance

It is important that you take a caring type of relational stance with your learners in your field experiences and in your own future classrooms. Relationships are the heart of teaching and learning. This **relational stance**—wanting what is best for a learner and attempting to achieve what is best through a positive relationship with the learner—will need to be based on what is both true about learners and true to what you hold theoretically most dear about learners. That is, your theory should have integrity. It should fit closely with what is known about learners and with what you believe to be factual about learners. You can best care for learners when you know in what ways individual learners need to feel cared for. But no single theory explains learners. No single worldview, regardless of how deeply held, explains learners. We encourage you in this chapter to combine perspectives about learners into your worldview, perspectives taken from your readings, partner teachers, and field experience. We encourage you to be open, holding your theories of learners with the same firm tentativeness that you might hold a butterfly—carefully, thoughtfully, and firmly, yet ready to let it go when necessary for the sake of the butterfly.

A typical Grade 7 class in Canada: Notice the developmental differences among these students.

Assumptions and Learning

We invite you to begin your theory building by considering some assumptions, or ideas, about learners that are common among educators. Consider how each assumption affirms what you believe or do not believe to be true about learners. In this way, you will begin clarifying and informing your own theories of learners. Next, we will introduce some major contemporary theories of learners, drawing from three areas of human development (cognitive, physical, and social). We intend that our description of major theories will deepen and broaden your emerging theory of learners. We will also invite you to consider ways that the historical and cultural settings of learners influence learners and their development. We will invite you to consider the philosophical question, What is the nature of a learner? In this regard, we will consider whether learners are free and able to freely choose their responses in classrooms; or whether learners' natures are determined in ways that influence what they can indeed learn. Finally, we will investigate issues that influence both learners and teachers in today's classrooms. These include issues of ethnicity, gender, abuse, diversity, and special needs.

Focus Questions

1. What approaches to teaching might best create an inclusive classroom, open and effective for all learners?
2. How do the needs of learners change as they grow and develop?
3. In what ways are all learners alike in their needs and desires?
4. What developmental tasks are most likely to help learners succeed in school and in life?
5. How might schools be designed to provide those developmental tasks for each learner?
6. What conditions create communities of care and success for learners in classrooms?
7. Why is it necessary to view learners as being more than a physical beings with basic needs to eat, sleep, and have shelter?
8. What is special about the special needs learners in classrooms?

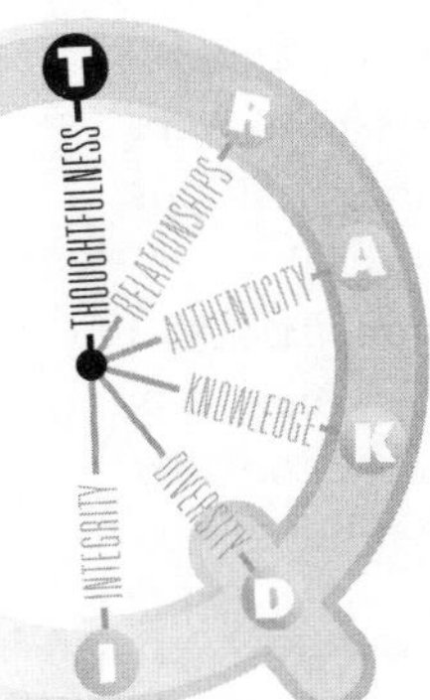

Assumptions About Learners

The following statements invite you to engage in thoughtful reflection on your own assumptions. We invite you to begin building your own theory of learners by considering how each assumption affirms or disaffirms your own emerging theory of learners. Most importantly, however, we invite you to use your own understanding of learners to call into question these assumptions.

Assumption 1: Learners are passive reactors to their environment and passive recipients of information.

This assumption has served to guide decision making in schools for a long time, perhaps too long. The classroom climate in schools where learners are considered passive is often created through "teacher talk" (Good & Brophy, 2000). In this climate learners succeed in proportion to how well they can listen. Management of behaviour and discipline is directed from teacher to learner. Goals and intended outcomes are decided ahead of time by the teacher, and are deposited into the supposedly receptive minds of each learner. Demands are often high for mature behaviour, as are conditions of restrictiveness. However, when demands are high, and warmth and communication low, learners rarely learn to be sufficiently competent (Baumrind, 1991). Also, in schools and classrooms where learners are seen as passive recipients of information, the notion of schemata (see Chapter 1) means simply that learner's minds are not active constructors of meaning, but are "file folders" waiting to be filled with information. How do you respond to this assumption in consideration of our discussion of constructivism in Chapter 5?

Assumption 2: Behaviours are fixed; interventions and learning conditions created by a teacher make little or no difference to the behaviour of older learners.

You have no doubt heard some of your friends claim that teachers make little, if any, difference to them and their learning. Your friends seem unable to learn and surprisingly helpless to change. Perhaps you wondered how they learned to be helpless? Can these learners be helped? Can they learn to learn?

Have schools been successful in maintaining young learners' intrinsic motivation to learn? Many educators believe the answer is no.

> Much of the attention to motivation in recent years has been due to the widespread perceptions that many students are not motivated by school. Worse still was the realization that the low motivation may not be due to inherent deficiencies in children (for particular children), but rather that schools as they now exist shape up learned helplessness. That is, many students come to believe that there is nothing they can do to achieve at a high level in school, and thus they do nothing. (Pressley & McCormick, 1995, p. 138)

You have already considered the answer to this question of learned helplessness through your reflections on individual learning. Chapter 4 discusses a number of insights regarding designing learning experiences and teaching methods that fit individual learning styles and thinking pre-dispositions.

This assumption presents you with a very basic philosophical problem: if you believe that behaviours are fixed, and that teacher interventions will not make any difference, then why are you going into teaching? The question for us to consider in this chapter is not whether behaviours are fixed and whether learning conditions make little or difference to learners, but rather, to what extent is it possible to help learners learn?

Assumption 3: Learners can always find something in school to be good at.

It is intuitively reasonable for you to believe this assumption. It is logical to believe that if learners do poorly in academics, they will compensate and do well in something else, such as art or basketball. Unfortunately, far too often, compensation does not happen (Le Francois, 2000). Young people do not always make up for their inability to learn in one area by necessarily being good learners in another. The reasons are many and varied. Students may not know that a strategy used in one situation can be applied in another (Gick & Holyoak, 1983). Poorer students have not developed a wide enough repertoire of strategies that would serve to help them learn across different subject areas.

> Good students definitely know and use more strategies (as well as more effective strategies) to accomplish school tasks than do weaker students. Good students take more notes, they plan essays, they prepare strategically for tests and they schedule their time so schoolwork and everything else in their lives can occur. (Pressley & McCormick, 1995, p. 47)

Learners need many complex, interrelated skills, attributes, and pieces of knowledge to learn. If learners believe that their efforts make little or no difference in their learning, or that they are "dumb," the result can be reluctance to attribute any success, anywhere, to effort or skill (Weiner, 1990). Learners can be expected to want to succeed, to value success, work hard for it, and most importantly, know how to achieve it, when they have had early, consistent experiences of success during their elementary school years. This is the critical time period Erikson (1968) describes as industry or inferiority, when young learners' identities, or sense of themselves, are developing toward competency or inferiority. The eventual outcome is always determined in relation to other people. How competent a learner comes to be is influenced by others' responses and by the learner's resultant sense of success. Learn to fail early during these years, and a learner learns to be helpless.

Assumption 4: Learners develop in stages, just as their learning develops in stages.

It is a popular idea that learners develop in stages. Stage theorists, such as Piaget (1983) in cognitive development, Erikson (1968) in psychosocial devel-

What ideal learning conditions might be present in this classroom?

opment, and Kohlberg (1969) in moral development, suggest that there are distinct stages, invariant and predictable, through which young people develop. In part, they are right. It is good if your assumption about learners includes this idea. However, there is good reason not to invest too much intellectual and professional capital into stage theory as the only way to understand learners. Many of the important skills you learned in your favourite sport or hobby or in social settings were learned incrementally, through a continuous gradual acquisition of skills and declarative and procedural knowledge (see Chapter 1). We invite you to consider stages of development in learners as only predictive of what learners might be expected to do at certain ages. However, we also invite you to think about learners as developing quantitatively, growing taller, thinking more complex thoughts, and acting in increasingly pro-social ways.

Assumption 5: Boys and girls are significantly different learners and should be treated as such.

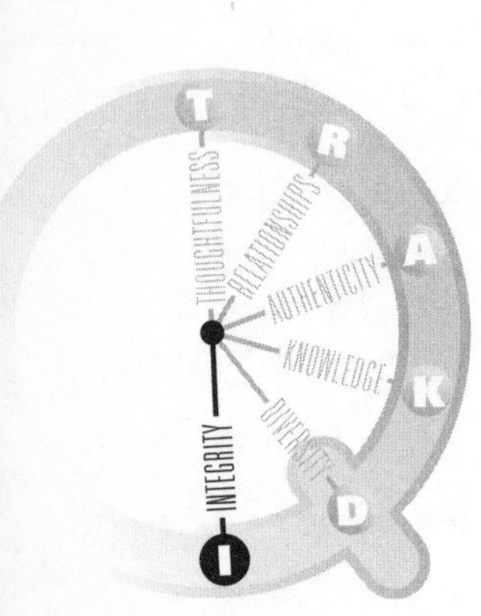

As you look around in most university classrooms you see males and females. That is obvious, isn't it? However, far less obvious are the implications of this observation. What difference does it make that there are both males and females in your class? The current, contemporary approach in working with learners is to identify and emphasize differences (Gilligan, 1982). Gilligan's conclusions about male and female differences seem to resonate with others (Noddings, 1984). Gilligan suggests that females are more likely than males to consider issues of interpersonal caring and person-to-person connections as they reason about moral dilemmas (Pressley & McCormick,1995). We invite you to consider whether this approach of emphasizing differences creates more or less separation between sexes. Also, consider whether there might be greater differences among people within the same sex group than between people of opposite sexes. In other words, might there be more significant difference among the fifteen or twenty males with whom you attend classes than among the females with whom you attend classes? It is intuitively appropriate for teachers to consider differences where they are important, as with learning styles, personality types, or learning difficulties. It may not, however, be appropriate to consider differences where this might lead to alienation, breakdown of integrity, and fragmentation, such as in cases of race, age, and ethnicity. Is sex also an example that could be included in this latter category?

Assumption 6: Learners can learn anything; they just need the right learning conditions.

An important statement of truth about human development says, "Structure precedes function." This means that a child must have the appropriate structure in place before he or she can adequately perform the function (Thelan, Ulrich, & Jensen, 1989). Learning is dependent on the development of cognitive and physical structures. In the physical area of development, an illustration might help you understand this axiom. Consider the relatively simple act of running and a two-year-old. A two-year-old cannot truly run. At no time during a "run" does a toddler "gain air" below his or her feet: one part of either foot is on the ground at all times. The best a two-year-old can manage is a glorified walk. The leg and body structure prevents proper running. A two-year-old simply does not have the muscle mass, the bone structure, and the brain development to accomplish a true run. The structure precedes and strongly influences the function a child is able to perform.

Next, consider the cognitive-development-based function of taking turns. During the first two or three years of life young learners are highly egocentric (Piaget, 1983)—they have difficulty taking on another person's perspective. They cannot, as a result, easily assume how another person will feel, think, or respond to a decision they make. They have difficulty taking turns, sharing and giving, not necessarily because they are selfish, but mostly because they have not developed the required cognitive structures and may not be able to take on another person's perspective. If they share a toy, they do not always know that they will get it back. If they take a turn, they do not know that they will get a turn back.

Consider the function of Grade 1 and 2 children sitting still in class. They can't, because they have less than half the muscle mass of an adult (structure), and have great difficulty performing the function of sitting still, a function that requires greater strength than the learner in Grade 1 or 2 can possess. Again, structure precedes function. It will be important for you to design learning experiences with this as part of your theoretical makeup about learners.

You may be aware of other assumptions. As you continue to read this chapter, and work on building your theory of learners, we ask you to consider those assumptions.

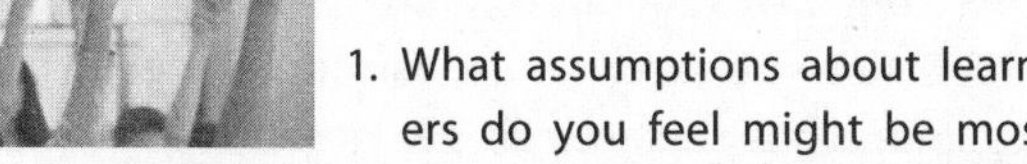

6.1 FOR YOUR CONSIDERATION

1. What assumptions about learners do you feel might be most helpful in your development as a teacher? What assumption might be least helpful?
2. Think of your behaviour as the "tip of an iceberg," and your assumptions and values as what is below the surface. Is it important for you to have right assumptions below the surface? What could happen to your teaching if your assumptions are wrong?

Cognitive Development

Cognitive development refers to the orderly changes in the way learners think about their world. *Cognition* refers to knowledge, or to what learners think about. One important assumption you should have about younger learners is that they are not miniature adults with cognition that is similar to but smaller than an adult's cognition. Children's cognition is qualitatively different from an adult's cognition. Children's development, or changes in the way they think and construct their knowledge, progresses over time through a normal change in thinking structures (Piaget, 1983) and through the acquisition of knowledge. As children develop and grow, they replace one set of ideas and assumptions with others. For example, one author's daughter once commented, "The sun shines in my back yard so my tree can grow." For a five-year-old this is a logical way of thinking about the reason that there is a sun up there shining down on things. At sixteen the same girl knows that the sun shines in her back yard because of the south exposure of her back yard, that there exists a mass of burning gases some 150 million km away, and that there is an ozone layer that permits rays of sunshine to pass through.

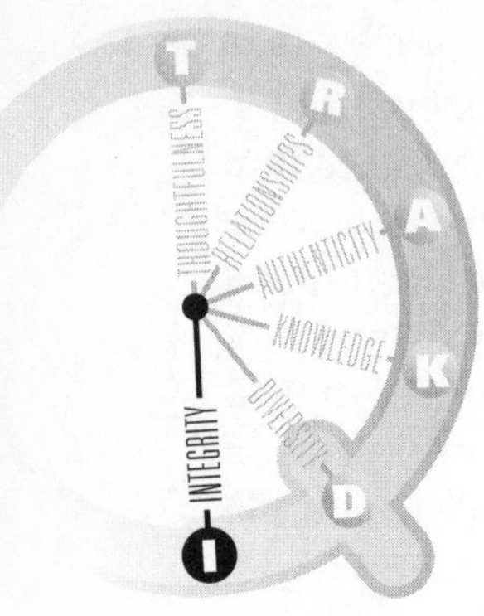

Learners' thinking accommodates to new information and to changes in their cognitive makeup. **Accommodation** means changing schema to fit new realities. Accommodation happens in many important ways. Consider how teachers can help accommodation to occur by creating the conditions under which the changes can occur. Teachers need to understand the limits that should be expected in learners' thinking, and how they might thoughtfully, with integrity, teach so that accommodation can occur.

Play

In play, younger learners' thinking is full of pretend and imagination (Parten, 1932). Play becomes symbolic quite early, around eighteen months of age, and the use of symbolism develops in its breadth and expression through the early elementary school years. Around twelve or thirteen, however, sticks no longer are spears, bikes no longer motorcycles, and a gathering of children in a back yard no longer a tea party. Something changes in learners as they mature. In the early years of symbolic play, playthings readily become other things. A sense of wonder accompanies this play and characterizes the learner's way of symbolically representing the world. One of the authors of this book would tell his four-year-old son stories of kings, queens, knights, dragons, as well as outer-space adventure stories. His son would listen with eyes full of wonder, the blankets pulled up to his chin, cries for more coming from his four-year-old mouth. As a twelve-year-old, the son yawns and falls asleep whenever his father tries to tell the same stories. Language has replaced imagination, real people and events have replaced wonder, and his far-reaching sense of imagination has been replaced by dreams of becoming a professional skateboarder. His imagination is still alive; now it just takes other things to fill his soul with imagination.

Good teachers recognize that wonder, curiosity, and imagination are always a powerful impetus to learning, and they work hard at creating the conditions through which imagination and mature symbolic play can have its age-appropriate place in the classroom. Play allows children to develop many skills and roles that become building blocks for healthy growth and development, because play requires children to assume many different roles. As Bretherton (1989) puts it, "[C]hildren must become co-playwrights, co-directors, co-actors and vicarious actors without getting confused about which of these roles they or a playmate are momentarily adopting.... [T]hey must repeatedly alternate between stage managers and actors because the creation of make believe plots proceeds on a make it up as you go principle" (Bretherton, 1989, p. 384).

Memory

Memory is an important part of a learner's cognitive makeup. Early in a learner's life, memory just happens. Young learners simply remember faces, people, and voices. Teaching is not required for learners to remember. By the time a learner is ten or eleven, this simple type of memory is not sufficient for learning in school. Simple recognition is not helpful in remembering the steps in writing an essay, doing a lay-up in basketball, or completing mathematics word problems. Learners need to be taught to "do something" with information that is more complex than recognizing faces or voices. They need to be directed to make sense of and organize information in ways that make it transferable and usable in new situations (Tulving, 1983).

The best teachers know that memory is enhanced when unfamiliar ideas are taught from familiar ideas. They know that learners, even older learners, learn best through opportunities to relate new information to what they already know. The best social studies teachers, for example, teach six-year-old learners unfamiliar ideas such as the general differences between human needs and wants by first having them consider what their own needs and wants are, and what are the differences between the two. Were your best teachers able to make the strange known, the unfamiliar familiar? Did your best teachers make connections for you between what you knew and what was being taught?

Attention

The ability to pay **attention** is another important aspect of cognition. How young learners actually pay attention can provide important information for teachers in the designing of learning experiences. How young learners pay attention can also be frustrating for teachers. As learners mature, their ability to attend to messages improves (Case, 1985). Attention becomes more selective (able to block out what is irrelevant), more persistent (able to maintain itself for longer periods of time) and less "captured away" by **discrepant stimuli** such as unusual noise or movements. Thoughtful teachers use learners' natural tendency to be captured by discrepant, or unusual, stimuli in designing learning experiences that have lots of changes, unusual stimuli, and variety. Like *Sesame Street*, learning experiences that thoughtfully attend to the natural tendencies of learners to pay attention are more successful than those that do not.

Abstract Thinking

Before we leave this discussion of cognitive development, you might consider for a moment the assumption that began our chapter: that *your* theory of learners is an important consideration in your development as a teacher. You will recall that a theory helps teachers choose appropriate teaching approaches when they design learning experiences. Theory helps teachers understand what learners might do while learning, and why. Before we begin our final discussion regarding another aspect of learners—adolescent abstract thinking—we invite you to consider your current theory regarding your own history of abstract thinking, your abilities to think "outside of the box," and why you sometimes (perhaps often) disagreed with your parents.

Abstract thinking is the ability to form hypotheses and reason from premises that are not part of a learner's concrete experience. When you disagreed with your parents, what was your hypothesis? Was the "problem" with your parents (and how "dumb" they were)? Or was the problem in your ability to imagine other possibilities regarding parenting? Do you recall thinking that other parents might be smarter than your parents? In other words, was the "problem" that you could think abstractly, logically, and formally (Piaget, 1983) about what your parents did wrong, why they did what they did, and how they might have done things differently? The normal transition into this "thinking in a new key" (Elkind, 1984) meant that you saw the world, including your parents, in very different ways than you did when you were ten or eight or even six years old.

The good comes with the bad, however, when considering this new way of thinking. You might recall that you imagined that no one else could possibly understand you and what you were going through. You imagined that when you walked through the hallway at school everyone looked at you and noticed that single small pimple on the tip of your nose and that you were wearing the same clothes you wore two weeks ago last Tuesday. Good teachers try to understand the far-reaching implications of abstract thinking in a learner's life. Abstract thinking is the "finding of distinctive features or invariant relationships" (i.e., relations that remain constant for a class of events [Pressley & McCormick, 1995, p. 183]). Abstraction is like squeezing the oranges to get the orange juice. For example, after catching a number of different balls—hard ones, soft ones, small ones, large ones—a learner hopefully abstracts that it is important to keep one's eyes on the ball throughout the throw, or that hard balls hurt more than soft ones. Through the ability to think abstractly, the learner can learn to filter out irrelevant information, decide what peripheral information to use (e.g., should I focus ahead or behind the ball), and make conclusions about what is most important to know in a new situation.

According to some psychologists (E.J. Gibson, 1982) the world presents itself to us with distinctive features and structures. In this view we can learn to use the objects in our world only because they have inherent structures. Things that are round roll. The world affords us with meaning to be abstracted from things and events (E.J. Gibson, 1982). Letters contain meaning that permits some predictability in learning to read. Abstraction, then, is about squeezing out what is already in events. Perception helps us abstract. As Eleanor Gibson (1991) puts it, "[W]e perceive to learn, as well learn to perceive" (in Pressley & McCormick, 1995).

On the other hand, some psychologists believe that there is no meaning inherent in objects, that we learn to perceive meaning in things as we touch, use, and understand the personal relevance of objects for our lives. We will let you and your colleagues in class discuss this distinction.

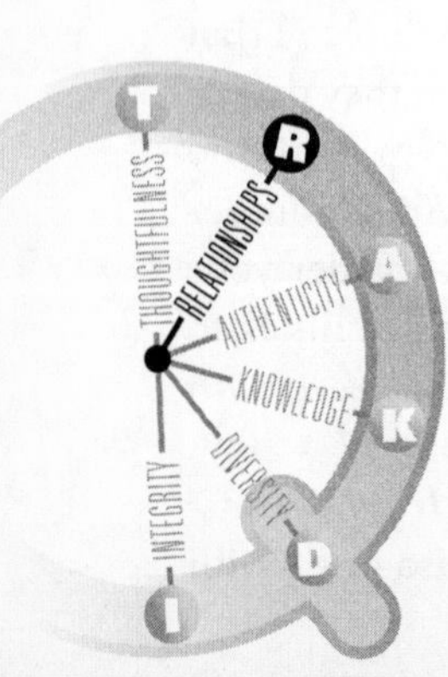

Regardless of whether learners learn to perceive or perceive to learn, good teachers try to be thoughtful regarding cognition and how learners think. The ability of a learner to think abstractly should be central to the design of learning experiences. Learning experiences can be designed to tap into this ability to think about the world in wonderfully idealistic ways. Teachers should hear young people's ideas about how the world can be made a better place to live, how to solve problems such as poverty and hunger. But perhaps even more important for teachers is that the relational stance of caring is enhanced through understanding a bit more about who learners are and how they think. In what ways might a teacher guide and encourage this type of abstract thinking in classrooms? What questions did you most enjoy being asked during your high school years?

Physical Development

Movement

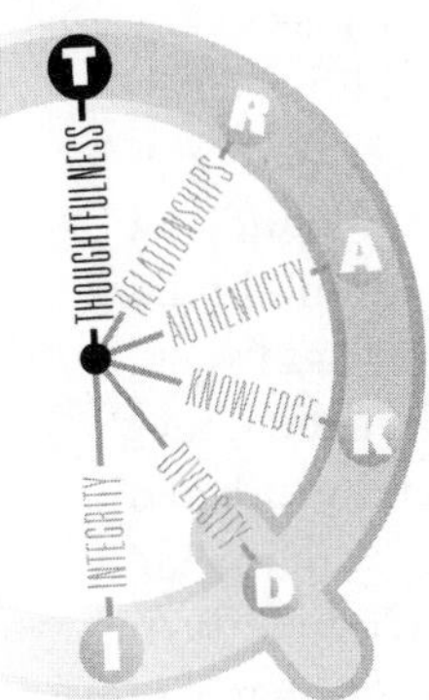

Accurate knowledge of learners is important in a teacher's emerging theory of learners. Knowledge regarding who learners are and why they behave as they do, leads to wise, practical decisions when teaching them. Knowledge of physical development is particularly important for teachers (Shonkoff, 1984). Without accurate knowledge of physical development, a teacher might expect inappropriate things from learners. For example, it would be inappropriate for a Grade 1 teacher to ask six-year-olds to run long distances. The physical structure of a six-year-old is not designed for long-distance running; a six-year-old's heart and lungs are small and unable to utilize oxygen in the same way an adult can. Joints are still developing and can be damaged by overuse and repeated movements. Young learners are sprinters, not marathoners, both physically and psychologically. Physical activities should be designed using this knowledge.

The next time you are in a Grade 1 classroom, pause to feel the energy in the air. You will notice, among other things, that movement—lots of movement—characterizes children's time sitting at desks. Imagine asking a group of five- and six-year-olds to sit perfectly still, not squirm, shift in their desks, or want to stand up. Should you expect young learners to sit still for long periods of time? Do you know why they cannot sit still? The reason is partly a physical one. The average five-year-old has less than half the muscle mass of an adult. Their muscle fibre is smaller, more watery, and less developed than that of an adult. Since it takes strength to sit still, and since younger learners do not have the same strength as adults (because they have less muscle), they grow tired more quickly trying to hold themselves still and upright. You squirmed, too, when you were five years old, for the same reasons. The shifting and squirming (and the energy that is produced in a classroom) is directly related to young learners tiring out and having to move to new, less tiring positions. Good teachers, in their theory-building, understand that and try to become increasingly appropriate in what they expect from children. They do not expect physical responses that children cannot give. More importantly, teachers design learning experiences with particular knowledge of learners' physical development in mind. They have regular exercise breaks, allow movement in their classrooms, and generally try to accommodate their classroom and its activities to children's innate need to be active.

Skill Development

Child development appears to have **sensitive periods** (Le Francois, 2000), times when a child is most susceptible to environmental influences and when learning might best occur. Psychomotor skills are best learned at certain times rather than other times. A **psychomotor skill** is the ability to perceive and respond to environmental influences, such as the speed of a ball, and respond accordingly. Learning to catch a small ball is best done when the physical development of a learner's muscles, bones, and nervous system has resulted in developed fine motor skills in hands and arms. Learners do not catch small balls very well before the age of six because their physical development will not permit them to do so.

Reaction times are relatively slow for younger learners. Good teachers recognize this and allow balls to bounce in volleyball classes. They modify learning tasks to fit the child rather than try to fit the child into the learning task. They design modifications such as bounces, which slow the ball down, to allow learners to succeed. That is being thoughtful. Thoughtful teaching recognizes that larger pencils are easier to hold in the chubby, small, less-developed hands of five-year-olds. Thoughtful teachers recognize that, in running, children should stop against walls, that balance among younger learners up to seven or eight years of age is poor, because the centre of gravity is higher and heads relatively larger than in adults. Thoughtful teachers recognize that learning is somehow affected by how children view themselves physically, that it "pays" to be an early maturing boy, but not necessarily an early maturing girl, that self-esteem is tied directly to how children view themselves physically. A thoughtful high school teacher will encourage positive body image, discourage critical body-directed remarks, and promote healthy, balanced physical development. Timing may be everything in learning. Is that statement too far-fetched for you?

6.2 FOR YOUR CONSIDERATION

With a partner, estimate your height by standing five metres from a wall and pointing to spot on the wall where you think your height fits. Ask your partner to pencil a dot there. Walk to the point on the wall and measure to see if your guess was correct, What does this activity tell you about self-concept?

Patterns of Development

A number of important patterns characterize learners' development. We have referred to some already: The **cephalocaudal pattern** refers to growth proceeding from the head to the caudal, or tail, region of the body. Young children's heads are relatively larger than older children's; this has implications for balance, self-concept, and injury prevention decisions (e.g., wearing helmets when riding scooters). Development also proceeds from the core of the body to the hands and feet. Development of children's fine motor coordination (in hands and feet) follows after development in the centrally located regions of the body (trunk). Younger children generally face bigger challenges than do older, more mature children when catching small balls with their hands. Pubescence is a major pattern, a period when physiological and psychological changes occur. Boys' growth spurts happen later and last for a shorter time than girls'. Girls experience pubescent change differently from boys. Girls and boys experience pubescence in social contexts that create unique challenges and needs. For example, early-maturing boys are often viewed by their peers as leaders, whereas, later-maturing boys may be teased and bullied (Pollack, 1998). Boys in North America are often confused about the meaning of being a "man" (Pollack, 1998), and many teachers and counsellors comment on gender role confusion that typifies many boys they work with.

Girls may be significantly taller than boys in the middle years (seven to twelve), leading to confusion and ambivalence regarding relationships between sexes. Growth is asynchronous, meaning that body parts do not grow uniformly. Learners' feet and hands will often grow to adult size before learners reach their final adult height. Because self-esteem issues accompany growth and skill development, thoughtful teachers structure learning experiences so as to preserve dignity, avoid creation of unequal competitive situations that may undermine confidence and success, and remove the fear of failure in learning situations.

Do you recall having to line up for a relay race? What created the most anxiety for you, the actual race or the waiting and worrying about what your friends might say if your mistake caused your team to lose? Good teachers do not create learning experiences in which children of different sizes and different abilities have to "compete" directly against one another. Is such a policy good and appropriate? Are there occasions when it is necessary and good to create competitive situations for learners?

Social Development

You have no doubt heard the expression "Values are caught, not taught." Do you believe this is true? If so, what are the implications of this for teachers? Learners are great imitators, as we read in Chapter 5. They have a natural tendency to observe and copy behaviours. Somewhere around the age of eight years the influence of peers takes on greater significance in learners' lives (Gupta et al., 1995). Peer influence peaks at around fifteen years of age and levels off during the late teen years and early twenties. Children's independence seeking is often troubling to parents; it is troubling to feel their children "pull away" toward their friends. Young people form groups and make "best" friends, usually through physical closeness early on, then through shared interests later in the adolescent years. Parents recognize that groups and friends represent a cohort, a sociological group representing certain values and lifestyles. Parents hope that their children's friends are "good" ones. Should teachers be equally concerned? Our discussion in the next pages will be about the social and historical contexts that influence development.

The Historical Context of a Learner's Behaviour

The historical antecedents of a child's behaviour are of some interest to a teacher. Teachers want to know what earlier experiences gave rise to a learner's behaviour. In your classroom, you too will want to know what is behind your learners' behaviour. You will want to know how permanent that behaviour is. For example, is a sexually or physically abused child's behaviour of mistrust, alienation, and caution permanent? Unchangeable? You may see evidence of their mistrust in many different ways, even in the course of a single day in the classroom. Such behaviour is fairly stable, but is it impossible to change? If you assume that the learner's behaviour is impossible to change (or that mistrustful behaviour is simply a function of the child's personality), your teaching will be characterized by a different set of behaviours and conditions than if you believe that the abused child's behaviour is changeable. The question that remains for the more optimistic teacher is, How can it be changed?

6.3 FOR YOUR CONSIDERATION

There was something different about Melinda that day. Her eyes twinkled and her head was held a little higher. As the class tumbled out of their desks for the end-of-day activities, Melinda lingered behind, just long enough to catch the teacher's attention. She looked at the teacher as if to say, "I have something to tell you."

Melinda rarely spoke in class. She was painfully shy and often teased by her peers, who described her as weird. The teacher found herself pulling away from her too, not deliberately, but because she had too many other needs that demanded attention. Melinda's needs did not.

But this day was different. Melinda ambled up to the teacher's desk and began to talk about going to her grandmother's house in another city, about the airplane ride, the turkey dinner, and the sledding in the first winter snowfall. The teacher listened. When Melinda stopped talking, the teacher asked questions, far less interested in what happened at her grandmother's than with this wonderful moment. Melinda had a voice and the teacher was determined to hear more. For a few moments, Melinda came outside of layers of shyness and quietness. The teacher felt she was listening to the real Melinda. She entered into Melinda's excitement, her fun, and her appreciation of a new experience.

The other story of Melinda, though, turned out to be much sadder. Melinda moved away from the school later in the school year. The school was told she had been abused and physically maltreated by caregivers. She had been moved into foster care in another city. No one said good-bye to Melinda. But that teacher will always remember those few precious moments when a little girl talked about something so simple and human, yet profound and real as airplane rides, sledding in snow, and turkey dinners.

Teachers often refer to a larger historical context that concerns the culture in which learners live, expressed in this way: Are learners different today than they were a generation or two ago? Some teachers believe learners are different today, that they are shaped by their culture and by pervasive media influences. Do you believe that sexual practices among youth and openness to discussion of sexual practices are evidence of the influence of culture on learners? In the next section we consider how Canadian culture has shaped learners.

The Contextual View of Human Development

The contextual view maintains that learners are influenced by their settings, through their interactions in home, school, neighbourhood, and culture. It is intuitively correct of you to assume that learners are influenced by where they live, including the cultural and ideological ideas in which they live. In Japan, conformity and teamwork are valued cultural ideas. In Canada, independence and individualism are valued cultural ideas. Do you think that the learning experience in schools and homes is different for learners in Japan than for learners in Canada? Why? One theoretical explanation for differences is found in Urie Bronfenbrenner's ecological theory of development.

Learners live among a number of influential settings, cultural and ideological (Bronfenbrenner, 1989). Think of these settings in the same way you would think about an ecology in nature. In any ecology there is a progressive, mutual accommodation of a living organism, a plant or an animal, with the settings in which an organism finds itself. Changes in one part of the ecology mean that changes, sooner or later, will happen in another part of the ecology, eventually affecting a living organism. As one part of the ecology, a living organism, mutually, progressively accommodates to the ecology, the entire ecology is affected.

Learners live in an ecology, a culture, that influences, and is in turn, influenced by, the learner (see Bronfenbrenner's model, Figure 6.1).

The most immediate ecological or cultural setting to influence learners includes the learner's health and biological well-being. The next part of the ecology includes the learner's physical environment, the family, neighbourhood, school, and immediate friends. Further away yet, but still influential eventually in a learner's development, is

Figure 6.1
Bronfenbrenner's model

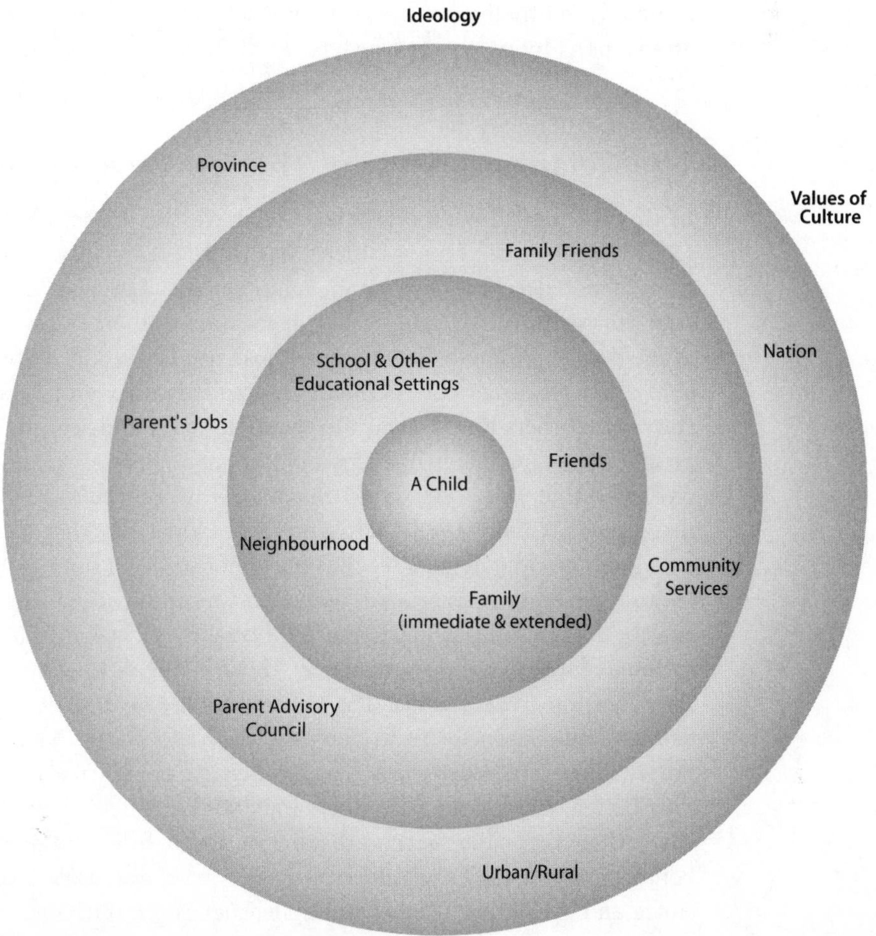

(Source: Based on information from U. Bronfenbrenner [1989], "Ecological Systems Theory," in R. Vasta [Ed.], *Annals of Child Development* [Vol. 6]. Greenwich, CT: JAI Press.)

the part of the ecology that includes the social and economic environment, the wealth, poverty, social class, and other general influences such as schools, health care services, and social services. Finally, the part of the ecology that influences the learner from the greatest distance is the ideology of the culture, the values and principles on which that culture is based, (e.g. materialistic, humanistic, religious, and so on).

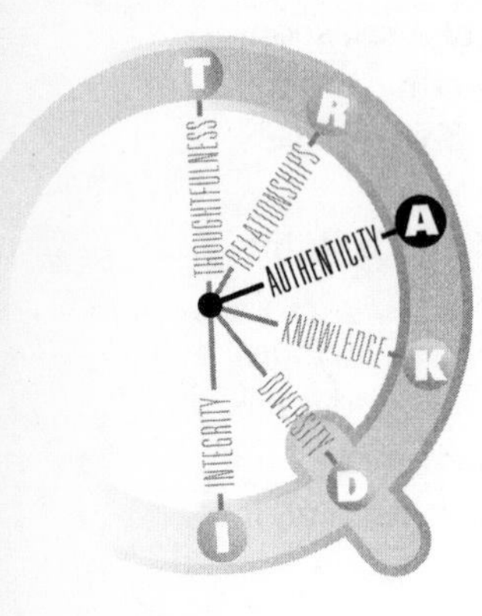

The thoughtful teacher realizes that a learner's development is in large measure influenced by the learner's accommodation to the demands that a particular culture places on that learner. Development again is by accommodation. If a learner lives in a culture that expects conformity rather than individualism, the learner develops tendencies to conform. A young person's attitudes toward and practices regarding sexuality will be accommodated, influenced by the learner's culture, the ecology within which the learner lives. The learner's culture and the various parts of that culture, from families to the cultural ideology, influence how the learner will develop. If most or all parts of a culture emphasize self-control, responsible behaviour, and religious-based thinking, then it is likely that a learner's sexual choices and attitudes will eventually come to reflect the same. The learner will progressively accommodate to the culture. The question for you is, So what? Is there anything you might do, thoughtfully and with integrity, to help young people progressively, mutually accommodate to the best of culture? Do teachers have a right and responsibility to help learners avoid the worst of culture?

The Relational View of Human Development

In this theoretical perspective learners have two basic, deep needs, the need for security and the need for significance (Crabb, 1988). A learner meets, or attempts to meet, those deep needs through relationships. Learners do not leave their deep needs for security and significance at the door of their classroom. Nor do they leave at the door their means for meeting those needs: through forming healthy relationships. Why? Learners are personal beings. It is through positive personal relationships with others that we learn to feel significant and secure. However, when other people, including teachers and peers, do not adequately meet these needs, learners will layer themselves up with behaviours that reflect their own attempts to meet these needs (Crabb, 1988). A twelve-year-old learner who is experiencing rejection by friends or ridicule by a teacher may choose to act out aggressively with peers to try to be liked or appreciated. A sixteen-year-old learner who does not experience healthy, loving, physical touch in the home may choose to use sex to get love and feelings of security and significance. These acting out behaviours may not reveal to a teacher the "real" learner. The behaviours are layers—actions and roles that are deliberately chosen to try to meet the two deep needs. The "real" person is often buried beneath a number of layers by the time the learner reaches high school, and may be very hard to find. Teachers may not recognize or understand the "real person" when there has been a disintegration, a fragmentation of the person into behaviours and roles that are inauthentic, to compensate for feelings of insignificance and insecurity. The layered up learner lacks integrity.

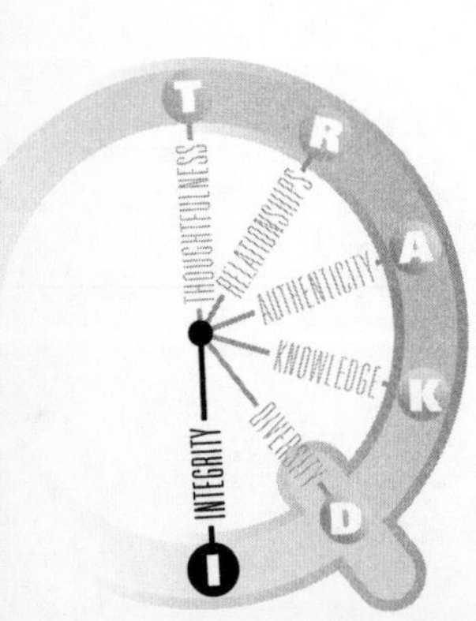

We have asked you to consider integrity as one important teaching quality. Let us give you one example of how learners might learn to have reduced integrity, to fragment into layered behaviours and roles.

One day, one of the authors decided it was time his six-year-old daughter learned to clean up her room. Her room was a mess. A tornado could do no more damage in her room than she could do in five minutes of playing. On the first Saturday of the "lesson plan" the daughter came downstairs to face the question "Is your room clean?" With a surprised look (this was the first time she had been asked the question) she replied honestly, "No, it isn't." In his most authoritative voice he told her to march up right now and clean her room.

She went upstairs, only to return in a few minutes ready for the day's activities. Her father asked her if she had cleaned up her room and she relied, again honestly, "Yes, Daddy, I cleaned my room." She had shuffled a few things around and for her, that meant "cleaning her room."

Her dad went upstairs with her, to see her room in the same mess that had become her trademark. In an angry voice he demanded that she clean her room, and told her she could not leave the house until it was clean. With tears in her eyes, she set about shuffling some clothes and toys into different constellations, but really accomplishing very little toward the goal of a clean room, at least as her father defined it.

The following Saturday, they repeated the lesson. When she came downstairs, her dad asked if she had cleaned her room. Once again, she replied, honestly, "No, I forgot, Daddy." Her father became obviously annoyed and he demanded that she go upstairs and clean her room. She returned and again said, honestly, that she had cleaned her room (her idea of clean). Again he expressed annoyance and disapproval. Again she responded in tears and appeared unsure of what to do next.

The next time, when she came downstairs and Dad asked if her room was clean, she lied for the first time, saying, "Yes, Daddy, I cleaned my room." She had wisely decided that lying was the way to preserve her dignity, her sense of security, her significance. Every time she had told the "truth" about the state of her room, it resulted in her father's anger, threats and disapproval. Why bother telling the truth? It doesn't work. It only results in greater feelings of insecurity and insignificance. Lying might work better. She put a protective barrier around herself to keep her safe from her father's reactions. Had one small seed been planted of her disintegration, her fragmentation of her real self into roles and behaviours?

Consider what this author now knows, ten years later, about his daughter. She is not a neat person. Her learning style and personality, her outlook on life, and her predispositions are random and scattered. That is who she is. Does this story invite some painful memories regarding how you have learned to be layered?

Teachers see "layered" learners in their classrooms every day and in many different manifestations of layering. They see the rational, deliberate decisions learners make to avoid homework (it might result in teasing), volunteer answers in class (it might result in being laughed at), take no risks in art class (it might lead to ridicule). Teachers also see how emotions reveal deeper and more profound realities in their learners. Like the low-oil warning light in a car, emotions show what is going on deeper and below the surface (Crabb, 1988). Anxiety might reveal goals that are not clearly understood or shared; anger might reveal desires that are being blocked, perhaps desires to be liked by friends; frustration reveals goals and desires that might be unreachable, too high for learners. These and other emotions are layers, hiding what might be more integral, authentic, and real.

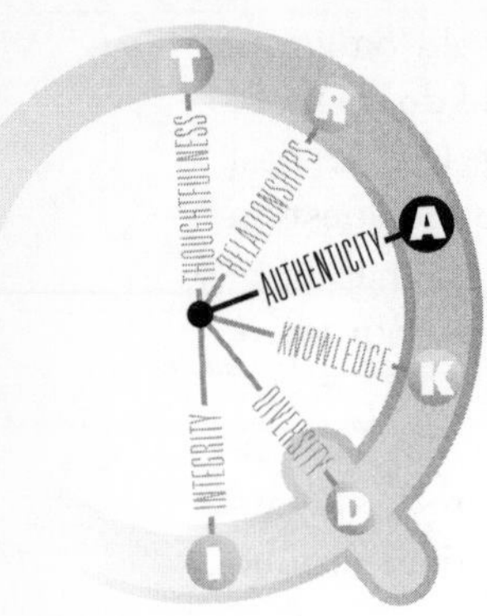

We do not want you to settle for simplistic understandings and solutions to what is a far more complex psychological matter than we have discussed here. We leave this section with a reminder: Young people will try to preserve their dignity, and layers can become their way of preserving dignity. We invite you to keep developing your theory of learners to understand why. Some young people are influenced by their culture, and choose harmful, yet dignity-preserving activities and addictive behaviours such as eating disorders and withdrawal. Other young people choose sporting activities and other legitimate means to preserve their dignity, gain significance, and achieve some personal measure of security. The question we leave you with is, How can teachers be part of the solution?

Issues Affecting Learners

The life young people experience and learn from is often confusing, painful, full of mixed messages, and scary. Learners come into classrooms every day with a history, a set of experiences that has left its mark. When a young learner's experience has been abusive, that mark is often reflected in the deep insecurity and insignificance that the learner feels as he or she tries to pay attention and participate in the activities teachers have designed. The abused learner does not leave those feelings of insecurity and insignificance at the classroom door. You may be one of these learners. As painful as the next sections might be for you to read and consider, we invite you to enter into the discussion regarding the issues that mark young learners and make the work of a teacher very challenging but rewarding.

Abuse

It is difficult to be accurate regarding how many children in Canada are abused. Many cases go unreported. Abuse is not perpetrated only by parents. Siblings and family friends abuse as well. There are some disturbing signs, however, that abuse is most common among immediate family members and that fathers are responsible for seventy-three percent of the physical abuse and ninety-eight percent of the sexual abuse that happens in the home. Perhaps more disturbing is that the abused child often has characteristics that may contribute to the abuse. They may be sickly, have difficult temperaments, be overactive, and be less physically attractive then their non-abused playmates (Berk, 1994).

Abuse may be difficult to detect. Certain behaviours might indicate that abuse has occurred. These include an unusual or sudden change in a child's behaviour, noticeable changes in a child's energy levels (more listless, dramatic increases in energy), strong indications of changes in a child's self-esteem, or physical changes such as rapid loss or gain in weight. Physical signs of abuse are easier to see. Bruises, fractures, and burns are to be treated suspiciously. Abuse in the form of neglect can show up as listlessness, poor hygiene, or absences from school.

In Canada, both child protection and education are provincial jurisdictions. Teachers are responsible for reporting abuse to the appropriate provincial agency.

In fact, teachers may be held liable and face legal consequences if they fail to report suspected child abuse. If you think a child has been abused, neglected, or in any way mistreated, your responsibility is to get involved, first by reporting your suspicions to your principal, then by following whatever provincial guidelines regulate reporting of abuse in your province.

Self-Concept

What is self-concept? How is self-concept different from self-esteem? **Self-concept** is the self-portrait—the "picture"—hung in the gallery of a learner's mind. Self-esteem is how a learner feels about that picture. Learners may have vague or unclear self-concepts, but they do not have low or strong self-concepts. Those adjectives can be used for self-esteem perhaps, but not for self-concept.

Self-concept is a composite idea of who we are (Marsh & Shavelson, 1985). Early in a learner's development, before the age of eight, self-concept is amorphous and undifferentiated. Young learners have a general self-concept, physically, intellectually, and socially. Their self-concept (like yours) becomes more differentiated and hierarchical as they think about and evaluate themselves in different situations. Am I good-looking? Am I doing well in school? Am I a good athlete? These are evaluative questions whose answers determine self-concept. Learners will behave in a way that is fairly consistent with their self-concept (Marsh and Shavelson, 1985). They will act out from who they think they are. If a learner thinks he is stupid in math, the pattern is for that learner to do poorly in math and be reluctant to try to improve. Good teachers recognize that it is often through comparisons with others that learners construct their self-concept. Social comparisons may leave a learner thinking that he or she is too fat, too short, or unattractive. School programs can be designed to reduce comparative bases for measuring success and enhancing clear, accurate self-concepts. For example, instead of promoting competition that involves comparisons of performance between young people, schools can promote competition that includes comparison of performance with a standard, a previous best, or a time.

Eating disorders such as bulimia and anorexia arise, in part, because young learners (both male and female) succumb to an unhealthy preoccupation with their bodies and to worry regarding whether their bodies "measure up" to other people's bodies. Both conditions are serious and pose potential health risks. We invite you to consider getting involved and becoming part of the solution in helping young learners grow to accept their body image. Is your image of yourself physically a close match to what you really look like? We invite you to predict the space that it takes for you to go through a partially opened door, frontward, sideways, and backwards. After predicting, actually go through a partially opened door and see how close your prediction was to how you actually did. If you predicted that you would need a larger space than you actually did need, what conclusions might you draw about your self-concept?

Divorce

More than half of Canadian children do not live with both their biological mother and father (Statistics Canada, 1999). The effects of divorce on children vary but are significant. The most pervasive one is often financial. Not all children have the same financial opportunities for recreational pursuits or educational programs. However, often the more subtle effects of divorce are the most difficult to deal with. The psychological effects of divorce include fear of abandonment, mistrust of males or females, and anger (Wallerstein, 1991). Many learners are unable to articulate clearly what they are feeling and how the divorce of their parents has called into question their deep needs for security and significance. We invite you to consider the inclusion of programs that emphasize the relational stance of caring for all children. Find ways in your classroom for each learner to be the "special kid of the week," the big fish in the small pond, the king or queen of the hill. Are these self-esteem building activities valuable? If so, why?

Drugs

Learners receive conflicting messages regarding drug use in Canada. Some television commercials associate the best of times with alcohol use, while other commercials call into question the use of alcohol and driving. Adults buy over-the-counter drugs for relief from many of life's stresses, yet these adults may caution young people to avoid using street drugs. Coffee shops sell millions of dollars worth of coffee, while talk shows lecture young people against the use of stimulants such as amphetamines. Learners will need to not only be clear-headed and long-sighted regarding drug use, they will need to approach their decision making regarding drug use through healthy self-esteem and strong social skills, both of which will be effective antidotes to repeated drug use. Can teachers help learners choose from among the conflicting societal messages regarding drugs?

Individual Differences

The following chapters will invite you to consider more closely individual differences in the context of designing learning experiences, organizing schools, and arranging classroom conditions in ways that help all learners learn. In Chapter 9 (Schools) we investigate inclusion, the practice of including all learners, regardless of abilities, in a school's classrooms. In Chapter 11 (Curriculum) we examine how the subject matter of science, physical education, art, and so on can be designed to create the best possible opportunities for all learners to learn. In closing this chapter, we will look briefly at three expressions of difference—ethnicity, giftedness, and learning disabilities (including developmental delays)—and invite you to consider how best to think about differences in these three areas.

Ethnicity

At one time, one of the authors taught in Zambia, Africa, at a boy's secondary school. When this author walked into the classroom, all the boys stood at attention and in unison said "Good morning, sir." They sat down, prim and proper in their grey slacks and white shirts, ties neatly arranged, feet flat on the floor and pencils at the ready beside their papers. You could have heard a pin drop. This author had spent the previous two years teaching in a rural junior high school in Canada where the response to the teacher walking in the classroom was quite unlike the one received at the school in Zambia. We are quite sure that you know what some of the differences were. The culture and the history of education in Zambia, including a deep respect for teachers, influenced the Zambian students' response to this particular teacher. The culture and history of education, along with the expectations and ideas about teachers, influence Canadian learners' response to teachers. Is it helpful to compare cultures and their response to teachers?

In discussing differences, ethnicity is an important consideration. The typical Canadian classroom is a composite of ethnic groups. Some ethnic groups in a school may struggle with personal identity and collective identity. **Personal identity** is one's sense of who one is and what one stands for; **collective identity** is one's sense of what one's ethnic group is and what it stands for. The pride in family, heritage, and history, so important to individuals from some ethnic backgrounds, is not always shared by second-generation Canadians, whose parents were born and raised in Canada. It might be useful for you to consider ethnic differences as the tip of an iceberg. What appears above the surface (e.g., physical features) may not appear to be substantially different. However, below the surface, the thinking patterns, the values and issues that are most important may be larger and more influential than what a teacher might see. We invite you to think about which differences should be celebrated and which ones should be ignored.

Giftedness

The one group of learners most often neglected in schools is the gifted group. Exceptionally talented or gifted learners often seek out alternative educational opportunities because schools do not always meet their needs. Giftedness is difficult to define. For our purposes, we invite you to think of **giftedness** as above average in ability, creativity, or intelligence. You may be surprised to know that gifted learners are not always easy to identify. Teachers may have gifted learners in their classroom and not recognize them. Do you know why that might be?

If you are able to recognize a gifted learner, you have some important decisions to make. Should you accelerate the learner? Move the learner to a special school? Encourage different programming? The answer is not simple. What about the learner's friends and normal socializing opportunities in the learner's age group? What about the need, even for very creative people, to learn the basics required to pass university classes?

We invite you consider the possibility of creating learning conditions that follow the advice of gifted learners themselves. Following is a list of recommendations from thirty-three academically gifted learners at Vancouver's University Hill Secondary School. They were asked, "If you could provide the very best learning situation for you, what would you have us do?" Responses included the following:

- Let me go ahead and work at higher levels.
- Let us work with older kids. We can fit in.

- It's not an age difference but an attitude difference that's important here. Older kids are more accepting.
- Give us independent programs. Let us work ahead on our own.
- Know that everyone has talent. Provide challenge in our talent area.
- Have totally hands-on lessons.
- Use more video, films, and telecommunications.
- Use humour.
- Provide independent study opportunities.

(Source: From *Gifted Education: A Resource Guide for Teachers* [p. 14], 1996, Victoria, BC: British Columbia Ministry of Education. Reprinted with permission.)

Learning Disability, Developmental Delay, and Emotional Disability

A group of experienced Grade 4 teachers was asked to watch a film of a Grade 4 classroom and predict the behaviours they might see when observing a particular learner in the class. In the first instance, they were told the learner had a **developmental delay,** that the student was lagging behind similar-aged children in the orderly sequence change, cognitively, physically, and psychologically. In the second instance, they were told the learner had a particular **learning disability,** that the student was manifesting difficulties in acquiring knowledge. In the third instance, they were told the learner had an **emotional disability,** manifesting unusual levels of psychological and physiological arousal. Before observing the class and the particular learner they were asked to watch, the teachers were asked to write down what they expected to see. Given that they were experienced teachers, one might expect that what they wrote down would be a close match to what they actually saw. As it turned out, after watching their particular students, writing down what they saw that student do, and how the student behaved, their observations turned out to match very closely what they had expected to see. No surprises here right? Except for one thing. In each case, there were no special needs students. The teachers had been set up. They had observed a randomly chosen, typical, and quite average learner. They saw what they expected to see (Foster & Yesseldyke, 1978). What conclusions do you draw from this example?

We conclude the chapter with this account to remind you to be knowledgeable, thoughtful, and reflective regarding your care and teaching of all learners. You will have many decisions to make when it comes to all learners, including special needs learners. Should you read and study previous records of learners? In some cases, this is unavoidable and helpful, as in the case of mentally challenged or physically restricted learners. In other cases, it may not be, as in the case of learners who have been described as emotionally challenged or hyperactive. We invite you to read on in the following chapters as we discuss in more detail the nature of special need learners and the design of learning experiences in schools.

Reflection and Perspective on the Chapter

A thoughtful teacher once remarked that what makes the biggest difference in teachers' work is what they see when they look at their learners. One development in the teaching field that we commend is the openness for teachers to view learners from a more holistic, even spiritual, perspective. This development matches more closely who learners are. If teachers see each learner as a masterpiece, a beautiful work of art, a poem of profound meaning, they will certainly treat learners differently than if they see them as nuisances, jerks, and hopeless losers. Does this high view of a learner trouble you? Does this perspective raise questions for you? What if learners do not look like beautiful works of art? Should teachers still be expected to see them that way? The reality is that most teachers today view learners somewhere in between these two extremes. The difficult challenge for you will be to come to some accurate, theoretically sound, and helpful perspective of who learners are.

In conclusion we ask you to begin your teaching career with this thought, that you and your colleagues, your classmates, and partner teachers accept the truth about learners, no matter how beautiful it is.

Key Terms

Suggested Further Reading

Elkind, David. (1981). *The Hurried Child.* Reading, MA: Addison-Wesley. A thought-provoking and still timely discussion about the perils associated with fast-tracking young learners into activities normally reserved for older youth.

Pipher, Mary. (1994). *Reviving Ophelia*. New York: Grossett/Putnam. A timely and insightful discussion about the deleterious societal influences on female adolescents. The book looks closely at self-esteem and the media's impact on the poor self-esteem of young North American females.

Levine, Mel. (2002) *A Mind At a Time*. Toronto: Simon and Schuster.

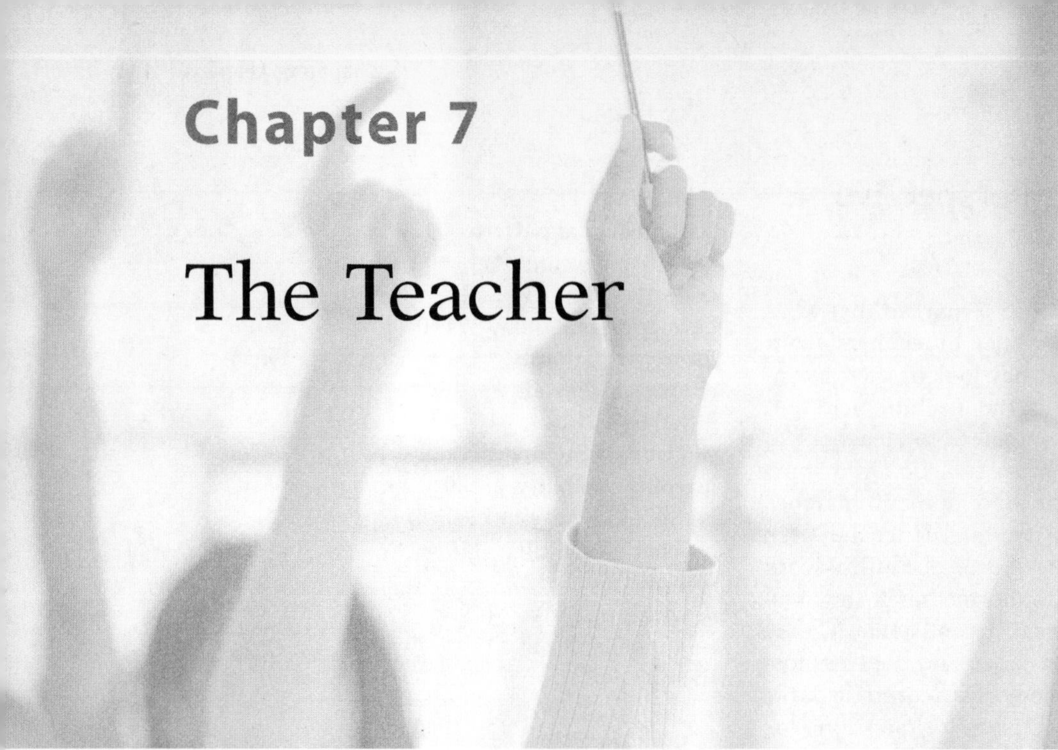

Chapter 7

The Teacher

Chapter Focus

A person's **worldview** is that mental model, or inner representation, of the outer world that is composed of theories, assumptions, and beliefs we hold about the big issues of life. Teachers live in a very complex world of education, and their preparation for this position in life does not involve the exploration of a precise discipline. It is important, therefore, that pre-service teachers as well as experienced teachers approach both their understanding and practice of teaching through a thoughtful worldview framework. Teaching is a profoundly ethical and moral activity, one that requires the making of sound practical judgments, arrived at through thoughtful reflection on and during practice.

In this chapter we attempt to uncover some commonly held assumptions about teachers for you to consider as you enter the profession. After reading and discussing this chapter, prepare to integrate these ideas into your view of the professional and personal "teacher" phenomenon.

Focus Questions

1. What is an ideal teacher?
2. What knowledge skills and attributes are expected of teachers?
3. What keeps the love of teaching alive for practising teachers?
4. Philosophy plays a significant role in a teacher's approach to learning and teaching. To what extent do effective teachers embrace one particular philosophical orientation to teaching or draw upon a number of orientations in their ways of responding to young people?
5. With the current fears of teacher shortage, there has been more active recruitment nationally and internationally. What implications does this have for job opportunities for new teachers?

6. To what extent is professional development an essential component of a teacher's professional life? How do teachers continue their professional development?
7. What is the value of a professional portfolio?
8. As a pre-service teacher, how do you start to develop your teaching portfolio?

Teaching Qualities

Before we begin to consider the many facets of being a teacher, we would like you to revisit the teaching qualities introduced in Chapter 2. The qualities are presented as fundamental areas for thought and reflection in decision making and praxis related to learning, teaching, and schooling (please refer to the six teaching qualities in Figure 2.1, p. 22). We ask that you consider these teaching qualities as a useful foundation upon which to engage in reflection and contemplation about assumptions, topics, and issues that may be called into question as you read this chapter.

The meaning and understanding you will gain about *teacher* will change, and it should. Thoughtful teachers constantly understand theory and practice differently as they are exposed to new knowledge, concepts, and ideas.

Diversity includes differences and variety in all aspects of being a teacher. The students as well as the teachers come to school with various backgrounds, experiences, and needs as learners and as individuals. Authenticity is the "genuine" quality the teacher brings to the profession in his or her relationship, learning, and leadership with all stakeholders in the schooling enterprise. The thoughtful teacher is one who engages in reflection and research, is able to identify and question assumptions, and has the capacity to think of others. As you read this chapter consider this idea of thinking of others as it relates to the role of being a teacher. A teacher who acts with integrity is one whose actions are not separate from his or her thinking, beliefs, or assumptions. The commonplace of knowledge is the foundation, so that pre-service teachers enrich their perspective and general worldview of learning, teaching, and schooling.

Assumptions About Teachers

You have been a student and have had teachers for at least twelve years of schooling. Because of this you hold a number of assumptions about teachers, whether you currently are a student, a parent, or practising teacher. You acquired these beliefs and assumptions accidentally, or tacitly. They shape your understanding of education and serve as reference points. Many people are not aware of the assumptions they hold, but this does not mean that their assumptions should go unchallenged. What assumptions do you hold about teachers? We invite you to consider a few common assumptions. The assumptions are not presented in any order or importance. You may find yourself calling into question some assumptions you hold. We also invite you to think about an excerpt from Teddy's story and the research and stories we present, with the hope that you will gain a deeper and broader understanding of what it means to be a teacher.

Assumption 1: Those who can, do; those who can't, teach.

Some people seem always to have known they wanted to become teachers. From an early age, they took on the role of teacher in play with other children or with their dolls or stuffed animals. Was this the case for you? Others may have been strongly influenced by a very special teacher held in high esteem, a significant adult or someone who made a difference in their lives, much like Miss Thompson, who influenced Teddy Stallard's learning and life. Still others have fallen into the career of teaching either because they didn't know what else to do after completing a few years of post-secondary education, or because they fell in love with the job after working with young learners. One of the authors of this book did not have a clue that teaching was an option in her life. She wanted to be an artist, but then discovered the effect the arts in schools had on young students. She was captured by the satisfaction of teaching and making a positive difference in student's lives in the development of self-confidence through expression in arts education.

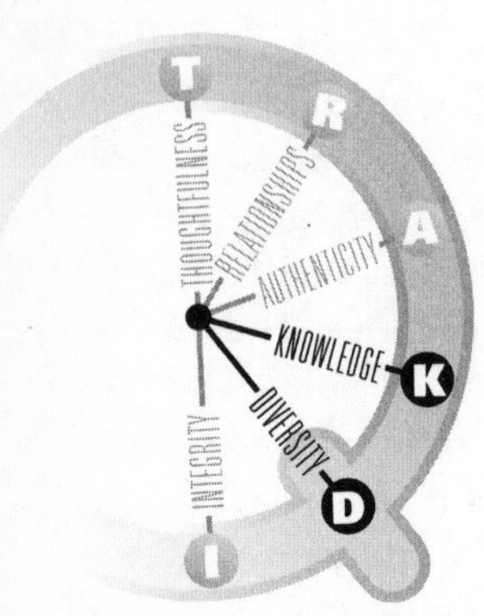

Recall the professor from Chapter 1 who remarked that elementary school teaching isn't rocket science. In fact, teaching is extremely demanding. The fellow was speaking from a single perspective, the narrow teaching worldview of a post-secondary professor, whose teaching consisted primarily of lecturing. He understood only one aspect of teaching.

Once you have decided to become a teacher, it takes years of education and experience, peer-collaboration, and self-reflection to develop the "art" of teaching. As one teacher put it, "When I graduated with a bachelor's degree in education, I thought I knew it all and could do it better than any teacher I had observed or worked with in my field experience practicum. I realized this was a misconception on my first day of 'real teaching'."

A related assumption frequently held about teachers is, "Teachers are born, not made." What are your thoughts about this assumption?

Assumption 2: Teachers choose the job because of long vacations and short working hours.

Perhaps you have heard this assumption stated by parents or in the media. We ask you to explore this assumption by talking to both new and experienced teachers. Follow a teacher around for a week or more. Create a chart of hours in a day and days for a regular week; in the spaces, write some of the activities with which the teacher is occupied. Compare your chart with those of others. Ask the teachers about what they do on their "days off," their weekends, and their holidays. Are they able to totally leave schoolwork and concerns behind at the school? What are your conclusions? Is Assumption 2 a valid one?

Assumption 3: Teachers teach subjects, not students.

When you find yourself in front of a class instead of being a member of the class, how do you think you will feel? By the time you have your teaching certificate, you will have completed at least twelve years of elementary and secondary school, and at least four years of post-secondary education. You know the subject or subjects you are assigned to teach very well. You know you know more than the students assigned to you. However, every teacher is at least a little apprehensive about the first day of class. What might you be worried about?

One author's husband commented that over the years he knew when September was approaching because his wife ground her teeth in her sleep. As she gradually gained experience and a greater understanding of the learners in her charge, this outward sign of stress disappeared. But her concerns were real. What would the students be like? Could she meet their needs? Would they like her? Should she not smile until winter break, so that the students wouldn't "walk all over her"? Does the first day of class set the tone for the whole year? If she had considered her job as "just" teaching the subject, there would have been little stress.

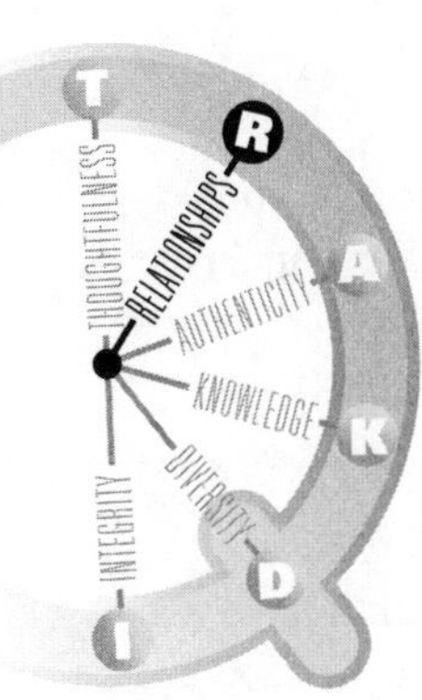

Think back to your grade school experience, how important was your relationship to your teacher compared to the importance of what she knew? What might be your concerns about the first day of school? Where does knowledge of subject matter fit on a scale of concerns?

Assumption 4: A teacher is not a substitute mother, social worker, police constable, or nurse.

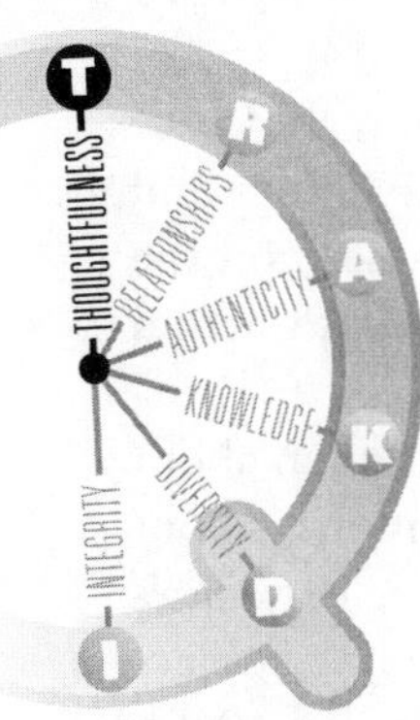

Teachers, students, and parents often hold assumptions and misconceptions about the role of teacher. What assumptions do you hold regarding the responsibility of a teacher to take on the role of mother, social worker, police constable, or nurse? Think back to the story of Teddy Stallard in Chapter 3. What role did Miss Thompson fulfill? What was her responsibility to her young learner? There was obviously a void in Teddy's life, and Miss Thompson happened to be able to fill it. What might have happened to Teddy if Miss Thompson had not altered her attitude? Have you had a teacher who really made a difference? Was there someone who actually helped you make your decision to become a teacher?

There is a cost to caring for your charges. Consider this tragic story. A sick man walked into a Scottish school one day, and proceeded down the hallway into a gymnasium, where close to thirty five- and six-year-old children were being children, enjoying activity and fun. The man pulled out a gun and calmly began to shoot and kill sixteen of these children. When this great evil was spent, people rushed into the gymnasium and found the children's teacher, Gwen Mayer, lying dead over two children, covering their bodies with hers in an effort to save their lives.

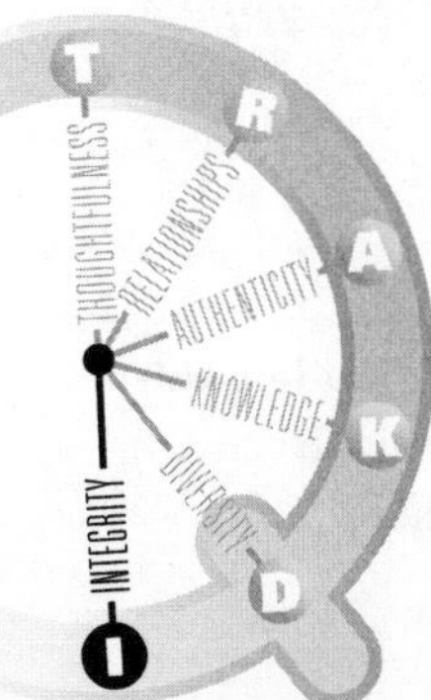

Unfortunately, there are many stories like this. What is the role and responsibility of teachers when it comes to the safety and security of their charges? As you reflect on the sacrifice of Gwen Mayer and the sad story of the Scottish school children, is there anything to which you can connect your own experience as a learner? While we hope that you never have to lay down your life in the same way Gwen Mayer did, are there other ways that teachers can give unselfishly of themselves?

Assumption 5: Teachers are not highly respected.

The notion that you will be a nobody when you become a teacher was mentioned in Chapter 1. The assumption was followed by the question, Who taught today's great world leaders? There have always been teachers who inspired and motivated people to enter a life of public service and creative expression. Who was influential in creating the passion for music or art that inspires the expression of the human soul that lifts us up out of the daily drudgery? Who were these nobodies? Sometimes we don't know, but often, when leaders in science, music, art, dance, literature, sports, or even teaching, write their autobiographies we learn that there was an important teacher in their lives. Teachers are the "moulders of dreams" who can spark the flame of a poet or songwriter, or on the negative side, crush tender beliefs.

What was the reaction of your family and friends to your decision to consider teaching as a career? We're they supportive? What were their main concerns, cautions, or comments of encouragement?

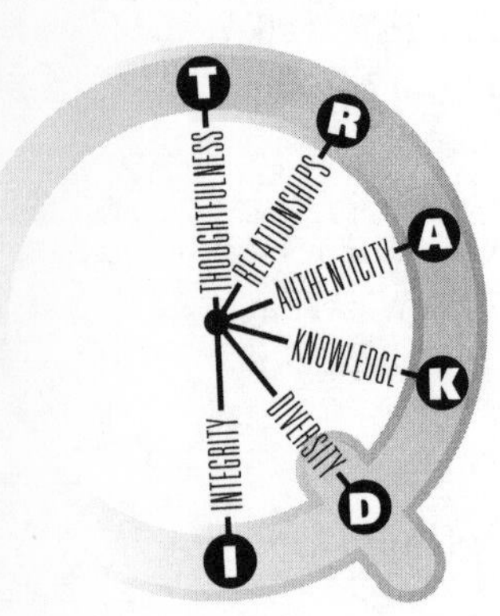

So You Want to Be a Teacher?

Take a moment and write your reasons for wanting to be a teacher. There are probably many, but list five or six. Compare these with your colleagues'. Ask a practising teacher the reasons that led him or her to choose teaching as a career.

Teachers' early experience as pupils is related not only to their choice of teaching as a career, but also to their expectations about teaching. F. Fuller and Brown (1975) identified several stages a beginning teacher experiences on the journey of learning to teach. The first stage, after the first contact with actual teaching, changes from idealized concerns about pupils to a concern for survival: "These are concerns about one's adequacy and survival as a teacher, about class control, about being liked by pupils, about supervisors' opinions, about being observed, evaluated, praised, and failed" (p. 37). This is the, How adequate am I? concern, the concern regarding class control, understanding subject matter, knowing the answers, being able to say "I don't know" (F. Fuller, 1969). This is a time of great stress for the pre-service teacher. What are your primary concerns about beginning to teach?

Teachers Who Made a Difference

Everyone has had a teacher, formal or informal, a special adult who made a difference in his or her life. We all are indebted to these special individuals. Here are three historical figures who owe much of their success to their teachers.

Pablo Picasso

"School was, from the beginning, an ordeal for Pablo. A restless boy, he hated obeying the rules and most of the time did not." (Huffington, 1988, p. 21) Picasso

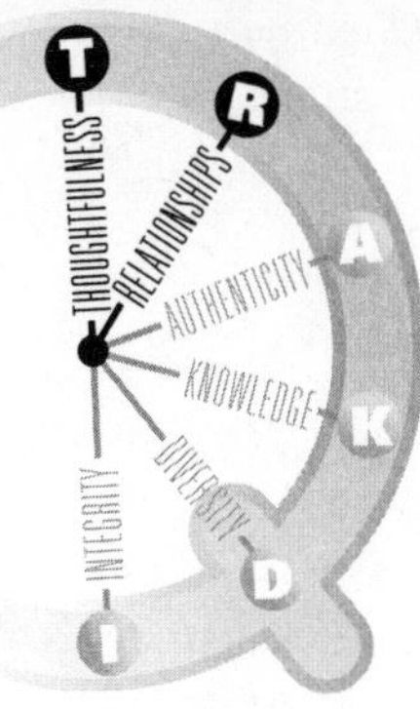

could not master the basics of reading, writing, and arithmetic. School was a nightmare for him, but painting and drawing became his way of displaying and creating his own reality. For punishment, students were sent to "the cell," a room with whitewashed walls. Picasso loved to be sent there with his paper, where he would draw nonstop. From the time Picasso was nine, his family saved virtually every scrap of paper on which he drew (Gardner, 1993). His father became his formal teacher in a school of fine arts and knew that his son was a prodigy. Without the support of his family and teacher-father, would Pablo Picasso have become the most renowned artist of the twentieth century?

Igor Stravinsky

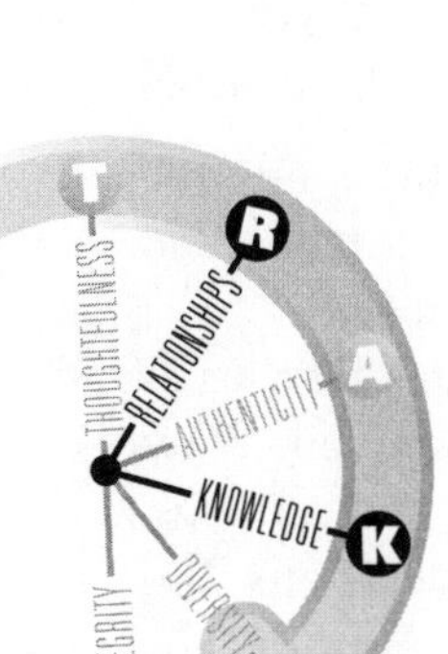

Igor Stravinsky composed some of the most expressive music in twentieth-century Europe. However, he was not a good student; he usually performed at or below the average level for his class—he was simply uninterested in formal schooling (Gardner, 1993). But music always seemed to be of interest to him, and his most vivid memories involved sound. Fortunately, Stravinsky "grew up in an atmosphere conducive to his musical and intellectual development" (Gardner, 1993, p. 191). Further support came from composer Rimsky-Korsakov, who took on the young Stravinsky as a student. For many years, until this teacher's death, Igor was his student and friend. Do you find it wonderful to hear that gifted individuals find appropriate mentors?

Albert Einstein

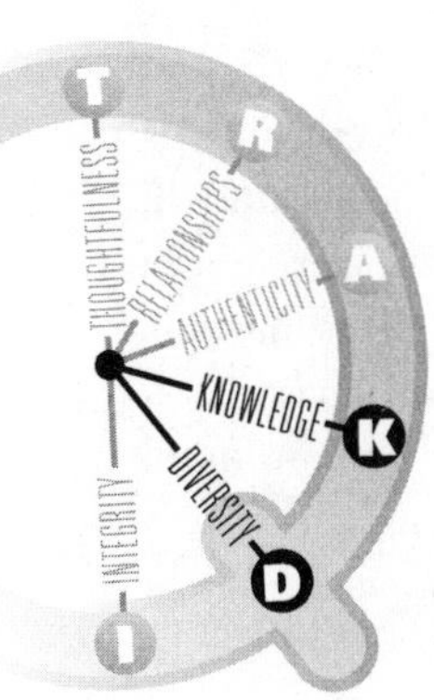

Albert Einstein has been described as dyslexic and a poor student. "He exhibited a strong dislike for the regimentation that characterized most German schools at the time." (Gardner, 1993, p. 91) But he loved to question things and make constructions of all sorts. Fortunately, when Einstein was a young adolescent, he met Max Talmey, who took a liking to him and gave him many books to read, from classic literature to scientific material. Later he attended a "progressive" school that was influenced by the pedagogical philosophy of Pestalozzi. (You will hear more about Pestalozzi and his philosophy in your studies on teaching.) Einstein enjoyed the emphasis on "hands-on" learning with his science theory studies. Einstein recalled, "The school made an unforgettable impression on me, thanks to its liberal spirit and the simple earnestness of the teachers who based themselves on no external authority"(Gardner, 1993, p. 92). This school and the unnamed teachers made a huge difference to the young learner, whom many consider to be a genius.

Think back to your early years. Was there an adult, a formal or informal teacher, who made a difference in your life?

An Ideal Teacher

Think back to your childhood, to yourself as a young student. Did you encounter an ideal teacher? What did this ideal teacher do, or not do, to help you learn? First,

How do you think this teacher makes a difference in the lives of her students?

imagine a composite of all the best teachers you have ever had. In this composite ideal, include all you can remember about your best teachers' skills, attributes, and behaviours. Now imagine rolling those best features into a single person.

Consider this composite teacher for a moment. Let's refer to this teacher as she, and imagine you had the privilege of having this teacher teach you. What would her thinking look like? To begin, her cognition, her thinking about things, would be full of wisdom and quite effective in helping you make decisions. Did she patiently correct and gently guide you to make better decisions? How did she do this? Let's look more closely at what the composite, ideal teacher understands in the light of what we know about learning.

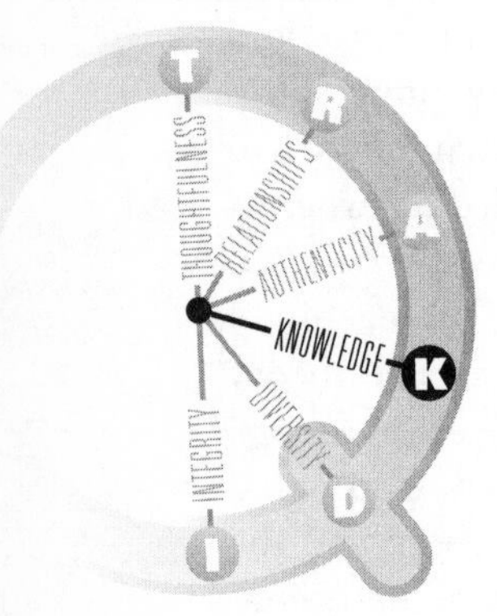

Teaching Strategies

This ideal teacher needed many teaching strategies. She probably used various strategies to help your thinking and decision making as the situation demanded. She often put herself "in your shoes" to help you make sense of what you were going through. She creatively put you in her situation as well, to help you see what she was going through. She had specific tactics for getting things done, and recognized the importance of remembering important details. Remember how she reminded you to take your science experiment home? She knew that memory sometimes cannot be trusted, so she wrote down a lot of things and had her students write things down, too. She made lists of things to do, things to bring, things to remember, birthdays, and rarely left anything out. She taught you to think about your thinking, to manage and control your own learning with some very "nifty" techniques.

Take an opportunity to observe teachers in action. Think about the strategies teachers use to meet their students' learning needs.

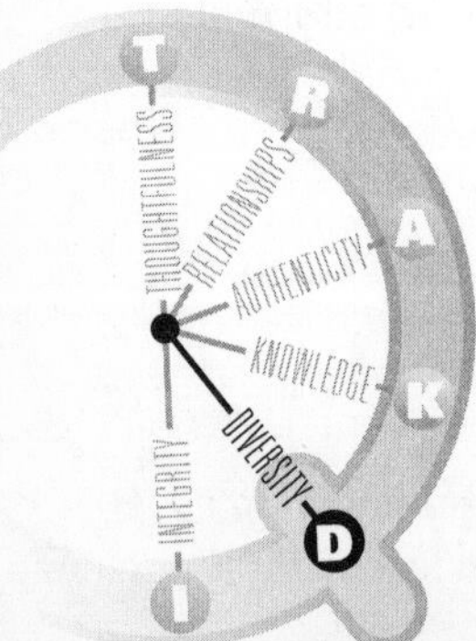

Executive Control Strategies

You came to realize one day that your teacher understood you pretty well. She monitored her use of strategies according to your needs. She treated all her students differently. You did not like it then, but perhaps now appreciate more the wisdom of not teaching all students the same way.

This ideal teacher adapted what she had intended to do in class when new strategies were needed. She could be determined and effective when certain things needed to get done; or more relaxed when the outcome was not so important. Remember when your classroom needed tidying before dismissal, how she got the whole class to work together to get the job done?

Memories, Stories, and the Social Construction of Knowledge

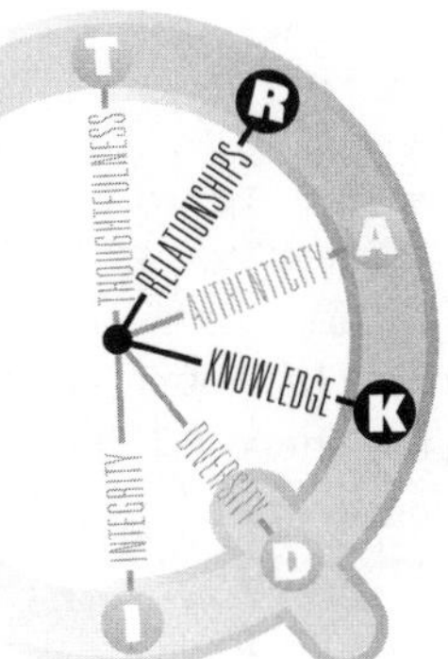

The ideal teacher had a rich storehouse of stories and anecdotes. She told great stories, preserving in the narrative many important memories and traditions, and illustrating many important ideas. The stories were the glue that somehow kept the students caring for each other's well-being. She knew how important it was to share opinions, to get everyone to contribute something to the knowledge base of the class. Her understanding that meaning is socially constructed was intuitive, yet profound. She knew and practiced the value of collaboration and talk.

Motivation

Her repertoire of motivational approaches was rich and varied. She knew how to help children decide for themselves what was important, before they set out to accomplish that task. She knew that when her children were not convinced of something's importance, it was going to be difficult for them to "go after" that something. She worked hard at putting others in control, at minimizing their sense of helplessness. She asked questions, often giving lots of information in the question. She preserved your dignity when the answer was wrong. She listened to your questions carefully, and encouraged you to be as self-reliant and self-directing as you could be. All the while, she gave you a safe and secure base from which to be a risk-taker.

The Individual and Environment

She balanced work, play, and nourishment, demonstrating her understanding that a healthy, functioning brain requires them all. She also nourished her children's creativity by creating a rich, stimulating environment. She encouraged proper language development and use, leading class members to express themselves often and in many different ways, from drama to science. She encouraged her children to talk their way into clarity. Do you remember your ideal teacher treating every student as a learner with a unique history and individual needs?

Humour

This ideal teacher had a great sense of humour. All the students in your class enjoyed it when she shared jokes, funny stories and anecdotes. She recounted and embellished funny things. She never used sarcasm or put downs, even in a playful

To what extent is humour important in learning?

way, never joked at the expense of the students or herself. The classroom humour energized and motivated the students. In the rare tough situations, she used humour to defuse an angry student. "It has long been the advice of wise ones to laugh and look for the lighter side in our daily journey." (Pearce, 1999, p. 50)

Which of the five strategies described above do you consider to be most important in your composite of an ideal teacher?

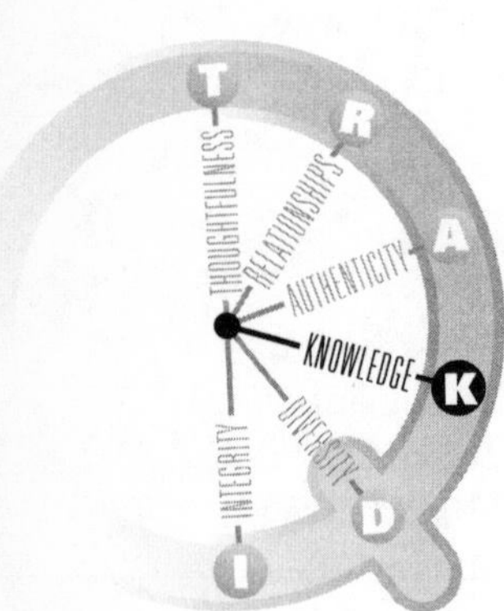

Who Is a Teacher?

Consider your image of the ideal teacher. Did you think more about skills than about attributes? Do great teachers do something better than less great teachers, or are they simply better people? What is it about them that makes a difference?

Attributes, Skills, and Knowledge

School administrators, school boards, and department of education divisions have attempted to create criteria for observable teacher attributes, skills, and knowledge. The following list (Table 7.1) is one example. These items are sometimes placed into the six categories of personal characteristics; relationships; cur-

7.1 FOR YOUR CONSIDERATION

We often think of observing as a passive activity—simply watching what is going on at a given time and place. Practice being a reflective practitioner by taking careful notes on what you observe. We ask that you pay special attention to what your co-operating teacher says and does. Learn from the techniques you observe (Manafo, 2000). Resist the temptation of making snap judgments about your co-operating teacher. Spend time being actively involved in her classroom. A well-run, pleasant learning environment is not created without a great deal of effort.

7.2 FOR YOUR CONSIDERATION

In a group of colleagues choose five characteristics shared by good teachers. With this list discuss the following questions.

1. How do you rank the importance of the characteristics?
2. In what way does the ranking change according to the age, needs, and learning characteristics of the students?
3. Discuss your personal strengths and characteristics in terms of the age level you will choose to teach.
4. How do your personal characteristics match your list? In what areas will you have difficulty?

riculum knowledge and instructional competence; classroom management and organization; professional growth and leadership; and contribution to the total school program. Consider each item from your present position as a pre-service teacher. What do you consider to be the most critical attitudes, skills, and knowledge a teacher should possess?

Table 7.1 Teacher Attributes, Skills, and Knowledge

A. Personal Characteristics

1. Models good work habits, deportment, and dress.
2. Exhibits poise and confidence.
3. Exhibits flexibility and enthusiasm.
4. Possesses a good sense of humour.
5. Exhibits a positive outlook and co-operative attitude.
6. Demonstrates creativity and initiative.
7. Demonstrates concern for student welfare.
8. Uses appropriate language.
9. Offers assistance to students outside regular class hours.

B. Relationships

Relationship with students

1. Demonstrates friendliness, courtesy, and empathy toward students.
2. Communicates with students at their level.
3. Is liked by students.
4. Behaviour generates high expectations for all students—proximity, reinforcement of responses, questioning techniques.
5. Demonstrates consistency and fairness in interaction with students.
6. Makes effective use of praise and recognition of student work and effort.

Relationship with adults

1. Demonstrates collegiality.
2. Demonstrates the ability to work in a team situation.
3. Communicates effectively with parents.

C. Curriculum Knowledge and Instructional Competence

1. Demonstrates satisfactory knowledge of curriculum and methodology.
2. Practises daily plans that reflect an understanding of the elements of effective instruction and the principles of learning.
3. Personalizes instruction:
   - Student-centred; balance between teacher talk and student activity.
   - Attends to student learning styles.
   - Uses a variety of instructional techniques.
   - Provides opportunities for student participation, initiative, and creative expression.
   - Continually assesses student work and development using teacher observations, assignments, tests.
4. Reports student growth regularly to students and parents.
5. Uses school and community resources effectively.

D. Classroom Management and Organization

1. Teaches from a daily plan.
2. Establishes and implements short- and long-term curriculum plans.
3. Makes efficient use of instruction time and ensures that student engagement time is high.
4. Organizes for individual instruction and continuous development.
5. Establishes effective routines, for example, attendance, material distribution, etc.
6. Employs appropriate disciplinary strategies to develop positive student/teacher relationships.
7. Strives to develop student self-discipline.
8. Creates an inviting and interesting classroom environment.

E. Professional Growth and Leadership

1. Participates in curricular and professional workshops, in-service programs, specialist councils, and conferences.
2. Assumes responsibility for professional self evaluation.
3. Keeps informed on current educational trends, procedures, and practices reported in literature.
4. Demonstrates professional leadership.
5. Demonstrates initiative in sharing ideas with colleagues.
6. Is willing to serve as a co-operating teacher.

F. Contribution to the Total School Program

1. Sponsors extra-curricular activities.
2. Serves on school committees.
3. Shows initiative in accepting duties beyond the classroom level.

(Source: From *EDTS Student Handbook*, n.d., Calgary, AB: Faculty of Education, University of Calgary. Reprinted with permission of the University of Calgary.)

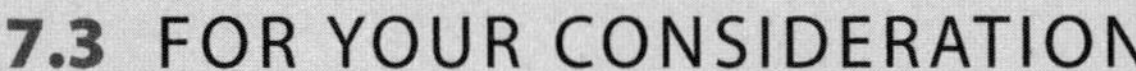 7.3 FOR YOUR CONSIDERATION

Task 1. The following is a list of characteristics for the ideal teacher. They are all wonderful characteristics, but we would like you to choose the five you most prefer and the five you least prefer in order of importance. You will notice that this list is similar to the list of knowledge, skills, and attributes in Table 7.1.

The Ideal Teacher

The Ideal Teacher is one who:

A) has a good sense of humour

B) makes learning an enjoyable adventure

C) cares about each person in the class

D) has an excellent knowledge of the subjects they teach

E) is creative and imaginative

F) believes that each child can succeed

G) is flexible and can adapt to a variety of situations

H) is well-groomed and presentable

I) communicates and gets along well with parents

J) has very good control of the class and has few discipline problems

K) ensures that lessons are relevant to the needs of the learners

L) focuses on teaching skills and processes, over content

M) is respected by colleagues as an ethical professional

N) gets involved in "extra" activities beyond their job description

O) is fully aware of the latest research into effective teaching

P) is able to communicate/interact with the students on their level

Q) has high expectations for themselves and their students

R) makes regular use of professional development opportunities

S) constantly reflects/evaluates to guide and adjust their practice

T) attempts to meet the individual needs of each student

U) works to establish a supportive and respectful community

V) is willing to put in long hours to do a good job

W) involves students in class decision making

X) can cover the entire curriculum set out for their grade level

Y) ensures that all students are treated equally

Z) is well organized and prepared

(Source: From *The Ideal Teacher,* by Steve Dunsmuir, 2001 [handout at the Westcast Conference, Calgary, AB, February, 2001]. Reprinted with permission of Steve Dunsmuir.)

Task 2: In groups of three or four, share your list and discuss, negotiate, and create a group list of the five most desirable and five least desirable qualities of an ideal teacher, in order of preference. Have each group share its list with the whole group. Discuss the differences and similarities between the attributes each group chose. As a whole group, can you reach consensus on the five most desirable and least desirable attributes?

What teacher attributes, knowledge, and skills are evident in this photo?

Professional Growth

Recruitment and Retention of Dedicated Teachers in the Classroom

> Teachers across the country explain the burnout phenomenon by pointing to higher public expectations, more integration of special needs children without extra support, a demanding new curriculum introduced with little teacher training and children who are more troubled and less prepared to learn. (Fine, 2001, p. A3)

After reading this quotation from *The Globe and Mail* newspaper, you might wonder why anyone would choose to be a teacher or stay in teaching. There are reasons and ways to keep dedicated teachers—new, experienced, or seasoned—in the classroom. Many school districts understand this and some are actively addressing this issue because burnout inevitably affects the learning environment (Guglielmi & Tatrow, 1998). Some school boards have made an effort by varying work routines, clarifying expectations, and introducing stress management and relaxation programs (Schamer & Jackson, 1996).

In any profession it may sometimes be difficult to maintain enthusiasm for the job. Here is one teacher's comment about how she stays interested in teaching.

> **The Rhythm of the Year**
>
> I've come to see the school year as a cycle of seasons. In summer the teacher recharges energy and plans for the coming year. In autumn she or he studies the children's skills and their parents' values, and teaches the children routines which help them to find independence. In the winter he or she teaches in order to augment children's skills and confidence. And in the spring the teacher, children, and parents celebrate the achievements of the year.... Whatever the drawbacks of having the same assignment for seven years, the chance to see the year unfold was there, and it has colored all my perceptions of teaching. (Clemens, 1983, p. 82)

Think of the teacher as an adult learner, and consider Erikson's Eight Stages of Psychosocial Development (briefly discussed in Chapter 5, pp. 92–93). Where does the experienced, adult teacher fit into this framework? Would the teacher be at the middle adulthood age of generativity versus stagnation, when the adult must find some way to satisfy and support the next generation? Or would the teacher be at the ego integrity versus despair stage, where one reflects on and accepts one's life with a sense of fulfilment (Woolfolk, Winne, & Perry, 1998)? Have you met or learned under teachers who would fit into one of these stages? What factors might assist the teacher in moving from stagnation to generativity or despair versus ego integrity? What keeps teachers going year after year? How do teachers sustain their enthusiasm for teaching and avoid burnout?

There are many ways that teachers can "keep the flame alive." They include the influence of research, an attitude of life-long learning, mentorship, professional growth plans, empowerment, leadership, collegiality, and an ability to embrace change, as well as reflecting the many enriching possibilities that being a teacher can bring. For a list of attributes that contribute to being a happy and successful teacher, see Table 7.2 on p. 147.

Teacher as Leader

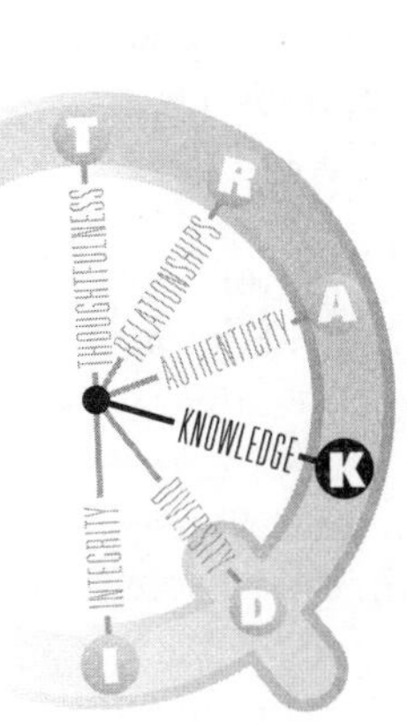

There is a difference between being a teacher and a teacher leader. This does not imply a formal administrative leadership position, but a situation in which the teacher feels empowered in the teaching environment and is authorized to make choices and decisions. When a school operates democratically, students as well as teachers benefit from teacher leadership. A school that has few discipline problems and high pupil achievement is one where decision making and leadership are significantly more democratic (Barth, 2001). According to Barth, "Teachers' lives are enriched and energized in many ways when they actively pursue leadership opportunities" (2001, p. 444). Becoming knowledgeable about and actively involved in the workings of the school and choice of courses to teach and textbooks to use, to list a few things, can enhance job satisfaction. In what other ways can teachers be leaders in their working environment?

Influence of Research on Teachers

A teaching colleague of ours once stated, "After studying Gardner's theory of multiple intelligence, I altered the curriculum delivery and assessment. I will never teach the same way again." This statement illustrates the influence educational research can have on a teacher's practice. Gardner's work excited teachers. As an elementary teacher stated, "Suddenly one finds it necessary to be an astute observer of children's behavior; a critical listener of their speech; an assessor of their thinking abilities; a stimulus for provoking their thought" (Athey & Rubadeau, 1970, p. 13).

From the 1920s to 1960s Jean Piaget wrote about children's development, language, intelligence, play, construction of reality, and schooling. During this time he influenced the way teachers thought about their role as teachers. Throughout the years, many educational theorists, such as Vygotsky, Dewey, and Gardner, have influenced the teaching practice.

Teachers' professional development has become an increasingly important focus for senior administrators promoting school reform and educational excellence. Great teachers make an effort to stay abreast of current educational theories. Other effects of studying educational research and other professional development activities include teacher's well-being, renewed dedication to teaching, and possibly teacher retention, keeping dedicated teachers in the classrooms. Unfortunately, when there are budget constraints, professional development funds and other resources generally are the first to be whittled away.

Mentorship

The Baby Boom generation, born between the late 1940s and 1960, has influenced education in a variety of ways. Through a population explosion it increased demands for more schools and resulted in an aging teaching force today. This has caused recruitment and retention problems for school boards and has also influenced some pre-service teachers' views about senior teachers. People are often judged not by their behaviour or personality but by their age, a stereotypical view called ageism. It is sometimes thought that older employees cannot perform as well as their younger counterparts and that they are set in their ways and unable or reluctant to learn. "Fortunately, recent research has shown that ageist stereotypes tend to be false or, at a minimum, overblown.... [C]ontrary to popular conceptions, people's curiosity and their desire for information and knowledge is stable and does not decrease as they grow older" (Reio & Sanders-Reio, 2000, p. 11).

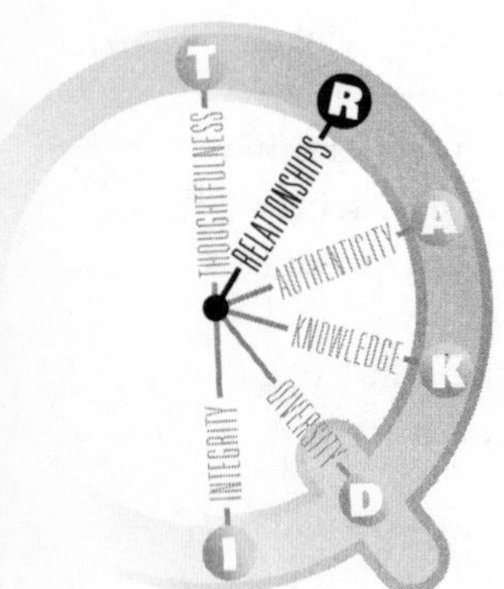

How do you view the "greying generation"? Is this factor significant for you as you enter the field of teaching? We believe this is important to think about as you enter your first teaching position and search for or are assigned a mentor, or "system buddy." This mentor will be your experienced counterpart, who can provide advice on many aspects of the job, the school, and the students. According to Lucksinger (2000), "Mentoring appears to be beneficial for both the novice teacher and the experienced teacher and helps improve teacher retention for both groups. Mentoring gives novice teachers support and encouragement and gives the experienced teacher a feeling of satisfaction and professional growth" (p. 14). If you are not formally assigned a mentor, it is a good idea to choose one. What qualities will you be looking for in your mentor?

Code of Ethics and Moral Conduct

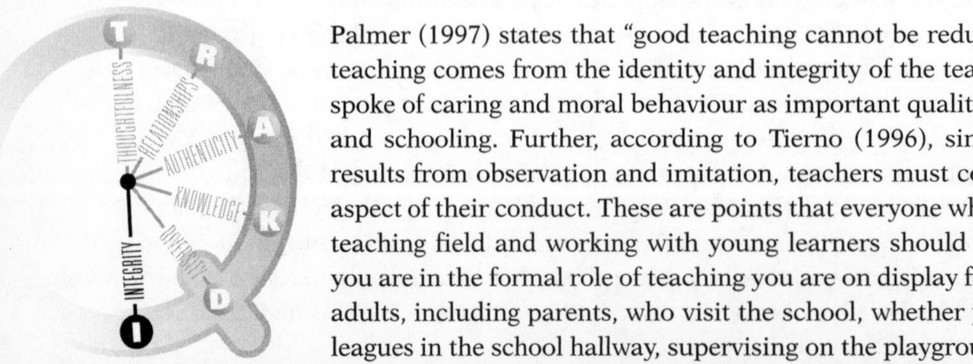

Palmer (1997) states that "good teaching cannot be reduced to techniques; good teaching comes from the identity and integrity of the teacher" (p. 14). Earlier we spoke of caring and moral behaviour as important qualities in teaching, learning, and schooling. Further, according to Tierno (1996), since most social learning results from observation and imitation, teachers must consider every observable aspect of their conduct. These are points that everyone who considers entering the teaching field and working with young learners should be very aware of. When you are in the formal role of teaching you are on display for your students and any adults, including parents, who visit the school, whether you are talking with colleagues in the school hallway, supervising on the playground, or conversing in the

Table 7.2 Should You Teach?

Teachers' associations believe there are certain characteristics that teachers should possess to ensure that they will be happy and successful. Below are several questions that you should ask yourself:

1.	Do I like to be with and to help children?
2.	Do I possess above-average intelligence?
3.	Do I like to read and study?
4.	Do I like working with ideas?
5.	Do I like to lead group activities?
6.	Do I have patience with and understanding of others?
7.	Do I have good physical and mental health?
8.	Do I like making and carrying out my own plan of work?
9.	Do I have a sense of humour?
10.	Do I accept criticism and use it for personal improvement?

(Source: From a pamphlet distributed by the Alberta Teachers' Association, Edmonton, AB. Reprinted with permission.)

teachers' lounge or prep-room. This is not a role you take on as you would in a play on stage; it is an identity that professes integrity, caring, and moral behaviour. Teachers are obligated to follow a code of professional conduct, and this code of conduct cannot be left when you go out the school yard gates. Whether you like it or not, you are a teacher twenty-four hours a day, fifty-two weeks a year.

Teachers in Canadian public schools are eligible to become members of their provincial or territorial teachers' organizations. These organizations are in turn members of the Canadian Teachers' Federation, which is a member of Education International. Various teachers' organizations have adopted codes of ethics, and several are empowered under provincial legislation to investigate cases of unprofessional conduct. A **code of ethics** stipulates the minimum standards of professional conduct of teachers, although the wording may vary from province to province. In the following example (Table 7.3 on the next page), from the Alberta Teachers Association, these are placed into four categories: in relation to pupils, to school authorities, to colleagues, to the profession. The Newfoundland and Labrador Teachers' Association Code of Ethics has similar categories. The Ontario College of Teachers provides members with a list of professional misconduct (Ontario College of Teachers, 2002).

Do you have a clear understanding of the significance of each item in this code of professional conduct? Discuss and clarify the impact these requirements have on teachers and their daily conduct, in and outside of school. Contact your local teachers' association for a copy of its code of conduct or search the association's Web site. At the end of this chapter is a list of Canadian teachers' associations and their Web sites. Compare codes of conduct of various teacher associations.

Table 7.3 Example of a Teacher's Code of Professional Conduct

In Relation to Pupils

1. The teacher teaches in a manner that respects the dignity and rights of all persons without prejudice as to race, religious beliefs, colour, sex, sexual orientation, physical characteristics, age, ancestry, or place of origin.
2. a) The teacher is responsible for diagnosing educational needs, prescribing and implementing instructional programs, and evaluating progress of pupils.

   b) The teacher may not delegate these responsibilities to any person who is not a teacher.
3. The teacher may delegate specific and limited aspects of the instructional activity to non-certificated personnel, provided that the teacher supervises and directs such activity.
4. The teacher treats pupils with dignity and respect and is considerate of their circumstances.
5. The teacher may not divulge information about a pupil received in confidence or in the course of professional duties except as required by law or where, in the judgement of the teacher, to do so is in the best interest of the pupil.
6. The teacher may not accept pay for tutoring a pupil in any subjects in which the teacher is responsible for giving classroom instruction to that pupil.
7. The teacher may not take advantage of a professional position to profit from the sale of goods or services to or for pupils in the teacher's charge.

In Relation to School Authorities

8. The teacher protests the assignment of duties for which the teacher is not qualified or conditions which make it difficult to render professional service.
9. The teacher fulfills contractual obligations to the employer until released by mutual consent or according to law.
10. The teacher provides as much notice as possible of a decision to terminate employment.
11. `The teacher adheres to agreements negotiated on the teacher's behalf by the Association.

In Relation to Colleagues

12. The teacher does not undermine the confidence of pupils in other teachers.
13. The teacher criticizes the professional competence or professional reputation of another teacher only in confidence to proper officials and after the other teacher has been informed of the criticism, subject only to section 23 of the Teaching Profession Act.
14. The teacher, when making a report on the professional performance of another teacher, does so in good faith and, prior to submitting the report, provides the teacher with a copy of the report, subject only to Section 23 of the Teaching Profession Act.
15. The teacher does not take, because of animosity or for personal advantage, any steps to secure the dismissal of another teacher.
16. The teacher recognizes the duty to protest through proper channels administrative policies and practices which the teacher cannot in conscience accept; and further recognizes that if administration by consent fails, the administrator must adopt a position of authority.
17. The teacher as an administrator provides opportunities for staff members to express their opinions and to bring forth suggestions regarding the administration of the school.

In Relation to the Profession

18. The teacher acts in a manner that maintains the honour and dignity of the profession.
19. The teacher does not engage in activities which adversely affect the quality of the teacher's professional service.
20. The teacher submits to the Association disputes arising from professional relationships with other teachers which cannot be resolved by personal discussion.
21. The teacher makes representation on behalf of the Association or members thereof only when authorized to do so.
22. The teacher accepts that service to the Association is a professional responsibility.

(Source: From Alberta Teachers' Association, *Code of Professional Conduct,* 2002 [pamphlet], Edmonton, AB. [**www.teachers.ab.ca/professional/code/html**]. Reprinted with permission of the Association.)

Philosophical Orientations to Teaching

As teachers, we all operate from beliefs, theories, and assumptions about learning and teaching that drive our ways of working with and responding to students. Collectively, these drivers describe a personal philosophy of education, which most teachers are able to articulate

Sometimes teachers do not consider philosophy kindly. The reasons are often difficult to determine, but chances are it has a great deal to do with pragmatism. Schools are very busy places and time is usually in short supply. When issues of philosophy are raised, people can think of a multitude of other things that need to be done rather than discuss issues that don't seem to be grounded in reality. Remarks such as, "I have papers to mark," "I have phone calls to make," "I have kids waiting in the gym for basketball coaching," "I have to plan my classes for tomorrow," and "I have to attend a meeting," are common. No doubt these reasons are all quite legitimate, but are they sufficient to deny the value of considering teaching and what it means from a philosophical framework of ideas?

Philosophy is sometimes seen as abstract; philosophy courses tend to deal with abstractions, and perhaps memories of these kinds of experiences linger in teachers' minds. However, philosophy can be very useful in helping teachers to improve schooling through discovering solutions to educational issues and problems, as well as clarifying beliefs and assumptions. Wilson (1983) notes that educational philosophy, "merely asks people to consider whether they are doing, or meaning A or B; whether their aims are clear, admirable, disastrous, wicked, muddled, or whatever. The philosopher simply interrogates" (p. 91). The relative intransigence that schools experience in responding to change in this ever-changing world may have a great deal to do with a reluctance to respond to the philosophical challenge (Waldron et al., 1999, p. 34).

Two simple questions are useful with regard to the philosophical challenge: Why do we do the things that we do? and, Are the things we do consistent with current professional knowledge? These simple questions can be useful for clarifying professional practice. There is good reason to question assumptions that describe any number of things that take place in schools, but questioning and challenging will not take place without meaningful application of philosophy. The reminder provided by Wilson, above, places a particularly practical perspective on the matter. Unless we are able to provide clear, professionally defensible reasons for our teaching and learning practices, we are clearly open to being questioned about our teaching. What if a parent challenged our practice? What if a young person challenged our practice?

Philosophical Questions

There are many profoundly philosophical questions that teachers must confront as they contemplate professional practice. Note the following:

- Are people inherently good or bad?
- What is good and what is evil?
- How should other people be treated?
- What is truth and is it ever attainable?
- What knowledge is most valuable?
- What values are most worthy to guide our lives?
- Can morality be taught?

These profound questions are rooted in branches of philosophy such as epistemology, metaphysics (or ontology), axiology, logic, ethics, and aesthetics. Out of these disciplinary roots, and in response to the questions posed above, six coherent orientations to teaching have emerged: progressivism, essentialism, perennialism, existentialism, reconstructionism, and behaviourism.

Progressivism

John Dewey can perhaps be considered the father of progressivism. His work in the early part of the twentieth century placed what we now call progressive ideas on the educational landscape. Progressive teaching begins with the child, from whom we take cues and clues about what is to be learned and taught. **Progressivism** views knowledge as somewhat tentative, and incorporates change as a fundamental part of life.

Progressive teaching has the following major implications for learners:

- The whole person is considered.
- The focus is on interests in all forms of learning.
- The learner is intimately involved in decision making.

Progressive teaching also has some major implications for teachers:

- Content is derived from the interests of the learners rather than from teaching subjects.
- Learning is active, stressing learning by doing.
- People are taught to be logical, rational decision-makers and problem-solvers.

- Young people become contributing members of society toward a more prosperous future.

Progressive teachers view young people as, essentially, good. Freedom and liberation are two key words that would fit easily into their vocabulary. Rigid, authoritarian practices are foreign to their teaching and resource selection. Instead, inquiry through questioning and guidance are strong emphases in any progressivist classroom. Direct experience activities encourage young people to build upon prior knowledge as they inquire into their environment, making meaning and understanding from new knowledge, leading to proposals, suggestions, and further questions.

Essentialism

Essentialism emerged in the 1930s and is largely attributable to the work of William C. Bagley (1934). In general, essentialists believe that young people must be trained to be good and useful members of society. Many of the assumptions that mark traditional schooling would be easily embraced by essentialist teachers: compliance, conformity, selecting and sorting, uniformity, and authoritarian uses of power and control, for example. Typical values would be hard work, discipline, obedience, and respect for authority. The back-to-the-basics movement that emerged in the 1970s and is still active today was really intended to encourage essentialist practices in schools.

Interestingly, the emergence of essentialism coincided with the spread of progressivism and it may well be that progressivist advocates provoked a reaction, which then became the essentialist tradition. One facet of your chosen profession likely to intrigue you is why teachers (and teaching) seem to react to and follow societal expectations and ideas. Certainly Bagley and other like-minded educators believed that progressivist beliefs and practices were damaging to young people.

So what are the core beliefs of essentialism?

- There is a core body of knowledge and skills that young people must have if they are to become productive members of society.
- Reading, speaking, writing, and arithmetic are basic, or core, to an elementary education.
- The most important core, or essential, knowledge is in the sciences and technical/vocational areas, because of their utility in society.
- Other studies such as fine arts and humanities are "frills" and therefore not essential in the quest to become a useful member of society.
- Schooling should be very practical.

Essentialist practices in schools mean that learners are required to

- learn and retain factual information
- respect and obey the teacher
- understand and value discipline, hard work, and respect for authority
- develop habits and knowledge to become good people

Within the essentialist framework, teachers are expected to

- provide sound practical and intellectual training for students
- focus learning on the acquisition of basic skills
- impart information to learners quickly and efficiently
- develop good character in students through instruction and example
- instil in students an appreciation for discipline, hard work, and respect for authority

Clearly, essentialists would see little value in student-centred approaches to teaching because "Essentialists tend to believe that people are not basically good and that individuals who are left to their own devices will not develop the habits and knowledge necessary for them to become good people" (Armstrong, Henson, & Savage, 1997, p. 156). Essentialism attempts to suppress non-productive tendencies in young people, such as in-school play and games, aggression, expressions of emotion—basically, everything that detracts from strictly formal student–teacher relationships.

7.4 FOR YOUR CONSIDERATION

The implications for approaches to teaching inherent in essentialism are probably quite clear to you. It might be useful to consider the teaching qualities in light of an essentialist orientation. Use the information grid below to jot down your personal thoughts. Use them as a reference to test your views against the views of others when you engage in small-group discussion. Is your philosophy of education challenged by the discussion?

Teaching Quality	**Implications for Essentialism**	**My philosophy**
Relationships		
Authenticity		
Diversity		
Thoughtfulness		
Integrity		
Knowledge		

Perennialism

Perennialism views truth as constant and unchanging, or perennial. An early founder of perennialism, Robert Hutchins, worked in the 1930s at the same time as Dewey was advocating progressivist methods and Bagley was countering them with essentialist philosophy. It would seem that schooling was receiving a pretty thorough analysis during those years.

Perennialists believe that education should focus on the search for and dissemination of the great unchanging truths and great ideas contained in the great books of arts and science. These works are believed to be great because they have withstood the test of time. The truths contained in them are enduring and therefore constant. Perennialists acknowledge that change occurs in society, but believe that this change brings only superficial changes to people's lives. The real substance of life remains essentially unchanged over time.

Perennialists support schools that develop the intellect of all learners in their preparation for life. The fundamental preparation is accomplished through mastery of constant truths, validated over the years and drawn from the most significant works of human excellence. From enduring classics such as Plato, Shakespeare, Dickens, and Einstein students explore the constant, unchanging truths to help them become critical and independent thinkers.

Perennialists believe that Western society has lost its way through an over-reliance on scientific experimentation and technological progress. Because of this over-reliance, society has suffered a decline in the importance of human reasoning and logic. Perennialists denounce futurist tendencies, training in research skills, and vocational training. They believe these emphases represent a compromise to the real intentions of schooling and a capitulation to the commercial pressures of business (Hutchins, 1963).

You may come across work by another, more recent, proponent of perennialism, Mortimer Adler, who has developed a program for schools called the Paideia Program (Adler, 1977). "Paideia" is from the Greek *paidos*, which means the upbringing of a child. The program, released in 1982, provides a rigorous liberal arts education that will allow young people to gain the necessary skills to earn a living, think and act critically as responsible citizens, and continue educating themselves as life-long learners.

Within the perennialist framework, learners are expected to

- master "truths" presented by teachers
- appreciate the arts and sciences as central to intellectual growth

Perennialist practices in schools mean that teachers are required to

- recognize truth as unchanging, constant, or perennial and to teach this to young people
- develop the intellect of young people and prepare them for life
- focus learning experiences within a curriculum that emphasizes arts and sciences
- teach students to become independent and critical thinkers

You may notice many characteristics of perennialism that appear to fit well with more progressive approaches to teaching. Life-long learning, critical thinking, responsibility, reasoning, and logic all lend themselves to transformational teaching and student-centred orientations.

There is a tendency to label perennialist approaches to teaching as "traditional" and somewhat out of step with contemporary thinking. What are your views on this? In For Your Consideration 8.8 (p. 184) we ask you to respond to a soliloquy from *Hamlet*, the famous "To be, or not to be..." passage. In our comments, we suggest that the soliloquy would be typical of a perennialist classroom. Do you agree? Do the great unchanging truths of the classical books of our civilization have to be confined to more traditional approaches to teaching?

Existentialism

A critical aspect of **existentialism** is its focus on experiences of the individual. Existentialists believe that people must confront the inevitability of death and that, preparatory to the event, they should be free to make choices and be clear about reasons for their existence. Existentialists are neither theo-centric nor particularly spiritual. They believe people are born, live out their lives, and then simply die and become nothing other than part of the earth. They do not subscribe to any grand plan for the universe or for humankind. Each individual has to define right and wrong. Each person has to come to terms with beauty, goodness, and truth. The French philosopher and writer Jean-Paul Sartre (1905–1980) was a well-known existentialist. He believed that individuals have the responsibility to fathom and assign meaning to their existence. In short, each of us must determine who he or she is (Sartre, 1972).

Existentialist teaching challenges young people to make their own meaning and understanding. Learners are encouraged to have a strong voice in decisions about their learning. Perhaps one of the best examples of existentialism in schooling was at Summerhill, a school established by A.S. Neill in England in the 1960s. Neill's school had no fixed curriculum; learning was organized around the needs and interests of students so that they might understand themselves in their process of becoming. His philosophy of education spread to this continent, though mostly only to a few private schools in the United States. Public schooling paid attention to his work but existentialism made few significant inroads into the daily life of schools. Existentialism has had perhaps less impact on school curriculum than most other philosophies.

Within an existentialist teaching approach, learners are expected to

- express needs and interests freely
- respect the opinions of others
- ask questions
- participate in the governance of the school

Existentialist teachers aim to

- involve learners in the design and development of individualized programs for learning
- recognize the uniqueness of each student
- help learners explore their world in a spirit of freedom
- provide learners with experiences that will allow them to make meaning in and of their lives

Behaviourism

Behaviourism holds that learning means a change in behaviour; if behaviour is caused to change then learning has occurred. The implication for teaching is that desirable behaviour can be achieved by design. Whereas existentialists believe that human beings should exercise free will to understand who they are in the scheme of things, behaviourists believe that free will is an illusion.

The two people usually credited with the founding of behaviourism are John Watson (1878–1958) and B.F. Skinner (1904–1990). Behaviourism, as you recall from Chapter 4, associates specific stimuli with certain responses. Watson was a great proponent of classical conditioning and the work of Ivan Pavlov (Watson, 1925). Skinner went beyond classical conditioning to develop what he called operant conditioning (Skinner, 1950).

Three prominent theories of behaviourism are presented in Chapter 4 and we invite you to revisit that section of the book to review these theories.

Within the behaviourist approach to teaching, learners are expected to

- respond well to a structured learning environment
- respond to reinforcement and group dynamics

Teachers using a behaviourist approach in their classes believe that

- desirable behaviour can be achieved through planning
- rewarding desirable behaviour is more effective that punishing bad
- learning means a change in behaviour
- consequences are important for good and bad behaviour

Reconstructionism

Reconstructionism holds that society needs to construct a new social order. Theodore Brameld is usually credited as being the founder of reconstructionism. Brameld believed that society was deteriorating, and he suggested that in order to combat this deterioration, human beings should capitalize upon their incredible potential to create a better civilization (Brameld, 1956).

Reconstructionists believe that schools should be catalysts in society's efforts to effect reform: "Schools should not only *transmit* knowledge about the existing social order; they should seek to *reconstruct* it as well" (Parkay et al., 1996, p. 196). Within the reconstructionist framework, a critical role for schools is to analyze all aspects of society so that when students leave school they will be capable of independent thinking and of actively working toward societal reform.

Reconstructionist teachers require learners to

- question the views of those in political power
- challenge the status quo and social conventions
- inquire into significant world issues and crises
- interact with the immediate community through social involvement and field trips

Reconstructionist teachers themselves

- draw heavily on insights from the behavioural sciences
- raise issues and use appropriate resources to guide students toward reconstructionist solutions
- actively engage students in learning
- model justice and reform of an enlightened society within the classroom

The Philosophical Orientations in Perspective

A good maxim to follow when inviting young people to learn something new is to provide opportunities for them to do something with what they have learned. We would like you to complete the exercises in For Your Consideration 7.5, using the philosophical orientations to teaching to help strengthen your understanding and to place them in perspective on the teaching–learning landscape.

7.5 FOR YOUR CONSIDERATION

a) Divide the class into groups and provide each group with a package of a proprietary brand of freeze-dried macaroni and cheese.

b) Each group should select one group member to be the "teacher."

c) The "teacher" should select (or perhaps the professor may wish to assign) a philosophical orientation to teaching.

d) Using that philosophical orientation, the teacher should then teach the remaining group members how to cook the package of macaroni and cheese without telling the group members which philosophical orientation is in effect.

e) When the teacher has finished, the group is to identify the philosophical orientation the teacher has been modelling. It is important that the group be able to say *why* the teaching behaviours of the presenter/teacher reflect the philosophical orientation being modelled.

The whole group might then usefully engage in a discussion about the merits of the teaching session using that framework and about why, in their collective view, the representation was accurate or inaccurate.

Once again we remind you that teachers and teaching cannot be compartmentalized. You will seldom find a teacher who adheres exclusively to only one philosophical orientation to teaching. Many teachers tend to work predominantly within two or perhaps even three orientations. Most will move in and out of quite a number. No matter which orientation(s) you choose, your primary motivation should always be determined by what is in the best interests of meeting the learning needs of your students.

Career Planning

Teacher Shortages

The importance of teacher recruitment and retention with school boards varies, depending on many factors, but the most significant factor is teacher supply and demand (Canadian Education Association, 1992). Currently there is a great deal of concern regarding teacher shortages across Canada. Baby Boomers are retiring, and school boards have discontinued the early retirement packages they once used to cut operating costs. (A senior teacher is higher on the pay scale than a beginning teacher.) Furthermore, American school boards and other overseas schools are offering attractive opportunities and salaries both to new and to experienced, seasoned teachers. The following news headlines illustrate this concern:

- "The Province of Ontario is facing serious teacher shortage since the teachers of the baby boom generation are approaching retirement age." (*Sunday Report*, CBC, 1999)
- "Retired teachers urged back to the classroom to solve a teacher shortage plaguing school, the province." (*Hamilton Spectator*, 1999)
- "Substitute teachers see hope for permanent placements." (*Times Colonist*, Victoria, 1998)
- "Nova Scotia school boards are worried about a looming teacher shortage." (*National Post*, 1999).

What does this shortage mean for beginning teachers? It means that you are embarking on a very exciting career in which there are greater and more varied job opportunities than in recent years. These include not only positions in your local community, but also overseas and at virtual schools!

Teaching Possibilities: Urban, Rural, and Northern

School boards in Canada have compiled information to track teacher shortage, recruitment, and retention, and have found that recent teacher education graduates are more interested in locating closer to cities than in rural school divisions. School boards in isolated geographical regions find it increasingly difficult to attract teachers. The highest concern about retaining beginning teachers was expressed by representatives from the Northwest Territories and Ontario school boards in a conference report (Canadian Teachers' Federation, 2000). The reasons for this vary, but include the avoidance of remoteness, fear of isolation, and inadequate housing. When possible, school boards offset this tendency with incentives, for example, supplementing living expenses, offering higher salaries, covering relocation expenses, developing housing, and enhancing professional development funds. Furthermore, school districts often institute special programs for new teachers, such as mentorship with seasoned teachers (Canadian Education Association, 1992; Ganzer, 2000; Rogers & Threatt, 2000).

Recruitment

Faculties of education are the most obvious sources for supplying new teachers. A few school boards also find that they can recruit through the pool of student teachers posted to their schools. Therefore it is advantageous for pre-service teachers to request that their practicum experience be in a school or district where they may wish to gain employment (Canadian Education Association, 1992).

Several areas of teacher expertise are in higher demand. They vary depending on the job market in competing occupations, but often include mathematics, science, technology, French, Native education, and fine arts, especially music. Aboriginal and other visible minority teachers are in constant demand as role models and to better reflect the diverse student population, especially in urban schools (Canadian Teachers' Federation, 2000).

International and Overseas Workplaces

"We live in an increasingly interdependent and rapidly changing world. Globalization in the cultural, economic, political and social spheres is reaching the farthest corners of Earth" (Kirkwood, 2001, p. 5). Globalization has great implications and presents many opportunities for teachers. There are numerous possibilities for new and seasoned teachers to work in overseas placements. These include international and American schools, international development agencies, organizations concerned with teaching English as a second or foreign language, and religious and government school systems (Travers & Lalonde, 2000). Many listings of international schools and Web sites give information on recruitment fairs in various parts of the country. You will see advertisements like this: "Seeking enthusiastic and dedicated educators who will play an integral part in fostering excellence and a sense of community within a student centered environment.... Benefits include tax-free salaries,... round-trip transportation,... housing,... health insurance, accident insurance, summer leave airfare, end-of-service award and moving-in allowance" (The American School of Kuwait. Retrieved March 18, 2003, from www.ask.edu.kw/jobs.html). Sounds wonderful! However, many teachers who have been suddenly transplanted abroad face an occupational disease—culture shock, which results from losing one's familiar signs of

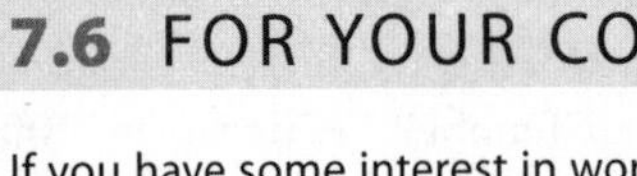

7.6 FOR YOUR CONSIDERATION

If you have some interest in working abroad, these Web sites may be useful:

European Council of International Schools: **www.ecis.org**
International Schools Services: **www.iss.edu**
Overseas Placement Services for Educators: **http://www.uni.edu**
Search Associates: **www.search-associates.com**
Placement Office: **http://educ.queensu.ca/~placment/int.html.**
The American School of Kuwait; **www.ask.edu.kw/jobs.html**
Association of American Schools in South America: **www.aassa.com**
CUSO: **www.cuso.org**
World University Service of Canada: **www.wusc.ca**
Canadian Crossroads International: **www.toronto.com/E/V/TORON/0012**
Canadian World Youth: **Cwy-jcm.org**
Volunteer Service Overseas: **www.vsocan.com**
Volunteer International Christian Service: **http://www.web.net/~interchg/96.html**
2Learn.ca: **www.2learn.ca/Profgrowth/uniqueoppelsewhere.html**
Learning Network Educational Services: **http://www.learning-network.org/teacherexchanges/otherprogramsandoptions.html**
York University: **http://www.edu.yorku.ca/InfoResources/TeachingOverseas.cfm**

social connection. Travers and Lalonde (2000) give several cautions and suggest that before accepting any position, "be sure that you have all possible information about working and living conditions. Be wise and research cultural features, political conditions, climate, diet, adjustment problems, the curriculum, etc. In other words, *know what you're getting into*" (p. 84). Do your homework—find out all you can about the country and culture to minimize effects of culture shock and the unknown.

Cyberspace: Virtual Instruction

How will computer technology, distance education, and virtual instruction affect the role of teaching? Some people believe virtual instruction signals the end of traditional education and fear that the need for teachers will disappear (Palloff & Pratt, 1999). What exactly is virtual instruction, or distance education? **Virtual instruction** has been seen as one of the most significant contributions to education in this new millennium. It takes place through computer-mediated communication, typically at a distance. "Exciting possibilities related to virtual instruction include an expansion of the range of courses and types of educational interactions available to learners" (Feyten & Nutta, 1999, p. 38). According to Palloff and Pratt (1999), "Electronic pedagogy does not advocate the elimination of faculty in the delivery of online courses" (p. 159).

What implications does the trend toward new technology in education have for you as a beginning teacher? Will it influence your role in the classroom and your relationship with your students? What do you believe you need to know and understand about virtual instruction and distance education? We will discuss the implication of technology on curriculum and course delivery in later chapters.

Minority Teachers

A group of people bound together by common traditions, values, and customs share a culture. They create their ever-changing worldview in values, tradition, and social and political relationships (Mullins, 2000). Canada has a distinct culture, however broad it may appear. Thiessen, Boscia, and Goodson (1996) believe that the fundamental purpose of the institution of schools is to pass on the values and traditions of society to the next generation formally, through textbooks and examinations, and informally, as demonstrated through routines and student–teacher relationships. If this is true, then what difficulty might this belief pose when the majority of the teachers in Canada (as well as the United States) are white, Christian, middleclass, and female?

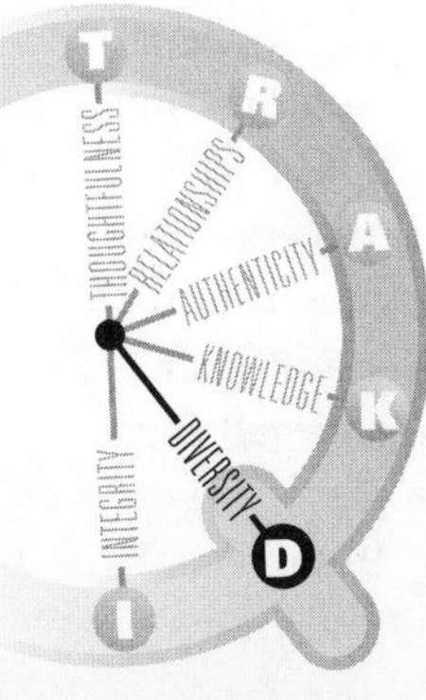

It has been well documented that many minority youth suffer from a school curriculum that does not match their experience because there are few visible minority teachers to serve as role models (Rettig & Khodavandi, 1998). The white, middle-class teaching force often has difficulty identifying with students from diverse backgrounds. Minority students need positive minority role models in their schools. They need visible minority teachers who understand their special requirements. These teachers can also assist Anglo-Saxon teachers in having a greater understanding of their diverse students. The Aboriginal student population in Canada is growing, especially in the western provinces. The Saskatchewan public school system projects that thirty percent or more of its student population will be of Aboriginal descent in the next ten years, but the number of Aboriginal people going into the profession does not reflect this percentage. This creates a challenge for the integration of Aboriginal culture into the school curriculum in addition to a staffing challenge (Canadian Teachers' Federation, 2000).

A curriculum developed to meet student needs would be beneficial, but Mullins (2000) suggests that we encourage "learning across cultures"—*across* defined as "to be understandable." Multicultural and anti-racist curricula and programs need to be developed, as we need to increase the number and proportion of racial and ethno-cultural minority teachers (Thiessen, Boscia, & Goodson 1996). It is imperative that educators seek to understand, and be understood by, their diverse student populations. What programs and curricula do you think need to be developed to encourage this understanding? We will look further at curriculum and curriculum delivery in later chapters.

Fewer minority than non-minority young people choose education as a career. Part of the reason may be the lack of minority teacher role models. Several minority teachers have suggested that "the novelty of visible minority teachers in their schools might contribute to educators questioning their legitimacy and seeing them as tokens" (Thiessen, Boscia, & Goodson, 1996, p. 163). Teacher education programs in post-secondary institutions, government policy makers, and senior school board administrators are looking at alternatives to increase the percentage of minority teachers in the schools. Some of the incentive programs include financial incentives such as scholarships and early recruitment involving parents (Solomon, 1997; Futrell, 1999; Haberman, 1989). What are your thoughts on this imbalance? Do you have any suggestions?

Women in Education

"Women came both early and late to education. From the beginning of human society it was woman's role to teach the girls what was required of them as members of society, from tribal rites to weaving, from child care to child training" (Shack, 1973, p. 47). Boys worked in the fields with their fathers or became clergymen or academics. Later, women took on the job of teacher when there was no one else to do it, often when men went off to war. The position came with low pay and low job security.

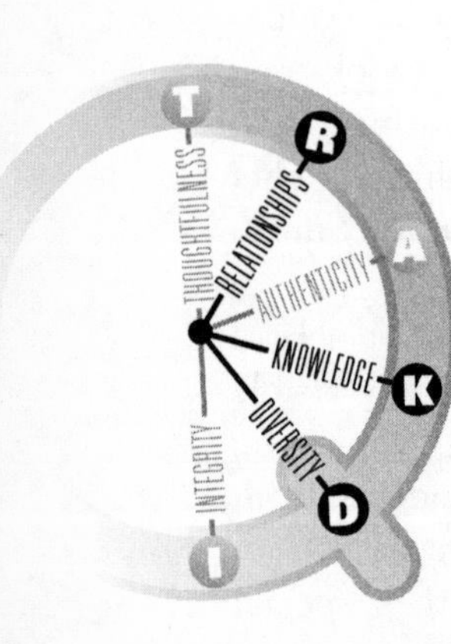

In the past half-century, women have made up the majority of the teaching force. Statistics Canada, in May 2001, reported the number of male teachers in Canada, in both elementary and secondary schools, at 107,630 and women teachers at 192,631. Seventy-seven percent of the administrators in elementary schools (in 1998) and 51 percent in the secondary schools are women (Benedict, 2000).

Benedict (2000) considers the increase in female administrators interesting as this is happening when the job of school administrator has become much more demanding. Some employers may feel that women's outside activities might negatively affect their work duties but a survey of Canadian managers considered the non-work activities of parenting, community service, and recreation to be of benefit to the job as they developed new skills and job enrichment (Jenkins, 1996). What do you think might be the difficulties women face in gaining leadership positions?

The Teaching Portfolio

An important consideration in career and professional development planning is the compiling of a teaching portfolio. This process and product will help beginning teachers as well as seasoned teachers in gaining employment or special positions.

A **teaching portfolio** is a document that details, in an organized way, a teacher's efforts and accomplishments. "Portfolios not only document teaching effectiveness but also provide opportunities for reflection, collegiality, and professional development" (Fahey & Fingon, 1997, p. 354). The portfolio can be either showcase (showing your best work and final drafts) or developmental, each approach involving different guidelines and a different purpose for construction. A developmental portfolio documents the teacher's professional growth over time. "Either way, one can use a portfolio to sell his or her skills and abilities. A portfolio can, therefore, be a very valuable tool in obtaining a teaching position" (Barry & Shannon, 1997, p. 322).

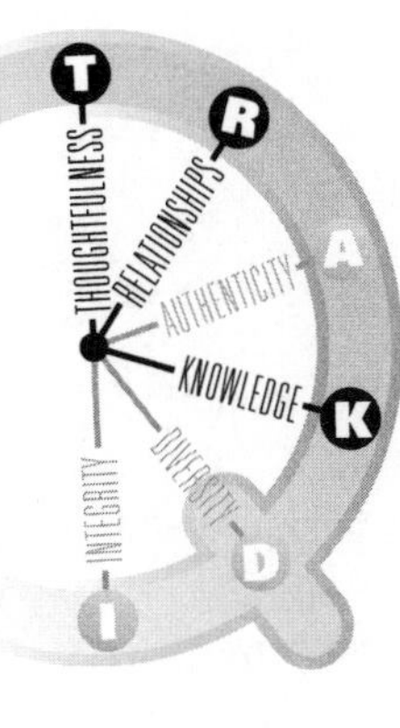

The portfolio usually includes information about a teacher's philosophy, methods, materials, participation in courses, workshops, and other professional development activities. It may also include evaluations from students, peers, and supervisors, as well as examples of students' work that concretely demonstrate learning. Although containing similar items, each person's portfolio represents the uniqueness of the individual who created it.

Portfolios are living documents that chart a teacher's growth and development. As new items are added, old ones can be discarded; as old goals are achieved, new ones take their place. Keeping a portfolio current becomes a process of continually reflecting on one's teaching and learning.

The portfolio is best contained in a generously sized three-ring binder because it provides security and flexibility. Materials can be organized into separate sections and labelled with tabs or section dividers. Items can easily be added or removed as needed.

Teaching portfolios can serve a number of purposes. They can help student teachers

- describe and document a growing body of work
- make visible some dimensions of teaching and learning that may have gone unnoticed

An example of a teaching portfolio.

7.7 FOR YOUR CONSIDERATION

Creating a teaching portfolio can be a valuable experience for both beginning and experienced teachers. It's an opportunity to take stock, to set goals, to reflect on what you've done and where you're going, to select your best work, and to present everything you've chosen in a colourful way.

What to Include in Your Teaching Portfolio

Essential Items

____ table of contents

____ a statement of your personal philosophy of teaching

____ a personal growth plan that includes your mission statement and your goals

____ your resumé, including employment, volunteer experience, and any other relevant experience

____ your education, including high school, education courses, and other post-secondary courses

____ a sample lesson plan you've developed

____ a written reflection on your learning from your journal on your teaching experiences

____ samples or photos of creative and technical work and abilities, fine arts projects, computer layout and design, etc.

____ photos showing your classroom and child-related activities, special interests, achievements, field trips, and other relevant experiences

____ a list of books about teaching you've enjoyed and found meaningful for teaching, and reasons why.

Other Suggestions

____ personal information on your leisure activities and interests, family, unique positions and experiences, etc.

____ medals or awards you've won, certificates you've earned, etc. in non-academic areas such as athletics, music, coaching, first aid, CPR, lifeguard, etc.

____ samples of work you've done: research or position papers, lesson plans, videos, creative writing, technical writing, computer disks, games you've created, and other artifacts

____ curriculum materials you've developed

____ bulletin board ideas and other forms of classroom displays

____ work that's been published or publicly recognized in some way

____ a list of your teacher role models and reasons for their influence

____ drawings of your ideas about what the perfect classroom is and an explanation of why

____ notes, cards, and thank you letters from students, teachers, etc.

____ list of references: the names, addresses, and phone numbers of people who can act as referees for you

____ a list of people who make up your network of contacts in the teaching field: co-operating teachers, principals, guest speakers in your classes, other contacts

____ letters of reference, recommendations, performance appraisals, and other forms of evaluation

____ a photo of yourself

(Source: From "Portfolio Checklist," by Carol Gerein, 1997 [unpublished classroom resource]. Reprinted with permission of the author.)

- demonstrate tangible, concrete evidence of their achievements, capabilities, and skills in teaching and learning
- improve their teaching and learning through the process of reflective writing and self-reflection
- present themselves and their accomplishments effectively in job interviews

The Pre-Service and New Teacher

Your pre-service practicum experience with a co-operating teacher may or may not be a positive experience, but you will have learned a great deal from all stakeholders on your journey toward becoming a certificated teacher. You may not believe it now, but you will not know everything you need to know when you graduate from a post-secondary school after four, five, or even six years of education. It is the authors' observation and personal experience that it is not uncommon that first-year teachers are placed in the least attractive schools in the district or that their teaching assignments don't quite match their course or grade-level expertise. This will cause some stress in your life. What are some of the ways you might assist yourself on your teacher journey? We have mentioned a few, which include collegiality, mentorship with a seasoned teacher, and lifelong learning. Several Web sites also specifically address the concerns of the beginning teacher. Here are three for your interest:

http://www.peaklearn.com
http://www.wsd1.org/PC_LMS/pf/new_teachers.htm
http://www.tcdsb.org/newteacherinduction/NewTeacherResources.html

Reflection and Perspective on the Chapter

We hope this chapter has helped you to consider your role in your chosen profession as a teacher—to think about your worldview of what a teacher does and needs to understand, and about your philosophical orientation.

A good teacher is thoughtful, constantly reflecting on his or her practice. Reflection can be *on* practice as discussed outside the classroom, as you might be doing now, as well as *in* practice. Reflection in practice is when teachers think about actions and decisions made at the time they are occurring in the classroom or school. Reflection on practice or teaching qualities for decision making and praxis involves the teacher's relationships, authenticity, integrity, thoughtfulness, and understanding of diversity. Many opportunities are available to new and seasoned teachers. Consider the well-publicized teacher shortage, aging workforce, globalization, and distance education. We hope you will start to develop your own teaching portfolio and find seasoned mentor–teachers to help you on your journey in becoming a teacher.

Key Terms

Suggested Further Reading

A. Travers and D. Lalonde. (2000). *What's Next? A Job Search Guide for Teachers*, 7th ed. Lakeside Publishing. This book gives teachers who are searching for international/overseas experiences advice and job search strategies.

Resources

A number of Web sites also specifically address the concerns of the beginning teacher:

http://www.peaklearn.com

http://www.ed.gov/pubs/firstyear/index.html

Canadian Education Association: http://www.acea.ca/english/publications.phtml

Canadian Teachers' Federation: http://www.ctf-fce.ca

Newsmagazine of the B.C. Teachers' Federation: http://www.bctf.ca/ezine

Canadian Teachers' Associations

Yukon Teachers' Association: http://www.yta.yk.ca

Northwest Territories Teachers' Association: http://www.nwtta.nt.ca

New Brunswick Teachers' Association: http://www.nbta.ca

Newfoundland and Labrador Teachers' Association: http://www.nlta.nf.ca

Nova Scotia Teachers Union: http://www.nstu.ca

Association Quebecoise de Pedagogie Collegiate: www.aqpc.qc.ca

Ontario Teachers' Federation: http://www.otffeo.on.ca

Elementary Teachers' Federation of Ontario: http://www.etfo.on.ca

The Ontario Secondary School Teachers' Federation: http://www.osstf.on.ca

The Manitoba Teachers' Society: http://www.mbteach.org

Saskatchewan Teachers' Federation: http://www.stf.sk.ca

The Alberta Teachers' Association: http://www.teachers.ab.ca

British Columbia Teachers' Federation: http://www.bctf.bc.ca

Chapter 8

Teaching

Creative teachers often forego the insistence upon clearcut behavioral objectives and predictable and measurable learning outcomes for the freedom to adjust and to explore new avenues with unpredictable learning outcomes. They realize there are multiple ways to teach and often watch for and develop teaching opportunities as they arise during class. Teachers who take advantage of the sudden appearance of a rainbow to shift the focus of the writing lesson, or who decide to combine the writing exercise with a science lesson on prisms, are exercising flexibility, not a lack of organization. (B.R.C. Barrell, 1995, in D.C. Jones, 1995, p. 28)

Chapter Focus

Teaching is successful when learning is the result. A teacher's task is to understand and work with learners in ways that motivate them to learn through invitations that appeal to interest, comprehension, and application. Teaching is a complex task that may, at first, seem relatively simple. Barrell reminds us that successful teaching is a constant search for ways to engage and motivate young people to learn. Teachers engaged in that search work from very definite theories and assumptions about teaching. Their worldview embraces a breadth of thinking that incorporates into teaching those things that children and youth believe to be important. It is what Duckworth (1996) would call an effort to understand the understanding of children.

This chapter will provide you with a sound foundation for your study of teaching.

Focus Questions

1. In what ways are power and control employed in the quest for learning in classrooms and to what extent is it of concern to you?

2. The way you define children has an awful lot to do with the way you work with them." (H. Levin, 1992, p. 20) What does this quotation mean to you?
3. How would you describe the difference between a teacher-centred learning environment and a student-centred learning environment?
4. In your quest to demonstrate effective teaching, in what ways is it necessary to exercise astute professional judgment?
5. Why is *teaching for transfer* a critical consideration in the learning process?
6. To what extent would it be useful to listen to the views of young people and to give them choices in their learning?

Assumptions about Teaching

The following story describes a mathematics class in which the teacher responds to students in a very definite way. How does he "understand the understanding" of young people? Do you see any "rainbows" in his lesson?

> Jim Schmidt enjoys mathematics. He had been a top student in school and his prowess continued when he attended university. Jim has taught high school now for fifteen years. Mathematics is his passion, and he expects his students to feel the same way. He controls learning from his favourite place on the elevated platform in front of the board, from where he can see all his students clearly. Lessons for Jim follow a predictable pattern. He expects students to settle down quickly so that he can begin his lecture. Students are expected to make their own notes. This practice usually occupies the first twenty-five minutes of every class. Following the lecture, he assigns questions from the end of the chapter to determine whether students have learned what Jim has taught. Often, toward the end of his class, he will assign problems to complement what he has covered in his introductory lecture.
>
> Jim runs tightly structured classes. He expects students to adhere to his lesson plans. Questions are entertained for a limited time, but they will not be allowed to interfere with the planned content coverage and completion of Jim's carefully planned lessons.

Think about Jim Schmidt and consider the following questions. (These questions are not asked for discussion purposes, but rather to encourage you to contemplate your assumptions about teaching.)

- What would Jim take into consideration when designing lessons?
- To what extent do you think Jim would be interested in finding out what his students already know about what is to be taught?
- Would you expect this teacher to attempt to understand differences in young people?
- Would you expect Jim to attempt to understand the understanding of students in his class?
- What kinds of exams and tests would you expect Jim to set?

Now, consider the following description of a teaching situation.

> "Hi, Jeremy, nice shirt!" "Noriko, how was the movie last night?" "Gretchen, you never said you were getting your hair cut. I really like it."
>
> As young people enter Sharon Kolchinsky's room to begin their day, each is greeted with some personal comment. Sharon takes an interest in all her students, and these expressions at the beginning of each day are her way of making connections with them.
>
> Sharon's classes usually begin with students sitting around her as she introduces the lesson and shares with them what it will be all about. She asks them what they know about the topic. She tries to find out what interests them. Above all, she asks them how they would like to learn about the topic. As Sharon listens to the students she is processing their input and deciding how she will begin the class so that the contributions of the students are taken into account. She is thinking about the students' needs, their ability levels, learning styles, and preferences, and throughout she is making professional judgments about how to proceed with the lesson preparations she put together the night before.

Consider, again, the questions posed after the first teaching scenario. What assumptions about teaching would a person likely hold if this second description resonated strongly with his or her beliefs?

Admittedly, the two teaching descriptions above are quite different, polar opposites perhaps. At this early stage in your pre-service preparation you might find yourself somewhere between the two, agreeing with some points and disagreeing with others. Thinking in this way helps to reinforce the point that good teaching is always a matter of sound professional judgment. A good teacher must always understand what needs to be taught, or what children are expected to learn. In Canada, provincial governments have jurisdiction over education, and each province and territory mandates particular learning requirements for school curricula. The question of how to meet these requirements, however, is the responsibility of a teacher, and in this regard good teaching engages what we term two constancies. Given that a teacher's prime responsibility is to effect successful learning, it follows that a first task is to understand the people who are to be engaged in learning, and how they learn best. On the basis of this analysis, a teacher then applies professional judgments to determine how best to engage learners in learning. A framework for the constancies of teaching may be seen in Figure 8.1.

Figure 8.1
Two Constancies of Teaching

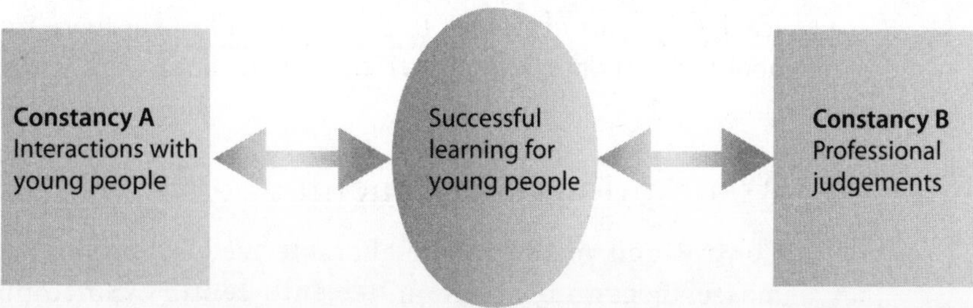

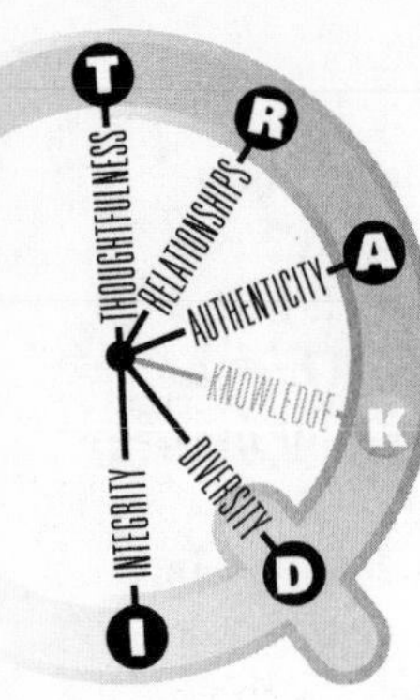

Frameworks of this kind are always arguable. They are visual representations of thoughts that mean something to the people who create them. In the case of the two constancies, the authors offer a framework for you to think about, perhaps even debate. Why do you think we use the word *interaction* in Constancy A? Think about the teaching qualities detailed in Chapter 2. How important is it to know the students who are to be learning with you? To what extent are relationships critical to successful learning? Is an understanding of authenticity important? Does diversity assume any significance in successful teaching? Integrity surely demands consideration, but to what extent and how? Do you agree that thoughtfulness should pervade everything that you do?

Constancy B uses the term *professional judgment* to invite consideration of the commonplaces of knowledge. A practising teacher must call upon many branches of professional knowledge to successfully engage young people in learning. (In this book, we provide you with a place to begin by identifying five commonplaces of knowledge with which to start: learners and learning; teachers and teaching; schools and classrooms; curriculum and subject matter; society, culture and history.) The focus of this chapter will be on foundations of thought for effective teaching, rather than the more specific "how to" knowledge required for lesson planning in subject areas, which we discuss later in Chapter 11 (Curriculum).

The key thing to remember is that, regardless of the professional knowledge to which you will be exposed, it is the judgments you make on how and why the knowledge is applied that are most important. In short, the level of thoughtfulness you apply to knowledge is what will often determine your success as a teacher. It is quite possible to gain an impression that you will be a good teacher because you are "good with children." Simply being around teachers in school settings allows a prospective teacher to observe behaviours and activities that appear to be successful in keeping children busy and occupied. When these observations are coupled with being "good with children" it is easy to be left with the impression that school, more than a university teacher preparation program, is where real teacher education happens. Courses may be viewed merely as requirements to be checked off for a degree before one can obtain a permanent job in school. Think about this attitude and ask yourself what assumptions it holds about learning to be a teacher. What implications does the attitude hold for the whole question of thoughtfulness? How would you anticipate those who hold that attitude to feel about ongoing professional development once they are in teaching positions? Does this serve students and the profession well?

The iceberg analogy shown in Figure 8.2 serves to remind us that a tremendous amount of unobservable behaviour goes into a teacher's decisions and actions in a classroom. Good teaching may be viewed as simply a series of activities that seem to work. An observer walking into a classroom sees children engaged in their work or attentively listening to a teacher and perhaps thinks, "Yes, this is how to be a good teacher." Is this accurate? In the context of our iceberg model, what do you think about as you observe an experienced teacher at work with children?

Assumptions and Teaching

Control and management characterized schooling when education for the masses began in the late nineteenth century. Since the institution was new,

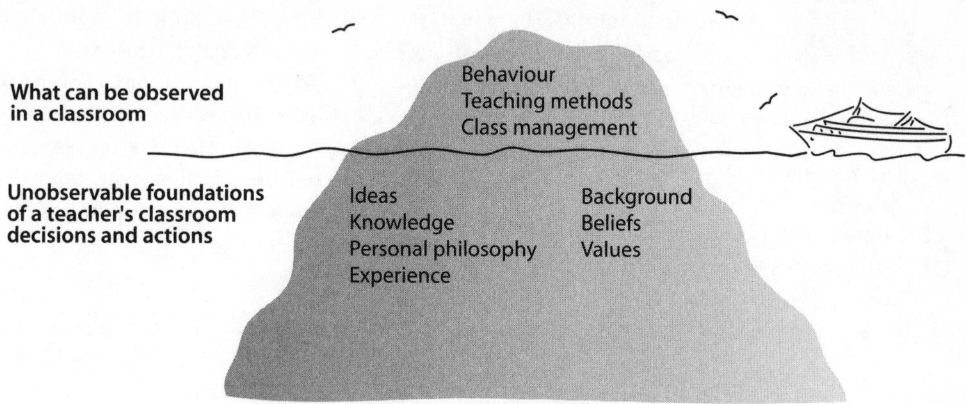

Figure 8.2 *Unobservable Dimensions of Teaching*

administrators turned to conventional wisdom of the times for guidance, liberally employing models from industry in the organization and administration of schools (Taylor, 1911). The military had more than a little influence in the methods of learning. These early, impressionable years established schooling on a path that many would argue is still quite evident today. The vestiges of the early influences on schools are manifested in power and hierarchy. We will discuss these matters in later sections of the book, but we ask you now to think about assumptions. Sarason (1990) advises that "the school and school system generally are not comprehensible unless you flush out the power relationships that inform and control the behavior of everyone in these settings" (p. 7).

Below are five assumptions evident in schools today that reflect the power and hierarchy mentioned above. We invite you to think about the degree to which they are evident in the teaching you have experienced.

1) The organization of young people in schools is characterized by selecting and sorting.
2) Conformity and uniformity are prominent practices in classrooms.
3) A narrow range of assessment practices is used in schools.
4) Bureaucratic control is favoured over moral control.
5) The role of teachers as donors of content and knowledge is still quite prevalent in classrooms.

Discuss these assumptions with your classmates. Listen to the views of others and try to gain some perspective on the matter. Remember, if your schooling experience has been in only a few schools in a settled community, then your perspective may be limited.

Further to this work on assumptions, let us pay some attention to practical situations that may be readily observed in most classrooms. Consider the following teaching strategies and ask what assumptions they suggest.

8.1 FOR YOUR CONSIDERATION

What assumptions do you hold about teaching, based on a) your experience in elementary school, and b) your experience in secondary school?

1. Do you detect any notable differences in your responses to a) and b)?
2. Should we expect there to be differences?
3. What assumptions seem to describe hierarchy in schools and classrooms?
4. What assumptions seem to describe power in schools and classrooms?
5. What assumptions about teaching did Jim Schmidt and Sharon Kolchinksy hold? Think back to earlier chapters on learners and learning and decide whether you would challenge Jim and Sharon on any assumptions they appear to hold.

- All students work on the same text questions.
- Students work in co-operative groups.
- A whole class learns in the same way.
- Students demonstrate their learning through methods other than pencil and paper instruments.
- The teacher demands that students may raise their hands if they wish to ask questions about a class assignment.
- Students have some genuine control over their learning and have opportunities to make their own choices.

For each example, try to determine the underlying assumptions about learners and learning. Refer to the iceberg model (Figure 8.2), and ask yourself what would be the prime motivations of a teacher employing these activities? To what extent are the two constancies evident in the teacher's behaviour?

Power and Control in Teaching

Teachers are, without question, in positions of authority. They are responsible for responding to the learning needs of young people in classrooms that are orderly, efficient, and safe. The question of power and control is not about whether teachers have it, but rather how they use it in the best interests of learning. Nearly every matter that is discussed about successful teaching should be grounded in knowledge about learners and learning. Teaching decisions are based on judgments about what we anticipate learners will learn. How we use power and control then, should be rooted in what we anticipate children will learn. From actions as varied as chastising a class for inappropriate behaviour to setting on-task requirements in co-operative group work, the teaching behaviour should reflect what we anticipate the learners will learn. Let us examine a story from the classroom to illustrate different approaches to power and control in teaching.

> Sven Anderson's Grade 8 class was entering his wood shop for the start of their double period. Sven knew, from his years of experience, that Grade 8 young-

sters are unpredictable, and he was expecting difficulties this particular afternoon. Sure enough, before he had a chance to say anything, three students were acting up in a far corner of the room. One boy was menacing two others with the hose from a Shopvac. They knew Anderson didn't allow this kind of behaviour, but as usual, they didn't think. Sven bellowed at the boys, "Will you idiots put the hose down and get your brainless heads outside the shop door until I have time to see you? I suppose you left your brains at home again." His voice dripping with sarcasm and put-downs, Anderson dealt with the boys swiftly.

At the sound of his booming voice, a hush fell over the room, lasting long enough for him to continue his tirade at the class in an effort to ensure that the rest of the afternoon ran smoothly.

Once the class was working, he shouted at the delinquents and dispatched them to the office for engaging in dangerous behaviour in his shop.

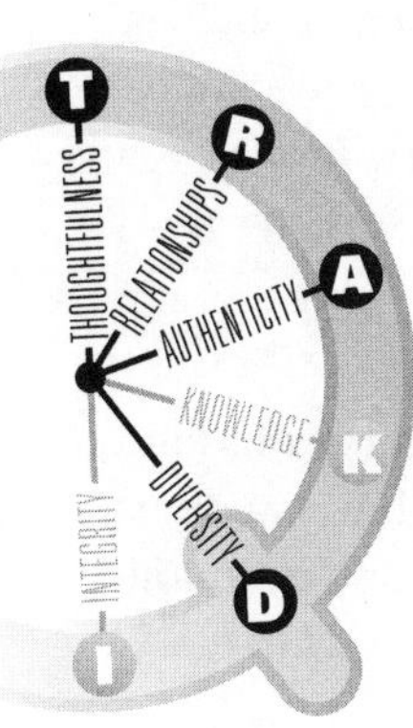

Clearly Sven's teaching style involved a certain use of power and control. What do you think the boys learned from the way Sven treated them? What role did Sven expect the principal to play once the boys reached her office? Do you have any predictions about the remainder of Sven's afternoon shop class? Think about the teaching qualities from Chapter 2. To what extent does he reflect upon the qualities and apply them in the course of his work with students? From which particular qualities could Sven benefit?

Sven Anderson's teaching style is based on power and control and relies heavily on *making* and *telling* his students what to do. Young people who experience this form of teaching have little or no voice in their learning; the teacher is the ultimate authority.

To explore this further, it is necessary to revisit the chapters on the learner and learning. When students are constantly being told what to do, what do you anticipate the outcome to be? Moffett (1994) speaks rather bluntly about this institutional tendency toward power and control: "Years of not being allowed to relate with humanness in class have taught apathy and alienation. Years of being herded, prodded, goaded, ordered, and otherwise manipulated have taught passivity and fatalism" (p. 57). This statement is extreme but worth thinking about. Is Moffett off the mark, or do you think he has grounds for such a strong comment? He further states, on a more benign note, that "making people learn, and making them learn certain things in certain ways, teaches them to abide by decisions from above, instead of learning to think for themselves" (p. 6). This last comment is perhaps more helpful, from a teaching point of view. Young people learn from the ways in which they are treated. McNeil (1988) extends this point somewhat with her comment that,

> ...when the school's organization becomes centered on managing and controlling, teachers and students take school less seriously. They fall into a ritual of teaching and learning that tends toward minimal standards and minimal effort. This sets off a vicious cycle. As students disengage from enthusiastic involvement in the learning process, administrators often see the disengagement as a control problem. They then increase their attention to managing students and teachers rather than supporting their instructional purpose. (p. xi)

It is unfair, of course, to make blanket judgments about schools. Wonderful teachers in many schools are doing wonderful things for learners. It is interesting, however, to consider the impact of too much control. Think about your own school experiences. Do you recall examples of high levels of control from teachers? What kinds of classes did these teachers have to deal with? What were the students learning? Why do teachers exercise control anyway?

Control and power are evident in many forms. We have discussed authoritarian teachers such as Sven Anderson and Jim Schmidt, who operate from a base of power.

Now consider some uses of power and control that appear to be more benign. Teachers often use these behaviours in their teaching:

> Students are compelled to learn required work with intimidating remarks such as, "This is worth 30% on the report card," "Do this tonight or you will face a detention," "If this isn't done by tomorrow you will lose 10%," "If this work isn't finished you will stay in for recess," "Do you want to miss phys. ed.?" and so on. (Waldron et al., 1999, p. 38)

What kind of learning would students experience from a steady diet of this kind of comment? Where is the line drawn between a teacher's efforts to have students become responsible, to meet their learning obligations, and coercion and intimidation? Kohn (1993) provides insight into these behaviours when he asks us to

> ... consider the conventional response when something goes wrong (as determined, of course, by the adults). Are two children creating a commotion instead of sitting quietly? Separate them. Have the desks become repositories for used chewing gum? Ban the stuff. Do students come to class without having done the reading? Hit them with a pop quiz. Again and again the favourite motto of teachers and administrators seems to be, "reach for the coercion," rather than engaging children in a conversation about the underlying causes of what is happening and working together to negotiate a solution. (p. 10)

Do you think Kohn is overstating the case? Think back to our discussions in previous chapters on learners and learning, and engage in some personal professional judgment. Is he being unreasonable? Overgeneralizing?

Looking at the negative perspective of power and control in teaching perhaps has caused you to experience some dissonance in your views about learning and teaching. To what extent do power and control, as discussed to this point, enter into the assumptions you hold about teaching? How do the teaching qualities fare as you reflect upon your prior knowledge and assumptions about teaching?

Teachers, then, have power as part of their authority. It comes with the territory, one might say. Let's revisit the question, What do you anticipate young people will learn from what you do in the practice of teaching? A response to this question must entail professional judgments about professional knowledge. Let us rephrase the question, What do I hope young people will be learning, as I respond to their needs in the practice of my teaching? We discussed Mr. Anderson and his methods. We now ask you to think about Lorenzo Sanchez, in the following scenario:

> Lorenzo was enthusiastic about teaching. He wanted the best for his children. On this Friday morning as they arrived at school, he was contemplating the class preparations he had made the previous evening. He greeted the children as they entered and wandered around the room, chatting with individuals and groups as they settled into their workspaces. "They seem a little subdued this morning," he thought. "I wonder how my preparations for discussion will fare in my language arts lesson." The weather was very oppressive that morning—high humidity and an incessant drizzle from an overcast sky. "Perhaps I should ask the children how they are feeling this morning."
>
> So Lorenzo drew four faces on the board, from very happy to a little sad. "Who feels a bit like this face this morning?" he asked the class. He went through the faces, gaining an impression from the class of how they felt that morning. He modified his preparations to include more kinesthetic tasks and informal group conversations. Lorenzo believed that to continue with his original preparations would likely have resulted in his "fighting" the class. He might well have found himself trying to *make* the children learn and this was anathema to his personal philosophy of teaching. Instead, he tried to respect the humanness of his children through being sensitive to their feelings, but always being mindful of his professional teaching obligations.

How do you feel about Lorenzo and his attitude to the learners in his class? What was motivating Lorenzo as he interacted with the students when they were entering his classroom? What would you have observed if you had been a fly on the wall? Think back to our iceberg model and ponder the below-the-surface decisions and actions in which teachers engage.

- What were Lorenzo's decisions and actions?
- In what ways was Lorenzo using power and control?
- What differences do you note between Lorenzo's use of power and control and that of Sven Anderson in the earlier scenario?

Empowerment and Learning

Empowerment is the act or process of bestowing power on others. It is like sharing power. Another word often used to describe this action is devolution. When power is devolved, it is moved from one source to another. The authority that teachers have bestowed upon them has many facets, but its use in learning contexts has significant implications for the learner.

> Empowerment concerns the learner's need to be active in his or her own education. For this to occur, educators must have a fundamental belief in the learner's ability to learn. Armed with this belief, this faith in the students' capacity to understand that

> which relates directly to their lives, teachers move from directing to facilitating, from talking to listening, from doing to observing. School leaders, in turn, must think less about administrative efficiency and more about student learning, instructional facilitation and long-term change. (Freire, 1988, pp. 63–64)

The primary question is, once again, What do we anticipate children will learn? The answer falls within a number of contexts, but of great significance will be a teacher's personal philosophy of education. Notions of empowerment, of sharing power, invite consideration of learning such as responsibility, ownership, independence, decision making, and co-operation. The skills and abilities to acquire these competencies require young people to take some control of their own learning. It is difficult for a child to learn responsibility unless she is allowed to be responsible. The same may be said of independence, decision making, and ownership. A teacher must let go, give up some control, so that a youngster is able to experience these characteristics in unfettered ways. Young people do not learn well within the unrealistic constraints of another person's opinions. This does not mean an absence of guidance. As adults we wouldn't allow children to decide to play in traffic, for example, because it is potentially life threatening.

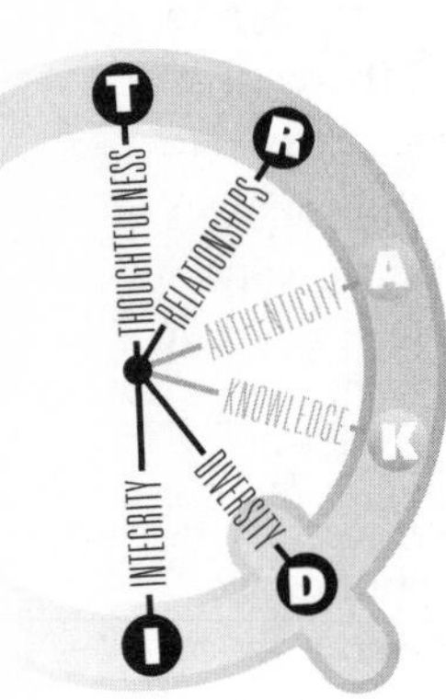

In concluding this section we are reminded of the remarks of one Grade7 girl: "I think I'm a pretty good learner, but I could learn a whole lot better if my teachers would move over a little" (Stacy, quoted in L. Smith & Johnson, 1993, p. 18). We could do worse than listen to the request of this young woman. We could learn a great deal from thinking deeply about the concept of "moving over."

Defining Learners

You will notice that we use the term *young people* quite frequently in this book. Why would we not simply use the term *student*? Our emphasis is on the word *people*. Student is a role that young people fill. A role is particular to the performance of a specific function. Admittedly you are still a student even when you are out socializing with friends on weekends, but during these times you are not fulfilling the role of a student. However, in whatever role you fill in life, you are always a person, a human being with all the attendant human needs. Think of the implications of a teacher who sees a class of thirty students, and another teacher who sees a class of thirty people. Sven Anderson's disposition toward his Grade 8 class would serve as an interesting case study in this regard. How did he approach his class? Was he concerned in any way with their feelings, emotions, attitudes, and developmental needs? Now turn your thoughts to Jim Schmidt. He is a different kind of teacher, perhaps, but how does his approach to teaching define his class of youngsters? What is important for him? How do Sven and Jim define the learners in their classes?

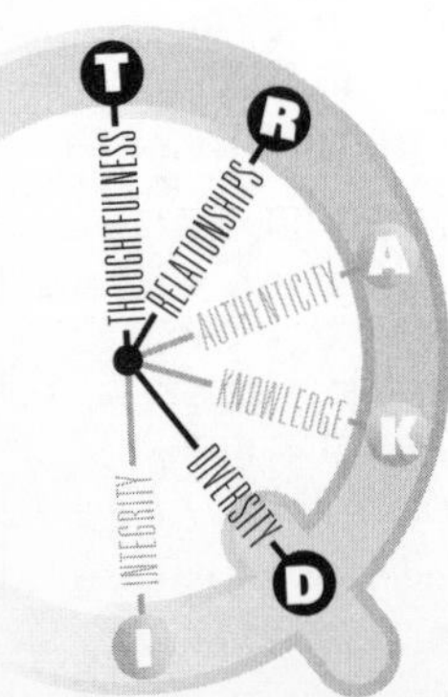

Clearly, Sharon and Lorenzo present different perspectives. These two teachers display much more attention to human qualities in youngsters. Was Sharon wasting valuable teaching time as she greeted her class? Could a similar question be asked of the time she spent with the children sitting around on the floor asking them questions to determine their prior knowledge and experience? What is your opinion about the way Lorenzo adapted his lesson on the basis of how he believed the children were feeling? Isn't it a child's responsibility to learn in school? Shouldn't children get on with what a teacher requires them to do? Was Lorenzo being too soft with his class?

Teaching is a human endeavour. People are complex beings with constantly changing feelings, emotions, and needs. As adults we are expected to get on with our work and do what our employers require of us, but don't we sometimes perform less well when we are "under the weather" or feeling some kind of stress? We are simply not able to leave our personal difficulties at our workplace door. How does this relate to learners in school? Should they be expected to leave their personal difficulties and human needs at the school entrance?

Young people are in school to learn. Your task, as a teacher, is to engage children in learning. Can you make them learn? Can you use your power and authority to tell them to learn? The nature of your students is that of growing, developing, maturing young people who are learning about their world. They are trying to make sense of their world and to learn the interpersonal and intrapersonal skills of socialization. They seek models for emulation and guidance. To what extent should your teaching respect and attend to these human needs? To some extent, the responses you give to this question will determine how you define people in your classes.

To conclude our discussion about defining learners, we invite you to respond to the following questions and ask yourself not only how you define learners, but also what this definition implies for your teaching.

- To what extent should young people be respected and understood as human beings in schools?
- Do our learning environments offer a moral context that promotes personal ownership?
- Do teachers provide opportunities for young people to experience authentic responsibility?
- How do we understand teachers and students as co-learners within a context of the social construction of knowledge and meaning (see our discussion of constructivism in Chapter 5, pp. 83–85)?
- Are young people provided with an active voice in decisions about learning and life?
- To what extent do we give young people control over learning choices to satisfy the need for intrinsic motivation?
- How do we understand and take into consideration the importance of a young person's intention? (Waldron et al., 1999, p. 58)

H. Levin (1992) believes that "the way you define children has an awful lot to do with the way you work with them" (p. 20). Teaching is working with young people, it is responding to their learning needs. How, then, do you define young people in ways that will allow you to work with them to successfully meet their learning needs?

Teaching Approaches

We have considered power and control in teaching, and the importance of defining young people. Let us broaden the discussion to look at ways of approaching the practice of teaching. A generalization we are confidently able to make is that successful teaching results in successful learning for young people. The goal for a teacher, then, is to create external conditions within which successful learning might take place. If we begin this discussion in broad terms we may more effectively bring the understanding of teaching to more practical considerations.

There are two broad understandings of teaching that may be described as direct teaching and indirect teaching.

Direct Teaching

In **direct teaching** a teacher is responding to the entire class. A teacher, usually at the front of a classroom, is talking, explaining, showing, giving seat-work, and generally controlling the classroom activity. Any interaction between teacher and students is usually in the form of questions directed by the teacher to students who indicate they would like to give answers. Direct teaching relies heavily on explanations, examples, review, and practice. The teacher is the main source of information, with students' contributions accepted only when they are requested. In short, direct teaching is centred on the teacher.

Typically, then, direct teaching may be used for presenting and structuring new content and guiding student practice. Also, it may be useful for the introduction of new skills, the review of previous work and to provide feedback and correction.

Indirect Teaching

Learning through **indirect teaching** emanates largely from young people in a class. A teacher establishes internal cognitive and psychological conditions with-

In direct teaching the teacher is in control of classroom activity—any interaction between student and teacher is controlled by the teacher. The student teaching her peers in the photo shown on the left is an example of direct teaching. Indirect teaching means the teacher acts as a guide to learning rather than controlling the process. The classroom in the photo on the right depicts an indirect teaching scenario.

in a learning environment to facilitate learning. Young people then engage in a variety of learning experiences based on inquiry, problem solving, investigation, and discovery. There is rarely a single best answer to a question. Instead, indirect teaching deals with concepts, patterns, and abstractions, leading to further questions and learning. The teacher motivates and guides young people to explore learning possibilities through the use of questions and challenges to guide the search and discovery process. Prior knowledge plays a significant role in indirect forms of learning and teaching.

Reflection on Teaching Dispositions

All teachers have certain dispositions toward their practice based on assumptions, personality, personal persuasion, and professional knowledge. Whatever the disposition, the approach to teaching should be based on a professional judgment regarding the best way to meet the learning needs of young people. We ask you to recall what you read in Chapters 5, 6, and 7 about learners and learning. Pay particular attention to the philosophical orientations to teaching in Chapter 7. With this information in mind, what disposition toward teaching would be most helpful for you to promote learning?

8.2 FOR YOUR CONSIDERATION

You are responsible for teaching social studies to a Grade 6 class, and you will have nine forty-minute periods in which to study urban planning.

- How would you begin to prepare for these classes?
- What would you think about first?
- When your preparations were completed, how would you begin your class?

Be prepared to give reasons for whatever decisions you make.

Discuss the above in groups. When the group discussion is completed, see how the group feels about the disposition of each person toward teaching, in the context of this discussion.

Learner-Focused Approaches to Teaching

Teachers who may be described as **learner-focused** tend to keep the nature and needs of people to the fore when preparing for teaching. Sharon and Lorenzo would be considered very learner-focused teachers. Both give a great deal of attention to Teaching Constancy A (Figure 8.1), and both would see great value in all the teaching qualities.

Learner-focused teachers begin preparations for learning by reflecting on the people they are to engage in learning. What is the nature of the learners? What do I know about them? How do they learn best? What skills do they need to learn? What do they already know? Throughout this reflective process, a learner-focused teacher would, as much as is possible given the large numbers of students often placed in a class, consider the individual needs of learners.

Teacher-Focused Approaches to Teaching

In a **teacher-focused approach** a teacher is focused primarily on deciding what is to be taught and what is to be done by a class. The teacher, exclusively, decides what will take place in the classroom and students will experience the lesson plan as constructed by the teacher. You may also see the term expressed as *teacher/subject-focused* because teachers who tend not to give due consideration to the nature and needs of students focus heavily on the subject they are teaching. It is not overstating the case to suggest that teacher-focused teaching tends to give little or no consideration to diversity in student needs and interests. To what extent would a teacher-focused person respect the teaching qualities from Chapter 2?

Reflection on "Focus" in Teaching

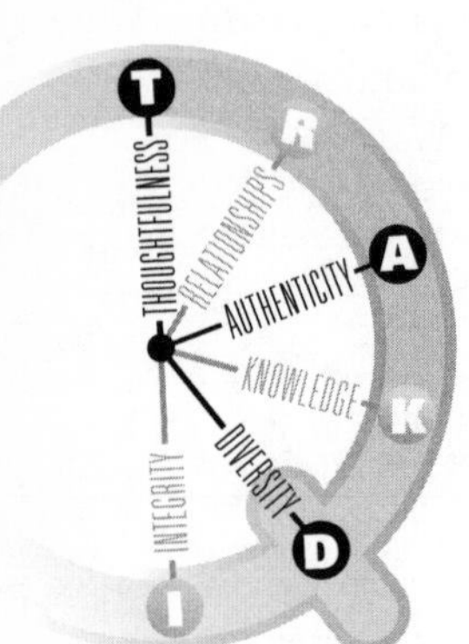

If you engaged in class debate around these teaching approaches, you know that teachers are never easily categorized. Just as young people are diverse, so are teachers. Our questions should focus not so much on labels as on reasons why teachers choose to teach as they do. Consider, again, the two constancies from Figure 8.1 and the learner/teacher-focused discussion to gain some perspective. To what extent should Constancy A be a factor in a teacher's practice? Should there be any difference in practice between a primary school teacher and a high school teacher? Remember our earlier exhortation that teaching is successful when successful learning is the result. What conditions should a teacher try to create to effect successful learning? You may have heard the expression "You cannot create a silk purse out of a sow's ear." Young people are not "sows' ears," but they can be "silk purses." A teacher has the task of discovering in young people those qualities that can produce a silk purse. How would a teacher begin to approach this teaching task? In Table 8.1 we offer a number of topics for you to consider and ask you to think about the degree to which each should be important to teaching a class of young people.

Table 8.1 Some Important Considerations for Teaching Effectively

A. Nature of young people:	■ Developmental characteristics ■ Attitudes and social traits
B. Learning styles and preferences of young people	
C. Conditions for learning:	■ Seating ■ Use of space and time ■ Access to resources ■ Learner choice? Voice?
D. Flexibility in teaching:	■ Rigidity of lesson ■ Assessment of learning and possibility of modifications
E. Teaching methods and styles:	■ Engagement in learning ■ Extrinsic/intrinsic motivation ■ Direct/indirect
F. Other?	

We include a box for "other" so that you can include your own ideas about what things are essential to the teaching process. When you have finished reading the list of important considerations, perhaps groups could engage in an exercise to rate them. Rate each item in Table 8.1 according to importance on a scale of 1 to 5, with five being "essential" and one being "least important." Explain the rationale for a particular rating.

Such an activity will help group members determine their own dispositions. Is the group disposed toward more direct teaching, a more teacher-focused approach? Are some groups disposed more toward a learner-focused position, with an orientation toward more indirect approaches to teaching? How are power and control evident in the group deliberations and rating? Whatever the outcome, be very clear on the reasons why.

8.3 FOR YOUR CONSIDERATION

Take a poll among members of your group. How many people are attracted to the term "teacher-focused," how many to "learner-focused," and how many to "child-focused"? How many would like to come up with another term?

1. Divide into smaller groups according to the poll results. In these groups, discuss reasons for the way you feel. Arrive at a consensus for your group's position.
2. Move back into a whole-class context and debate the issue, with spokespersons for each group presenting their position. (Remember to establish some basic rules for debate to maintain some sort of order. Control is not all bad!)

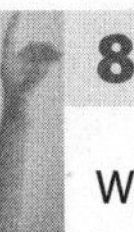

8.4 FOR YOUR CONSIDERATION

We have discussed the characteristics of student-focused and teacher/subject-focused training, as well as the nature of direct and indirect teaching. Two considerations we would like you to think about are power and control. Toward which end of the continuum, and within which philosophical orientations to teaching, would teachers tend to wield power, and at which end would they tend to share power, or empower? We invite you to decide this matter, and we urge you to be clear about the reasons for your beliefs. In groups, and using what you have learned, place the philosophical orientations to teaching on the continuum below, according to the degree to which they reflect student- or teacher/subject-focused tendencies.

Learner-focused ———————————————— Teacher/subject-focused

a b c d e f

- Each group should spend some time identifying their reasons for the position of each philosophical orientation on the continuum. Write your group's reasons on a large piece of chart paper and post them on the classroom wall.
- Each group should then be prepared to defend their reasons for placement order, and address questions from the larger group.

Understanding Teaching for Successful Learning

The primary goal of a teacher is to create conditions in which young people can learn successfully. Think back to our discussion so far in this chapter. How do you define children? What are your beliefs about power and control? How would you respond to Constancy A in Figure 8.1? Consider, now, a further refinement of the ways we might view learning and teaching.

Transmissive Teaching

Transmission is a process of moving information from one source to another. In **transmissive teaching,** this means moving information from one source (the teacher) to another source (the student). You may hear the term *transmission model* applied to this form of teaching. This means information and knowledge are transmitted-passed along-from a teacher to a student in what is, essentially, a one-way process. Teachers working in this way may see themselves as experts. How do you think teachers who use transmissive teaching would define students? Some terms that have been used to describe students receiving this form of teaching are *blank slate* and *empty vessel.*

8.5 FOR YOUR CONSIDERATION

If you used the term *blank slate* in reference to students you were teaching, what would you mean?

1. Working in groups, compose a one-sentence definition of the term *blank slate* on which your group agrees, and write it down on a piece of paper.
2. When all groups have written their responses, act out a one- to two-minute performance for the rest of the class that demonstrates the meaning you have agreed on.
3. Discuss the points in each performance that highlight the essential meaning of the term *blank slate.*

Your understanding of *blank slate* will also help you to understand the term *empty vessel.* Teachers engaging in transmissive forms of teaching often view their students as empty of knowledge, ignorant about that which is to be taught. They believe the student's role, therefore, is to receive the transmitted knowledge so that their minds may be filled from the transmission process.

In a transmissive approach to teaching, teachers are actively doing all the work to provide instruction. They decide what people will learn and how it will be taught. Transmissive teaching, as a rule, does not encourage students to have any say in their learning. Think back to the assumptions presented in Chapter 3. Also, reflect upon the previous sections in this chapter on assumptions in teaching and power and control in teaching. If you used a transmissive approach as a dominant form of teaching, what assumptions would you be demonstrating about young people and learning?

On the other hand, are there useful possibilities for transmissive teaching? What if you were introducing a new skill to your class, say, how to use a pencil sharpener in Grade 1? Perhaps you are introducing to Grade 10 students a new concept on castles as defensive weapons in European history. Can you think of other examples where transmissive teaching can be useful?

We must constantly remind ourselves that teaching is never a black-and-white process. Our reasons and justifications for using certain approaches come from professional judgments based on the needs of our learners. Just because teachers present something to the whole class does not necessarily mean they consider their students to be blank slates or empty vessels. Teachers may well be trying to determine prior knowledge and experience, but at some point see the value in transmitting knowledge through a whole-class presentation. Transmissive teaching as a dominant form of teaching raises many questions. However, we hope you will be able to articulate these questions as you engage in thoughtful inquiry into successful teaching and learning.

8.6 FOR YOUR CONSIDERATION

We invite you to conduct a small-group activity in which you carry out a PMI analysis of transmissive teaching, which views students as empty vessels to be filled. Refer to previous chapters of the book, particularly to Chapters 2 and 3, to help you complete this activity. Jot down points for each of the following categories:

P stands for Plus, or positive things.

M stands for Minus, or negative things.

I stands for Interesting: things neither positive nor negative, but which could have interesting possibilities.

After time for discussion, each group should take what it considers to be the strongest point from each category and write it on a master list on the board at the front of the class.

The master list should serve as an interesting catalyst for discussion, debate, and conversation.

Transactional Teaching

A transaction is a communication between two or more sources. This is usually an active process with a certain amount of free-flow movement between the parties. **Transactional teaching** is an active process in which information is communicated in free-flow processes, though direct teaching and directed learning are the norm. The teacher tends to exercise high degrees of control over student learning, though some ventures into indirect approaches are acknowledged. In teaching, this free flow is not only between teacher and student, but also among students. In other words, young people are learning from each other.

Teachers working within the transactional mode of teaching make use of transmissive methods, but also make use of approaches to learning that involve and engage students. Once again, it is a matter of degree. A teacher employing transactional methods communicates skills, concepts, and knowledge to the

Does this activity suggest a transactional approach to teaching?

class and sets students to work on various activities to reinforce their learning. Such a teacher may use some transmissive methods, but will more than likely also set whole-class activities. It is perhaps a one-or-the-other issue. Knowledge will be declared by the teacher (see Declarative Knowledge, p. 6), in some transmissive form, to be processed by students through activities determined by the teacher.

To illustrate transactional teaching, think about the following scenario.

- Teacher begins the class.
- Teacher calls the class to attention; asks students to watch the screen on which he projects a transparency containing information about the subject of the lesson. (3 minutes)
- Teacher proceeds to tell the class about the topic, referring to the transparency from time to time. He also uses a few visual aids to illustrate certain points. Students are expected to give their undivided attention to the presentation. (20 minutes)
- When the presentation is completed, students are placed into groups of four, in which they must work together, using their textbooks to answer questions given by the teacher. (20 minutes)
- The lesson concludes with students working in pairs to complete an exercise in which they are each to draw a picture showing their understanding of a major concept introduced by the teacher in the initial presentation. (15 minutes)
- Homework assignment is written on the board for completion by the next class. (2 minutes)

Teachers often refer to the need for variety when talking about well-planned lessons. The lesson described above contains three activities. To what kinds of activities is most of the lesson devoted? Who decides on the activities for the class? What degrees of freedom do students have when engaged in these activities?

8.7 FOR YOUR CONSIDERATION

Critique the above lesson scenario, using the following questions:

1. Is there anything inherently wrong with the plan?
2. What are the strengths of the lesson?
3. Do you have any concerns about it? What are they and why?
4. Consider the teaching qualities. How are they evident in or absent from the planning of this lesson?
5. What assumptions about learning and teaching would the teacher likely hold?
6. The grade level of this class was not specified, but would your opinions differ if the class was secondary or elementary? Why?

Decide, with your teacher, how to organize responses to these questions. Some ideas:

- whole-class discussion
- group discussion
- debate
- assignment to interview practising teacher(s) for analysis by the class
- assignment to interview grade school students for analysis by the class
- other...

Transformational Teaching

"Research in cognitive and developmental psychology, psycholinguistics, and psychogenetics has significantly affected the way we think about teaching and learning today, with emphasis on learning and the learner." (Chapman, 1994, p. 5) It is this emphasis on the learner and learning that marks the orientation to teaching identified by the term *transformational*. To transform is to change and thus, because **transformational teaching** emphasizes learning and the learner, transformation in the teaching context is concerned with change within the learner. Chapman (1994) further states, "Once the stage is set, the teacher retreats to get out of the learner's way. The teacher is facilitative and indirect; 'interventions' —direct instruction—are discouraged. Teachers who adhere to this philosophy are concerned that since learning cannot be forced, teachers should 'let children develop at their own rates'" (p. 5). It is this individual development that characterizes the transformational approach to teaching. Transformational teaching thoroughly embodies the belief that the focus should always be on the learner.

Consider the philosophical orientations to teaching. Which do you believe embrace transformational teaching most comfortably? As a corollary question, which ones would not? Remember, as you reflect upon these questions, that good teachers make judgments about professional knowledge based upon the needs and well-being of students. Could a perennialist embrace transformational teaching? Why would an essentialist teacher likely experience difficulty with transformational approaches?

8.8 FOR YOUR CONSIDERATION

Read the following soliloquy from Shakespeare's *Hamlet*:

To be, or not to be: that is the question.
Whether 'tis nobler in the mind to suffer
The slings and arrows of outrageous fortune,
Or to take arms against a sea of troubles,
And by opposing end them. To die; to sleep;
No more; and by a sleep to say we end
The heart-ache and the thousand natural shocks
That flesh is heir to. 'Tis a consummation
Devoutly to be wished. To die; to sleep;-
To sleep? Perchance to dream! Ay, there's the Rub;
For in that sleep of death what dreams may come,
When we have shuffl'd off this mortal coil,
Must give us pause. There's the respect
That makes calamity of so long life
For who would bear the whips and scorns of time,
The oppressor's wrong, the [proud] man's contumely,
The pangs of disprized love, the law's delay,
The insolence of office, and the spurns
That patient merit of the unworthy takes
When he himself might his quietus make
With a bare bodkin? Who would fardels bare,
To grunt and sweat under a weary life,
But that the dread of something after death,
The undiscover'd country from whose bourn
No traveller returns, puzzles the will
And makes us rather bear those ills we have
Than fly to others that we know not of?
Thus conscience does make cowards of us all;
And thus the native hue of resolution
Is sicklied o'er with the pale cast of thought,
And enterprizes of great pith and moment
With this regard their currents turn [awry],
And lose the name of action.-Soft you now!
The fair Ophelia! Nymph in thy orisons
Be all my sins rememb'red.

Hamlet, Act III, Scene 1

Hamlet's soliloquy, laden with value and spiritual connotation, would be typical of what you might find in a perennialist classroom.

How could the soliloquy be part of transformational teaching?

How were you asked to learn about Shakespeare's plays?

Check off the following categories in response to the statement, When I studied Shakespeare in school, the teaching was predominantly …

_____ Direct
_____ Indirect
_____ Transmissive
_____ Transactional
_____ Transformational

... and in my judgment, my teacher's philosophical orientation to teaching (see Chapter 7) was predominantly

_____ Essentialist
_____ Progressivist
_____ Behaviourist
_____ Existentialist
_____ Reconstructionist
_____ Perennialist

How much did you enjoy studying Shakespeare?

_____ I didn't.
_____ It was okay.
_____ Fairly enjoyable.
_____ Enjoyed it a lot.

1. Comparing your answers to those of others in your class, do your "enjoyment" responses compare with the predominant methods of teaching you experienced?
2. To what extent did your teacher reflect the teaching qualities?
3. How do you think your teacher's teaching could have been altered to make the learning more enjoyable?

J. Henderson and Hawthorne (1995) discuss transformative curriculum leadership in the context of constructivism. They use the term **emancipatory constructivism,** defining it as, "constructivist educational practices that help students become contributing members of a particular community of inquiry and active members of humanity's age-old struggles with enlightenment and liberation" (p. iii). This interesting use of the term *emancipatory* helps us gain insight into the concept of transformational teaching. Constructivism, as we know from Chapter 5, establishes conditions within which learners build new knowledge upon prior knowledge, toward gaining greater meaning and understanding. A student transforms himself or herself to become more informed and aware than before. The process is emancipatory in that the learner is freed to explore, experiment, and expound independently, and more importantly, with others in social contexts. The concepts of freedom, liberation, and enlightenment fit well within transformational teaching practices and conditions.

A key component of transformational teaching is creating learning conditions that allow learners to experience the freedom and enlightenment that will lead to responsibility and ownership. Transformational teachers work toward encouraging a deeper sense of ownership in learners so that, when ownership is experienced, the young person can bring a powerful sense of commitment to an endeavour. Think about occasions in your life when you have experienced strong personal resolve. How strong was your commitment and dedication to bringing about that toward which you were working? It is truly amazing the transformations the human spirit can accomplish when the power of will is intrinsically engaged. Perhaps you have heard stories like that of Norman Cousins' (1979) successful fight against terminal illness and other self-healing stories about people who have fought serious illness. Such stories entail people's learning about their misfortune and turning the power of indomitable will against the illness. These people learn how to take ownership of themselves because they have an acute need.

Transformational teaching attempts to tap into this same inner resolve by motivating young people to take ownership of their learning. It allows them to pose their own problems in response to their own inquiries. Problem-posing is a critical element in making personal meaning. Whereas transmissive teaching would tend to simply present meaning to students, transformational teaching encourages them to make meaning for themselves.

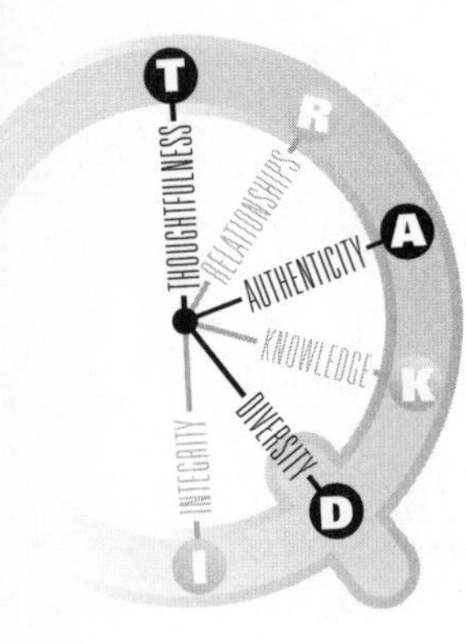

Can you think of occasions when you have experienced the "Aha!" of self-realization, those memorable moments when you have come to an understanding, when you have made your own meaning? It is those same inner workings of the mind that transformational teaching appreciates and respects. Freire (1988) alludes to transformational teaching and learning as a way students "develop their power to perceive critically the way they exist in the world with which and in which they find themselves ... [and take humanity's] historicity as their starting point. Problem-posing education affirms [people] as beings in the process of becoming...." (pp. 71–72).

The implications of the concept of becoming are very pertinent to transformational teaching. Think again about defining learners and the concepts of blank slate and empty vessel. If we accept the notion of "becoming," in this human, learning context, then who decides what learners will become?

- Does a teacher, as a seemingly all-knowing, all-powerful presence, deem to know what is best for learners?
- Or does a teacher, seeing a learner as a phenomenon, attempt to understand the phenomenon to work with and guide the learner toward becoming who he will become?

The former would suggest a teacher as an expert who knows what is best for all students. Teachers of this type may breed dependency and compliance in their students. Is compliance necessarily an undesirable thing for children? What does dependency mean to you? We ask you to think carefully about this concept, because it is a particularly significant characteristic of more traditional schooling. The latter would see a teacher as co-learner and co-teacher, where a considerable amount of "moving over" allows young people the freedom, liberation and enlightenment to transform themselves through the powerful, willing engagement of the inner self.

Key Considerations in Teaching

We have referred a number of times to the concept of constancies (Figure 8.1). Professional judgment always looms large because it implies thoughtfulness about the commonplaces of knowledge and the teaching qualities. Judgments made on the basis of considerations from Constancy B are premised on considerations similar to Constancy A to determine ways of working and responding to young people in learning contexts. In this chapter, in addition to constancies, qualities, and commonplaces, we have introduced you to ways of thinking and talking about teaching through understanding dispositions, orientations, and teaching for successful learning. We ask you to think about a number of statements during the course of this chapter, of which the following are particularly significant:

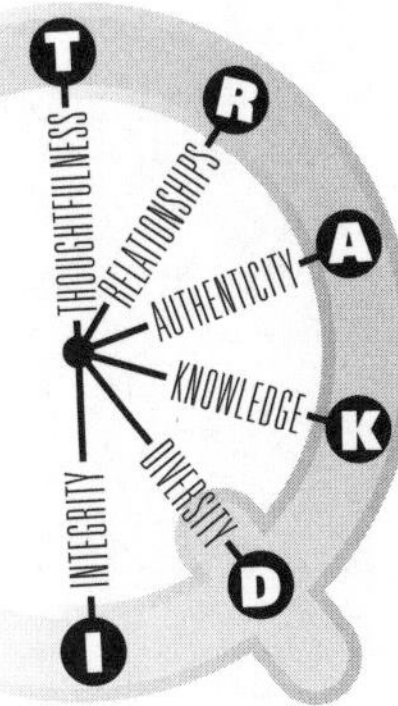

- Teaching is successful when young people learn successfully.
- Teachers are, without question, in positions of authority.
- The question of power and control is not about whether teachers have it, but rather how they use it in the best interests of learning.
- Teaching decisions are based on judgments about what we anticipate young people will learn.
- We could learn a great deal from thinking deeply about the concept of "moving over."
- Teaching should respect and attend to human needs.
- A fundamental goal for a teacher is to create conditions within which successful learning can take place.

The ways you respond to these statements will be strong indicators of your philosophy of teaching. Young people with whom you will be working will likely be a diverse group. Young people learn in different ways, and the rate at which learning occurs will vary among learners. What implications does this have for preparations to teach? Within any typical class of youngsters you may have those who are gifted and/or talented, are learning disabled, experience learning difficulties, exhibit attention deficit disorder (ADD) or attention deficit hyperactivity disorder (ADHD), are learning English as a Second Language (ESL), or come from various cultural backgrounds. Respecting diversity means that you must prepare for your classes in ways that provide all learners with the opportunity be successful.

At the beginning of this chapter we presented stories about Jim Schmidt and Sharon Kolchinsky, two different kinds of teachers. We asked you to think about assumptions toward teaching that flowed from the stories. Would diversity receive favourable consideration in either the Jim or Sharon scenario? Think about your response to the significant statements above in the context of the two stories. Do you feel any clarity beginning to emerge regarding your personal philosophy toward teaching? It is never too early to reflect upon your philosophy. Indeed, it is essential that you do, because it should become habitual, a normal professional behaviour in which you constantly ponder, wonder, contemplate, question, support, even challenge, professional practice. You will find yourself in many stages as you move through life, but try to avoid becoming entrenched in a professional status quo.

The following knowledge about learning and teaching (Figure 8.3 below) is generalized from many sources of educational research (Cone of Learning; Integrated Technologies, Inc. [from Edgar Dale, Audio-Visual Methods in Technology, Holt Rinehart and Winston]; retrieved August 1, 2002 from **www.intech.com/education**; The Learning Cone, Jiva Institute, 2000; retrieved August 15, 2002, from **www.jivaworld.com/keys/learning_cone.htm**).

We invite you to consider this generalized model of research about learning, and discuss it in your class. What implications does the information have for teaching?

Figure 8.3
The Building Blocks of Learning

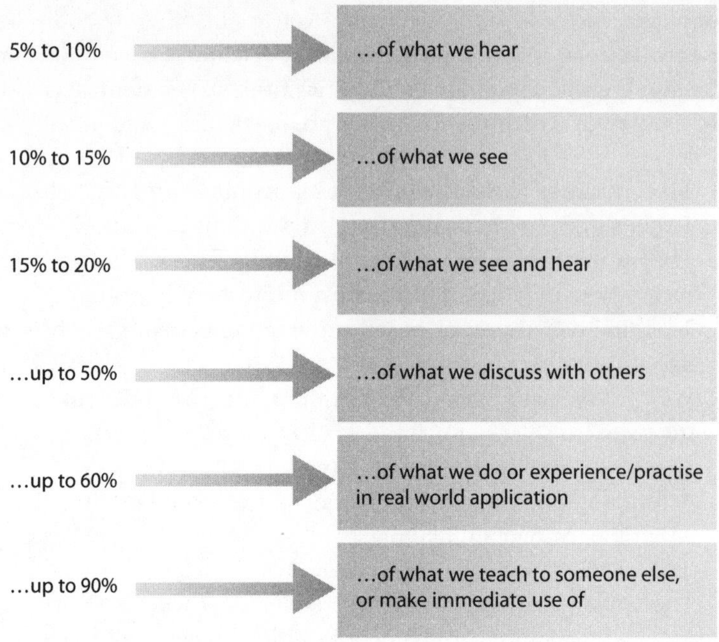

(Source: Cone of Learning; Integrated Technologies, Inc.[from Edgar Dale, Audio-Visual Methods in Technology, Holt Rinehart and Winston]; retrieved August 1, 2002 from www.intech.com/education; The Learning Cone, Jiva Institute, 2000; retrieved August 15, 2002, from www.jivaworld.com/keys/learning_cone.htm)

Think back to the chapter discussion so far and revisit For Your Consideration 8.2. Has your approach to the Grade 6 class changed? Perhaps the most interesting consideration would be to see how your personal philosophy of teaching withstands scrutiny alongside the building blocks of learning. Teachers must constantly reflect upon their pedagogy and be prepared to challenge their ideas, theories, and assumptions about teaching. Earlier we cautioned about becoming "entrenched in a professional status quo." Change is a phenomenon of any contemporary society.

Learning and teaching are as much a part of society as any other endeavour and it is incumbent upon teachers to be aware of current professional knowledge, so that young people might prosper. Bolman & Deal (1991) suggest that those who are reluctant to look at pedagogy and schooling practices in different ways tend to "live in psychic prisons because they cannot look at old problems in a new light and attack old challenges with different and more powerful tools-they cannot reframe. When they don't know what to do they simply do more of what they do know" (p. 4). Think about teaching for successful learning and the question of inner resolve. Think deeply about your personal philosophy of teaching.

Teaching for Transfer

One of the generally accepted aims of teaching is that learning will be transferable, that learners will be able to apply what they have learned in different contexts. "Broadly defined, **[teaching for] transfer** involves prior learning affecting new learning or performance. The new learning or performance can differ from original learning in terms of the tasks involved (as when students apply what they have learned on practice problems to solve a new problem), and/or the context involved (as when students apply their classroom learning to performing tasks at home or work)." (Marini & Genereux, 1995, p. 2, emphasis added) Regrettably, the quest for transfer of learning continues to be elusive.

Research on effective transfer of learning dates back more than a century. Many of the studies document examples of failure. It is not the purpose of this book to delve into the extensive research on transfer of learning, especially the examples of failure, but there are positive signs in more contemporary research (Lupart, 1995) that may serve as useful reference for our discussion. Before we explore the positive signs, we invite you to think about your learning experiences in school. In what kinds of learning situations did you find yourself learning most successfully? We suspect there were perhaps three primary motivations at work:

1. You needed to understand because it was necessary for your future goals.
2. You were intrinsically motivated to learn.
3. Through your high interest in the topic, you were able to actively help others to learn.

You may be able to identify other motivations, but these three are particularly significant.

8.9 FOR YOUR CONSIDERATION

Write the above three motivations on the board for the entire class to see. Divide the class into groups of four. Have group members share stories about school experiences in which they experienced learning that had application in other contexts.

a) To what extent do the three motivations on the board resonate with your stories? Have each group compose one phrase that describes the most important points from the stories that you all shared.
b) Merge two groups into a single group. Now share the phrases each group has composed. Explain them and discuss them. Can the newly combined groups agree on a single statement? It need not be one of the existing statements, but can be a newly worded phrase.
c) Continue to combine two groups, using the same process as in stage b), until the whole class has become one large group again.
d) What is the final phrase the class has agreed on and to what extent does it accurately describe the essence of the three motivations on the board?

Two issues are pertinent to the matter of transfer in learning: self-regulation and connectedness. The three motivations, above all, entail a high degree of personal commitment from a learner. The motivation for the commitment may well be different, but it is, nevertheless, apparent.

Self-Regulation **Self-regulation** is an individual's ability to make decisions about learning and life that will serve to enhance personal well-being. Lupart (1995) posits the existence of four perspectives in self-regulation.

1. Learners must be encouraged to be dynamic participants in the learning process. Static learners are passive recipients and therefore relatively inactive.
2. Learners also need to learn how to become self-regulated. It is not sufficient to afford the opportunity and assume that young people can, therefore, become self-regulated.
3. Teachers must also consider unique characteristics that learners possess and reflect these characteristics in invitations to learn.
4. Finally, teachers should recognize the role of motivation and attitudes toward learning within students and consciously include them in their teaching preparations.

Think about self-regulation in the context of this chapter. Toward which type of focus would a teacher lean if self-regulation were being encouraged? Could transmissive teaching comfortably embrace self-regulation in students? Which disposition toward teaching would better accommodate self-regulation? What role would self-regulation play in transformative teaching? These kinds of questions and the surrounding conversations should constitute important steps in the formulation of your personal philosophy of education.

The conclusive point in this consideration is the degree to which an individual sees some utility in learning. There are interesting parallels to some of our earlier discussions. Constructivism, for example, values prior knowledge and attempts to engage learners, through degrees of freedom, in decisions about what and how to approach new learning. Constructivist learning is compatible with self-regulation. Social learning, generally, engages young people in various social contexts and, through these engagements, nurtures individual expression. The social contexts encourage control and shaping of learning by groups, which, through individual expression, facilitate self-regulation.

We invite you to think about other approaches to teaching and learning where self-regulation could be encouraged.

Connectedness Learning in schools has sometimes been described as fragmented: learning time is broken up into blocks during which different subjects are taught. Any connection between learning in different subject areas is inadvertent, at best, and left up to learners, who are really least able to make those connections. You will read more about efforts to redress this problem in Chapter 11, on curriculum, but generally speaking, programs in schools remain disconnected, and learning remains disconnected to children's lives.

Connectedness helps students understand relationships within a subject, between subjects, and between the subject and life itself. Connectedness in learning eliminates fragmentation, facilitates relevance and authenticity, and contributes to the meaningfulness of learning. Duckworth (1996) speaks about learning with "breadth and depth," which she feels is a matter of making connections: "Breadth could be thought of as the widely different *spheres of experience* that can be related to one another and depth could be thought of as the many different kinds of connections that can be made among different *facets of our experience*" (p. 70). If we were to add a third dimension to Duckworth's seemingly two-dimensional view of learning, then it would be connections to life itself. In Chapter 2 we presented a model for Reflection on Authentic Learning (see Figure 2.2). To effect successful transfer of learning it is important to focus the breadth and depth of learning on the third dimension, life itself. Learning should help young people understand their world, their life. And life for a youngster is immediate—it's now.

Connectedness in learning is a skill that needs to be taught. Simply declaring knowledge within and across subject areas is not likely to effect transfer. Assumption 3 in Chapter 3 (p. 51) is "Children automatically apply their learning." In the discussion of this assumption, we note many hypotheses for the failure to transfer phenomena. A key consideration in the transfer process is providing sufficient procedural activities (Chapter 4, p. 77). Young people need opportunities to practice strategies of transfer so that transfer becomes a skill. Teachers are encouraged to understand their worldview as they engage in teaching; so also should young people. It is important that our worldview be integrated, so that we understand the influences on our lives (Chapter 1, p. 8). Young people, for whom life tends to be immediate, have an even greater need for their worldview to not only be expanded through learning, but also integrated so that learning is relevant and meaningful.

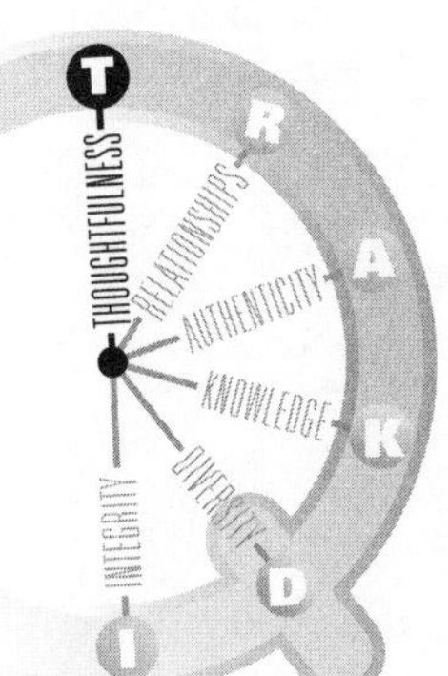

For learning to be meaningful, to have utility, it should have some relevance to learners. The making and telling to which we referred earlier in this chapter represent approaches to teaching that do not sit well with our three motivations. You will notice that the essential conditions of self-regulation and connectedness are similarly incompatible with making and telling learners to learn. Teaching for transfer is a difficult task. As you think deeply about its merits, reflect upon the degree to which young people should be involved in their own learning if transfer is to be successful. In this regard, then, to what extent would your teaching lean toward indirect, transformational approaches? Your personal philosophy of education should consist of clearly held views on this and similar questions. Thoughtfulness is the mark of a good teacher.

Designing for Learning

Once talk about learning and teaching has quietened, the time will arrive when you have to walk into your class and be ready to work with young people. At this point, we suspect, the thought that leaps to mind is "lesson plan." What is a lesson plan? Think about this seemingly obvious question for a while and then consider the students with whom you will be working. We would like you to consider another word alongside *planning* and that is the word *preparing*. Perhaps you are thinking that this is a little incongruous, debating word meanings when talking about something as concrete and practical as planning! A plan is a concrete procedure that one follows to achieve a specific intention. It is usually a series of steps to be followed to arrive at a specific end. A plan to build a house, for example, instructs the builder on specifically how to construct the house to satisfy the buyer. Any changes to the original plan that the buyer might wish to make during construction are incorporated by the architect and communicated to the builder. Plans are usually inflexible. Now, back to our earlier question about plans in the context of teaching and young people. Do words like *concrete* and *inflexible* seem compatible with learning?

Let's revisit for a moment some of the things that we are reasonably sure of as far as learning and young people are concerned. We know that learners learn at different rates and in different ways. We also know that learners are unique individuals. From a developmental perspective, young people reflect great disparity physically, intellectually, socially, and morally. And we must also consider diversity. Learners may be learning disabled, may be gifted and talented, or may experience learning difficulties. Some children may be socially challenged, especially those exhibiting behaviour problems. Others may be from cultural backgrounds where English is their second language. And, perhaps most important as far as lesson planning is concerned, learning is not predictable. Some of these conditions may be evident in your classes, certainly the last one. Another thing that we know with some certainty about learning is that it is most effective when learning conditions are structured for success. So, anticipating diversity, disparity, and unpredictability, how do you get ready to work with a class of young people in ways that are set up for success? Admittedly this is a challenging task, but it is one you cannot take lightly. Often teachers talk about "designing for learning" instead of doing "lesson plans." Which phrase do you prefer?

8.10 FOR YOUR CONSIDERATION

You are to teach a Grade 6 class of thirty students, in which there is quite a bit of disparity in both ability and behaviour. Your lesson is in social studies and you are beginning a study of ancient Greece. In the forty-five minutes you have allocated to this class, how would you approach the task of getting ready for the lesson?

Work in groups of four. Each group will need one large piece of newsprint and felt pens.

1. On one half of the newsprint make a diagram of the classroom, showing workspaces, resource locations, desks, wallboards, and equipment.
2. On the other half of the newsprint indicate what you intend to do with the children during the forty-five minutes.
3. When this task is completed, post your newsprint sheet on the wall.
4. Invite the whole class to wander around the room and visit the work of all the groups.
5. When the visiting is finished, each group should sit by their work and describe it, providing explanations and responding to questions. Note how many groups show the following conditions in their posted work: flexibility, uniqueness of children, and knowledge about learning. Be sure to give clear reasons for your observations.

Approaches to Lesson Preparation

We understand that you will not likely be preparing to work with young people in formal practicum situations until later in your teacher preparation studies.

However, it is useful to begin reflecting on some models for lesson preparation, so that your thoughts might be grounded in the eventual task of working with young people. We invite you to consider three approaches that appear to be widely used.

Model A

1. Specify your objectives for the lesson.
2. Design and organize learning activities to meet the objectives.
3. Evaluate students to determine the degree to which the learning has been successful.

(Parkay et al. 1996, p. 307)

The next model follows a similar traditional format, but contains a little more detail.

Model B

1. Rationale: purpose of the lesson—link to prior knowledge and skills
2. Objectives: what the students will learn
3. Material/resources: supplies and equipment to be prepared before lesson starts
4. Procedure: step-by-step specific procedure to be followed to introduce, develop, and finish off the lesson
   - introduction
   - body
   - closure
5. Student description of how to evaluate the attainment of objectives

(Source: From "Lesson Plans" by I. Naested, 2000, [Mount Royal College student handout document]. Calgary, AB: Copyright 2000 by I. Naested. Reprinted with permission.)

Brownlie and King (2000) present an approach to lesson preparation that they offer as "a viable model for planning for productive learning" (pp. 51–53).

Model C

1. What are the key concepts which the students are required to learn?
   - Big ideas, major focus, or purpose to guide the learning events.
   - Planned activities will make the big ideas clearer to the students.
2. What specific learning outcomes will be addressed in this lesson or lesson sequence?
   - Teacher chooses, from curriculum guide, suitable outcomes on which to focus.
   - Outcomes could be from different subjects to foster integration.
   - Engaging students through including them in building lesson criteria is a priority.

3. How will students demonstrate their learning?
   - Students give evidence that they have achieved the learning outcomes.
   - Students required to reorganize material learned and connect to information previously learned.
   - Criteria for demonstration of learning developed with students or given to students.
4. How will we assess student learning?
   - Criteria, established before lesson begins, are always available and visible to students.
   - Teacher uses criteria to judge demonstrations and student products.
   - Students encouraged to assess their own work:
   - What do I need to know?
   - How will I show what I know?

(Source: From *Learning in Safe Schools: Creating Classrooms Where All Students Belong,* pp. 51–53, by F. Brownlie & J. King, 2000, Markham, ON: Pembroke Publishers. Copyright 2000 by Pembroke Publishers Ltd. Reprinted with permission.)

In which of these models is the teacher more prepared? Perhaps we are splitting hairs with this question, but it is useful to contemplate the differences between the three models, especially in light of our earlier comments about learners and learning. Teaching must be practised with the willingness to be flexible always present. We urge you to think about the characteristics of being well prepared. Does designing learning experiences result in being well prepared?

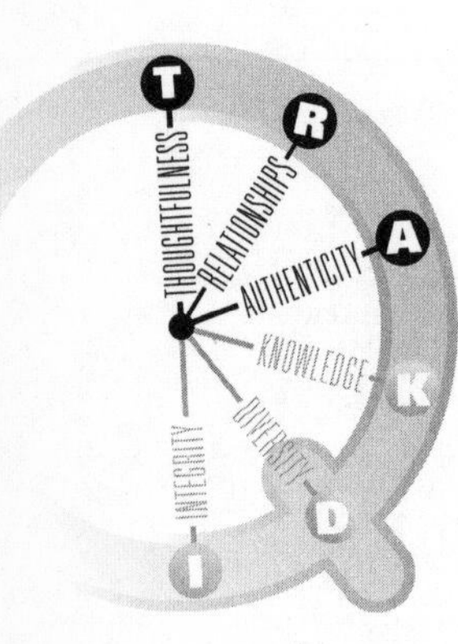

The degree to which a model for teaching accommodates, indeed encourages, a teacher to be responsive to differences and disparities of learners and learning during the course of a lesson indicates to us the degree of a professionally defensible approach. Being prepared for teaching is being prepared to respond to difference and disparity when learning is intended to occur, not as an afterthought. Being prepared also means having the flexibility to respond to emergent situations. We presented one such example earlier in this chapter with Lorenzo Sanchez. Here are three other settings for you to consider if, say, you intended to engage your class in a formal debate/discussion type of activity.

1. The weather has turned overcast and rain is falling heavily. Your class is subdued and seemingly without energy.
2. Because of a favourable weather forecast, the principal has decided to move the sports afternoon from tomorrow to today. Your class is now "off the wall" with excitement.
3. An unscheduled assembly was called for the period before yours. During the assembly a fundraiser representative motivated the students, "pumped them up" for a successful fundraising drive. The youngsters are excited about the prizes being offered for most fundraising items sold.

If you were confronted with situations like these, would you continue to teach your lesson as planned, regardless of unexpected changes? Why would you do this? Perhaps you will find this topic to be a lively source for discussion in your

The design process draws on both resources (left) and colleagues and conversation (right).

present class. We invite you to try such a discussion and if you do, be sure to ground your reasoning in sound professional judgment. What rings true for you?

Finally, think about the three models of designing for learning and decide, not so much which you prefer, but what features you would adopt in building your own approach to teaching preparedness that would allow you to respond to the learning needs of students.

Building a Personal Philosophy of Education

In the process of becoming a teacher and in the practice of teaching you will accumulate knowledge about the profession from books, courses, conversations, readings, observations and on-the-job experience. All this accumulated knowledge will pass through your personal filter, where it mixes with your beliefs, values, attitudes, and assumptions about education and life to manifest itself in the ways you present yourself to the world. Personal philosophies change with time. Your task is to gain clarity about your personal philosophy so that you are able to speak and act in ways that you find comfortable and defensible in your professional life. Preservice teachers, in interviews for a first teaching position, are often asked to articulate their philosophy of education. We strongly encourage you to make as explicit as possible the fundamental convictions and beliefs you hold about learning, teaching, morality, and personal conduct. Figure 8.4 on the next page may help you to articulate your philosophy of education.

Figure 8.4 *Toward a Personal Philosophy of Teaching*

Purpose of Education:

Role of teacher: ____________

Role of Parents: ____________

Role of Young People: ____

Success in Learning

Young People:

Nature: ____________

Development: ____________

Preferred Learning: ____________

Defined as…: ____________

Curriculum:

What should be learned? ____________

What knowledge is of most worth? ____________

Relevance/connectedness: ____________

Conceptions of: ____________

Beliefs about successful learning: ____________

Success in Teaching

My disposition:

My Philosophical Orientations

Methodologies

Behaviour/Responding to Others

Morality/Ethics

Professional Behaviour

Professional Development

Professional Involvement

Reflection and Perspective on the Chapter

Teaching is a complex process and the danger of over-simplifying it cannot be overstated. Our discussion of power and control is important to think about. Authoritarian practices, used to control students, often signal a situation in which a teacher wishes to subdue a class to impose a teacher-preferred agenda. In such cases, a lesson is delivered to an entire class, with all students working on the same things, in the same ways, and at the same rates. The teacher decides and the students must conform, differences and disparities notwithstanding. Constancy A in Figure 8.1 is bureaucratic and superficial at best.

Another caution about rendering the complex simple is what may be termed the "good with children" view. In the early pages of this chapter, we discussed observation of activities that appeared to be successful in keeping children occupied, and that coupling these observations with a characteristic of being good with children could result in the formula for being a good teacher. This unfortunate interpretation is easy to accept, especially during early years of teacher preparation. Visiting classrooms as a volunteer and assisting teachers can sometimes be an awesome experience. The euphoria of being seen by youngsters as a "teacher," of being addressed as Miss or Mr., is a seductive experience at first. You may well feel that you want to get into this teaching business as quickly as possible so that you can experience these rewarding feelings on a regular basis. Enthusiasm for the teaching profession is laudable, but be very clear about the deeply professional nature of the responsibility.

The complexity of which we spoke is firmly rooted in the complexity of people, learning, and the depth of knowledge and interpretation that surrounds both. Constancy B in Figure 8.1 should not, in any sense, be rendered simple. The discussion and considerations in which we have invited you to engage are but a small step into the professional landscape of teaching. As you progress with you professional preparation, step surely, confidently, and openly into the landscape. There is much to learn. The landscape is broad, rich, and exciting. Enjoy your journey. You have far to go. Travel in the knowledge that your journey will never really end but that you will reach a comfort level that will allow you to not only enjoy the landscape but enrich it as well. Remember that the one quality that will keep you on course is thoughtfulness. A good teacher is a thoughtful teacher.

Key Terms

connectedness 190
direct teaching 176
emancipatory constructivism 185
empowerment 173
indirect teaching 176
learner-focused teaching 177
self-regulation 190
teacher-focused teaching 178
teaching for transfer 189
transactional teaching 181
transformational teaching 183
transmissive teaching 180

Suggested Further Reading

Fennimore, Beatrice S. (1995). *Student-centered Classroom Management*. Scarborough, ON: Nelson Canada.

Goethals, M. Serra, and Howard, Rose A. (2001). *Student Teaching: A Process Approach to Reflective Practice. A Guide for Student, Intern and Beginning Teachers*. Upper Saddle River, NJ: Merrill.

Kindler, Anna M., Badali, Salvador J. and Willock, Renee. (1999). *Between Theory and Practice: Case Studies for Learning to Teach*. Scarborough, ON: Prentice Hall-Allyn and Bacon Canada.

O'Sullivan, Edmund (1999). *Transformative Learning: Educational Vision for the 21st Century*. Toronto: University of Toronto Press.

Preskill, Stephen L. and Jacobvitz, Robin Smith. (2001). *Stories of Teaching: A Foundation for Educational Renewal*. Upper Saddle River, NJ: Prentice Hall Inc.

Tomlinson, Carol Ann. (1999). *The Differentiated Classroom: Responding to the Needs of All Learners*. Alexandria, VA: Association for Supervision and Curriculum Development.

Chapter 9

Schools

[W]hen a process makes people feel they have a voice in matters that affect them, they will have a greater commitment to the overall enterprise and will take greater responsibility for what happens to the enterprise.... [T]he absence of such a process ensures that no one feels responsible, that blame will always be directed externally, that adversarialism [sic] will be a notable feature of school life. (Sarason, 1990, p. 61)

Chapter Focus

Sarason reminds us of a very important consideration when schools are the subject of debate. Success of schools has a great deal to do with the degree and kind of involvement of all constituents. Teachers, especially, are the constituent group charged on a day-to-day basis with learning, the raison d'être of a school. As a group with equality in professionalism, it is important that they share voice, commitment, and ownership in the enterprise. We ask you to think about what "equality in professionalism" means for the ways in which schools are run. Sarason (1990) is of the view that "school(s) and school system(s) generally are not comprehensible unless you flush out the power relationships that inform and control the behaviour of everyone in these settings" (p. 7). How did you experience power when you were in school? As a student did you feel any sense of power as a member of your school community? Perhaps you felt powerless. At various levels of school hierarchies power and control, depending on the degree to which they are shared, have a significant impact on a school's effectiveness. People-intensive institutions, such as schools, are complex bodies. Harnessing the talents, expertise, and will of people into a cohesive, effective group takes leadership of the most sophisticated kind. It is not sufficient to simply create a congenial atmosphere and leave people to their own devices in a well-run building. Conversations about learning must be common practice, and a school benefits from clarity in meaning and understanding related to its direction and purpose.

Glickman (1990) speaks about "empowered" schools. This is not a new term in education, but we believe it is a useful one. If we are to initiate conversations among teachers, students, and parents with the intention of gaining clarity in meaning and understanding about a school's purpose and direction, then people need to be involved in taking action to move a school in intended directions. This is what we mean by empowerment, to bestow power on others. It is sharing power.

Empowerment can also be a guard against **reductionism**, the reduction of complex concepts and practices to simple understandings. Teaching and learning are complex practices, and in the busyness of school life sometimes complex concepts and understandings are inadvertently reduced to simple understandings, largely because of insufficient time devoted to meaning and understanding. Arguably, this has contributed to the accusation that schools tend to drift from one new trend to another without any lasting more than a few years. Ownership can be a powerful protection against reductionism. When empowered people are involved in taking action to move a school in intended directions, they are doing it themselves, taking ownership for the action.

> Life is simpler when we have an enemy to circumscribe our actions. Life becomes much more difficult when there is no enemy out there; if there is an enemy in empowered schools, the enemy is ourselves. No one tells us what we can't do; instead, they're asking us what we wish to do. (Glickman, 1990, p. 72)

Think about yourself in school. When you saw something inappropriate happening, what did you do? How often did you say, "That's not my problem; it's somebody else's responsibility"? In effect, you circumscribed the problem and absolved yourself of responsibility. When teachers and students are empowered to set directions for a school and to take action on those directions, they tend to have a stronger sense of ownership. Although this is a potentially difficult and sensitive process to enact, with strong leadership we believe that it will have impressive benefits for schools. When students and teachers feel ownership for a school, both feel better about their school, students tend to learn more successfully, and everyone benefits. We realize that you may find this to be a new way of thinking about schools. Keep it in mind as you read this chapter.

Focus Questions

1. What are some expressions of a school's ecology?
2. Why is it important for a school to be clear about its intentions?
3. How can schools pay attention to mission and purpose through the orchestration of day-to-day activities?
4. To what extent are administrative dispositions toward management or leadership factors in school success?
5. To what extent is power a factor in school success and what is the most desirable manifestation of power?

Understanding Schools

Assumption 1: School is a social institution where intentions for the whole school will be accomplished whether students, teachers, and parents, understand them or not.

The Ecology and Ethos of Schools

The above assumption introduces the idea of the school as a whole and raises questions about the need for interconnectedness and orchestration of relationships and functions toward achieving success in learning and teaching.

How do you think of a school? Is it a place you attended to learn about different subjects? Was it where you went to socialize with your friends, where your activities were subject to control and discipline? How were you treated? What was the attitude of the adults toward you and your friends? Many questions could be asked about this place that society calls school. It is important that you come to your own understanding of school because, as a future teacher, it is the place where you will most likely practice your profession. You should be clear about it because the school contributes to your effectiveness as a teacher. More importantly, the school contributes to the effectiveness of learning for young people.

A school is a place where there is constant interaction among functions and intense interrelationships among people. *Functions* refers to activities such as communication (newsletters, staff meetings, assemblies), budget (resources purchases, annual requests from teachers, subject allocations, school operating expenses), and facility maintenance costs. *Interrelationships* refers to staff collaboration (team teaching, committees, opportunities for social interaction, professional development), parent meetings (parent councils and advisory committees, ad hoc sessions), and student meetings (student council/representative groups, staff/student councils, planning sessions). The totality and interconnectedness of these interactions and interrelationships constitutes the ecology of a school. The health of a school is the degree to which these interactions and interrelationships are effective.

The word *ecology* is borrowed from the scientific community and means a system in which there is a symbiotic relationship between all life forms and their sustaining environment. The **ecology of a school** is the symbiotic relationship between functions and people toward the essential purpose of successfully meeting the learning needs of all people in the school's learning environment. The way a school operates and the way it is understood by all its constituents is vital to its healthy ecology. As you read the following story, think about the school's ecology. How healthy is the school?

> Renee and Lisa teach grade two and three respectively at Lester B. Pearson Elementary School. Both teachers have become interested in a concept of combining grades called *multi-age grouping,* which accommodates children learning at their own rates and learning from each other. The principal likes their ideas and encourages them to try the concept in January after the holiday break.

Renee and Lisa enter into their project with enthusiasm and spend countless hours ensuring the success of their venture.

Pearson's February newsletter to parents mentions nothing about the multi-age grouping venture. Teachers are given only a brief update at the January staff meeting.

The venture is working well as far as Lisa and Renee are concerned, and the principal appears to be positive about their work.

However, as spring break approaches, parents begin to call the principal expressing concern about "these teachers experimenting with my daughter."

Other staff members are disgruntled. "What's going on in those grades? Are we expected to do that when those children move into our grades next year?"

The caretakers are also upset about all the changes with furniture and space configuration.

Lisa and Renee's initial excitement is being severely challenged.

To what extent do you see ecological problems in Pearson Elementary School? How do you think the ecological difficulties could be solved?

9.1 FOR YOUR CONSIDERATION

Scenario: You are working in an elementary school of 400 children and 22 professional staff. The school is located in an upper/middle class socio-economic community in which parents take an active interest in their school. 60% of the children stay at school for lunch.

Divide the class into groups of four. Assign each group to one of the following tasks.

1. Decide on four approaches to social learning to be adopted by the whole school.
2. Decide on four ways that parents might become involved in the school's curriculum.
3. Decide on four ways for dealing with discipline that would complement children's growth and development.
4. Decide on four features of a lunchroom/lunchtime program that would ensure learning, order, and efficiency.

Each group post their decisions on chart paper displayed around the room.

As a whole class, compare the decisions of each group and determine the implications of the decisions for the other three groups. Where do you detect incompatibility? Where do you see compatibility? What kind of impact do you think the decisions made in your class would have on a school's ecology? Be prepared to give sound reasons for your answers.

Two significant factors contribute to the health of a school's ecology:

1. beliefs about learning and teaching that unite functions and interrelationships
2. ways of working within a school that promote dialogue, discussion, and decision making toward common understanding and implementation of school beliefs

The integrity of a school's beliefs and ways of working, and the manifestation of that integrity in day-to-day life, defines a character and moral nature that collectively creates a school spirit, or ethos.

We invite you to think carefully about the concepts of ecology and ethos. A **school as an entity** is a place with a unity of purpose where parents expect their children's learning needs to be met. The functions and interrelationships of a school's ecology combine with its character and moral nature to form a whole, an entity whose functions, interrelationships, and ethos are orchestrated to provide for the learning needs of all people.

School Intentions

Young people benefit from consistency in approaches to learning, and in this regard schools should pay attention to aspects such as mission and purpose. Most schools have developed statements that declare the school's intentions about learning and teaching. Often parents and occasionally students are involved in creating these intentions. A typical mission statement might read as follows:

> John G. Diefenbaker School celebrates learning through responsibility, diversity, and relevance.

Mission statements are usually succinctly stated indicators of approaches to learning that a school values. The implication is that all people who work in the school have a clear understanding of what is intended by the concepts embodied in the mission statement and can incorporate them into their work with students. Some schools develop intentions a little more thoroughly in statements of purpose. A typical statement of this kind might read as follows:

> John A. Macdonald School is a bilingual school where the celebration of learning and personal accomplishment results in people assuming responsibility for and taking pride in themselves and their school.
>
> Young people attend school to learn. As we all salute the primacy of learning we are motivated and have the responsibility to learn how to learn. Learning embraces academic, social, emotional, artistic, physical, moral, and ethical dimensions. Therefore, our broad curriculum actively considers the diverse nature of students and the ways in which they learn.
>
> People at Macdonald work closely in a multicultural community of learners to create a learning environment that nurtures caring and responsibility, and which encourages the demonstration of learning. We will continue our tradition of working together in collaborative ways to acquire knowledge, skills, attitudes, and personal qualities integral to self-direction, competence, and societal contribution.

This somewhat lengthy statement contains many important beliefs and concepts, all of which should be understood by staff, students, and parents, and embodied in the day-to-day work of the school. Also, all staff (including non-professional people), students, and parents should collaborate in the composition of a purpose statement so that all take ownership for it.

We would like you to understand that teachers need to be clear about the implications for learning and teaching of a school's mission or purpose. We are not suggesting that teachers be "homogenized"—be all the same. We have said that young people are all different. Adults are also unique. Teachers must be allowed to be themselves so that their individuality, even their idiosyncrasies, can flourish. However, with this in mind, we believe it is important for teachers to possess a clear understanding about ways of responding to the learning needs of young people consistent with the school's declared intentions.

The Institutional Focus of Schools

As people in a school and its community attempt to define and implement intentions for the school, they must pay attention to ways the intentions are to be orchestrated and enacted in the school's day-to-day life. Figure 9.1 illustrates how this attention can be given through what we call an "orbit of response," signifying ongoing professional activity within three areas of focus. In this way a school staff creates ecological health and well-being. In the period between a school's stating and successfully achieving its intentions, the staff, students, and parents need to do some rather specific work.

Some questions one might ask of schools as they seek to achieve a healthy ecology include, What is the school in the life of a young person? What constitutes a successful and dynamic school for young people? How do young people position the school? How does the school position young people? What is at work between young people and their school? Is it possible for the school to become something different? Figure 9.1 requires a school to be clear about its learning intentions so that beliefs and values, relating to all forms of learning, are made explicit in formal statements of mission, purpose, or goals. How would a school respond as an entity to the broad panoply of student learning needs?

Figure 9.1 *Institutional Focus in Schools*

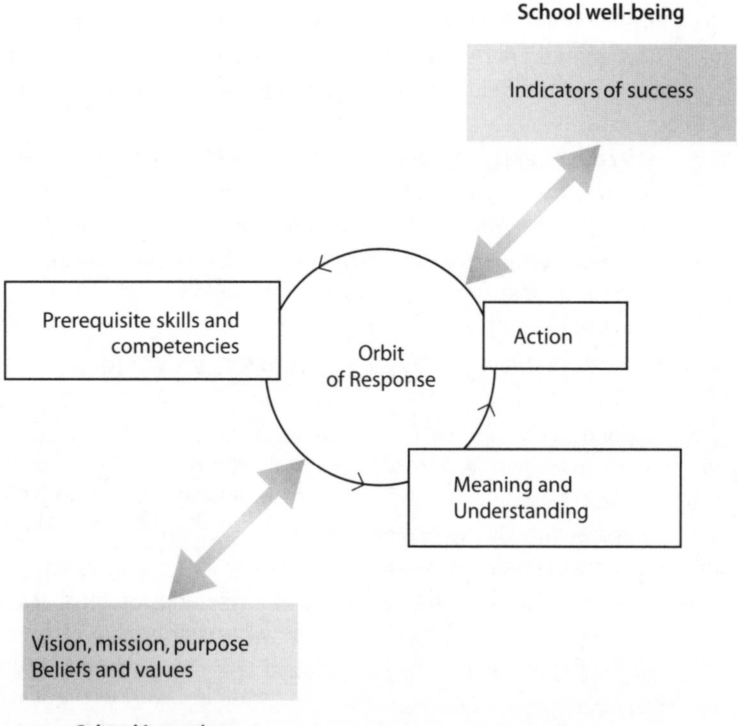

Source: Adapted from P. Waldron, T. Collie, & C.M. Davies, *Telling Stories About School* (1999), p. 122. © 1999. Reprinted by permission of Pearson Education Inc., Upper Saddle River, NJ.

Figure 9.1 presents three areas of focus: meaning and understanding; prerequisite skills and competencies; and action. Each area of focus operates continuously and simultaneously. The following discussion of these areas of focus provides some insight into their intent.

Meaning and Understanding Invariably, in intention statements schools will include terms such as self-discipline, responsibility, social behaviour, concern for others, and respect, in addition to goals for academic achievement and results. A good question to ask about these intentions is, How are they enacted in a school's day-to-day life? Two further questions need to be asked as well: How do we understand these intentions? and, What do they mean? It is in the meaning-and-understanding area of focus that critical inquiry and professional development activity take place. Staff must have opportunities to discover their prior knowledge about the intentions, to talk about them, and to gain new knowledge so that conversation and dialogue are informed by research and practice. Workshops, conferences, and seminars are typical activities that contribute to a staff gaining meaning and understanding. An important part of the meaning and understanding focus is honesty in acknowledging current reality in a school. In this way assumptions are aired and challenged—a necessary aspect of making meaning and gaining understanding.

Prerequisite Skills and Competencies When a school seeks meaning and understanding regarding its intentions or new knowledge and attendant assumptions, teachers may realize that they do not possess the necessary skills and competencies to implement the practices. The school must make decisions about the professional development necessary for teachers to acquire the skills, attitudes, concepts, and competencies to effectively implement new ways of working with young people.

Action Clearly, people will quickly reach frustration levels if all they do is talk about concepts and ideas. Schools are pragmatic places, and teachers will find time only for things they consider useful. Implementing new concepts in school occurs in concert with other areas of focus depicted in Figure 9.1.

9.2 FOR YOUR CONSIDERATION

Respond to the question, How are school intentions enacted in the day-to-day life of a school?

Using the intentions of self-discipline, responsibility, respect, and results, discuss ways in which these intentions could be woven into the daily life of a school.

Some questions to think about:

- What do we understand by the intentions?
- To what extent should students be involved?
- To what extent should parents be involved?
- How would teachers be involved so that the intentions could be enacted as part of a school's ethos, in aspects such as hallways, lunchroom, extra-curricular activities, main office, school buses, as well as classrooms?

We understand that this topic is, perhaps, a little advanced for the early years of teacher preparation programs. However, although the subject may be complex, we believe it is essential that prospective teachers begin thinking about it.

If you completed For Your Consideration 9.2, we are sure you found many questions about a school's purpose beyond fostering proficiency in subjects. Think back to your experiences in school and try to identify how your school fostered positive attitudes and behaviours relating to respect for people and property, responsibility, achievement, self-discipline, and empathy. If these particular qualities were not apparent in your schooling then think, instead, about discipline. What was your school's approach to discipline, however you understand that term? What do you believe the teachers anticipated you would learn as a result of discipline used in the school? Were the school's intentions clear to you, or did it appear to be left to the whims of teachers? Other than the more obvious matters such as fighting, throwing snowballs, firing paper pellets, and engaging in abusive behaviour, what was the broader perspective on discipline?

As you contemplate these issues, let us consider a deeper question: What constitutes a successful and legitimate school experience?

9.3 FOR YOUR CONSIDERATION

What constitutes a successful and legitimate school experience?

Obviously the key words are *successful* and *legitimate*. Decide as a group how you might best deal with this question and set your own process in place. Try to position yourselves in terms of what the school *should* be in your lives.

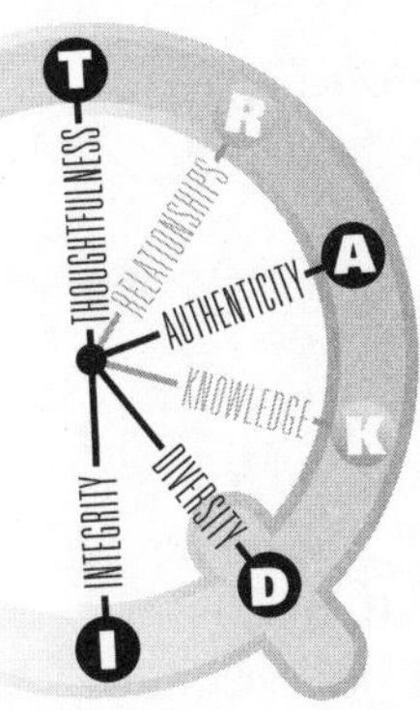

Legitimate may refer to effective teaching and learning associated with mandated subjects, as evidenced by student satisfaction and the results of assessment processes. *Successful* demands a broader understanding. In addition to student satisfaction and good assessment results, *successful* may refer to knowledge, skills, and attitudes related to life itself. How does a school pay attention to developing skills related to self-discipline, empathy, responsibility, and altruism, for example? How does a school nurture student attitudes such as ownership for learning and behaviour, trust, and risk-taking?

Consistency Within a School

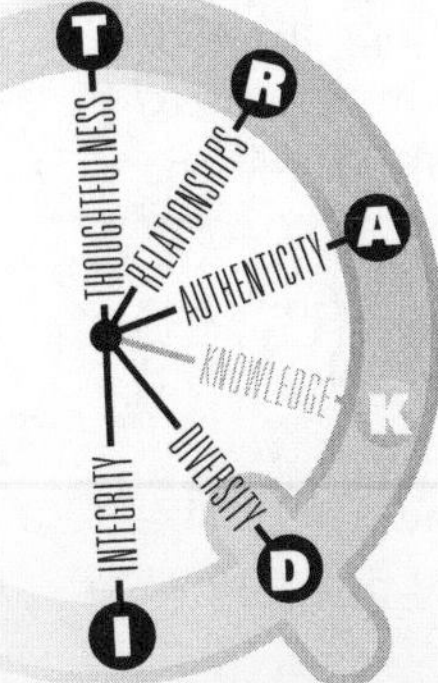

Assumption 2: Adults in a school do not need to work together to achieve consistency in the implementation of school goals. Students accept differences in adults.

Given that schools are social places and that the central purpose of school is learning, how does the institution embrace learning in its day-to-day operation? Is learning confined to classrooms? Have you considered learning that takes place in lunchrooms, hallways, and the office, for example? How important is it that adults respond to young people in consistent ways when dealing with them in various areas of the school?

It is not unusual for teachers to hold the assumption that students learn to accept differences in the professional behaviour of adults in classrooms and in other places around the school. If Teacher A employs a very autocratic, somewhat punitive approach to dealing with students in the lunchroom, for example, and Teacher B in that same lunchroom attempts to teach responsibility through humanness and caring, what effect would this have on learning? Would there be a difference if this disparity occurred at a primary school level as opposed to high school? Think back to our discussion in Chapter 8 and the attitudes of Sven Anderson (p. 170) and Lorenzo Sanchez (p. 173). What if these two teachers were on supervision together in hallways or lunchrooms? Do you see potential problems for learning in the conflicting messages young people might receive? The question of a school's orientation to learning—cognitive, social, psychomotor, moral-ethical—becomes germane. Teachers are unique individuals with their own personalities and idiosyncrasies, but when they are teaching young people to show respect and consideration to others, for example, then they must do so in ways that are consistent with good learning and their school's declared intentions. A special approach to leadership is required in a school to ensure that students experience consistency in the ways they are treated by adults and in the ways of learning that the school values.

Administration in Schools

Assumption 3: Administration is simply getting things done efficiently and using the power of authority to ensure that people in non-leadership positions do their jobs.

Connections between Administration and Learning

We would like you to think deeply about this notion of "providing for learning needs" and the resulting implications for a school environment. For example, how does a school's use of time—its timetable—accommodate differences in the ways people learn? To facilitate students in learning how to become responsible, does a school actively seek student opinion on matters to do with policies and procedures regarding discipline? Teachers should be encouraged to ask deeper questions about dwelling in the teaching world. Typical of these deeper questions are, Who am I in the lives of children? How am I positioned by others? How do I position them? In short, this kind of question invites us to contemplate living in the world of a teacher, as opposed to simply doing the "job" of teaching.

Similar questions may be asked of schools, but before these questions are raised let us think about the purpose of schooling. Why do young people attend school? We are sure you are ready with the obvious response: "They have to." Of course the law requires young people to attend school up to the age of sixteen. Given that school attendance is mandatory, what then is the purpose of schooling?

9.4 FOR YOUR CONSIDERATION

Here are four conceptions of school to think about:

a) school as place to prepare young people for a role in the "workplace"
b) school as a place to prepare young people for life
c) school as a sanctuary
d) school as a place to prepare young people for post-secondary education

Which of these conceptions do you consider to be most appropriate for schooling? Why?

Questions relating to the purpose of schooling invite a variety of perspectives and responses. We believe that one response should rise above all others. Schools are places young people attend for the purpose of learning: about themselves, about others, about their world, and about who they are in that world. We would like you to be clear on the nature of these places called schools, where hundreds of people (possibly thousands in larger high schools) attend each weekday with a common purpose. How would you describe such an institution? We would like you to understand the social nature of the place. A school is very much a social institution and it is within this context that the central purpose of school—learning—takes place.

Schools today are, arguably, quite similar to schools of decades past. To what extent is the essential way of organizing and running schools different from, say, thirty years ago?

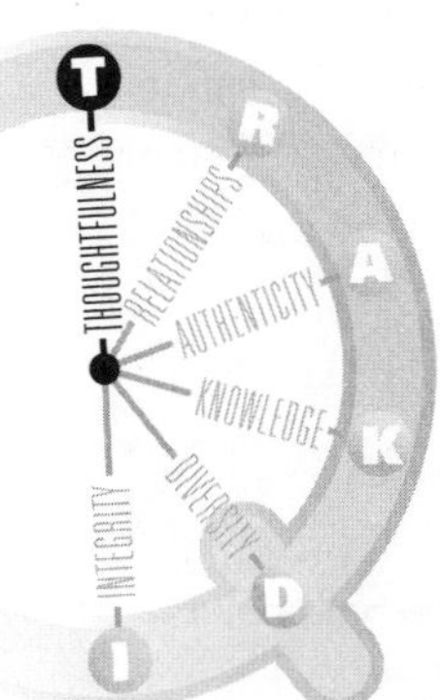

Administration to Effect "Meaning and Understanding"

A teaching quality promoted in this book is thoughtfulness. We believe that a good teacher is a thoughtful teacher. Meaning and understanding are critical elements of thoughtfulness. In every chapter of this book we have invited you to think about the importance of assumptions. Teachers must understand clearly the intention of any agreements developed and presented by a school as indicators of purpose and direction. As a principal new to a school, one author of this book remembers engaging teachers in a conversation about discipline.

9.5 FOR YOUR CONSIDERATION

1. Decide, as a group, how schools are organized and run today, in a general sense. Break your responses down into categories, e.g., buildings, resources, subjects, timetables, rules, discipline, attitudes of teachers toward students, teaching methods, and attitudes of students toward school.
2. Ask your parents and/or grandparents how school was organized when they attended, according to the categories you used in part 1. Compare the two. What are the significant differences in the ways that schooling is practised today as opposed to thirty years ago?

The discussion was impassioned and intense. After about fifteen minutes, three or four differing understandings of discipline were evident, resulting in people talking past each other with little agreement on anything, let alone an understanding of discipline. Here, in summary, are the approaches to discipline taken by the staff:

A. Hard line	Kids must learn the hard way."You goof up, you pay the price." (Hard consequences)
B. Tough love	Distinguish between the person and the misbehaviour."I like you as a person, but you made a mistake. Tell me the rules. Now, you also know that when you break them you face the music."
C. Natural/logical consequences	Life has consequences for rule (law) transgressions."Do you understand what you did wrong? Here are some consequences. You messed up the washroom. See me after school for a mop and cleaning fluid and be prepared to clean up."
D. Learning from mistakes	Sit down and talk to the child. Involve the child in decisions about consequences. May involve a letter expressing feelings of regret or remorse.

The discussion was useful but clearly we needed to do a great deal of work to gain any sort of useful consensus for a consistent approach to discipline in the school. The objective was not that everyone should think the same way. Remember our recognition of the uniqueness of people. The need was to gain clarity on the kinds of social learning the school would work toward and then seek meaning and understanding about that learning. Once again, the deeper questions become germane. Who are we in the lives of young people? How do they position us and vice versa? We need to deepen the questioning to move beyond the *what* and *how* questions to *why* and *who* forms of inquiry (Palmer, 1998, p. 4).

9.6 FOR YOUR CONSIDERATION

Take the generalized teacher responses A, B, C, and D from the summary of teacher positions given above, and place them on the continuum:

Weak student learning ———————————————— Strong student learning

a b c d

Toward which end of the continuum would you expect student learning to be strongest? Why? (Use the following references from this book to guide your decision: Chapter 4, pp. 72–75; Chapter 6, 7 and 8.)

1 Discuss your position in a small group and try to gain consensus. Then move into a larger group and try to expand the consensus.
2 How would you respect and reconcile differences among your larger group so that, if you were part of a school staff, children would not get mixed messages?

As we move to discuss administration and its impact on learning, think back to Assumption 3. Is administration solely a matter of efficiency, of using authority to ensure that people do their jobs? How should the principal deal with the disparate views on discipline?

Administration for Learning

Leadership and management are inextricably interwoven in the course of practice. However, we believe that teachers and administrators exhibit certain dispositions toward management or leadership, and that the particular dispositions displayed will have a significant impact on learning in a school.

Assumption 4: School administrations that exemplify extreme dispositions toward management develop rich learning environments.

A Management Disposition Toward Administration in Schools

You may encounter people in schools who believe that a well-managed school is sufficient to ensure an effective learning environment. We agree that good management is a necessary condition for an effective learning environment, but we do not believe that it is sufficient.

In a rather strict interpretation, management looks after the business at hand and gets things done in the most efficient way possible. Indeed, in this strict interpretation of a **management disposition,** the completion of tasks and the accomplishment of goals are ends in themselves, and are often the internal standard by which role effectiveness is judged. Teachers who hold the attitude, "Leave me alone and let me get on with my job" appreciate administrators with a management disposition because things that need doing can be shuffled off to the administrator for completion. The teacher doesn't have to deal with it, and the administrator perhaps gains satisfaction from completing the task and doing something for the teacher.

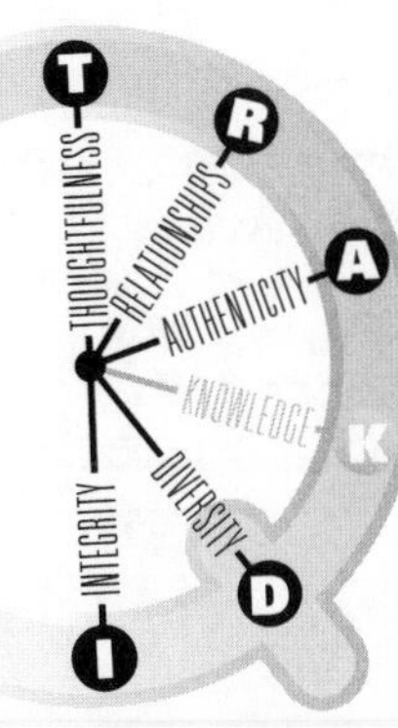

This behaviour is acceptable if the requests pertain to things such as building maintenance, acquisition of supplies, and social services involvement, but the inherent attitudes and assumptions tend to manifest themselves in learning-related matters as well: "Go down to see the principal, Johnny. Perhaps your father would like to hear about your poor behaviour." "If this is the best work you can do, perhaps you should explain yourself to the assistant principal." "Why are you two boys pushing each other around in the hallway? Get down to the office immediately." Who should deal with these classroom and hallway concerns? Without knowing the context for any of the incidents, what response would you expect from the principal or assistant principal? What administration response do you think the teacher would expect? What would the students be learning from the ways they were treated? (Waldron, 1996)

We would like you to imagine yourself as a professional. You have a considerable amount of professional knowledge from your studies. Increasingly, as time goes on, you absorb a great deal of practical wisdom from the practice of your profession. You learn from young people, from colleagues, from parents and from others with whom you have contact who have an intelligent interest in teaching and learning. Essentially you are a competent professional who has a great deal to offer in your chosen field. If you worked in a controlling and controlled environment, how often would you become involved in ways that shape your working environment? When you work continuously in a controlled environment, what do you think it does to your worldview? How might it affect your professional outlook? We believe that strong management dispositions tend to reduce teaching and limit teachers to a role that does not allow the full blossoming of their professionalism. Others with greater responsibility (power?) know best how the shoe fits.

"Wellness" in Schools

Wellness is a term you will hear often in workplaces. It refers to the feelings and attitudes workers have toward their roles in the workplace. What conditions in the workplace contribute to feelings of wellness? People who feel they have some control over their working conditions tend to feel more positive toward work. Because they have some degree of control they are able to effect change and shape things for the better. Most endeavours in life are accompanied by stress, and stress can be positive or negative. When people experience negative stress it is likely that feelings of being unwell permeate their workdays. Negative stress is usually the result of overwhelming events one feels powerless to change. Interestingly, negative stress, a fairly common concern among teachers, tends not to be caused by, "too much work, too little time, or too little compensation. Rather, it is powerlessness—a lack of control over what one is doing" (Kohn, 1993, p. 10).

Wellness is promoted when people feel they have some control over their workdays, when the ways of working allow people to take action on issues that directly affect their roles. In schools, teachers and administrators tend to feel more positive when they have opportunities to take ownership for their lives in school, to have a voice in decisions and actions that directly affect their roles and responsibilities in the school. Words such as *liberation* and *freedom* are often heard when describing these conditions.

To what extent should schools be places for teacher well-being as well as student well-being?

This discussion should not be understood as a case against efficiency in schools. There are few things more debilitating than working in an inefficient environment. Teachers appreciate a well-run school. Concerns emerge when a particular disposition veers toward an extreme. Consider the following continuum:

Management disposition ———————————————— Leadership disposition

If an administrator's disposition is weighted too strongly toward the management end of the continuum we believe there is potential for some concern. Remember our comments about Assumption 4: An efficient management disposition is a "necessary but not sufficient" condition for an effective learning environment. Do you agree with this?

The Leadership Disposition in Schools

***Assumption 5:* A person disposed toward leadership tends to value and trust the competencies of people working with and through their passions to create successful learning environments.**

What differences, then, might we expect in a person whose disposition leans more toward leadership? A **leadership disposition** demonstrates the tendency to value and trust the competencies of people, working with and through their strengths and passions to effect a strong learning environment, establishing conditions for teachers to work in collaboration—not in isolation—to foster the most successful learning possible for young people.

As a transition to a discussion of a leadership disposition, read the following description of a school situation. Try to understand the motivation behind the staff's attitude and the administration's response to events. Also decide where you would place the administration on the management/leadership continuum above.

> Lunchtime was not a calm time in Ayshah's school. The school was noisy, there was litter on the floor, and teachers resented having to supervise large numbers of adolescents for an hour every day. They had more important things to do with their time. Increasingly, at staff meetings, teachers were registering their complaints with conviction.
>
> Ayshah and her assistant principal, Gareth, would retreat to her office after a staff meeting and contemplate a course of action that would calm the teachers down. Gareth, a practical man, proposed that the children be contained in a small area near the school's main doors so that they would be easier to supervise. Ayshah, listening intently, was warming to the idea for she saw this as a way of cutting down the supervision requirements. A period of silence fell over the office as both of them thought a little more about the suggestion before them.
>
> Then Ayshah had an idea: the children could be sent outside the building for forty minutes of the one-hour lunchtime period. Twenty minutes, she mused, should be sufficient for them to eat their lunches and then, presto! Out they go.

Supervision outside requires fewer people than inside the building, where children are wandering into every nook and cranny. They decided on concessions for inclement weather: lunchtime inside when wet (constant rain) or below -15C.

The plan was presented to staff at the next meeting and carried 15 to 3.

In this scenario, the administration dealt with a problem in an efficient manner. The plan was put into effect; the task was completed. What is your opinion about the attitude of the staff? What do you think about the administration's solution? Who owned the problem during the lunch period? The group that owned the problem should learn how to deal with it. In dealing with the problem they would learn valuable lessons about responsibility, ownership, and problem solving. The management mentality of the administration and the hierarchical subordinate mentality of the teachers resulted in appeals to the administration for a solution to the nuisance of students disturbing teachers' lunch period, and in the administration solving the problem by removing the students to a more distant location. Who learned what in this situation?

Characteristics of a Leadership Disposition

We believe that teachers need to experience a leadership disposition that encourages them to unleash their collective wisdom, experience, and professional knowledge, and to apply their insights to the greater success of the schools in which they work. Ways of working in schools benefit from leadership that encourages critical inquiry before taking action on any matter that directly affects learning and teaching. This disposition toward leadership establishes the conditions for teachers to engage in real collaboration to effect the most successful learning for all students.

Attitudes displayed by administrators with a strong leadership disposition involve devolution of responsibility to teachers on matters to do with learning and teaching. Typically this includes curriculum development and planning, class organization, use of space, communication with parents about preferred approaches to learning and teaching and about assessment methods, including exhibitions and demonstrations of learning. Administrators with leadership dispositions also trust teachers to know what needs to be done and to get it done effectively. They also value the importance of relationships so that they can work with and through the strengths and passions of staff, as they focus the school on meeting the learning needs of students. Leadership of this kind appreciates diverse views; dissent is dignified, and opinions are valued.

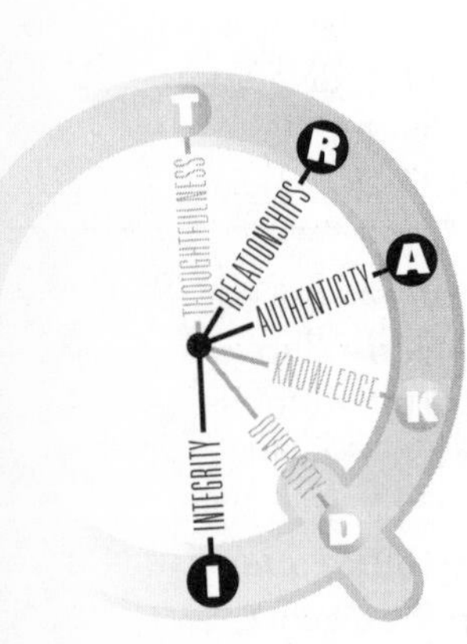

We believe that these leadership qualities enrich the necessary qualities of a management disposition to effect an administrative orientation that will create a strong learning environment in a school.

Ownership and Responsibility in Schools

Assumption 6: Learning is the responsibility of individual teachers working in their own classrooms. Administration should simply run an efficient school so that teachers can get on with the job of teaching.

We remind you once again of Glickman's caution about wanting to circumscribe situations. Lunchtime is the administration's responsibility, and teachers, therefore, don't have to do anything. This works fine, perhaps, until such time as teachers perceive lunchtime to be a problem. The circumscribed responsibility becomes something to which blame is attached. Staff meetings become the "official" mechanism for venting complaints, and the administration is required to act. Decision: get rid of the kids and, through this action, get rid of the problem.

We ask you to think about being practical. We are sure you see nothing untoward in this thought. Most of us have to be practical in our day-to-day lives. It's the only way we get things done. How is being practical, or pragmatic, problematic in Ayshah's school? If a school is a place for learning, in the broadest sense of the term, and we accept that social learning is a fundamental part of the learning picture, especially for young adolescents, then what patterns of behaviour, what attitudes, in Ayshah's school are proving to be an impediment? Why is this the case and what is being impeded?

We consider it important that schools experience leadership that is shared by all who are party to the enterprise, so that teachers are free to contribute openly to the ambience, ethos, and design of the whole school as a learning environment. The goal is to release any constraints that inhibit the powerful collective experience, wills, and spirits of teachers to meet the learning needs of young people. You will discover that teachers benefit from being liberated from the constraints of hierarchy and control so that they might take ownership and unfettered responsibility for the schools in which they are knowledgeable, competent professionals.

The Role of Learners under a Leadership Disposition

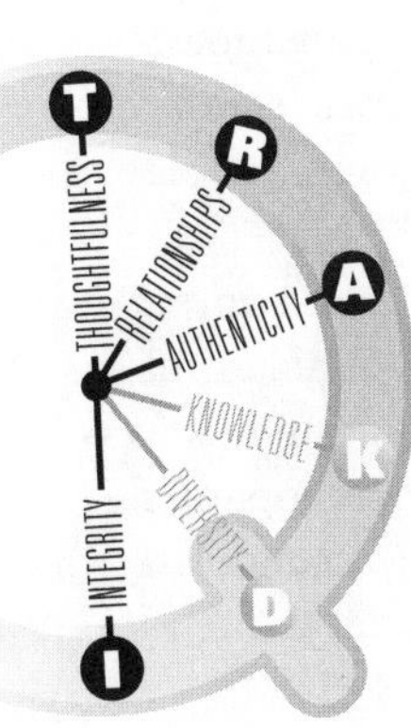

We are sure it is not too long ago that you were a student in grade school. Were you ever consulted, formally or informally, about the running of the school? Did anybody ever ask you for input when discipline policies were being set? Did the school ever ask for student representation on committees setting, say, homework policy? We suspect that for the great majority of you, the answer will be no. School was a fairly autocratic place where, as Kohn (1993) rather bluntly states, things are typically done to young people, rather than with them: "An array of punishments and rewards is used to enforce compliance with an agenda that students rarely have an opportunity to influence" (p. 10). Well, of course, there are exceptions to the picture that Kohn paints, but do you think that schools generally embody the principles of democracy that one might expect in a democratic society? If not, how do young people learn about social and political responsibility in these institutions?

People with a strong leadership disposition operate from a firm belief in the competencies of people and trust that these competencies will flourish in a supportive and liberating environment. A leadership disposition allows students to benefit through democratic approaches to consultation and involvement. Student voice is important, and opportunities to have meaningful impact on school organization, learning, and teaching are always present.

9.7 FOR YOUR CONSIDERATION

- How might principles of democracy be evident throughout an elementary school?
- Describe the form of governance you might expect to see in this school.
- What role would you see for parents in the school's ways of working?
- What role would you see for children up to age nine? What role for children from ten to twelve? Give reasons why, and consider the information in Chapter 5 in your reasoning.

Pragmatism and Practicality in Schools

Assumption 7: Practicality and pragmatism are sufficient conditions to bring about progress and change in schools.

If teachers are to work together to articulate and carry out a school's intentions, then meaning and understanding become very significant. The matter of action looms large in any school because pragmatism is almost a way of life. Whenever young people are present then teachers must also be present. Classrooms need teachers, and hallways, lunchrooms, and playgrounds need supervisors. A school's daily rhythm is one of constant interaction between teachers and students, with precious little time for professional conversation. Time spent talking about matters that teachers do not consider to be connected to the business of the day is often deemed dispensable.

This leads to what may be termed the **impediment of pragmatism,** which means that conversations needed to gain clarity about school-wide intentions, new knowledge, and the challenging of assumptions may easily be relegated to a later time in favour of more immediate tasks that need to be done. When this occurs, the practicalities of daily life in school—marking, coaching, organizing displays, preparing lessons, keeping records, consulting with colleagues, searching for resources, and so on—impede the time needed to give attention to whole-school matters.

Professional development days can fall into this category unless their content emanates from the day-to-day intentions of a school. One-shot professional development activity suffers from a lack of grounding in ongoing practice and tends to have limited enduring success. Attention to action should always be accompanied by attention to meaning and understanding. It is incumbent upon a school to establish conditions within which these practices can be considered.

Organism and Corporation: Two Metaphors for Schools

We have used Figure 9.1 to invite you to think about the need to orchestrate professional activity in a school toward achieving desired intentions. We now invite you to explore a little further the concept of a school as an entity, a place with the potential to have a powerful collective impact on student learning, rather than a place where learning takes place in unconnected ways, in quasi-isolated units of space called classrooms. In For Your Consideration 9.4, we invited you to discuss four conceptions of school.

We now invite you to read and think about two metaphors for school to further broaden your understanding of this place we call school: organism and corporation.

School as an Organism

Assumption 8: School is a people-intensive institution where the interconnectedness of people, activities, and functions occurs automatically to bring about success in learning.

An organism is a complex living structure with connected interdependent parts whose relations and properties contribute to the health and well-being of the whole. The whole is considerably greater than the sum of its parts. The school as a social institution is a hub of human interaction and may usefully be understood, metaphorically, as an organism.

In Chapter 5 (pp. 96–97) we claim that schools have little choice in being social institutions. They do have a choice in how they respond to the social characteristics in the name of learning. Remember, a school is a place with a purpose; it is not merely a place where random things happen. A school is a community where learning should happen by design rather than by chance. In the following story think about the metaphor of an organism, and seek to understand the school as a community where learning happens by design.

> The professional development day at Grenfell School was over and most staff members were satisfied with the outcome. After much debate, discussion, and soul-searching, the school now had a clear statement of purpose, a mission statement to publish and post, and a sense of vision to head them in exciting directions. The future looked rosy.
>
> Three weeks after the momentous professional day, Yasin and a few teachers began to talk about the new directions and moved to design some projects that reflected the new way of thinking. Other staff, a little more cautious, held off on becoming involved. A few teachers led by Simon, a man of some experience, simply refused to do anything; they didn't agree with the decisions on the professional development day and they were not about to change their ways.
>
> Yasin and his group, on their own initiative, began to implement some of their ideas and children found themselves learning in different ways. Mrs. Singh's child told of being in a group of amoebas and being required to dramatize a scientific experiment, to write a story from the perspective of an amoeba, extolling the merits of a single-cell existence. Mr. McKenzie's son was writing stories in mathematics and drawing sketches about equations in the life of a grizzly bear.

Parents started calling the principal. "What's going on?" asked one parent. "Why aren't these kids learning science?"

"You don't tell stories in math," challenged another irritated parent. "My son hasn't had any problems to do for over a week now."

"Why are kids working all over the school, lying on the floor, sticking stuff all over the walls?" complained another parent.

Questions about budget, space, and differences in approaches to learning, leadership, and general communication increasingly inundated the school. Simon and his cohort were dissenting voices. Yasin's go-getters were oblivious in their enthusiasm. The principal had an uneasy feeling that things were getting away from him, and many parents were simply upset. What had started with an exciting day was gradually turning into a troublesome experience.

Schools are people-intensive places where decisions and actions have repercussions in various dimensions of the school and into the parent community. If there is some difficulty in one facet of school life, then it will inevitably show up in another area as well. What dynamics were at work in the Grenfell example? People didn't seem to know what was going on, what was being done by whom, where, and with what resources. Parents were confused and staff divided. What was the problem?

Take a moment to think of your body. What parts of your body are absolutely necessary to its effective and efficient functioning? Let's say you picked arms, legs, brain, heart, kidneys, liver, lungs, and digestive system. What happens to a person when one or more of these parts is not working effectively and efficiently? Let's say you have a broken leg. Is your body able to function well? If you had a punctured or collapsed lung, could you perform at full capacity? We are sure you see the point. Of course you would be somewhat incapacitated by these impediments. The organism that is your body would not be effective and efficient.

A school, then, will not be efficient and effective if any of its elements is in some way deficient. What are the parts that make up a school? The essence of understanding a school as an organism is ownership. Designing processes for working together must be an internal matter. It is possible to enunciate some conditions that should be at work in such an environment.

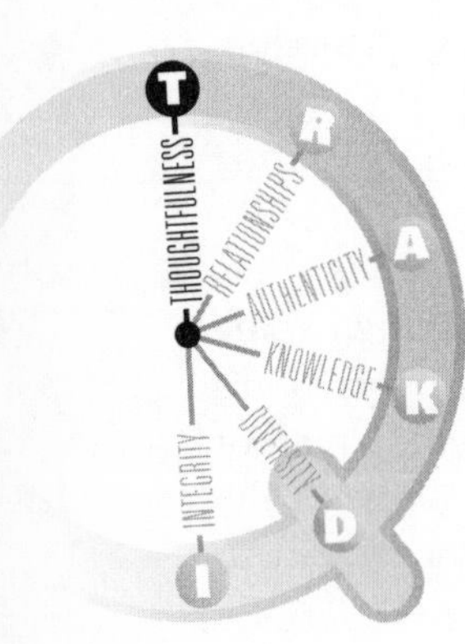

Elements that make up a school may be understood as dimensions, each connected and working in synergy. By way of example, consider a set of dimensions determined by a school with which one of the authors was once associated: communications; physical environment; curriculum (learning and teaching); management/administration; professional vitality; and social-emotional wellness. Before we move to the next condition, think about the following reminder from Senge (1990) as he discusses the need for communities (schools) to learn together:

> A school is a community where, "people continually expand their capacity to create the results they truly desire, where new and expansive patterns of thinking are nurtured, where collective aspiration is set free, and where people are continually learning how to learn together." (p. 3)

Understanding **school as an organism** would mean that a school must learn to foster and nurture its own health and wellness. In a healthy, fully functioning organism, there is a synergistic relationship among the parts. In a healthy school all people who make up the school must work and learn together to identify the school's dimensions, and define and describe the contributions of each dimension to the learning in the school. Also, they should understand the synergistic relationship among the dimensions so that the school will be a vibrant and successful place.

The very essence of understanding a school as an organism is ownership. Designing processes for working together in a school must be an internal matter characterized by collaboration and cooperation. Three key conditions should be at work in such an environment.

- Ownership is a very important condition for a dynamic school. People can experience ownership only when they have a hand in shaping the school. They know what is happening because they have been involved in shaping the way the school responds to its learning intentions.
- Empowerment is an essentially liberating condition. In the practice of their daily work, teachers and young people flourish when they experience a learning environment in which they feel free to take risks, to explore, and to experience an intimate involvement in *their* school.
- Shared decision making is a feature of school governance that truly embodies the previous conditions. True involvement in a school and the spirit of freedom that empowerment brings are really enacted when decision making is shared with teachers and young people.

Let us return to the Grenfell School example. What was the nature of the problem? Who seemed to own the problem? Who clearly *doesn't* own the problem? That question harks back to Glickman's position about the tendency for people to want to circumscribe problems so that they can assign responsibility to others, and to the situation at Lester B. Pearson Elementary School (pp. 200–201). Try to understand the situation at Grenfell School through our discussion of dimensions and the three key conditions described above. Imagine how many of the potentially negative aspects of the situation might be remedied if the school functioned more as an organism.

9.8 FOR YOUR CONSIDERATION

Grenfell School has established a purpose and direction.

1. If the dimensions and the three conditions described in the text were in effect at the school, how might the situation have been different?
2. How might a stronger leadership disposition have provided conditions that could avert the difficulties they were clearly experiencing? Remember the discussion of dimensions: staff, through some school-determined process, would be paying attention to all dimensions in an ongoing way. A further reminder: the dimensions all work together in a synergistic fashion. If an action or decision is made in the curriculum (learning and teaching) dimension then those implications would be considered within all others.

School as a Corporation

Assumption 9: The tall hierarchical organizational structures that tend to characterize schooling make wise use of power to create successful learning environments.

Typically, corporations are organized with boards of directors, CEOs, presidents, vice-presidents, senior managers, middle managers, and so on. The hierarchical nature of most business environments sees increasing levels of power, with each level of the hierarchy having power over those below. Social scientists refer to this kind of **hierarchy** as tall organizational or institutional structure. In education this hierarchy may be similar to the following:

chief superintendent of schools

superintendent of instruction

district level supervisor

principal

assistant principal

department head (in secondary school)

teacher

The hierarchy could be extended through provincial/territorial departments of education as well.

Some important assumptions are embedded in tall organizational structures, all having to do with power. One assumption is that the higher up the hierarchy, the more capable the person is. It follows that most of the important decisions will be made at the higher levels. Another assumption is that lower levels of hierarchies are staffed by people deemed to be less capable and with less power. Those at or near the bottom of a hierarchy need close supervision. This rather stark explication of hierarchical organization and attitude is important to note in a schooling context because of the implications it has for teachers and their involvement in decision making.

We invite you to consider again the management disposition toward administration. On page 198 we recognized the professional status of teachers and how this professionalism manifests itself in a thorough knowledge of the raison d'être of schools-learning and teaching. Teachers know the learning needs of students and how to respond to these needs. Can you think of any contradictions in a hierarchical organization in schooling? Would this hierarchical power allocation work effectively in a school setting? To what extent is this form of power allocation conducive to the nurturing of a vibrant learning environment? Apply your understanding of this metaphor to the situation at Grenfell School. Would co-operation and meaning and understanding result? Do you think it could solve the problem?

Let's explore the corporation metaphor a little further with a look at Champlain High School, in the following example:

Champlain High School was promoting its image as a strongly academic school, where results on provincial achievement tests were of the utmost importance, and as an athletic school, where the performance of athletic teams was a further indicator of the school's quality. Honour rolls were prominently displayed in the hallways on wall spaces not occupied by sports trophy display cases. Literature distributed by the school lauded former students who had achieved university entrance and success in the academic and business community. A special place was reserved near the main office for the recognition of those few students who reached the level of professional sports.

Thursday evening was the school's annual open house for students entering the school for the first time in September. Parents and their children were talking excitedly in the auditorium, waiting for the evening's proceedings to begin. Finally the principal arrived, flanked by his assistants, and the open house commenced. After a cordial welcome the principal began to tell parents and prospective students about the school and its expectations.

"When you come to Champlain, you will be joining a community of high achievers where success in all endeavours is demanded and expected. The teachers in this school are here to teach and you will be here to learn. If you do not learn, it will be interpreted as a choice you have made and serious consequences may result. The discipline in this school is ..."

Later in the evening, before the school tour, parents were invited to ask questions of the administration. Mrs. Chung asked, "My son has real difficulty with his mathematics and in his last school was getting special help. Will you be able to help him when he comes to Champlain?"

"Thank you for your question," said the principal. "As I have outlined during my introductory remarks, Champlain stresses high achievement in all endeavours. The teachers do their part to the best of their abilities, and we expect students also to work to the best of their abilities. If you think your son will have difficulties at Champlain then perhaps, in his best interests, he might be better off in another school. I suggest you give serious consideration to this suggestion. I'm sure you understand that we are all interested first and foremost in the well-being of students."

The principal then turned to the next question.

What do you think about the principal's attitude toward Mrs. Chung and her son? There was no mention of Mrs. Chung's son having a learning disability. She

9.9 FOR YOUR CONSIDERATION

Work in two groups and discuss the Champlain story, answering the following questions.

1 Position yourself as the principal: What place do the parents hold in his world as a principal?
2 Position yourself as Mrs. Chung: What is the school in her life as a parent?

After sufficient time for discussion, assemble your two groups facing each other along each side of the room. The two sides should then engage in an open debate, with each side taking the position of either the principal or Mrs. Chung. Which side seems to be more persuasive? Why?

said only that he was having, "real difficulty with his mathematics." What do you think of the school's apparent philosophy toward learning? Champlain is a public school, presumably there to work with any student who enrols, unlike many private schools, which select clientele to meet their espoused goals. What are the principal's goals for the school? Do you consider his goals to be those of a professional leader? We suspect he is trying to project the image of a well-run school, an efficient school, where high achievement on measures of learning will validate the school's effectiveness. In his efforts to project the image of a successful school, his admission policies prefer the more academically able students. We ask you to ponder the approaches to learning and teaching in the school. Which do you think should concern the principal more: meeting the needs of students, or meeting the needs of the school?

This admittedly provocative little story is not fictitious. We offer it for you to reflect on in the context of hierarchy and the metaphor of school as corporation. The principal is promoting academic excellence, and that is laudable. But is it not a school's responsibility to attend to the learning needs of all students? It seems that Champlain is interested only in those students who have the ability to achieve high scores on achievement tests. Is this an appropriate attitude for a public school principal?

Hierarchy denotes capability and power. The principal is responsible for his school, and with that responsibility come concerns about enrolment, staff, student behaviour, parent perceptions, perceptions of superiors, and money. What disposition toward administration do you think the principal of Champlain School favours? How do you think the characteristics of hierarchy are reflected in the principal's behaviour? As you contemplate the last question, give some thought to the teachers in Champlain School. Do you think teachers have been consulted about the learning needs of students such as Mrs. Chung's son? If they have and if they concur with the principal's philosophy, then what approaches to learning and teaching do you think they will practice? Chapter 8 provides some insight as to what these approaches might be. If the teachers do not concur, then what do you think the principal will do to ensure that his school gets the results he wants?

What does this photo reveal about this school's philosophy?

Reflection and Perspective on the Chapter

A particular tendency in schooling is the pitfall of reductionism, the proclivity to reduce the complex to the simple. Schools are very complex places. Institutions that deal with people are always fairly complicated places, because people are themselves very different. Schools deal with many kinds of people—young people, parents, professional staff, support staff, community, politicians, and so on. If management is the sole disposition displayed by those with assigned responsibility for school, then the complexity may well be reduced to something merely to be managed. Pre-service teachers are often warned not to be in too much of a hurry to teach. Before they start teaching, they must put a great deal of thought into understanding the young people they will be inviting to learn. The whole school is a learning environment, or learning community, where learning for teachers as well as young people should be nurtured. Understanding this is very important for a teacher to work comfortably and effectively. Teachers should view a school as *their* school, with all the implications of ownership that that implies.

Historically schools have reflected the cultures and societal influences of their times. As recently as fifty years ago society was generally stable, change occurred slowly, and times were less complex. The incredible pace of change in today's world places schooling in a seemingly paradoxical situation. The roots of schooling still anchor the institution to times past. Many people speak, almost romantically, about times when children in school experienced discipline and structure. They learned their subjects and knew how to read, write, and do arithmetic. "Let's get back to the basics," we hear. One might place many interpretations on this yearning for times past and it is not our place to get into subjective judgments here. It is interesting, however, to consider the paradox. We live in a world in which new knowledge and change is upon us with increasing rapidity. If one looks at society just ten years ago, one sees remarkable changes compared to today. Is it not reasonable to expect that schooling—society's way of helping young people to become competent, caring, and contributing citizens—should be experiencing similar changes?

Schools experience many pressures from all kinds of constituents. As public institutions, schools are of interest to many agencies, organizations, institutions, and governments. Universities, home and school associations, departments of education, charitable organizations, social services departments, fundraising companies, professional and amateur sports organizations, teachers' professional associations, and illness prevention societies are some bodies in society with agendas for schools. Schools also have obligations to become familiar with current professional knowledge. Schools, as the points of convergence, are expected to respond to the agendas. We encourage you to think deeply about the complexity of schools.

Key Terms

ecology of a school 200
hierarchy 218
impediment of pragmatism 214
leadership disposition 211
management disposition 209
reductionism 199
school as an entity 201
school as an organism 216

Suggested Further Reading

Bliss, Traci, & Mazur, Joan (2002). *K-12 Teachers in the midst of reform: Common thread cases*. Upper Saddle River, NJ: Prentice Hall Inc.

Bolman, Lee G., & Deal, Terrence E. (2002). *Reframing the path to school leadership*. Thousand Oaks, CA: Corwin Press.

Glickman, Carl D. (2002). *Leadership for learning: How to help teachers succeed*. Alexandria, VA: Association for Supervision and Curriculum Development.

Grudin, Robert (1990). *The grace of great things: Creativity and innovation*. New York: Ticknor and Fields.

Pellicer, Leonard (1999). *Caring enough to lead.* Thousand Oaks, CA: Corwin Press.

Stoll, Louise & Fink, Dean (1996). *Changing our schools: Linking school effectiveness and school improvement*. Buckingham, UK: Open University Press.

Chapter 10

Classrooms

Typically today's schools are organized in much the same way as they were in 1925. The basic organizational unit for instruction is the self-contained classroom containing one teacher—a subject matter specialist—and approximately thirty students. (Howard, 1996, p. 75)

Chapter Focus

Why classrooms? Young people are taught about their world primarily by significant adults in their lives. The hunter-gatherers/farmer-fishers passed on to their heirs important knowledge and skills they needed to know to survive, as well as their view of their world. As the knowledge base grew, individuals within the community took on special roles, such as spiritual leader, historian, and scribe. They became the holders and bearers of specific skills and knowledge that were passed on to each new generation. Gradually, specific environments were constructed for passing on this knowledge and skill more formally. Children were taken away from the environment in which they had learned to walk and talk and were placed in what Matthews and Kay (2001) describe as "a long-term, expensive intervention termed 'formal education'" (p. 113). This is how classrooms with four walls and one teacher came to exist.

Does it matter how classrooms are designed and organized? What options do teachers have? A teacher needs to be concerned about physical space factors such as lighting, windows, fixtures, equipment and technology, and the use of the space. What do the teacher's philosophical ideals about pedagogy—power versus a democratic model—have to do with classroom design? How can teachers create a learning environment conducive to the learning they wish to effect? Many questions, many assumptions, and many decisions call for consideration with respect to teaching and learning in classrooms.

This chapter will present ideas about classroom design, classroom grouping for learning, classroom management, as well as alternatives that go beyond classroom walls.

Focus Questions

1. Whose needs are being served when classroom space is organized? Where does the student's voice fit into the scheme of things?
2. Why do we use separate classrooms for separate functions?
3. Should learning styles influence classroom design?
4. How does classroom design reflect the teacher's philosophy of learning and teaching?
5. Where does technology, specifically computers, fit into the classroom design and organization?
6. What are the various ways of grouping learners and under what circumstances do teachers form these groups?
7. What are the issues surrounding team teaching?
8. Why should teachers give students experiences that go beyond the classroom walls?
9. What classroom choices are available to parents, teachers, and students beyond the self-contained classroom inside a school?

10.1 FOR YOUR CONSIDERATION

Miss Joan Jensen completed her Grade 12 in a small school in northern Manitoba. Her future, after high school, consisted of career options such as nurse, teacher, or housewife. She wanted to see more of the world than her small community, and she wanted to work with young children. She believed that becoming a wife to a local fellow would not be advantageous to see the world. Since she was always good at her schooling, especially in language arts, she opted to take the ten-month teacher-training course offered at the university.

Living in the city was an interesting experience for her, but it ended all too quickly. Joan spent the summer with her family and just after her eighteenth birthday she received a contract to teach in a southern community near Brandon. She was excited by this new prospect, but also fearful. The one-room schoolhouse had twenty-three students, ranging in ages from six to seventeen, Grades 1 to 8. Several were siblings. The two seventeen-year-olds were sons of farmers who spent most of their time on the fields, planting, harvesting, calving, and milking. Most were of English heritage, a few Ukrainian and German, two Aboriginal, and one other (you decide).

Joan had studied what she felt was a great deal at the time about teaching. She had completed thirteen years in the school system, and so knew a great deal about schooling. Was she prepared to meet the needs of these students? She hoped so.

1. What teaching qualities do you believe are essential for Joan? What specific knowledge and skills would she need to have acquired from her post-secondary school experience to be prepared to meet the needs of her students?
2. Imagine you are one of the students on her first day as a teacher. What age are you? What is your family's heritage? Does it matter? Do you enter the school alone or with someone else, maybe a sibling? What do you believe your thoughts, fear, or hopes might be for this new school year?
3. Imagine you are Joan (or Jon). What might your thoughts be on this first day of school? Compare them with your colleagues' thoughts.

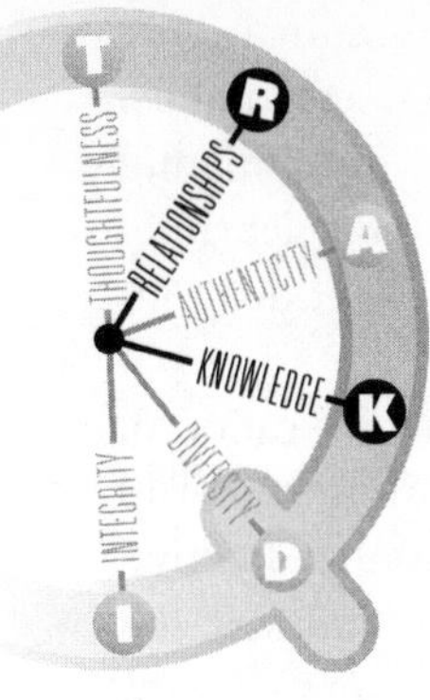

The Traditional Classroom

The terms *traditional classroom, traditional teaching,* and *industrial model* have been referred to in previous chapters. What images do they conjure up? Do they fit with your assumptions about classrooms—teacher at the front of the classroom and the young learners in rows, faces to the front? Is this a stereotypical image of a classroom or the real thing that is common in schools today?

Classroom Design

> Decisions about the layout of a classroom provide tangible evidence of beliefs about what the learning experience should be like and about the role of teachers and students in the learning process. (Merkel, 1999, p. 421)

One room, four walls, one teacher, thirty students, stereotypical classrooms, industrial model, kids in rows—the design and organization of the classrooms have mirrored society's expectations and the teacher's philosophy of how students learn and how teachers teach best. But we must ask the question, Whose interests are being served—the teachers', society's or the students'—in this design? Do the teachers shape the classroom design and create the atmosphere? How much does

10.2 FOR YOUR CONSIDERATION

When you hear the term *traditional classroom,* what do you think of in terms of classroom organization, seating plan, work areas, lesson presentation, questioning and discussion, student leadership, assessment?

1. Design a floor plan of what you consider to be a traditional classroom.
2. Does it make a difference how classrooms are organized?
3. Does it depend on grades or subjects?
4. Compare your design with your colleagues' designs. What are the similarities?

Does it matter how classrooms are designed and organized?

classroom design shape teaching? According to Hathaway (1986), educational facilities have the potential to aid or inhibit learning and human performance. Designing an educational facility that includes classrooms poses fundamental questions such as, "What are the instructional frameworks, pedagogy, learning resources, and delivery strategies that are to be accommodated in the educational facility?" (Hathaway, 1986, p. 3)

Merkel (1999) believes the organization of one's environment is not random. People shape their space through the way they organize the things in it (material lore), describe their environment (verbal lore), and perform the ritualized activities that occur in the environment (ritual lore). Where does the worldview of the teacher who works with students appear in the design of the classroom?

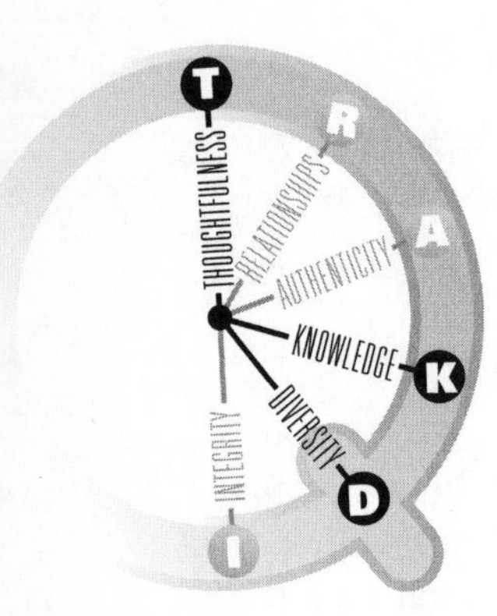

Classrooms are the places where students spend most of their daytime hours, working on courses of study with a group of students and one or more adults. Besides classrooms, other spaces within the school and in the community provide places where learning and social interaction may take place, such as the gymnasium; the library, art, music, or drama room; the special education, resource, or conference room; teacher workspaces; and industrial arts and home-economics shops. Equally important spaces that may have a huge impact on students include the main office, with the friendly or not-so-friendly secretary, and the sometimes dreaded principal's office. Each of these spaces serves a specific purpose in the learning and teaching landscape.

Other spaces that affect learning and social interaction are the playground, corridors, lunch room, washrooms, the main doors, the back doors, and other informal spaces where students congregate before, during, and after classes. How do you think these informal school spaces affect learning and social interaction? The accommodation of technology within the classrooms or in specific areas is a current learning-space innovation. As a student you have spent time in these spaces and they have had an effect on your social, emotional, and academic development. As you read this chapter, consider the design and use of these spaces.

Within the next five or ten years, the schools that were built for the baby-boomers will be in need of major repair, if not rebuilding. Architects are working with educators to create educational spaces that improve the health, safety, and learning of the young people who spend most of their daylight hours in these spaces. "Educators believe that classroom design and condition have a strong impact on overall quality of education, student self-esteem, and test scores." (McMorrow, 2000, p. 9) What are the effects of daylight and room temperature on learning? Surveys have indicated that "simple things, such as having windows and carpet in [the] classroom, may help students learn better" (Henry, 2001, p. D08). Another consideration in new school design is flexibility, as it is difficult to predict the future needs of teachers and learners. School safety is certainly a concern for all stakeholders.

As you read further and as you observe classroom spaces, think about the various areas of a school's design. Do you feel physical spaces are important considerations for students' education? How might the areas affect students' social, emotional, psychological, and academic development? How can you, as a teacher, alter your classroom and other school spaces to enhance your teaching and your students' learning?

Can school spaces affect learning?

10.3 FOR YOUR CONSIDERATION

Do you recall, from your student days, a classroom that made you feel uneasy, unhappy, tired or actually sick, or alternatively, a classroom where you felt comfortable, safe, excited, happy to be there? Describe that space. What was it about the space that affected you?

Natural Lighting and Climate Control

Lighting and climate control are two important classroom design considerations for educators. This includes the ability to organize and decorate teaching spaces and adjust the temperature and humidity.

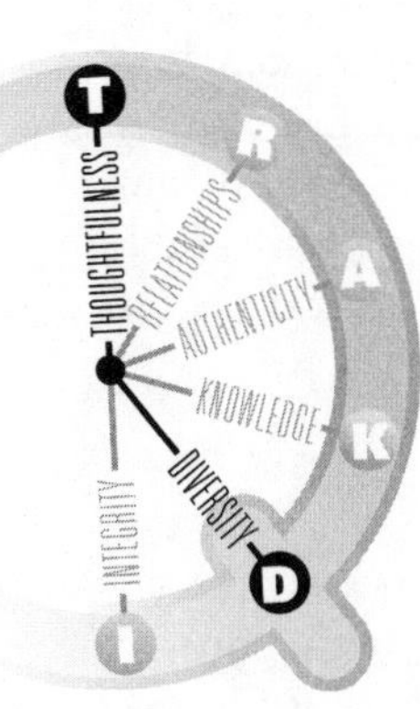

One of this book's authors had the opportunity to have input into the design of a high school in Alberta. Natural light was an important feature of the school's design. Every room had either direct or deflected natural light. A study conducted by Naested (1993) to discern the faculty's and students' thoughts about this feature of the school found that they appreciated the feeling of openness that the natural light and presence of windows created. However, some educators found it difficult to darken classrooms adequately for audio-visual equipment; others wished the windows were positioned lower in order to see out. With this in mind, lighting designers need to also consider the types of tasks performed in the spaces (J. Smith & Raiford, 2000).

More recent studies indicate that "windows in classrooms improve achievement; students in rooms without natural light suffer a kind of jetlag.... Experts agree most on the importance of daylight and windows in the classroom" (Zernike, 2001, p. 4A20). Many schools built thirty or more years ago were designed without windows because at that time windows were considered a distraction to learners, a safety concern with respect to vandalism and theft, and a source of energy inefficiency. Do we need to rethink natural light in our classrooms or should we still be concerned about our young learners' safety?

"Ventilation continues to be a big concern at schools teaching K-12 students." (C. Fuller, 2001, p. 64) Indoor air quality is important, not only for learning and teaching to be successful, but also for the health of the staff and students.

Unhealthy air quality may result in a "sick school" and affect the health and well-being of the people who spend most of their days in the school building. The ability of teachers to control temperature and humidity is also considered important for well-being (C. Fuller, 2001).

Hallways and Lunch Rooms

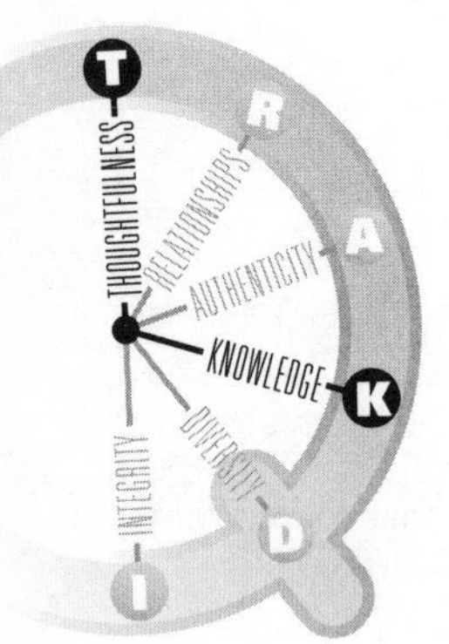

Schools have corridors where students move from space to space throughout the day. There are long and short, narrow and wide corridors. Does the shape and size of the corridor affect behaviour? Can the shape of a hallway discourage bullying (Zernike, 2001, p. 4A20)? In your mind, does a long, narrow corridor suggest a speed running course with an adult calling out, "Children, no running in the hallway"?

Have you had the misfortune of visiting a large, overcrowded, older school during a class change? Did you observe pushing and jostling? Have you visited a spacious school with wide short hallways leading off to different areas? As a student in elementary or secondary school, what were your feelings during student movement in the hallways?

Class change is an interesting occurrence that has a huge impact on both students and teachers. Consider how the faculty at a specific school has designed and orchestrated class changes, room changes, and lunch times. How have they determined to indicate these times—a bell ringing, music playing, lights blinking off and on? Does it matter what type of music is played? Does student movement happen

10.4 FOR YOUR CONSIDERATION

Take a tour of a school and draw a diagram of the school's floor plan. What do you observe in the corridors and work areas? Make note of the physical size of the school and the student population. Make note of student movement during class changes, recess, and lunch time. Compare your findings with those of your colleagues who have looked at different schools. What effect does the school population in relation to the school's physical size have on the movement and placement of students in the corridors and work areas? Consider the emotional, physical, and academic implications for the students.

Does the shape and size of a school's physical space affect student behaviour?

just as smoothly if there is no sound or light indication of the time to move on? Do these factors have an influence on learning?

Consider for a moment the school lunchroom or cafeteria. "Research has demonstrated a distinct connection between nutrition and a child's ability to learn" (E. Bergman, Buergel, Enamuther, & Sanchez, 2000, p. 696). Students need a pleasant, uncrowded surrounding where they eat an unhurried lunch and socialize safely and comfortably. If food is so important to learning, do you believe that school lunchrooms are well-designed for the purpose of eating? What might the faculty consider when planning the lunchtime and the lunch space? Would it be helpful if the school population had staggered lunch times?

Playgrounds

Have you wondered what conditions and equipment are needed to create a healthy, safe, and enjoyable school playground that encourages physical activity and congenial social interaction? According to Rivkin (2000), children appear to benefit from being outdoors, especially with the increase in indoor attractions such as television and computers: "[T]he richness and novelty of the outdoors stimulates brain development" (p. 4).

There are several things to consider in playground use. Do the design and the equipment in the school grounds depend on the age or grade of the student? Do the activities change depending on the time of day—before or after school, for example, at lunch time or recess, during physical education period, sports day or the sports season in the school term? Is there a place for natural gardens in the educational plan? Can the space enhance literacy, the arts, and science learning? What involvement or responsibility can and should the teachers and students take for this designated space to enhance curriculum connections? Is the space used in the most educational way possible? Could something more be done with the space, or time spent in the space, to make it more educationally valuable?

10.5 FOR YOUR CONSIDERATION

Observe a particular school yard over a period of a few days. What ages of children does this space accommodate? Make a sketch of the space. Describe how the space is used. Interview students, parents, teachers, and administrators to find out what they believe to be the best features of the space, how they feel the space is used, and how they might improve it or use it differently. What are your thoughts for improving the space? How might the space be re-designed to enhance curricula? Compare your sketch and ideas with those of your colleagues.

Classroom Arrangement and Paraphernalia

Classrooms can be arranged in ways that welcome students into the learning arena or exclude them. The placement of the teacher's desk in relation to the students and the placement of the students' desks in relation to fellow students can have a huge impact on the way learning and teaching happens. What non-verbal signals are sent to students when their desks are arranged in rows facing the teacher's desk at the front, as opposed to four student desks placed together in pods?

How do teachers include or exclude various students by the books they shelve in their room and the posters they hang on the walls? This may happen with the level of reading material (e.g., how primary or advanced it is), but also through content. Does the teacher light a menorah for Hanukkah or prepare red envelopes for Chinese New Year? Does she encourage students to dress up for Halloween or decorate the door at Christmas and give out presents? Does he recognize other religious, cultural, or seasonal occasions? How should teachers prepare their rooms to welcome the diverse students they may have in one classroom?

Where do animals fit into this landscape of books and desks and chairs? Rud and Beck (2000) investigated the role of pets in the classroom and found that interaction with animals has important implications for the physical and emotional well-being of children. Animals and fish can be useful for scientific or artistic studies, as well as provide an impetus for creative writing. Rud and Beck suspect that "having animals in the classroom adds to the ambience and emotional health of the room in much the same way as pleasantly decorated walls or sun-filled windows" (2000, p. 313). This opportunity also gives students a creature to hug and take care of. Why then are animals and other living things not seen more often in classrooms?

10.6 FOR YOUR CONSIDERATION

Design the classroom floor plan for a room in which you have been assigned to teach. Included the following: seats for twenty-eight Grade 4 students, two bookshelves, a teacher's desk, a reading area with sofa and cushions, and a large working table. Add or discard whatever piece of furniture you wish. Support aspects of your design with your philosophy of how students learn and how you wish to teach.

Learning Style and Classroom Design

Should teachers think about students' learning styles when they design their classrooms? (Consider the various authors on how students learn, such as Dunn and Dunn, Gardner, Vygotsky, Piaget, and Skinner from Chapter 3.) The way the teacher organizes a teaching and learning space reflects his or her belief about how students learn.

According to Dunn, students respond to their immediate environment, which includes sound, light, temperature, and formal or informal design. The physical stimuli include such elements as perceptual stimuli, time, and mobility. Sociological stimuli in the learning space include working with peers, in pairs or in teams, by oneself, or with an adult (Dunn, 1999). These are elements and stimuli that a teacher can influence. Would the classroom of a teacher who prefers the

10.7 FOR YOUR CONSIDERATION

You enter the school and make your way down a hallway and step into a self-contained kindergarten classroom. The classroom space is subdivided into "centres" including art, writing, sand/water, reading, math, manipulatives, blocks, science, and domestic/house and dramatic play area (Tarr, 2001). On the shelves are books of various sizes, and bright-coloured poster boards display posters on various topics from people at work to animals. A large calendar and a clock hang on the wall. Mobiles of various sizes, shapes, and colours, obviously created by young children, hang from the florescent lights. Coloured cellophane shapes are mounted on the windows that overlook the climbing gym in the school yard.

Based on this description of a classroom, what do you surmise about the teacher and her philosophy of learning and teaching?

10.8 FOR YOUR CONSIDERATION

Look back at the six philosophical orientations to teaching presented in Chapter 7: progressivism, essentialism, perennialism, existentialism, behaviourism, and reconstructionism. How would a teacher with each of these specific philosophical orientations arrange his or her classroom in relation to student seating plan, work areas, lesson presentation, questioning and discussion, student and teacher leadership, assessment, books, and posters? Consider your own personal philosophical orientation. How would your way of arranging your classroom differ from classroom organization arising from those orientations?

philosophies of Dunn be different from that of a teacher who follows Gardner's theory of multiple intelligences? If so, how would it be different?

Technology in the Classroom

The incorporation of technology has added to the cost of new schools because of the necessity to incorporate cabling, switching boxes, furniture, and technological hardware (Heavey, 2000). The cost of technology is considerable in older buildings that must be upgraded, as well. Incorporating technology into schools and classrooms has forced architects and educators to redefine the spaces for work, study, ergonomics, cyber-connections and power sources, security, vandalism and theft, and for future developments in technology.

Coppola and Thomas (2000) discuss "e-classrooms" in which computers are placed on tables, with monitors on top. The teacher's station is generally crowded on a desktop, with wires everywhere. More attention needs to be paid to research and design of the technology spaces. According to Riley and Gallo (2000), there is a need to reflect on current educational practices and the expected changes in pedagogy and technology when incorporating various technologies into our schools. These would include planning for a full range of teaching methods with built-in flexibility for changing needs.

Smart classrooms are spaces "where students can use personal computers or laptops at workstations to take notes, download information from the instructor's computer, or even take tests electronically ... [and] link to internet for research or to school intranets to collaborate with others in the room or throughout campus" (McMorrow, 2000, p. 18). Cheek (2001) writes about "Edlabs" where "there are no blackboards, no bookcases, no cartoon posters, no windows through which to ponder drifting clouds and daydream" (p. 39). Do educators wish to go to this extreme in their use of technology in learning and teaching, or is there room for compromise?

Many of the Canadian teachers' associations have specialist councils that address technology and computers in education, including curriculum and classroom design. A few Web sites are listed at the end of the chapter.

10.9 FOR YOUR CONSIDERATION

Consider the following questions:

1. Where is it best for computers to be housed in the classroom and in the school?
2. Should separate rooms be set aside as computer labs?
3. How could teachers use a pod of computers in the classroom?
4. Should all students be "connected" and use laptops? How do you see laptops being used in the classroom?
5. Does the degree of technology provided (amount of time and sophistication of programs) depend on the ages and grades of students?
6. What are your thoughts on ergonomics for young learners with small hands working with equipment designed for larger people? Can and should something be done?
7. In your experience in schools have you observed impressive teaching and learning happening with the use of technology? Do you have specific examples?

School Safety

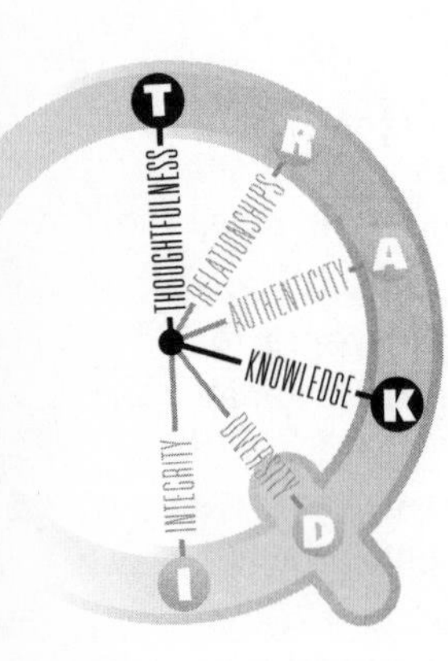

School safety is certainly a concern for all stakeholders. Principals have authority to limit access, and most school districts require criminal reference checks of school employees (Elementary Teachers' Federation of Ontario, 2000) and other adults, including parents who volunteer in the schools. "Many schools have taken steps to improve security, such as installing telephones and intercoms, providing resource officers, and adding video monitors or metal detectors" (McMorrow, 2000, p. 9).

There are few clear policies on the use of surveillance equipment, and there appears to be no single initiative that will eliminate violence from public schools (Green, 1999; Schneider, Walker, & Sprague, 2000). The National School Safety and Security Services (2002) suggests that relying on equipment or any other single-approach solution is unfair, and potentially costly, to schools. School safety needs to be a school-wide effort involving faculty, parents, and students.

The following is a list of questions you can ask yourself, teaching colleagues, or students to get a sense of what factors aid in generating the feeling of a safe school or to find out if a specific school feels safe. Develop other questions you feel are pertinent to this topic.

- Have you been in a school where you felt safe and in a school where you felt uneasy or threatened? What factors made the difference?

- In a safe school do you believe the principal and teachers display a common approach to abusive student behaviour, to drug and alcohol possession and use, and to unwanted visitors to the school?
- Do some physical areas of the school building feel less secure then others? Why?
- Do you feel more at ease in a smaller school, where you know the teachers and the principal and maybe the local school police officer? Please explain.
- How do you think a safe school enhances academic performance?

Grouping Students and Teachers in the Classroom

Teachers may group their students formally or informally, homogeneously or heterogeneously. They may stream, or track, the students into courses of study they deem appropriate for their physical, social, or academic ability. They may place students into groups or classes of multi-age, split grades, or multi-grades. Students may be segregated according to ability (gifted and talented) or special needs into pull-out programs (a teacher works with the student in a separate room), given tutoring, placed in special education classes, or even put into a segregated classroom in an alternative setting. The students may be included, or integrated, into classrooms of their peers.

The one-room schoolhouse in rural Canada in the 1920s was a multi-age classroom, generally with one teacher. At times, teachers may have joined efforts to team teach, often in open-area or large classrooms. These concepts of grouping have a history of acceptance, then rejection, and then renewed popularity, depending on the political climate and the school jurisdiction.

Teachers should consider what information they need to group students and what is the ultimate purpose or philosophy behind the grouping. Are the groups to become permanent for a term or longer? Or are they intended to be fluid, with the ability to move students from group to group with reflection on continuous authentic assessment?

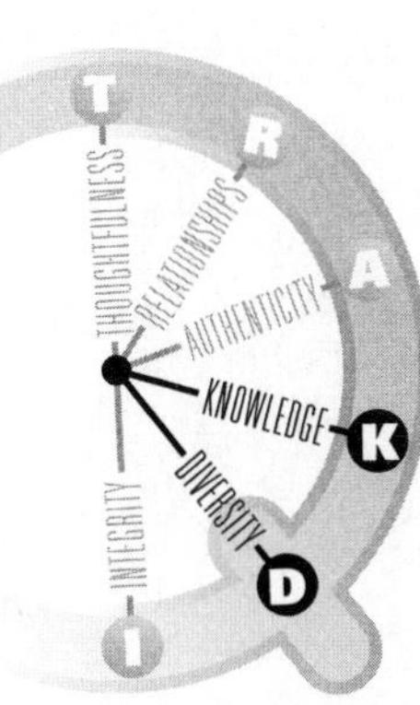

Tracking

Tracking (or streaming) of students is different from ability grouping in that tracking generally refers to a practice of separating students into different courses or course sequences, called tracks. The track is based on the student's level of achievement or proficiency (Haury & Milbourne, 1999). Tracking was questioned when it was found that students from higher socio-economic families tended to be in the higher level tracks. Students formerly in the lower tracks did better when moved into mixed-ability groupings (Naested, 1993; Haury & Milbourne 1999). Why do you think this would happen? Do the teaching techniques differ from one track to another? Do the teachers' or students' expectations change? Could something be happening with peer pressure? Should this form of grouping have implications for the way the classroom is arranged?

Multi-age and Non-graded Classrooms

Graded classrooms, with children of similar ages, became a popular tradition by the mid-1950s because of their administrative practicality (R. Anderson, 1992). Staffing formulas simply divided the number of pupils per teacher according to age or single grade. In graded classrooms teachers compare their students, and competition is encouraged.

Non-graded classrooms, a concept adopted particularly by private schools, feature the absence of grade labels and the use of competitive and comparative evaluation. In a non-graded classroom teachers work in teams with groups of students, and the curriculum orientation is flexible and organized to address the needs of the whole child (Haute, Heins, Tichenor, Coggins, & Hutchinson, 2000).

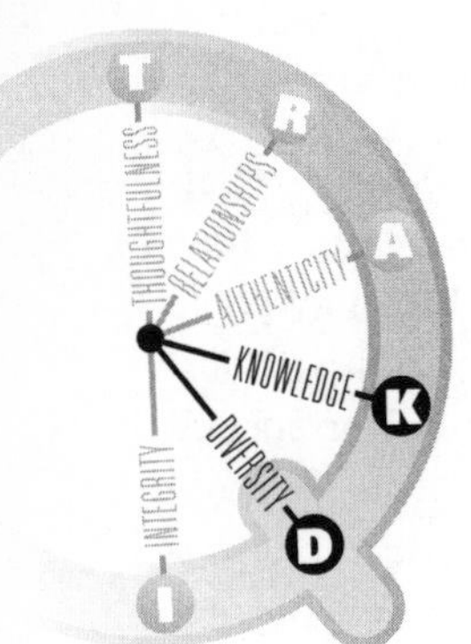

A **multi-age classroom** is one in which the developmental range is wider than that seen in a single-grade classroom. It attempts to break down the common categorization of students by not dividing them or the curriculum into steps through grade designation. Often the teacher or teachers observe and teach the same students over a period of time, sometimes even years. These classes are formed deliberately because of the philosophical commitment of the teachers to a "focus on individual progress through a developmentally appropriate curriculum" (Lloyd, 1999, p. 188). On the other hand, multi-age and split-grades (combining Grades 1 and 2) are sometimes formed for administrative reasons to even out the number of children in the classrooms.

The basic characteristic of a multi-age class may be tables that are rearranged frequently instead of desks arranged in rows. There is an emphasis on teacher-to-student interaction and co-operative learning (Haute et al., 2000, p. 30). Further information on multi-age education can be found on the following Web sites: **http://www.ncrel.org/sdrs/areas/issues/methods/instrctn/in500.htm** and **http://data.teachernet.com**

10.10 FOR YOUR CONSIDERATION

Teachers help each pupil master writing, reading, and curriculum rather than passing on the student to the next grade if he or she is not ready. If a teacher holds back a student, the student then becomes a failure. Where else in your experience do you become a failure in a way that stays with you for a lifetime?

Interview an adult or student who has failed a grade, or been held back to repeat a year of schooling. Does repeating grades help or hinder a student's self-concept as a learner and his or her ability to learn? Can you think of alternatives to failing a student?

The open-plan, or **open-area classroom** is often home to a multi-age grouping of students and the teaming of teachers. Open areas were popular with school boards and architects in the 1960s. Schools were planned around central areas, usually the library, with adjoining large spaces designed to house several groupings of students and teachers. Team teaching wavered, and by the 1980s teachers began to build walls to separate their classes. They were not given enough planning and professional development to maintain the integrity of the open-area concept. Administrative support, professional development, and planning time were found to be essential for the survival and flourishing of the open-area concept (Naested, 1993). In educational settings today, self-containment still prevails but some schools have open-area classrooms. Have you had the opportunity to observe this form of classroom?

Team Teaching

Team teaching is an approach to classroom instruction that involves two or more teachers who are responsible for co-operatively planning, teaching, and evaluating a group of pupils. Working teams, whether formally or informally arranged, are believed by many to be beneficial (Naested, 1993). When teachers are asked to identify their primary source of assistance, they reply that it is usually "other teachers" (Johnson & Johnson, 1987).

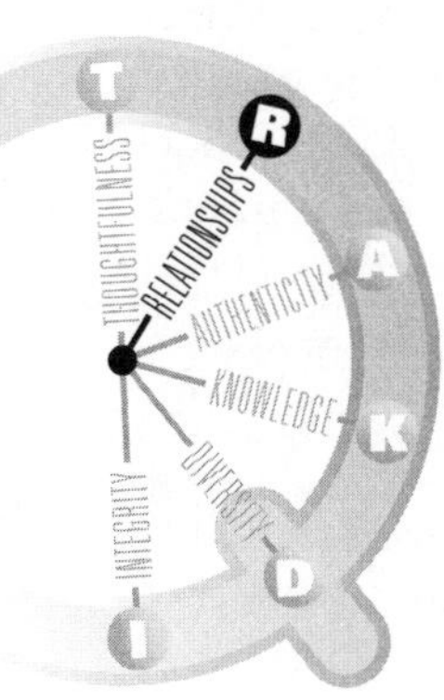

The 1960s were exciting times in education, with large financial grants from federal governments and foundations to encourage educational reform, including team teaching (Trump, 1985). Team teaching was studied and found to be "more intellectually stimulating" (R. Anderson, 1989) for the teachers and the students. The adults learned more about teaching, but it was also "much harder work" (Naested, 1993). For a team teaching approach to work successfully, administrative support is imperative. Team members need to view this process as an opportunity for professional growth and must be enthusiastic participants rather than reluctant draftees (Beggs, 1966). Participants also need to have a choice in the selection of partners. Other components for success include adequate time for planning, especially common planning time and space to plan; flexible scheduling; and flexible teaching spaces for large and small groups.

The members of the teaching team need to recognize and celebrate differences, and acknowledge how these differences enrich the relationship. Some teachers will need training and guided practice in collaborative and consultation processes (Thousand & Willa, 1991). Lack of money can be an impediment: "Very little in education can be improved without the expenditure of at least a little 'pump priming' money to get projects started" (Howard, 1996, p. 91).

Here are some questions to consider about team teaching:

- If the concept of team teaching has many strengths, why do we not see team teaching practiced more often in our schools?
- What are your views on teaming with another teacher? Are you uneasy about being part of a teaching team?
- Have you been in, or witnessed, a team teaching situation that was working or one that was not working smoothly? What were some of the reasons for success or lack of success?

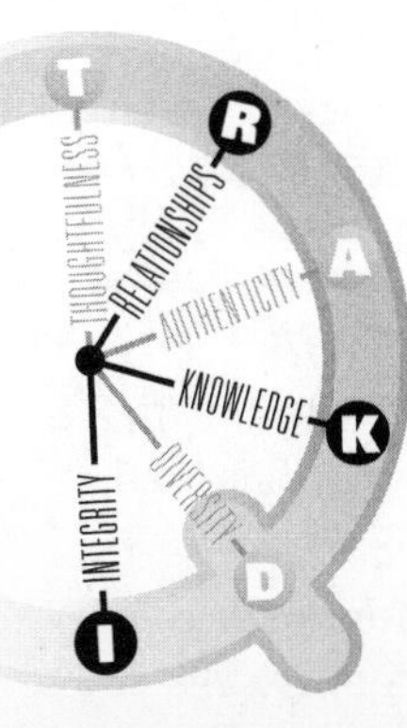

Special Classes, Inclusive Education, and Pull-out Programs

The question is not whether students with diverse backgrounds should be included in the general education classroom. Instead, the more productive question is how

> instruction might be provided most effectively for all students. (Hourcade & Bauwens, 2001, p. 243)

By the 1970s, children with disabilities were entering the public schools and were generally taught in separate classrooms with their own teachers. Inclusive and integrated classrooms, which don't exclude children with special learning or physical needs, have become more politically correct and more common. The terms *exceptional, non-exceptional* and *handicapped* are not useful, or used, for educational purposes (Brice & Miller, 2000). The main difference between inclusion and integration is that integration does not accommodate or restructure the environment for the student's needs, but assimilates the student into the existing environment (Avramidis, Bayliss, & Burden, 2000).

In **inclusive education,** Soto says, "Full inclusion occurs when students with disabilities are full-time members of age-appropriate, regular classrooms in their home schools and receive any support necessary to participate in both the learning and the social communities of their peers" (Soto, Muller, Hunt, & Goetz, 2001, p. 62). When inclusive or integrated models are practiced, the classroom teacher generally has a special education teacher and/or a teacher's aide, depending on the severity and type of special need the student or students may have. This model values interdependence and independence, and encourages a sense of community and understanding that all students are special. This is a democratic model that reflects the diversity in the broader community. However, even with assistance, teachers find inclusion an addition to their workload. Why do teachers feel this way and how can school systems further assist the teachers?

Programs for gifted and talented students exist in various forms, having the ultimate goal of meeting the needs of these learners. Students who are considered gifted may have a higher IQ than the "average" student, but they can also have learning difficulties. Attempts to meet their needs include pull-out programs; self-contained, or segregated, classes; mentorship programs; and advanced placement in courses of study, to name a few.

In a **pull-out program** a teacher with special training withdraws a student from the regular classroom and works with the student in a separate room usually referred to as a resource room. The value of pull-out programs for meeting the needs of students who are gifted or have English as second language is debatable (Viadero, 2001). Pull-out programs for gifted students have been viewed by some members of the public as elitist (Delisle, 1999).

Beyond Classroom Walls: Alternative Places for Learning

> "Education that is interactive, takes place outside school walls and in authentic environments." (Kluth, 2000)

Humans learn by reflecting on experience. Place-based education, pedagogy of place, or outdoor education, suggests going beyond the classroom walls to experience the world, as advocated by John Dewey. Dewey (1973) stated that "amid all uncertainties there is one permanent frame of reference: namely the organic connection between education and personal experiences" (p. 225). Outdoor environmental adventure and ecological education, experiential methodologies, as well as the common "field trip" to the local zoo, museum, science centre, or animal and bird sanctuaries help students connect with their environment.

The essential characteristics of off-campus education emerge from the attributes of the place. This approach is multidisciplinary and experiential to connect the learner to the experience or environment (Woodhouse & Knapp, 2000). For Dewey (1915), experience outside the classroom "has its geographical aspect, its artistic and its literary, its scientific and its historical sides" (p. 91).

Outdoor Education

Outdoor education initially started with school camping experiences in the 1930s and involved structured experiences and challenges (Richardson & Simmons, 1996). Outdoor experiences can occur in various settings, and over the years the concept of experience as education has developed into various pedagogical disciplines that require the educator to adopt a specific approach and undertake specific training. According to Cassidy (2001), for example, "Experiential education is more than just learning by doing. Experiential learning occurs when individuals engage in a concrete activity, reflect upon that activity and develop a new understanding that can be transferred to other situations" (p. 22). How does experiential education differ from environmental or adventure education? The advocates for each do not appear to see these approaches as similar. They advocate that these experiences are valuable for learners and that it is imperative that the educator have adequate knowledge and skill in such areas as safety, group management, technical equipment, environmental information (especially with respect to protection), and proper planning for the expedition, which must be appropriate to the learners' physical and mental development.

A great deal has been written on the approaches to education in the outdoors. B. Henderson (1992) wrote a book to assist educators in balancing classroom and library study with long days and short stays in the wilderness. He believed that students can never understand early Canadian history without experiencing similar travels to inspire a connection to the writer, explorer, and settler by sharing in the experience of life in the bush and on the water.

Rollans (1992) developed a handbook as a resource for teaching archaeology in Saskatchewan, describing classroom and outdoor activities to reflect the multidisciplinary nature of archaeology. Sharp (1943) simply stated that what can best be taught inside the schoolrooms should be taught there but what could be best be learned through experience dealing directly with nature should be learned there.

As a student, leader, or teacher have you taken advantage of some form of outdoor education? To your knowledge, have safety and liability concerns limited outdoor or off-campus experiences from taking place?

Service Learning

In graduation requirements, schools are including community service requirements that are directed to the "common good," a special challenge to the social studies curricula. Service learning has taken the place of "civic education," which also followed Dewey's melding of theoretical, practical, and moral considerations (Tice, 1999). Service projects can involve playing an active a part in "adopting" a highway, pathway, playground, or river bank for maintenance or cleanup, or some form of urban renewal. Other projects may involve the students working directly with people at drop-in centres or seniors' residences. Were you involved in some form of service to the community while attending school? What are your thoughts on the inclusion of this component in the school curricula? Should service to the community be a part of graduation requirements?

Science and Cultural Centres

Museums, zoos and science centres, philharmonic orchestras, opera and ballet companies, to name a few, have staff assigned as their institutions' educators. The primary purpose for these individuals is to assist the public, especially teachers, to integrate educational field trips into classroom studies. Educators from both institutions plan the excursions co-operatively to propose the best way to make the experiences relevant to curricular studies. Pre-and post-visit classroom sessions build on the visits. For many individuals, school field trips provide their first introduction to cultural and natural institutions. These trips provide experiences that make up lifelong learning (Hicks, 1986). Reflect on your experience of a trip to a science or cultural centre. Did this experience have a long-term impact on your learning and worldview? Why or why not? Can your support your response with an example?

Work-Site Learning

Students may be unaware of many occupations that are available. They may be unsure of the job experience, training, or educational requirements, and unfamiliar with what the occupation actually involves. Here is where work experience and job shadowing can be an asset, not only to the student, but also to future employers. Areas that need more exposure include the trades and teaching fields. The main difference between work experience and job shadowing is the length of time and commitment. High school credits are often given for work experience and sometimes students can actually start an apprenticeship program in areas such as welding, carpentry, automotive, plumbing, electrical, or forestry before graduation.

10.11 FOR YOUR CONSIDERATION

Have you been involved in some form of work experience or job shadowing that made a difference in your decision to choose or not choose a particular career? Was the work experience or job shadowing beneficial to you? Should these opportunities be encouraged and continued in students' high school experience?

Classrooms in the Home or During Travel

As mentioned in the previous chapters, parents, students, and teachers can choose among public, Catholic, private, charter, **magnet**, and home schools, based on ideology or pedagogy (program delivery). **Magnet schools** focus on a specific aspect of learning, such as fine and performing arts or courses of study for gifted and talented students, and parents choose the school because of this program. Home schooling has become an increasingly popular choice. The reasons for parents to educate their children at home or during travel are varied. The introduction and use of computer technology, the Internet, and other teaching resources have made it easier for students to study in locations other than in a school building. The locations often go beyond the family house and may include sailing around the world or living in a coastal lighthouse.

10.12 FOR YOUR CONSIDERATION

Though there are many opportunities for the young learner in homeschooling, there could also be some drawbacks. What might be the positives and negatives of homeschooling?

Virtual Classrooms

Students are being given the option to move away from face-to-face learning experiences to a Web-based synchronous and asynchronous learning environment, distance learning, or distributed learning (Kochtanek & Hein, 2000; Arbaugh, 2000), commonly called *virtual classrooms*. Synchronous formats require that all class participants be together (physically or on-line) at the same time, and asynchronous, which is more time-consuming for the teachers, do not. The learners can set their own schedule for participation in the asynchronous course (Arbaugh, 2000). Often students and their parents choose on-line education to enhance home schooling, holiday travel, or overseas work placements. The teaching approach in distance-based courses needs to be less focused on the dispensing of information and more focused on "creating virtual contexts where students can learn collectively and collaboratively" (Arbaugh, 2000, p. 233). What do you believe to be the difficulties, challenges, and rewards for distance education teachers?

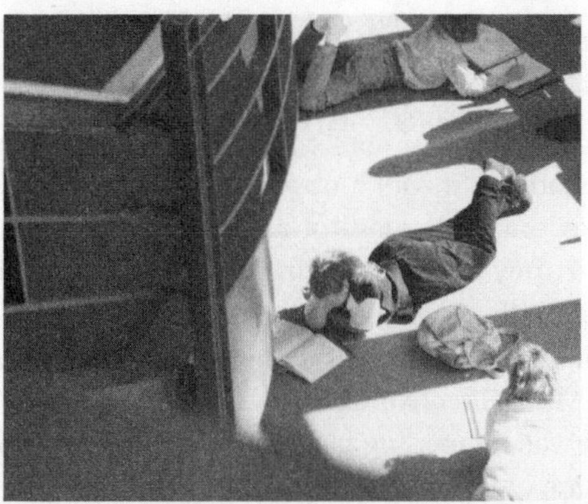

Should learners be given alternative spaces in which to study?

Classroom Management

Classroom management, which includes classroom control, discipline, and governance, encompasses an assortment of the techniques a teacher uses to create a positive learning environment. Principals, teachers, parents, and pre-service teachers view this as one of the most important topics in education. All of the provincial teachers' associations and some of the provincial departments of education offer handbooks and seminars on this topic. Many people consider it to be essential for a teacher's "survival" with a group of students. New teachers want to know how to manage a class. They want to know the steps to follow to avoid losing control.

Considering what has been discussed in previous chapters regarding the diversity of students as learners and as individuals with different backgrounds, experiences and needs—physical, psychological, as well as academic—does it seem reasonable that one set of guidelines is adequate for every teacher, who also has diverse needs? Furthermore, every classroom of learners is different from another. Do different rules and procedures pertain in a computer classroom, a woodworking shop, a band, drama, or art room, a field trip or other off-campus learning experiences? Who sets the rules and procedures, and how? What are students' and teachers' rights and responsibilities when classroom management is under consideration?

Often new teachers begin to model their teaching styles on those of teachers they have had or observed during their practica. In a well-managed classroom the observer has difficulty identifying the management signals. To the inexperienced observer, the learning and teaching just seem to be moving along without interference or need for intervention.

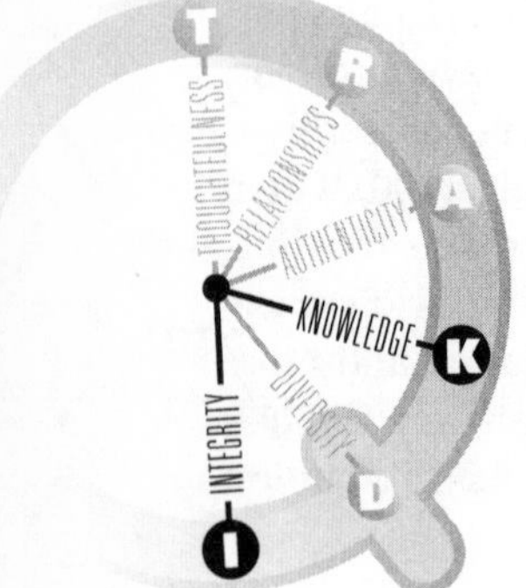

The new teacher's preferred style will change through experience in the classroom and further observation of colleagues. Many books and articles address the topic of classroom management and discipline. (Several are listed at the end of the chapter under Suggested Further Reading.) Some authors have developed questions and attempted to categorize teachers' styles and the styles' effects on the structure of the learning environment. Others offer various formulas and procedures for the teacher to follow in specific situations. The key to your learning about classroom management and governance is to read, to observe, and to reflect on experience. No style is wrong unless it interferes with or affects the positive well-being of others. Honour and dignity for all must be respected.

Monitoring, "With-it-ness," and Transition

Teachers monitor their students through observation and directing or re-directing students' actions or behaviour. This monitoring indicates whether students understand directions, whether they are engaged in the desired task. The teacher monitors student interactions with classmates. Are they on topic? Are students safe physically and emotionally? Borich has termed this technique "with-it-ness." According to Borich (1992), "Effective classroom managers who exhibited withitness were aware of what was happening in all parts of the classroom and were able to see different things happening in different parts of the room at the same time"

(p. 483). Is the ability to monitor—with-it-ness—an important aspect of classroom management? Is this a learned skill on the part of a teacher or does it come naturally?

Transition is the time when the learning climate changes from one topic or physical space to another. You have observed class transitions. Have you experienced smooth transitions? How do smooth and not-so-smooth transitions differ? How does this affect learning or classroom climate, management, and control? Closure is a time when students sense the end of a session, lesson, lunch hour, recess, or school day. How does closure and the way the teacher initiates closure affect the classroom environment?

10.13 FOR YOUR CONSIDERATION

Chapter 8 discussed power and control in teaching; empowerment and learning; and how we define learners. Refer to the section in Chapter 8 on understanding teaching for successful learning, which describes the transmissive, transactional, and transformational ways of teaching.

1. What are the primary teaching strategies for each?
2. Which style might include independent learning, *co-operative* learning, or drill and practice?
3. What implications does this have for a teacher's management and teaching style?

10.14 FOR YOUR CONSIDERATION

Observe teachers in their classrooms and consider some of the following. Remember—no style is right or wrong, as long as it honours the dignity of others.

1. Would you consider the teacher to be a facilitator, or discovery-oriented teacher? If so, what methods does she or he use to guide learning? Are students encouraged to explore and discover things for themselves?
2. Is the teacher directive, or authoritarian? Methods, process, and content are directed by the teacher. The students know what to expect. The purpose is to cover the curriculum on time.
3. The supportive, feeling teacher considers her or his students as equals in the learning and teaching area, and the primary concern is for the students to feel comfortable and non-threatened.
4. Other styles might also be considered as "roles," such as coach, cheerleader, counsellor, content expert, and researcher. Have you observed teachers who might fit these terms? What other terms would you use to describe a teacher's management or teaching style?

Reflection and Perspective on the Chapter

Classrooms and classroom design are important considerations in learning and teaching. We understand what the traditional classroom with four walls, many students, and one teacher looks like. However, we are entering a new era and must consider designing various teaching and learning spaces—on and off campus—that are flexible and safe, physically and emotionally. How we group students, as well as teachers, also has an impact on the learning environment.

The presence and placement of physical objects, artifacts, decorations, and furniture have an effect on the classroom environment. As a teacher you may have little opportunity to change the colour of the walls other than the bulletin boards. Lighting and windows, bookshelves and student desks might be beyond you control. One would hope not. This is why it is important that when school personnel are designing spaces and ordering furniture they consider flexibility for the changing needs of the learners and teachers.

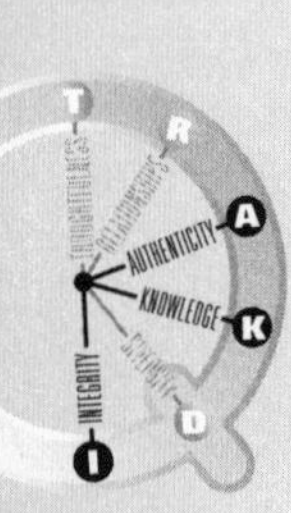

Educators have many assumptions about classrooms, their design, and the function they are to house. We have posed many questions in this chapter on classrooms. You will have the answers to some, and some answers may change over time and with experience in classrooms and schools.

Key Terms

classroom management 240
inclusive education 236
magnet schools 239
multi-age classroom 234
non-graded classroom 234
open-area classroom 234
pull-out program 236
team teaching 235
tracking 233

Suggested Further Reading

Multi-age Education

(NCREL) North Central Regional Educational Laboratory: **http://www.ncrel.org/sdrs/areas/issues/methods/instrctn/in500.htm**

TeacherNet: **http://data.teachernet.com** This site provides bulletin board messages on K-8 multi-age classes.

Team Teaching

Teamworks: **http://www.vta.spcomm.uiuc.edu/TWT/twt-ov.html**

Innovative Teaching Concepts: **http://www.todaysteacher.com/TeamTeaching.htm**

Outdoor Education

Henderson, B. (1992). Canada Experientially; Every Trail Has a Story. In G. Hanna (Ed.), *Celebrating our tradition, charting our future: Proceedings of the International Conference of the Association for Experiential Education.* Banff, AB: ERIC document ED353120.

Rollans, M. (1992). *A handbook for teaching archaeology in Saskatchewan schools.* Saskatoon, SK: Western Heritage Services. ERIC Document Reproduction Service No. ED393785.

Sharp, L. (1943). Outside the classroom. *The Educational Forum,* 7(4), 361–368.

Technology

Technology Educators Association of Manitoba: **http://www.technologyeducators.mb.ca**

Computer Using Educators of British Columbia: **http://www.cuebchorizons.ca**

The Association for Computer Studies Educators. ACSE-Ontario: **http://www.acse.net**

Classroom Management

The Manitoba Teacher's Society, *Beginning Teacher Handbook*: http://www.mbteach.org/beginteach.htm

Discipline with Dignity: http://www.disciplineassociates.com

Blum, Paul. (2001). *A teacher's guide to anger management*. London: Routledge Falmer.

DiGiulio, R. (1995). *Positive classroom management: A step by step guide to successfully running the show without destroying student dignity*. Thousand Oaks, CA: Corwin Press, Inc.

Evertson, C., Emmer, E., Clements, B., and Worsham, M. (1997). *Classroom management for elementary teachers*. London: Allyn and Bacon.

Hardin, C. (2000). *Managing classroom crises.* Bloomington, IN: Phi Delta Kappa Educational Foundation.

Martin, J., Sugarman, J., and McNamara, J. (2000). *Models of classroom management: Principles, practices and critical considerations*. Calgary: Detselig Enterprises.

Ontario Ministry of Education. (1986). *Behaviour: Resource guide.* Toronto, ON: Ontario Ministry of Education.

Ranallo, J., Bareham, S., and Chandler, M. (ed) (1997). *Student conduct management, the passionate side of teaching*. Vancouver, BC: Educational Services.

Seeman, H. (2000). *Preventing classroom discipline problems: A classroom handbook*. London: The Scarecrow Press.

Stanvitoff, L. (1997). *Support for classroom teachers involved in mainstreaming students with severe handicaps*. Regina, SK: Saskatchewan School Trustees Association.

Wiseman, D. and Hunt, G. (2001). *Best practice in motivation and management in the classroom*. Springfield, IL: Charles C. Thomas.

Ziegler, S. and Rosenstein-Manner, M. (1991). *Bullying at school: Toronto in an international context*. Toronto: Toronto Board of Education Research Services.

Chapter 11

Curriculum: Decisions, Development, Implementation and Assessment

> For it to come alive in the classroom, the curriculum itself has to contain, said or unsaid, an invitation to teachers and students to enter into it. Not only that, there needs to be a reciprocal invitation. The curriculum-as-plan must wait at the classroom door for an invitation from teachers and students. And when the curriculum, teachers and students click, we are likely to find a live tension that will allow the teacher and students to say, "We live curriculum." (Aoki, 1990, p. 40)

Chapter Focus

Understanding Curriculum: The Importance of What Is Taught in Schools

This chapter will help you understand what curriculum means and who makes curriculum decisions. We will examine the reasons certain curriculum decisions are made, who decides what subjects are taught in schools, what goals and intended outcomes schools should emphasize, and how these decisions affect learners in today's schools. We will also examine how you might begin to handle the complexity of decisions you will need to make in implementing curriculum.

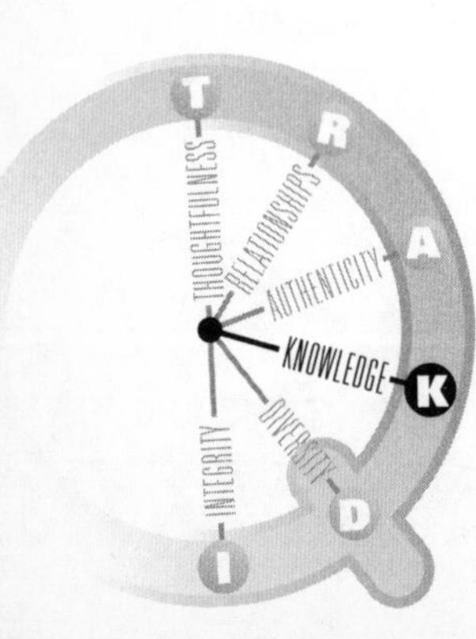

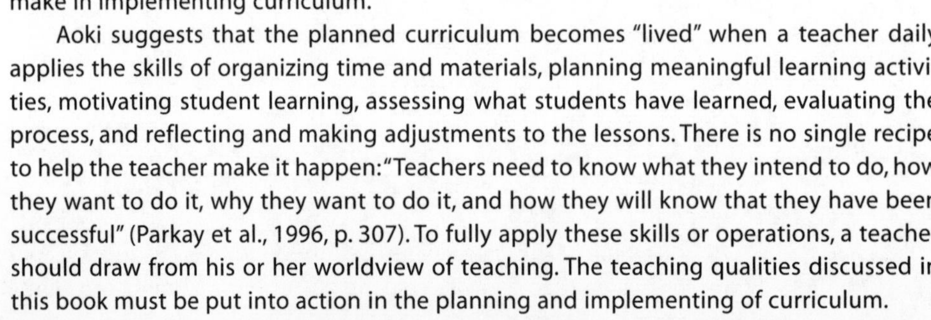

Aoki suggests that the planned curriculum becomes "lived" when a teacher daily applies the skills of organizing time and materials, planning meaningful learning activities, motivating student learning, assessing what students have learned, evaluating the process, and reflecting and making adjustments to the lessons. There is no single recipe to help the teacher make it happen: "Teachers need to know what they intend to do, how they want to do it, why they want to do it, and how they will know that they have been successful" (Parkay et al., 1996, p. 307). To fully apply these skills or operations, a teacher should draw from his or her worldview of teaching. The teaching qualities discussed in this book must be put into action in the planning and implementing of curriculum.

Your task in this chapter will be to integrate into your emerging teaching worldview some important and foundational ideas about curriculum: decisions, development, implementation, and assessment.

Understanding Curriculum: More Than Just Subject Matter

We will give you some examples of various Canadian school curricula and describe some current curriculum decision making. We will discuss the planned curriculum, the hidden curriculum, and the non-formal (or null) curriculum. We will examine extracurricular programs in schools, the sports and arts clubs, for example, through which much learning occurs and which provide both teachers and learners opportunities to grow and develop. We will also look at a number of curriculum innovations in Canadian settings and consider some trends and issues that teachers now face and will face in the future.

A discussion of curriculum would not be complete without some mention of four very important topics: assessment, evaluation, measurement, and reporting. We will look at how schools in Canada have decided to respond, in their curriculum decision making, to the current emphasis in Canadian education and society at large on accountability, competency, and outcomes.

Focus Questions

1. What is curriculum, and how does it influence a teacher's day-to-day work in schools?
2. What is the role of society and culture in determining what planned curriculum is used in schools?
3. To what extent should curriculum be designed to prepare learners for the real world of work?
4. Can curriculum be designed to serve the needs of both business and learners?
5. How should curriculum design respond to changes in society and the workplace?
6. How much of the planned curriculum should be devoted to development of competencies? To knowledge? To values, attitudes, and appreciation of the arts?
7. How might a teacher use the curriculum to help learners prepare for the real world of work and the familiar world of relationships, growth, and development of interests and desires?
8. What forms of alternative curriculum design and delivery can be developed to meet the needs of diverse learners?
9. What forms of assessment are teachers required to administer and what alternate forms are available?
10. What formats do teachers use to report student achievement?

Assumptions about Curriculum

The following assumptions are invitations for you to think about curriculum and how your own theories, beliefs, and assumptions have been shaped by your school experience.

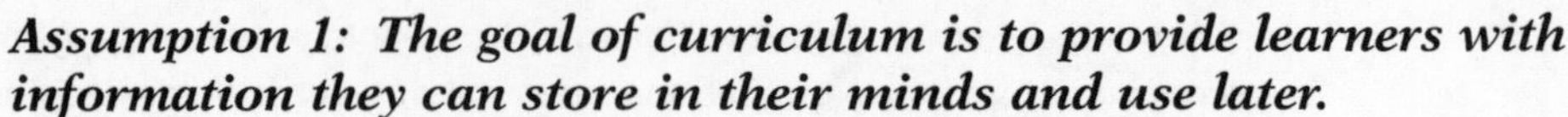

Assumption 1: The goal of curriculum is to provide learners with information they can store in their minds and use later.

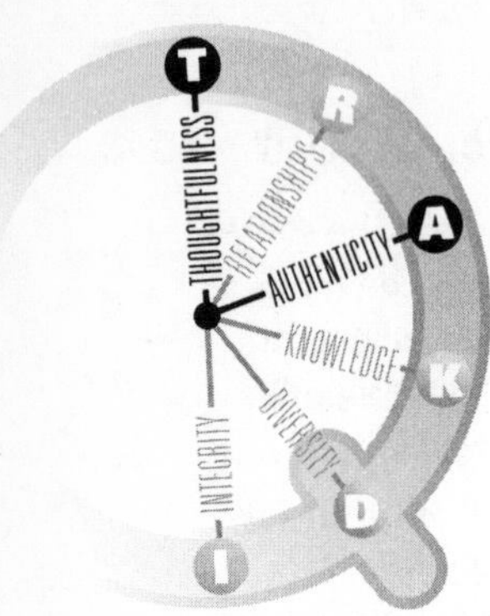

To assume that the mind can be provided with information is to assume that the mind is a thing, a place that can be filled up, a storehouse to be loaded up with facts. This rather mechanical view of the mind and learner fits neither what is known about learning nor what is true about the complexity of the real world, including the real world of work. Learners construct meaning. Curriculum that does not follow this idea will emphasize content, or information, over the processes that learners go through to learn something. Curriculum that attends to both content and the learning processes will more likely be relevant, exciting, and useful for learners. Such a curriculum naturally guides learners and their teachers to consider ways of connecting the content to the real world and transfer what they are learning to their worlds of work, play, and relationships.

Assumption 2: Curriculum should prepare learners for the world of work. History, drama, and other non-academic, non-work-related subjects are better left out of schools.

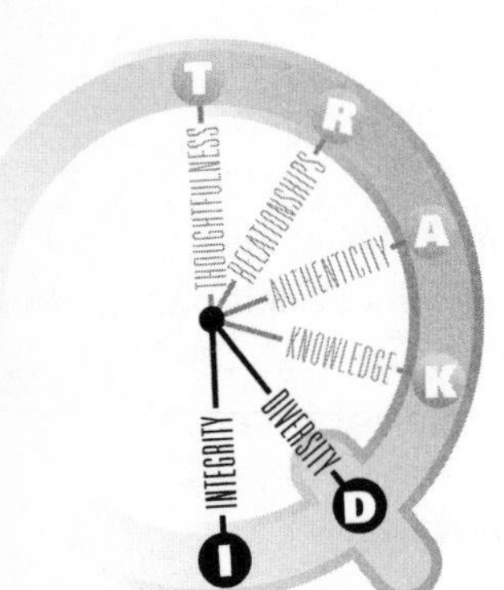

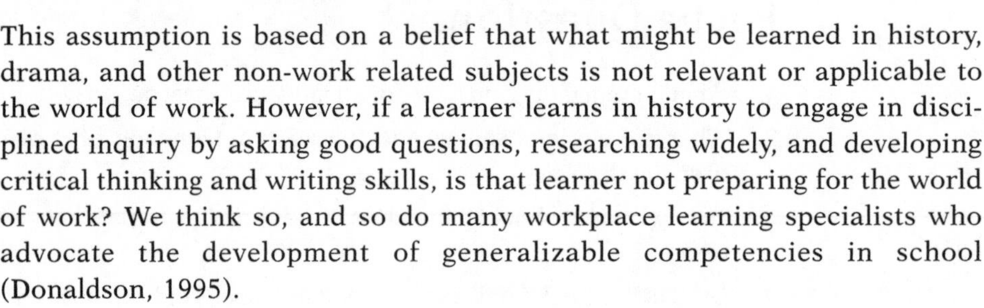

This assumption is based on a belief that what might be learned in history, drama, and other non-work related subjects is not relevant or applicable to the world of work. However, if a learner learns in history to engage in disciplined inquiry by asking good questions, researching widely, and developing critical thinking and writing skills, is that learner not preparing for the world of work? We think so, and so do many workplace learning specialists who advocate the development of generalizable competencies in school (Donaldson, 1995).

Assumption 3: Having student teachers write lesson plans is just an educational busy-work task that "real" teachers do not have to endure.

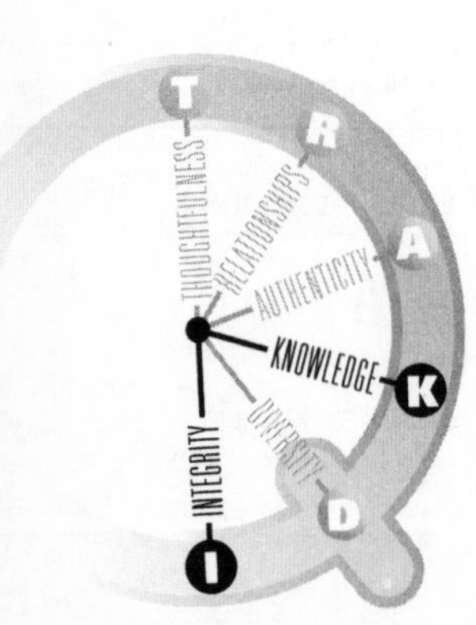

Most faculties of education require student teachers to develop detailed lesson plans. This includes outlining the learning objectives, the materials needed for the learning experience, a step-by-step procedure with approximate times for each step, including introduction and closure, and an evaluation component. Many student teachers feel that this is simply busy-work and they just want to get on with the task of teaching. Pre-service teachers may observe that "seasoned" teachers spend little time writing down their plans. It may be that these teachers have taught the lesson many times and know the process they will undertake and materials required. This works some of the time. However, successful teachers will constantly design new learning experiences and re-evaluate their teaching philosophy that affects how they respond to learning needs in classrooms. According to Winzer (1995), "There is not a single recipe for good planning. Teachers plan in many different ways and at varying levels of depth and complexity: They view planning as a means to an end, not an end in itself" (p. 501).

Assumption 4: Curriculum ties together teachers' needs (e.g., preparing children for examinations), and learners' needs (e.g., being successful in examinations) together in a neat, tidy package.

Many curricula are developed in a linear fashion. That is, teachers begin with their goals clearly outlined at the beginning of a course (their subject matter), and then work in a step-by-step process toward achieving these curricular goals. Yet, learning often happens in non-linear ways when a learner connects new information to previously learned information. For example, learners may understand a physics concept such as angles of thrust and maximum distance, not through trying to comprehend words in a physics textbook, but through throwing a javelin-like stick on the playground. Learning is often messy, non-linear, and serendipitous. Learning is often a discovery, an "Aha" moment arrived at through play perhaps.

On the other hand, for some learners, learning occurs when there is cognitive dissonance, an upset of some previously held idea that requires the learner to learn to right the dissonance (Piaget, 1963). For example, a learner in science may find it cognitively confusing to blow over the top of a piece of paper only to see that the paper actually rises up at the end. Why? The learner may need to experiment further, read, discuss, and consider applications of this famous Bernoulli principle.

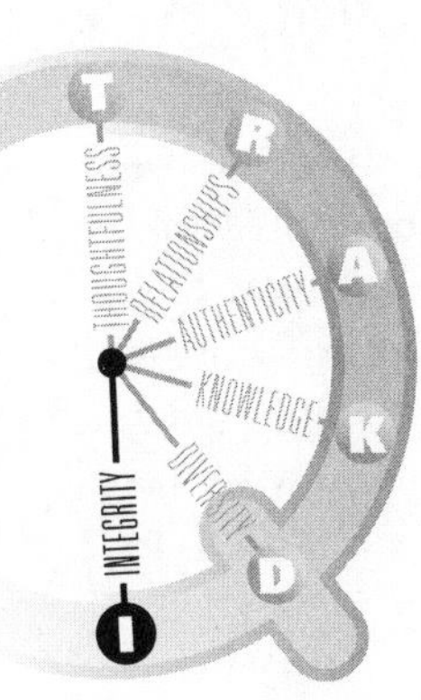

Think of a planned curriculum as one of many vehicles you will use in designing learning experiences for learners. In addition, school boards make available teacher resource manuals. Textbooks will also be available for you and your learners to use. You will go to conferences, workshops, and professional development sessions that will deepen and broaden both your understanding of curriculum and of ways to implement it. Finally, you will learn to trust your acquired acumen, your insights about teaching and learning, acquired through being a reflective, informed practitioner.

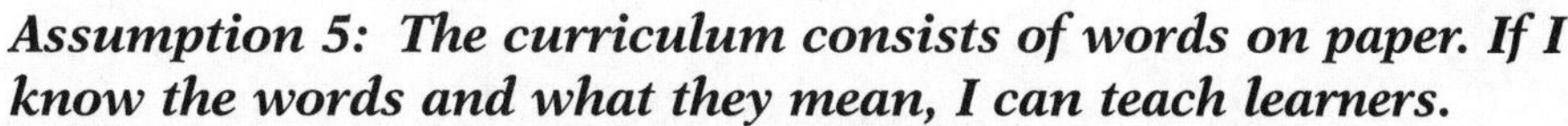

Assumption 5: The curriculum consists of words on paper. If I know the words and what they mean, I can teach learners.

If someone asked you to read and interpret a page of ancient Egyptian hieroglyphics, you would probably either get some help or would ignore the task completely. If you chose to get some help, you would be doing what is most central to implementing curriculum in schools. You would be engaging in a learning process involving others, experts who are willing and able to help. The outcome would be the ability to read and interpret the text. Curriculum looks as though it is just words on paper—goals and intended outcomes written down in programs of study and teacher resource manuals. Curriculum guidelines even seem to be more confusing than Egyptian hieroglyphics. But with your professors' help and the guidance of teachers with whom you will work in schools, the words on paper will soon come to be transformed into well-designed and carefully implemented learning experiences for learners.

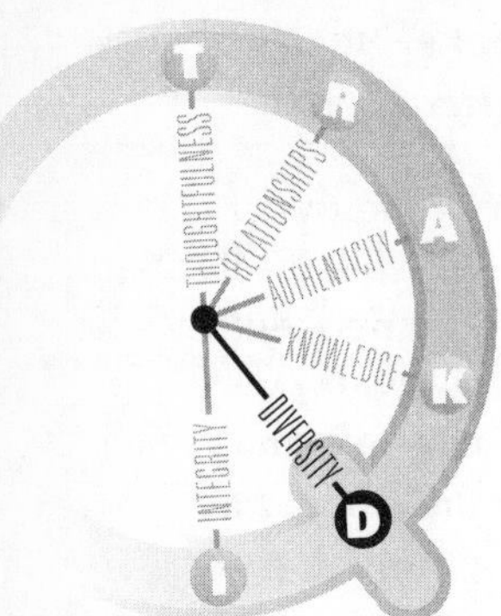

Assumption 6: Teachers need to change subjects and learning activities often to respond to students' short attention span.

Educators schedule the amount of time students spend on each subject over the course of a school year and designate the learning spaces in which the subjects will be taught. The way educators plan schedules has a great deal to do with their philosophical approach to and understanding of how students learn and how teachers and students should behave. Some educators believe that students need to change subjects often, that students' attention does not last, and therefore there is a need to open and close a math book within thirty to forty-five minutes and then open a language arts book, possibly including movement to another classroom. Other educators support the theory that students learn more and retain interest in and understanding of concepts when allowed longer periods of time for projects or experiments on particular areas of inquiry.

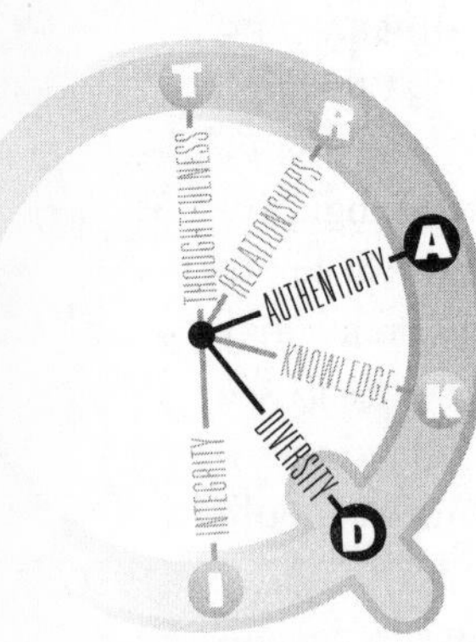

What experiences have you had with schedules and timetables in school? Does the amount of time students remain focused on a task depend on their age, the subject, the teacher's approach, the amount of interaction with other students, and the students' ownership of the learning or project or problem?

Assumption 7: Testing should have a strict time limit so that it is fair for all students.

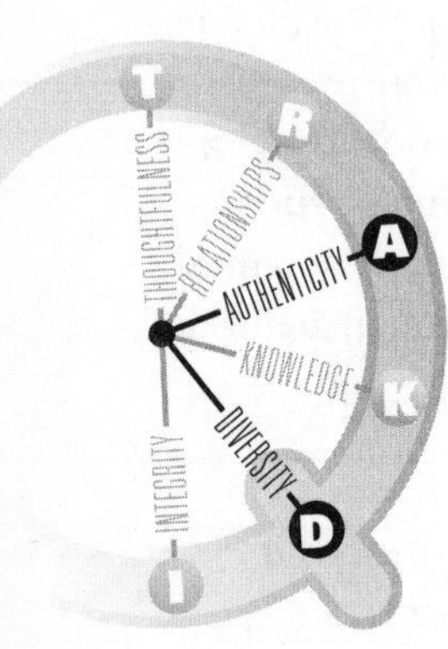

Can you give reasons why you believe this assumption to be true or untrue? We are sure by that this time in your years in school you have felt some pressure to complete a time-specific exam, especially standardized tests. Did you feel anxious due to pressures of time? Did consideration of time block out some of the answers you thought you previously understood? Do some students need more time to consider their responses? Does this have something to do with the uniqueness of children and how children learn in different ways and at different rates?

School Curriculum in Canada

Canadians, it appears, want education to prepare children for the workplace (*National Post* Survey, 2001). According to the same report, parents also want

11.1 FOR YOUR CONSIDERATION

1. What three problems in our society do you believe have the greatest influence on the school curriculum?
2. What three circumstances do you believe should have the greatest influences?

Compare your two lists. If there are any differences, can you explain them? Why do you think they exist? Also compare your lists with those of your classmates. How do you explain the differences between your lists and theirs?

education to prepare their children to be good citizens. In a survey of more than 800 respondents, only seventeen percent said that the purpose of education is to encourage the intellectual growth and desire of learning among children. Canadian parents indicated that character education is important, but secondary to preparing young people for the workforce. Are Canadians expecting too much from the education system? Or are they expecting too little?

Quebec and Nova Scotia are introducing a character-development component into their planned curricula. Other provincial decision-makers in education are faced with a growing body of research indicating that participation in the arts and drama increases learner achievement in academic subjects, improves chances of going to university, and decreases engagement in anti-social behaviour (*National Post* Survey, 2001). If that isn't challenging enough for curriculum decision-makers, many parents report wanting more of a values-based, religious orientation to what happens in schools. Given the complexity of demands, is it any wonder the decision-makers have both great challenges and opportunities when deciding what should go into the planned curriculum?

Your task as a teacher in implementing the curriculum will be equally complex. You will be held accountable for what your learners learn. That accountability shows up in many ways. Ontario, for example, has plans for teacher-testing programs and entrance examinations for the profession, similar to those taken by lawyers. In Alberta, school-based scores from achievement tests administered in Grades 3, 6, 9, and 12, are reported in newspapers. Your role as a teacher includes being able to translate the already challenging planned curriculum into actual learning experiences for perhaps thirty or more diverse learners.

How should you prepare yourself for that? We suggest that you begin now to be a conscientious, thoughtful, and reflective practitioner. This means carefully reading the planned curriculum and trying to understand, with others' help, what the words mean and how best to use the words in the design and implementation of learning experiences. The written programs of study, the curriculum documents prepared by a provincial department of education, will often specify the goals, intended outcomes, and purposes of education. They are often thought of as quasi-legal documents, specifying what it is that all learners are expected to be able to do or know at the end of particular grades.

In addition, teacher resource manuals, the provincially recommended supplementary materials that school boards provide, are designed to help teachers implement the curriculum and achieve the program of studies goals. They provide teaching ideas, resource suggestions, Web sites, and practical help in designing and implementing learning activities. It is important to be as familiar as you can with all the planned, written curriculum materials.

11.2 FOR YOUR CONSIDERATION

Interview three teachers about how they use planned curriculum materials. Ask them what challenges and opportunities are presented in the planned curriculum.

In groups, compare responses. Are there common themes or patterns in your findings? What conclusions might you make about the planned curriculum and how practising teachers actually use the curriculum?

Is there more to curriculum than words on paper?

Conceptions of Curriculum

In Canada, each province is responsible for the education of its children. Saskatchewan, for example, determines its own curriculum, the minimum standards for passing, and testing and other assessment procedures. A child who moves from Saskatchewan to Manitoba may find some differences in what is taught. Because of our highly mobile population, in part, some curriculum initiatives are underway among provincial departments of education to develop standardized, national-based curriculum. One example of such an attempt is the Western Canadian Protocol in mathematics education. Until, or if, nationalization of curriculum occurs, the legislative and design responsibility for curriculum remains provincially situated.

We define **curriculum** here as the programs of study, subject guides, and school-specific policy decisions that affect the ways of working and general conduct in a school. We will examine some contemporary conceptions of curriculum in the next few sections.

The Hidden Curriculum

When a middle-school boy comes home after school and tells his parents that teachers have favourite students and those favourites get better treatment, perhaps even better marks, he has learned something about school and teachers, and about how to succeed with both. He has learned that success in life depends on relationships. Be nice and well-liked, and your chances of success go up. Get in trouble with authority figures and be unpopular, and your chances for success go down. You might argue that the above example is based on a number of assumptions and misconceptions. What if the boy was wrong and teachers are all perfectly fair and unbiased? Is the boy's conclusion about teachers therefore not valid? Did he not learn anything?

The **hidden curriculum** is about unintended learning outcomes. No teacher sets out to teach favouritism, but many learners "learn" it and conclude that indeed this is the reality of teachers in schools. Sometimes the hidden curriculum is more powerful than the planned curriculum. Ask a few young children in your

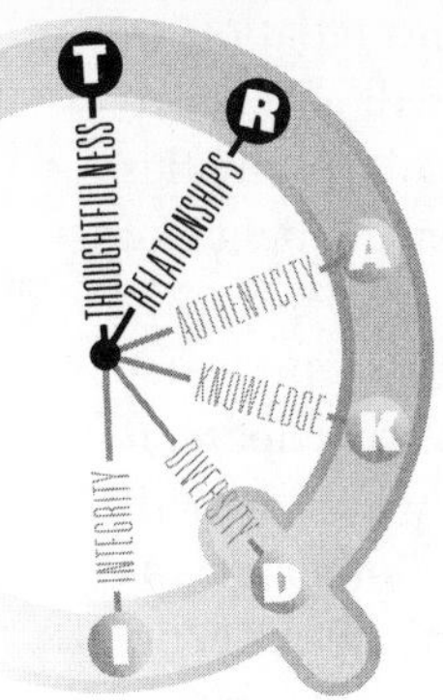

neighbourhood this question, What happened in school today? Listen carefully to their answers. If they reply, "Nothing," you might be tempted to say, "I know what you mean." On the other hand, they would probably be more truthful if they said that they learned to do whatever it takes just to get by. They learned that people can say mean things, but it is surprisingly easy to hide hurt feelings and broken hearts. They learned that creativity and imaginative expressions are okay in some subjects, but not others, that there is a right way to do things for some teachers, and a wrong way for other teachers. Figuring out the difference is the real key to being successful in school.

The Null Curriculum

The **null (or empty) curriculum** is about what is *not taught* in schools. If a school does not teach world religions, learners not only do not learn the knowledge, skills, and attributes that might have come with such a course, they learn that this must not be important knowledge. After all, if school does not teach it, how important can it be? That conclusion is a learning outcome, arrived at through the null curriculum. If a career and life-management class teaches everything about sexuality, the biology, the male/female response, the consequences of sexual activity and prevention of those consequences, and so on, but does not teach how to evaluate and make responsible choices about engaging in or refraining from pre-marital sexual intercourse, learners learn something very important, do they not?

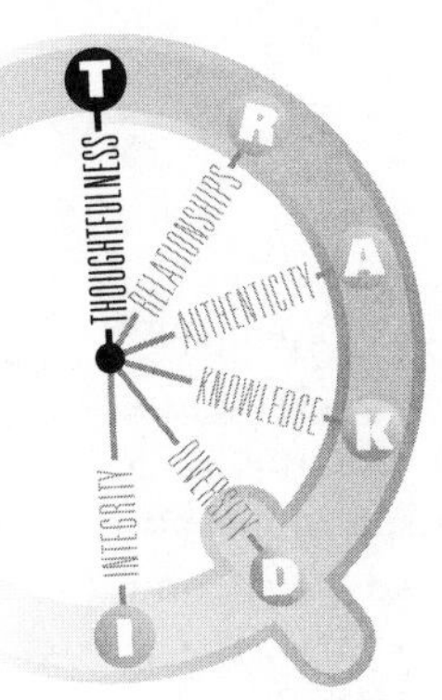

As a teacher, do you have a choice about bringing into your classroom some topic, concept, or idea that is absent in the planned curriculum? For example, can you bring into your classroom a discussion about a particular religious viewpoint? The answer is not a simple one. Every teacher has a position, a philosophical set of ideas about most of the problematic issues in our world. It is noble and perhaps appropriate to try to keep one's personal position out of the discussion. However, by remaining silent about your position, might you be comfortably teaching within the null curriculum as well? In some subject areas, neutrality is virtually impossible, because silence or objectivity are both full of value themselves, are they not?

11.3 FOR YOUR CONSIDERATION

With your classmates, think about possible topics you might not be able to discuss in your future classrooms. How might you handle discussions about those topics should they come up through student questions?

Extra-Curricular Activities

What many of us recall most fondly about school is our participation in extra-curricular activities. Often these activities—the sports teams we played on, the drama we participated in, the clubs we joined—were the best of all our school experiences. Why do you think this is true? Research indicates that participation in extracurricular activities contributes a great deal to a learner's growth and development (Sparkes & Dickensen, 1987). Participants in extracurricular activities generally have greater chances of going to university, display lower incidence of criminal behaviour, and perform better in academic subjects.

Think about who might benefit most from participation in extracurricular activities and how you might encourage the most needy learners to participate. If learners tend not to participate in extracurricular activities, yet would benefit from doing so, it could be important to consider incentives or some other means of drawing them into participation. Perhaps the new participant in an extracurricular activity might show improvement, over time, in academic performance and behaviour.

11.4 FOR YOUR CONSIDERATION

Imagine that a parent has questioned you about the value of school sport teams and the money that goes into funding school sports. The parent wants a justification for including sports in the school budget. You describe the research indicating that there are benefits for some learners who participate, yet the parent remains unconvinced. Is there another argument you might use to convince the parent?

The Planned Curriculum

A **planned curriculum** includes the expressed, or written, statement of goals and intended outcomes within particular subject matter. Typically two types of planned curriculum documents are used in each province. One document is sometimes called a program of study; it specifies the purposes, goals, and intended outcomes of a subject such as science or mathematics for each grade. A second type of document is sometimes called a teacher resource manual; it often specifies how a teacher might design learning experiences, what textbooks best support achievement of goals, and what alternative subject matter ideas might be introduced. The planned curriculum can also include the textbooks, worksheets, and other print or computer-based text.

A planned curriculum includes the content of that subject matter organized in ways that best achieve the goals and intended outcomes for that subject as determined by the province. For example, a physical education curriculum includes the goals of physical education. You would be hard pressed to find any teacher resource manual or provincial program of study that did not make a statement such as that the goal of physical education is to promote the life-long pursuit of physical activity and the consequent development of fitness and a healthy lifestyle. The general goals expressed in curricula among Canada's provinces can be quite similar. In addition, most provincial physical education curricula include the actual subject matter—the content of the program (e.g., games, gymnastics, dance-like activities, outdoor pursuits, track and field, aquatics, and fitness).

11.5 FOR YOUR CONSIDERATION

Imagine you have been hired to revise and improve the curriculum in a particular subject area in school. You might choose science, mathematics, or any other subject that you feel needs revising. Interview a teacher working in that area, and ask that teacher what he or she believes to be the main changes required. Come back to class and prepare a role-play with a classmate about the change and, in particular, the core belief of the teacher regarding that main belief about what needs to be changed. As a class, articulate the themes that appear in each person's presentation.

Textbooks are a third form of planned, written curriculum. They represent a point of contact between learner and subject matter. Today Web sites and on-line learning programs using software programs like WebCT™ and Infonet are replacing textbooks. Textbooks and on-line programs are selected by a school district, often on the recommendation of a school. Curricular resources must be approved by a provincial department of education.

Design of the Planned Curriculum

In some subject areas, the design of a planned curriculum is accompanied by some debate and contention from its main implementers—the teachers. For example, language arts curricula in Canada have been influenced at various times and in various ways by whole-language approaches to teaching, grammar–translation and phonics approaches, and even some emerging combinations of both. Mathematics is another case in point. Some advocate a concept-development approach, where learners learn mathematical concepts such as numbers, space, and distance as foundation to learning the arithmetic of actually manipulating numbers in adding, measuring, or calculating.

Who decides which approach to adopt? Sometimes provincial departments of education hire practising teachers as consultants and writers for particular branches of curriculum. At other times, a department of education will hire directors of instruction as full-time employees. Often it is a combination of both. However, the final decision about what appears in the planned curriculum rests largely with provincial departments of education, which must approve the documents used in schools.

Teacher resource manuals are often created by local school districts. Sometimes these manuals are developed by practising teachers, but more often they are developed by education specialists working in the school board and alongside practising teachers. These specialists are nearly always effective classroom teachers who have specialized in their field and perhaps hold an advanced degree in that field. Why do specialists take on this role? Often it is because they love their subject matter. Sometimes it is because their school board has asked them to do this for a year or two.

How Is Curriculum Developed?

Developing a planned curriculum involves putting words on paper, but what decisions lead to someone putting those particular words on paper? The design of any planned curriculum—such as programs of study and teacher resource manuals—is carried out by those who have a vested interest in the implementation of that curriculum. These individuals include teachers, administrators, and hired curriculum developers within school boards and departments of education. These individuals often work in teams and make a number of decisions in four general areas:

1. *Provincial department of education policy*. This determines the emphasis within a province on the parts and topics of a program of study. For example, a province may mandate daily physical education for all learners within the province, or mandate that each high school learner have a certain number of credits of science before graduating.
2. *School board initiatives*. Curriculum writers often serve within local and regional school boards, which often make situation-specific decisions regarding what should be taught and how that material should be taught. For example, a school board may decide that, given a rise in violence within a local community and school, a program on bullying needs to be introduced.
3. *Parent–teacher advisory groups*. Parents often work with teachers in the design of special events, the purchase of equipment, and the content of curriculum surrounding seasonal dramas and concerts. For example, a parent advisory group may raise money and promote the hiring of a drama troupe for a week-long fine arts development program in a school. They may also be involved in policy and practice decisions such as discipline.
4. *Teachers*. Planning here not only takes into consideration the present—the daily lesson plans and design of the learning conditions based on the learners' needs and the program of study requirements—but also weekly, monthly, and yearly planning. There is a future orientation to what will happen in a classroom and other learning environments. This area of short- and long-term planning is truly curriculum development. The roles of a teacher include the tasks of translating the goals and intended outcomes of programs of study and designing learning experiences based on these translations. In addition, teachers can be creative designers of curricular resources, such as Web sites and science experiments.

What would make this a lived curriculum?

Issues with Curriculum Design

Many design issues face curriculum planners and developers. Since you will be a key curriculum designer who ultimately plans and implements curriculum, it is important that you understand how some of these issues may affect your ability to do your job. Here are just a few:

- *Subject-matter-oriented versus nurturing-oriented curriculum*. Some educators argue for a nurturing approach to being a teacher. They argue that if learners' self-esteem is high, their sense of self-efficacy sound, and their motivation to learn attended to, then they will learn. Emphasis in classrooms is often on developing these positive attributes in learners. On the other hand, many educators argue for a subject-matter emphasis, maintaining that if learners master a subject first, their personal development will follow. These educators will also argue that the real world of the workplace is not nurturing, and therefore schools have some responsibility to reflect that real world.
- *Developmental versus outcome-based curriculum*. The world of education you will soon be a part of emphasizes outcomes and competencies. Curriculum design decisions are driven in part by the need that schools feel to be accountable to parents and society at large. The outcome-based camp of educators believes that if we can identify, teach, and measure learning outcomes in our learners, then we are doing our jobs. On the other hand, developmental-based educators believe that schools should be about the development of learners, the transformation of schemata, the development of capabilities and potential, and the formation of character.
- *Integrated versus subject-matter-focused curriculum*. Some educators believe that subject matter in the curriculum should be combined, or integrated, so that one learning experience includes, for example, elements of science, mathematics, and art. Many educators skilfully do just that, and more. Their thinking is that curriculum needs to be aligned, or integrated, so that learners experience the world as a whole rather than as isolated or fragmented parts (since life doesn't present itself in subject areas). These teachers believe there is efficiency and insight-generating potential when learners see how subjects can be connected and can inform each other. Other teachers, however, prefer to organize curriculum around specific subjects, such as discrete learning experiences in mathematics, science, and so on. These teachers believe that each subject has its own unique language and body of knowledge, and should be understood as such.

Each orientation mentioned above produces a different type of curriculum design. For example, a developmental-based orientation produces a nurturing type of curriculum that emphasizes a learner's values, assumptions, theories, and beliefs over society's (or the provincial curriculum development teams') values, assumptions, theories, and beliefs. You can recognize this type of curriculum because it is often designed to lead students to inquiry, around questions that guide them to uncover and question values.

An integration-based orientation produces a thematic approach to organizing subject matter. You would recognize this type of orientation when a teacher has

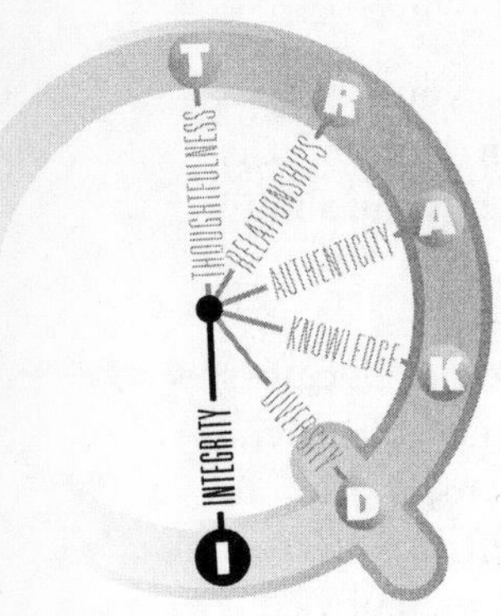

class time organized in themes. One example of integration could be when a teacher decides that May's theme might be culture. In this orientation the teacher can design curricular-appropriate learning experiences related to the theme of culture but use each subject as a vehicle to carry the theme forward and explore the theme from many perspectives. For example, in social studies the teacher might consider the influence of ethnocentrism in society. In language arts the teacher might assess selected pieces of literature from different cultural points of view. In physical education the design of learning experience might include dance forms representing various cultures. In fine arts the teacher might work with students to create art representing various cultures. This approach to integration is only one of many you may consider as you contemplate the design of curriculum that you will ultimately have to implement.

Curriculum Implementation

According to Canadian educators Davis, Sumara, and Luce-Kapler (2000), "[L]esson plans are most often conceived in terms of itineraries—that is, of step-by-step listings of specific activities, their duration and their pre-specified outcomes. In the extreme, some lesson plan formats are so specific as to prescribe almost every aspect of the teacher's and learners' activities (e.g., homework checks, formal lesson, two examples, seat work, etc.), timed to the precise minute" (p. 99). Some teachers prefer to create very specific lesson plans.

Beginning teachers especially may find them helpful in scheduling time and organizing materials. However, it is always important to remember to be flexible and that alternative plans are also useful. Three models for lesson preparation are presented in Chapter 8. There are many variations on the models as well as methods of evaluation. Generally lessons are prepared with a focus on one subject.

How did separate subjects come to be? Did the idea of creating linear, separate subjects or programs of study develop when our society entered the Information Age, or was it much earlier? There are ways to teach and learn that do not require subject separation. They might be called inquiry-based, integrative curriculum (Beane, 1993), integrated (Vars, 1991), interdisciplinary model (Jacobs, 1989; Clarke & Agne, 1997), integration (Beane, 2001, 1995; Jacobs, 1989; Irwin, 1993; Naested, 1998) or generative curriculum planning (Laminach & Lawig, 1994; Fisher & Cordeiro, 1994), to list a few. Many more models are being developed.

Course integration can be explained as a teaching and learning practice that stresses organization that cuts across subject matter lines to bring various aspects of the student's separate subject learning into meaningful association. Connecting learning in one subject to learning in another should lead to greater understanding.

Fogarty (1991) described ten models to integrate curriculum. He believed these models might give educators a foundation for designing curricula that help students make valuable connections for learning. The traditional design for organizing curriculum is the fragmented model, in which each subject is taught separately and involves little course connection. He describes the integrated model as having interdisciplinary topics that are rearranged around overlapping concepts and skills. For example, the concept of "argument and evidence" can be drawn from the math, science, language arts, and social studies curricula. According to Beane (2001), "Curriculum integration begins with the idea that the sources of curriculum ought to be problems, issues and concerns"(p. 184). These concerns can be personal or from the community.

Some educators are not totally sold on the idea of integration. Eisner (1991) supports integration of the arts and other subjects, "as long as the values of art are not diminished in the process"(p. 19). J. Smith (1989) does not advocate complete separation of disciplines as he can see some obvious connections in music, English, and social relationships to name a few, but he considers "music to be one of the most precise of disciplines" (p. 43).

As you might imagine, there are huge debates about maintaining the integrity of separate disciplines, while at the same time realizing that humans live in an integrated world beyond the classroom. Teachers need to understand that these models are just the beginning. "Teachers should go on to invent their own designs for integrating curricula. The process never ends." (Fogarty, 1991, p. 65) And if educators wish to pursue some form of integration or interdisciplinary curriculum, then teachers must have adequate planning time, professional development, and a flexible schedule or timetable to accommodate alternate frameworks for teaching and learning (Naested, 1993).

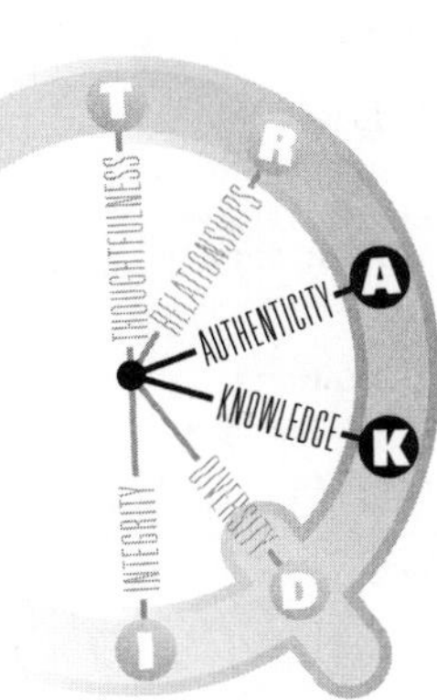

Have you, as a student in school or as a pre-service teacher, experienced a form of course integration? What do you believe to be the problems and possibilities in using this approach to learning and teaching?

The importance of teacher–student and teacher–teacher relationships as a teaching quality has been discussed earlier, as well as the benefits and problems of team teaching. Consider the following scenario.

King George Elementary School had four Grade 6 classrooms with thirty to thirty-five students in each, and four teachers. Two of the teachers, Monika and Tan, have taught at the school for the previous two years and enjoyed their conversations and enthusiasm for teaching. Roula, the third teacher, has taught at KGE for six years. She enjoyed working in this neighbourhood school. The fourth teacher, Jason, was a recent replacement.

Monika and Tan had many discussions of how they might work together on several topics of study, as they realized they had different areas of interest and expertise. Monika had interests in sports, music, and dance, and Tan favoured the math–sciences area. Topics for study in the Grade 6 social studies curriculum guide from the department of education stipulated the study of a country and suggested Brazil. Monika had just spent three weeks in Brazil with her husband, Juan, and was excited to share her understanding of this country, its culture, and its people with her students. Tan was very keen to team with Monika.

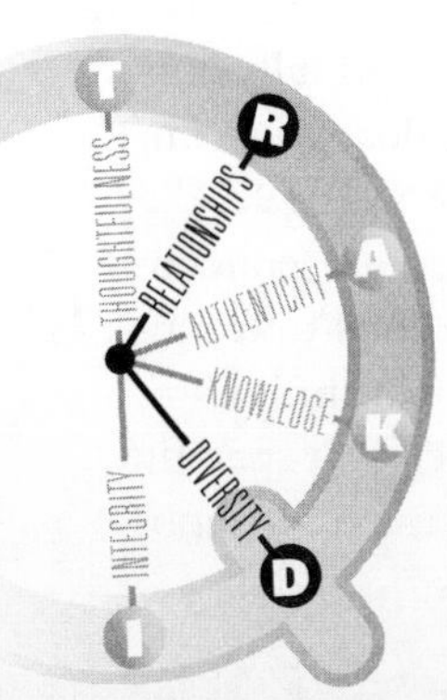

After the traditional start-of-school staff meeting, Tan and Monika cornered Roula and Jason to discuss their undeveloped idea to team-teach and integrate other topics of study for their Grade 6 students. Jason was interested but somewhat cautious, being the newest of the Grade 6 staff. However, he was a keen soccer player, had an interest in politics, and had a strong background in South American art history. He could imagine some possibilities. Roula was satisfied with the way she approached the topic and could not see the benefits of team-teaching as opposed to the many hours it would take to discuss and coordinate.

Figure 11.1 represents the start of the conversation of the four Grade 6 teachers. What do you consider to be the benefits and the difficulties for the teachers and students? What do you believe will be the effect on the students in Roula's class if she chooses not to be involved in this team-teaching, integrated effort?

11.6 FOR YOUR CONSIDERATION

Below is a mind-map of course integration, using the theme of Brazil. Other country and cultural themes might include China, Japan, First Nations of the Northern Woodlands, or the Northwest Coast. Study the curriculum guides in various grade levels of interest to you, and consider how you might integrate the learning for your students.

Another integration model could use more global themes such as world peace, harmony, or conservation.

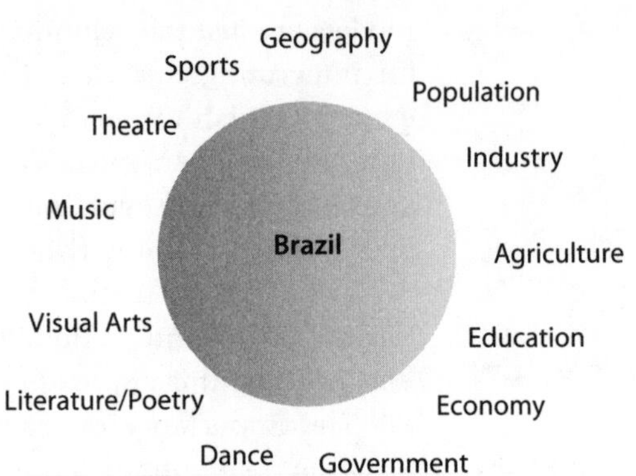

Figure 11.1
Brazil mind-map

Topics on the country of Brazil can be integrated into curriculum areas such as social studies, mathematics, science, physical education, art, music, dance, and language arts.

Approaches to Curriculum Implementation

There is a great deal of diversity in teachers' philosophies on what to teach and how to teach it. In Chapter 7 we discussed an orientation to teaching that has captured the imagination of many educators. Philosophical orientations are not totally accepted, and one's philosophical choice is always up to personal beliefs, just as religious or spiritual beliefs are generally personally interpreted.

According to Chartock (2000), **educational philosophies** are essentially curriculum theories concerning the relationship among a teacher's philosophy, content, and method she or he chooses to apply in the classroom: "For example, the theory of perennialism can be linked to a subject-centered curriculum conception" (Chartock, 2000, p. 65). Reconsider the philosophical orientations to teaching presented in Chapter 7: progressivism, essentialism, perennialism, existentialism, behaviourism, and reconstructionism. With reference to a specific grade level and subject, how might a teacher who follows one of these philosophical orientations implement curriculum?

11.7 FOR YOUR CONSIDERATION

In Chapter 7 we asked you to think about the teaching qualities in light of essentialist teaching and your personal philosophy. How might an essentialist teacher implement curriculum? What are your preferences? Discuss with your colleagues your philosophy and how it might affect your planning.

Segregated and Inclusive Educational Settings

Segregated education and inclusive education represent two diverse theories on meeting the needs of students with special needs. In **segregated education** the students identified as having special needs are taught in a segregated setting, a separate classroom or building, where they are set apart from their age peers. The goal of **inclusive education,** on the other hand, is to include students with disabilities or special needs in classrooms with their age group peers, with or without a teacher's aide or assistant. Special needs students may include those who are gifted and talented, disabled, or have a learning need. Disability generally refers to a physical, mental, sensory, psychiatric, or learning disability.

The authors of this book have taught in both types of settings and found advantages and disadvantages in both when addressing the needs of students. Teachers working in these settings are generally offered professional development, education, and support from the school jurisdiction, teachers' organization, and nearby university. A list of resources and Web sites for further investigation is presented at the end of this chapter.

Innovative Expressions of Planned Curriculum

You might be developing the idea that the planned, or written, curriculum is simply "words written down on paper." Let's examine some innovative expressions of curriculum in a few Canadian settings to illustrate how creative and complex curriculum design and implementation can be.

School jurisdictions may have specifically designed curricula. Politicians, parents, administrators, and teachers often perceive community needs that should be addressed in the classrooms. These might include alcohol and drug abuse, suicide, pregnancy, sexually transmitted diseases (STDs), violence, conflict resolution, and bullying, to mention a few. The manner in which the issue is addressed will vary depending on many factors, including money, personnel, and resources. The decision-makers may decide to bring in guest speakers, develop a lesson, connect the issue to curricula (for example, social studies), or develop a distinct course such as driver training. The Tamarac Education Centre in Port Hawkesbury, Nova Scotia, for example, enhanced anti-violence initiatives by supporting the students in developing an awareness campaign and intervention procedures to reduce the incidence of bullying at the school (Nova Scotia Teachers Union, 2002).

In one British Columbia school, a high school class is taken on an overnight trek into a wilderness area. The trek is intended for learners to experience a bit of what refugees have to endure as they are displaced in many of the world's countries. The learners are given minimal supplies. They experience reasonable levels of teacher-induced hardship along the way. For example, breaks are brief and overnight stays are in tents. This is an example of a curriculum innovation. This approach to curriculum involves designing learning experiences that are simulations of real-life situations. These types of innovations guide learners into experiences that classrooms simply can't provide. What do you think about the value of such curriculum approaches?

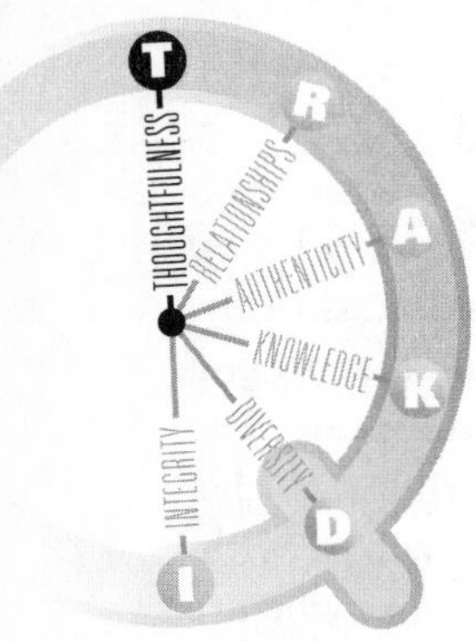

School jurisdictions and provinces have attempted to meet the needs of students by developing curriculum for selected student populations. These initiatives include Aboriginal education, gifted education, French immersion, religious studies, English as a Second Language (ESL), and others. Often the purpose is not to add on to existing curricula but to integrate the curriculum content to better address the needs of the particular population.

Apprenticeships and Workplace-Based Curriculum

In secondary schools in Canada, the issues related to curriculum are very complex. The rapidly changing worlds of technology, workplace demands for specialized and highly skilled workers, and societal expectations for a competent workforce influence the design of curriculum. The rapidity of change presents creative challenges and opportunities to put into schools curriculum that both meets the needs of learners and addresses the issues arising out of an ever-complex world.

In Alberta, for example, in the early 1990s, career and technology studies and registered apprenticeship programs were introduced into the secondary school setting. In career and technology studies, the focus is on students developing employability skills that are consistent with what the workplace identified as most important. These included budget-keeping, planning and implementing business plans, and organizing a work day. Businesses played a key role in the development of this curriculum, not only in supporting the initiative financially and philosophically, but also in designing the actual curriculum guidelines. Business representatives helped to design the program and to identify the goals and competencies required for young people to fit into the contemporary world of work.

The programs have had mixed reviews. Sometimes businesses have not been able to devote the time required to help determine goals. Sometimes the administration of these programs is costly and complex. In Alberta's Registered Apprenticeship Program, for example, the goal is also to address perceived deficits in the availability of trades workers. High school students work part-time, earn a minimum wage, and earn credits toward journeyman certificates. Schools and trades planning together to achieve this goal have both found it challenging.

Across Canada many other expressions of curriculum have attempted to integrate the needs of the workplace with what is done in schools. Technical preparation programs organize curriculum around transferable employability skills and give Canadian learners opportunities to succeed in subjects and learning outside the academic subjects. However, these curriculum innovations have their challenges. Sometimes a specific workplace experience in high school does not produce skills that are transferable to other, slightly different, workplace settings. It seems that learning may, indeed, be tied to the situation in which it occurs. Also, businesses that have the money to invest in such programs and the expertise to share in curriculum decision making often don't or can't do so. Another problem is that workplace needs often are tied not so much to competencies as to attitude. How do you design a curriculum that develops the right attitudes toward work, toward others, and toward problems often encountered in the workplace? These challenges remain to be addressed by curriculum designers.

Special Needs and the Emergent Curriculum

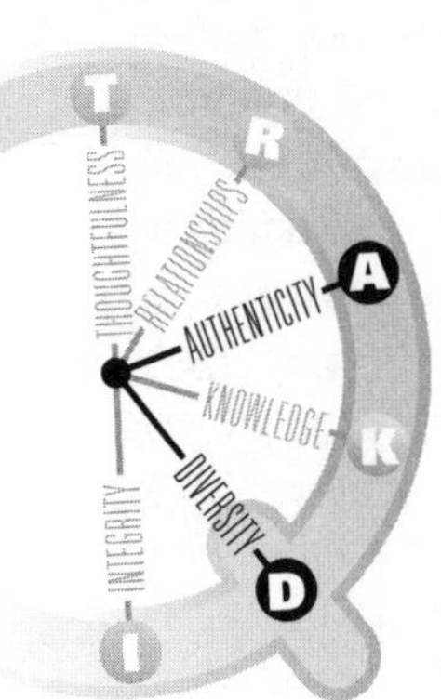

In the Vancouver Public School District, four full-time teachers work with one school district supervisor of instruction to design an emergent curriculum for the sixty or so legally blind children registered in the district. Emergent curriculum is developed on an ad hoc basis in response to learners' needs and system goals. Each of the four teachers travels among Vancouver's schools, meets with each child individually, discusses problems, challenges, and opportunities for learning with respective parents, and discusses ways of mainstreaming some of these children into regular classrooms where possible. There is no fixed program of study. Instead, this team of practising educators meets to pool ideas and resources found in searches through libraries and Web sites and to share research from their respective university programs to design this emerging curriculum. Does this approach to designing curriculum surprise you? It is not common in schools. The benefits include teacher ownership of the curriculum and relevance of curriculum to the students being served. As a practising teacher, you may be a participant in emerging curriculum design.

11.8 FOR YOUR CONSIDERATION

Many trends in approaches have characterized the design and implementation of special education curricula. To identify trends in current approaches to special education curriculum design and implementation, interview three teachers of special needs children: a teacher working with deaf children, a teacher working with a resource room and a non-mainstreamed education program, and a teacher who has an identifiable special needs child in his or her class. Ask them to describe their philosophies (their personal sets of guiding principles) on which they base their practices and what values they hold most dear regarding curriculum design and special needs children. Compare your findings with those of your classmates.

Aboriginal Education

The Western Canadian Protocol for Collaboration in Basic Education developed a common curriculum framework for Aboriginal language and culture programs for Kindergarten to Grade 12. The planning for this involved teachers and representatives from the ministries of education of Alberta, British Columbia, Manitoba, Saskatchewan, Yukon Territory, and the Northwest Territories. For non-Aboriginal students, the goal of this curriculum framework and others developed in various provinces is to increase the acceptance of, positive attitudes toward, and understanding of Aboriginal and Métis cultures in our Canadian pluralistic society. For Aboriginal students, the goals include the development of "positive self-identity through learning about their own histories, cultures, and contemporary lifestyles" (Aboriginal Education Directorate, 2002).

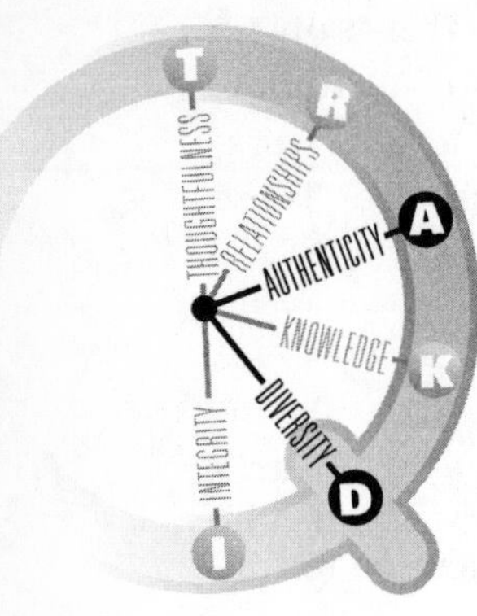

Many post-secondary teacher education programs also include programs for Aboriginal and Métis teacher preparation.

Gifted and Talented Learners

Educators have developed many approaches to the delivery of programming for the gifted and talented as well as for other select student populations (e.g., autistic, deaf). A gifted child may be defined as one who has exceptional potential and/or performance across a wide range of abilities in one or more areas of general intelligence: specific academic, creative thinking, social, musical, artistic, or kinesthetic (Alberta Learning, n.d., p. 41). For the gifted and talented student population, educators have considered the work of educational theorists and researchers such as Renzulli (1988, 1987), Gardner (1999, 1995b), R. Sternberg (1991, 1989), Treffinger (1991), Treffinger and Sortore (1992), F. Gagne (1995, 1991), and others. For example, if the model you are working with in a school setting is based on Gardner's theory of multiple intelligences (discussed in Chapter 4), what implications would this have for the way you teach and assess your students?

Imaginative Education

An interesting curriculum adaptation comes from a relatively new consortium of educators and researchers called Imaginative Education Research Group from the Faculty of Education at Simon Fraser University. This group is working to develop tools for teachers that include "Myth and Metaphor in Responsive Teaching." A goal is to engage students' imaginations in order to render learning more meaningful and emotionally satisfying (Imaginative Education Research Group, 2002; Egan, 1996). They believe "Students can understand almost any material when they are given the opportunity to 'romantically engage' with it. This can be successfully accomplished by humanizing the subject matter that is to be taught; that is, by locating the source of human hopes, fears or passions that were involved in generating the knowledge in the first place" (Imaginative Education Research Group, 2002). Much work needs to be done in this area in order to integrate this concept with curricula. As a pre-service teacher, to what extent do you find these ideas intriguing or difficult to consider?

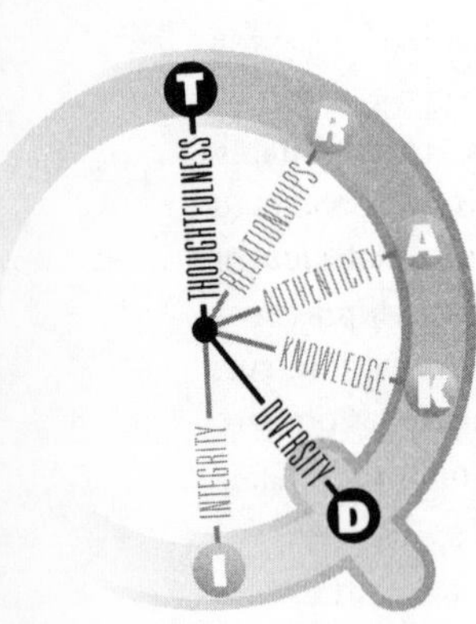

As a student have you been involved in some form of alternative curriculum that addressed a particular need in your school or classroom? How was it approached? Was it successful? Why? Why not? For years to come educators and researchers will continue developing and altering curriculum delivery to meet the needs of diverse learners.

Trends and Future Considerations in Curriculum Development

You will need to consider and make decisions about a number of trends in curriculum:

- *Inquiry-based curriculum.* In this approach to curriculum, learners are encouraged and given guidance to be problem-solvers, to develop the skills of the scientist by asking questions, organizing their learning approach to answering those questions, and arriving at their own answers (Short & Burke, 1996). Surprisingly perhaps, inquiry-based education was strong in the 1960s and 1970s as a result of the influence of Jerome Bruner (1971) and his notion that learners learn best within an inquiry framework. As you will see throughout your profession, trends and shifts in teaching practice are sometimes cyclical.
- *Emergent curriculum.* With this approach, the subject matter emerges as learners, teachers, and perhaps even the community of parents and business leaders work to decide what should be taught, when, and how. The planning is done among teachers in response to emergent needs of students.

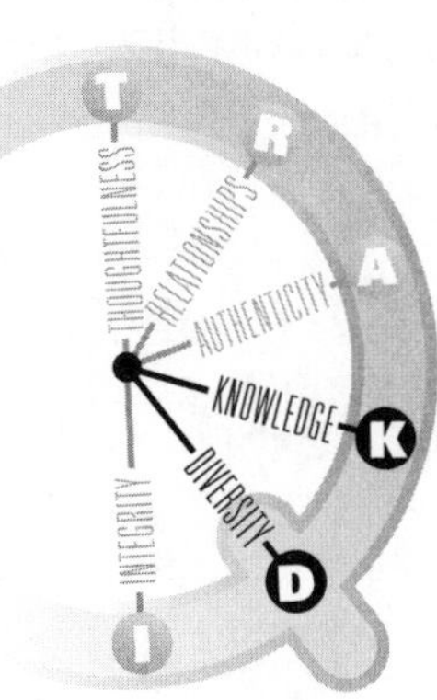

- *Action–learning curriculum.* In this approach, learners solve real-world problems and generate insights and conclusions through the solving of the problems. Some people view this form of education as training (Callender, 1994). The premise of this approach to curriculum is that life-long learning and the skills required to be life-long learners are best developed through real problem-solving opportunities. Provinces produce curricula that are designed to improve job-related skills such as technological literacy and to upgrade the quality of career programs. British Columbia's "The Skills Now" is an example of this.
- *Work-based curriculum.* Here learners learn while on the job. The difference in many work-based curricular approaches is that besides the "words on paper" we have talked about regarding curriculum, work-based learning uses movies, literature, mentorships, and learners' own projects for their learning (Oloroso, 1995). Some educators refer to this form of learning as *situated learning*, in which the learning premise is that the actual situation of work teaches more than a classroom learning situation, where work is just talked about, and that standardization of programs in schools across Canada will ensure that each learner has the opportunity to receive the very best education. There are many difficulties in developing a core, national curriculum. Countries such as Japan, England, and Korea have national curricula and national examination systems. The problems they have faced include the limitations that national curricula place on teacher creativity and their ability to respond to changing times and needs of the learning community. Also, national curricula do not effectively accommodate learners' individual differences and needs. We hope that you watch the trend in Canada toward a national curriculum and standardized testing.

Other trends may also emerge and result in some implications for how you do your job. There is a renewed interest in spirituality as it relates to curriculum in schools that promote spiritual values (Miller, 2000). The interest in spirituality in curriculum is happening at the same time there is a renewed interest in spiritual-

11.9 FOR YOUR CONSIDERATION

Design an overview for the ideal planned curriculum for a subject of your choice. Please keep your overview to one or two pages. In the overview, identify some learning goals, a number of appropriate instructional activities, and some main pieces of information that learners need to know. Specify the grade level and the materials needed for the curriculum to be successful. Also, if possible, connect the learners with the "real world" of work or business.

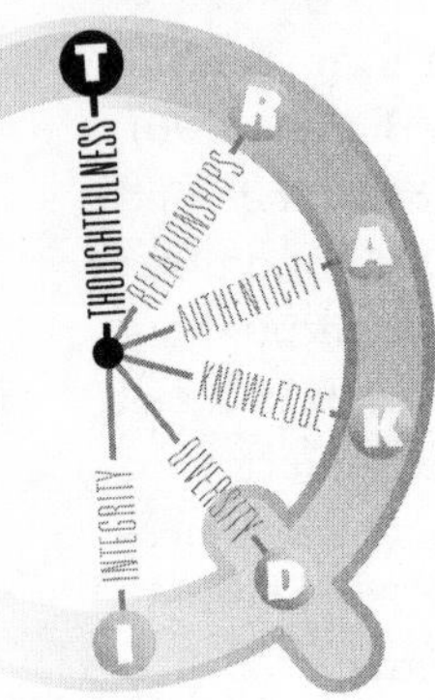

ity in other institutions and areas of public life, such as politics (Wallis, 1981), business (Secretan, 1997), and third world development work (Guitieriez, 1973).

It is unlikely that public schools will ever embrace a spirituality emphasis, particularly if it is one that is encouraged by a particular religious group. However, most people do share a number of common values, regardless of religion, and it will be interesting to see how this interest in spirituality plays out in schools.

Assessment, Evaluation, Measurement, and Reporting

> Not everything that counts can be counted and not everything that can be counted counts. (Herman, Aschbacker & Winters, 1992, p. V)

> Evaluation is shot through with issues of power, responsibility, sensitivity, and even personal taste (Fenwick & Parsons, 2000, p. 13)

Assessment, evaluation, measurement, and reporting are vast fields of study in education. Advanced-level courses, graduate programs, and post-graduate programs exist where years of concentrated studies are available to teacher researchers. "In assessing students' learning, teachers make judgments about the performance of students and about their own performance as teachers. Successful teachers continually evaluate the effectiveness of their own performance as teachers" (Parkay et al., 1996, p. 307). Assessment, evaluation, measurement, and reporting are critical components of your profession. Becoming knowledgeable in this area of teaching will greatly assist you in your work with students. We will briefly discuss a few aspects of assessment for you to consider.

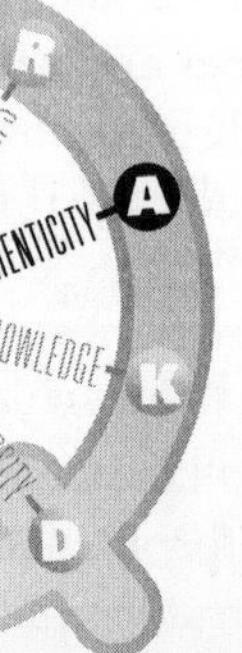

What you believe to be true about students and learning—your philosophy of learning and teaching—influences the way you will approach this area in your practice as a professional. "Students' experience in school is substantially shaped by the fact that they are evaluated and graded" (Young & Levin, 1998, p. 268). The process also has a huge impact on teaching and schooling, and therefore it is important for you to consider your philosophy of teaching. According to Fenwick & Parsons (2000), "To bring your evaluation and teaching practices into line with your ideas, you need to reassess your philosophy of teaching and ask yourself if your methods and criteria for evaluation match your beliefs about what and how [students] ... learn" (p. 21).

The job of a teacher includes the ability to assess learning, as teachers and administrators live in an age of accountability. We now examine four main considerations for a teacher in this field: assessment, evaluation, measurement, and reporting.

Assessment

Assessment means gathering information about learners' learning in order to make a judgment. For example, when a teacher gives a test, that is assessment. The judgment that follows may be to assign a mark for the test or a letter grade on a report card. Judgment may even mean a phone call home to parents. When a teacher observes a learner in class, that observation can be assessment as well. Much information about learning can be gleaned simply by carefully observing how learners approach learning and respond emotionally to learning. The information gathered through observation may not be the most reliable or used for assigning a mark, but it can be used to help the learner improve, to solve a problem, or to modify teaching and learning. This is called **formative assessment.** When teachers gather any information, through any means, including testing, and use that information to help inform the learner of ways they might improve, that assessment does not lead to a mark or grade. When teachers assess, gather information through testing perhaps, and use that information to assign a mark or grade, that assessment is called **summative assessment.**

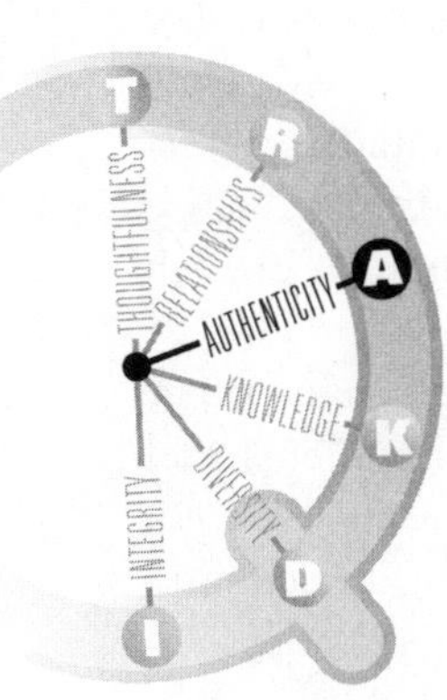

There are alternatives to the traditional standarized testing. This includes authentic assessment, or **performance-based assessment,** which invites students to demonstrate their learning with a response, demonstration, performance, or product. Generally performance assessment requires the students to "generate rather than choose a response. Performance assessment by any name requires students to actively accomplish complex and significant tasks, while bringing to bear prior knowledge, recent learning, and relevant skills to solve realistic of authentic problems. Exhibitions, investigations, demonstrations, written or oral responses, journals, and portfolios are examples of assessment alternatives" (Herman, Aschbacker & Winters, 1992, p. 2).

Student portfolios, which typically contain samples of the student's written work, graphs, charts, drawings, paintings, PowerPoint presentations, and audio and video tapes, can be used in student-led parent–teacher conferences, for example. Portfolios are used for a specific purposes or courses such as art, writing, mathematics, or music, where they provide records of learning and skill development. "Portfolios have the potential to reveal a lot about their creators. They can become a window into the students' heads, a means for both staff and students to understand the educational process at the level of the individual learner." (Paulson, Paulson, & Meyer, 1991, p. 61) However, portfolios are cumbersome and difficult to store (unless the information or images are stored on a disc), and the assessment of the work contained in them is at times interpreted as subjective.

Evaluation

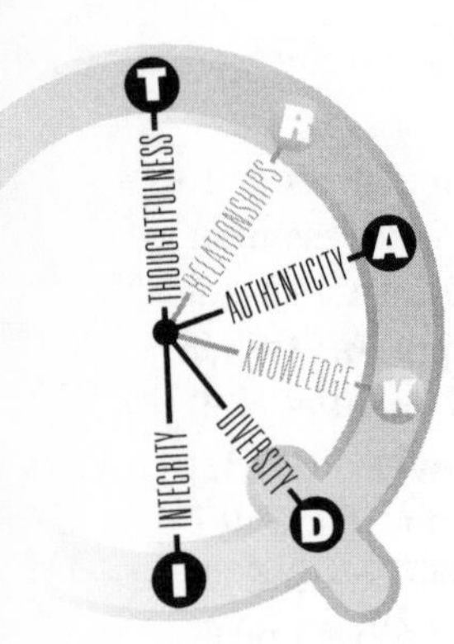

Evaluation is the judgment a teacher applies to the information gathered through assessment. For example, when a teacher asks learners to write essays and then gives letter grades on the essays, the teacher is evaluating. In some cases, evaluation is quite simple. If the teacher uses a multiple-choice test to assess learning, evaluation consists of adding up the right answers and putting that mark on the top of the examination.

But is it really that simple? Perhaps you have noticed that your report card does not include the mark you received on your examinations. Instead, you received a letter (A-), an averaged mark (62%), or a number grade (3.2). Teachers must follow the reporting system of their school and report in the required report card format. However, teachers still have judgments to make, and parents and learners may challenge them about those judgments. For example, if you mark an essay and assign a letter grade of B, the learner may want to know how you arrived at that mark. Some teachers use rubrics, clearly identified sets of criteria that describe what is required to achieve a particular mark. For example, the rubric for earning an A might read as follows: "A—essay was clearly written, with three or fewer spelling mistakes; a compelling and logical thesis statement was followed with grammatically correct sentences, orderly plot development, and logical ending."

Most Canadian children are exposed to standardized tests. **Standardized tests** are generally developed by provincial departments of education and are given to students in pre-selected grades at pre-determined dates and times. Debate surrounds the use of these tests. Parents and teachers voice concern about the affects of test anxiety on the young students and the cost to the taxpayers of administering the tests. Issues arise as to how the test results are used. How should teachers use the results in working with their students? Should administrators use the results to evaluate a teacher's performance? Should the media use the results to rank schools? (Kamat, 1999; Simmer, 2000; Ontario English Catholic Teachers Association, 2002).

In 1997 the Ontario Ministry of Education and Training joined many other provinces in implementing province-wide testing to public school students and annually posting the results of student achievement in specific subjects. By 1999 British Columbia's Ministry of Education decided to stop distributing student and school reports to the public (Kamat, 1999). Many of the provincial teacher associations and provincial departments of education provide the public with standardized test results, articles, links, and other resources. At the end of this chapter is a list of the provincial departments of education and their Web sites. At the end of Chapter 7 are the Web sites for provincial teachers' associations for your reference.

Read the following excerpt from *Teacher,* a newsmagazine of the B.C. Teachers' Federation, written by two teachers who spent several months teaching in Korea. What questions or concerns regarding testing arise?

> Koreans are flocking to Australia, America, Britain, and Canada. The reason? For many it is to ensure that their children avoid the Korean public education system, unaffectionately known by some students as "exam hell." We have seen and experienced here that increased testing does not make teachers more accountable or give students more

> choices. It has the opposite effect. The entire education system, year after year of schooling, is geared entirely to the tests. Principals and administrators are concerned only with how their schools fare competitively against others. The test results are only used to publicly determine which are the best students and then to categorize them. The students achieving the best scores are sent to specialized charter schools for an education in technology, science, or other pursuits. The poorer test achievers are sent to industrial schools. The career and lifestyle choices for both high achievers and low achievers are limited early in their life. (Woelders & Moes, 2002, p. 20)

Measurement

Measurement is about standards teachers use to determine whether learners have learned, how much they have learned, and whether what they have learned, is good, bad, or indifferent. If a teacher decides to use multiple-choice tests to measure learning, the multiple choice tests are also measuring sticks, the standards used to determine whether learning has occurred. If a teacher uses rubrics, these are the measuring sticks. Often, measurement is subjective. A teacher uses past experience with similar learners and may conclude that a particular learner is not doing very well. The measurement then becomes a teacher's professional judgment, sometimes developed through years of reflective experience.

Reporting, Interviews, and Conferences

Reporting student progress and accomplishments is also a teacher's responsibility. Reporting can be verbal, when parents talk with teachers about their children's progress and accomplishments. You may remember your own "student-led conferences," during which you, your parents, and your teachers discussed your work together at the school.

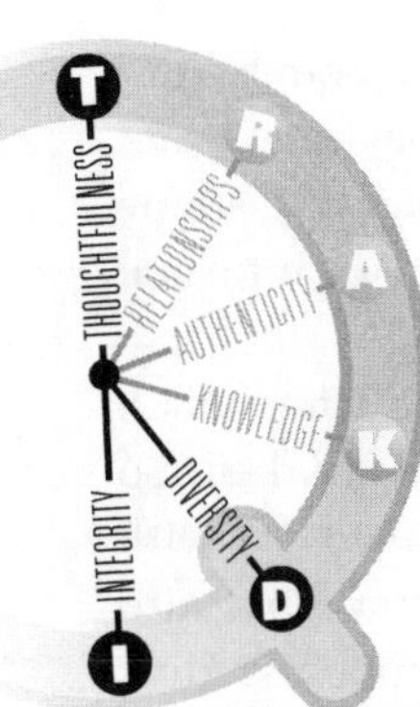

Another way of reporting student progress and accomplishments is by written report cards. For each of us, report cards bring mixed memories. For some of us, report cards meant waiting for that dreaded "report card day" to arrive. Most teachers report progress, or lack of progress, to parents via report cards. Teacher judgments are very important here. It is one thing to record an average mark on a particular spot on the report card. It is another thing for a teacher to decide and report to a parent whether that mark is good, average, needs improving, or is poor. A mark of seventy-five percent may look like a good mark when it stands alone, but if everyone else in the class is getting ninety-five percent, then seventy-five percent is not a good mark. On the other hand, if a learner who has never achieved above a fifty percent earns seventy-five percent, then that seventy-five percent may very well be considered an excellent mark, at least for that learner. Are you beginning to see some of the complexity in this part of a teacher's job? Teachers have to be careful, thoughtful, and above all, use criteria that are well-considered when reporting to parents on the progress of learners.

Reporting student progress has historically been a very difficult task for the teacher and sometimes painful for the students and parents. Often the faculty set up an initial meeting with parents early in the school term; it is often referred to as "meet the teacher night." Parents have the opportunity to meet, sometimes for

11.10 FOR YOUR CONSIDERATION

Search formal and informal report card forms from various schools: Kindergarten, early childhood, elementary, middle, junior high, high school, vocational school or special needs programs. Some of these can be found on provincial teachers' association or department of education Web sites or acquired from school boards, schools, or teachers. Compare various aspects of these report cards. What and how are they reporting information to the parent or guardian, or the student? Are they primarily anecdotal, with spaces for written comments, or numerical, with boxes for check marks? What categories do they use? What subjects are indicated for marks or comments? What subjects are omitted? Compare these report card forms. Which ones appear to be the most useful for parents and students? Give reasons for your decision.

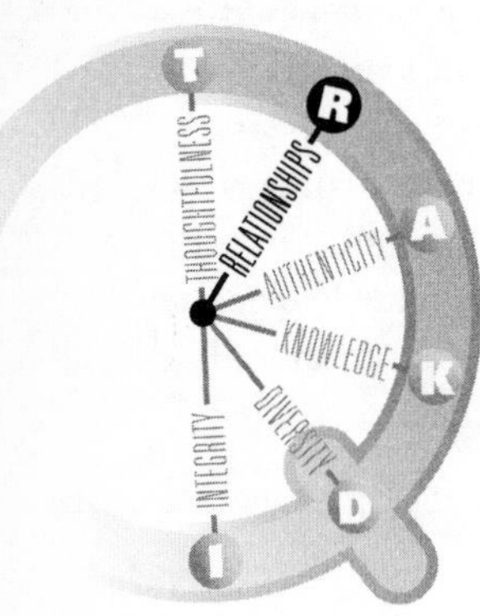

the first time, the teacher their child has discussed at home, and it is often a time when parents can informally alert the teacher to possible problems and provide insight into their child's learning or behaviour. This might also be a time when teachers discuss initial concerns about the student. These meetings are more popular with parents of younger students. The attendance is also greater with parents who are *very* interested in their child's education.

The initial meeting is generally followed by a more formal meeting called the parent–teacher interview, which generally takes place shortly after the first report cards are sent home. Teachers, especially new and inexperienced teachers, can become very nervous about this meeting. They often consult seasoned teachers or even take a workshop on the topic: how to sit, how to listen, what questions to ask. Concerned, conscientious parents will likely come with a list of questions to ask the teacher. Most of the provincial teachers' associations have developed resources and Web site links that offer advice to the beginning teacher.

Following is a story about Jasmine and her first experience with parent–teacher conferences. Consider your thoughts on this important event in teaching and learning.

> Jasmine's first year of teaching was teaching social studies at a "rough" junior high school. The school faculty was primarily made up of beginning and new teachers, with a few "seasoned" teachers. Over the first few weeks Jasmine observed these seasoned teachers and engaged a couple of them as informal mentors.
>
> By mid-October the teachers were into the reporting-period, during which they gave tests in every subject, which then, of course, had to be marked. So there went Jasmine's weekends! Her evenings were already taken up with course planning. The students not only got a final percentage grade but also anecdotal comments. Now, what do you say about each of your students? How do you make each comment positive, yet honest, reflecting the learning strengths and needs of the individual learner? Jasmine also wondered about the organization and routine for the parent–teacher conferences. Had her years of post-secondary education prepared her? What did she need to know and understand about these important events in teaching and learning? What are her options in seeking assistance?

11.11 FOR YOUR CONSIDERATION

Do you think your parents had valuable and informative or fearful and frustrating teacher interviews? Did you attend any of these meetings? Why or why not? If you did, did you find they were valuable to you as a learner? What made them so? How could these meetings be structured to become meaningful for parent and learner? Compare your thoughts with others.

11.12 FOR YOUR CONSIDERATION

The following is an excerpt from the British Columbia Teachers' Federation Web site, which includes many useful suggestions for new teachers, including reporting, planning, working with volunteers, and other topics of interest.

A Communications Checklist for Parent/Teacher Conferencing

The best communication climate is a comfortable one; if you are relaxed, parents/guardians usually will relax, too. There are many communication techniques that will lead to a successful conference. You may wish to use some of the following:

Before the Conference

- Before your first meeting with parents/guardians, review the school history of the student.
- Complete a data page on each child's strengths (emotional, social, physical, intellectual).
- Be well prepared: collect dated samples of student work completed throughout the term to show improvement or decline in quality and to substantiate your evaluation.
- Ensure privacy.
- Arrange informal seating around a table displaying the student's work.
- Post appointments outside the door, and keep to the schedule; invite parents/guardians needing additional conference time to come at a later date.
- Have chairs and coffee available outside the classroom.
- If the conference is part of the regular reporting period, send home a newsletter describing your programs and some of the topics being studied.
- If the students are not included in the conference, meet with them beforehand so that they are aware of what will be discussed.
- Prepare a conference form for record keeping to keep the discussion focussed and to be an aid for future conferences and for follow-up.
- Send out an interview confirmation sheet; ask parents/guardians to return it.
- Successful conferences deal with only a few issues because of time constraints; make sure you know what points you want to cover.

During the Conference

- Greet the parents/guardians at the door.
- Be clear and concise in your comments; be an attentive listener.
- Introduce yourself with a friendly voice, but keep opening comments to a minimum to allow for more discussion time.
- Keep the parents/guardians involved by encouraging them to share pertinent information with you.
- Maintain the focus, and keep the discussion on track.
- No matter how many problems a student has, find some positive things to report.
- With the parents'/guardians' help, develop some goals or an action plan for the rest of the year.

Concluding the Conference

- Check that the parents/guardians have a clear understanding of what was discussed.
- Highlight the conclusions and the agreed-upon actions.

- Set another date for another interview if one is needed.
- End as you began—on a positive note.
- Thank the parents/guardians, and walk them to the door.
- Summarize the points covered, and add them to your files.

Follow-Up

- Send a note home the next day thanking the parents/guardians for their time and interest.
- After a few weeks, phone the parents/guardians with a progress report.
- Keep your principal informed.

Ways To Communicate Regularly With Parents/Guardians

- Keep file cards for each child, noting the positive things that have happened; then send home a couple of happygrams during the term using the information.
- Make phone calls about good things the child has accomplished.
- Send newsletters containing student work.
- Think of Education Week as an opportunity to communicate with parents/guardians.
- When you discuss a problem with parents/guardians, be truthful, sincere, and objective; they will respect your integrity.

For further materials, contact the BCTF and/or your local. British Columbia Teachers' Federation Website, 2001, **www.bctf.bc.ca/beginning/handbook.**

(Source: From "Communication for Conferencing," *A Handbook for New Teachers*. Retrieved March, 2002, from **www.bctf.bc.ca**. Copyright by British Columbia Teachers' Federation. Reprinted with permission.)

Student-led conferences put the learner at the centre, in contrast to the previous model where the learner was usually excluded from the conversation. Student-led conferences have gained much attention and praise from parents. Parents have the opportunity to have a conversation with their child and her or his teacher to discover what their child is learning at school and what they believe to be the child's strengths and weaknesses in various subject areas. Students become actively involved in assessing their schoolwork. According to Borba and Olvera (2001), "[S]tudent-led parent-teacher conferences encourage students to participate actively in the evaluation of their academic progress, which motivates students to think about and act on personal initiatives to improve learning" (p. 333).

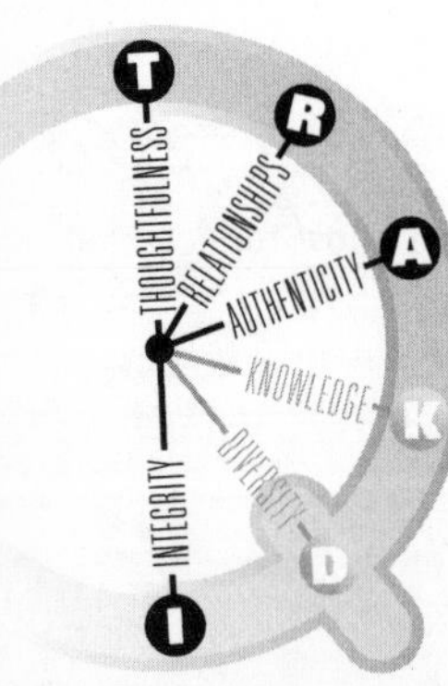

These student-led meetings, however, require a good deal of preparation and time on the part of the teacher and students. The teacher must prepare the students by helping them select appropriate examples to demonstrate their learning, often in the form of a portfolio. Teachers may organize class time for the students to role-play the conference with their classmates. Teachers may also provide parents with leading questions to ask during the conference. The conference may end with students writing their learning goals. Teachers, however, need to make sure that parents feel welcome for a follow-up meeting. The Calgary Board of Education (1993) encouraged teachers to conduct the conferences to "provide an opportunity for the teacher and student to give one another feedback and to negotiate assignments, goals and actions to promote continuity in the student's learning." Assessment and reporting should assist the teacher, student, and parent in the teaching and learning process.

Reflection and Perspective on the Chapter

Curriculum is one more piece of the teaching landscape. In our discussion about curriculum we have visited some important and current practices, issues, and trends in the field of curriculum. You might be surprised to learn that many professors teaching in faculties of education have earned doctorates in curriculum development. This field is growing and contributes to the profession a body of research and writing that may one day entice you to study more.

Your philosophy of learning and teaching affects the way you will approach curriculum in your practice as a professional. This is curriculum implementation: bringing to life the conceptions and decisions—the curriculum—in the classroom, where there is no single recipe for success. Your personal philosophy will also influence the way you approach assessment, evaluation, measurement, and reporting as regular duties that require a great deal of knowledge, understanding, and sensitivity.

Standardized tests will probably continue to be a part of your experience as a teacher. We hope that if they are a fact in your life as a teacher you will be able to use the data gained from these tests to enhance your teaching. Expand your approaches to student assessment with alternatives such as performance-based assessment and portfolios. Reporting to parents should become a regular occurrence. Using the student-led conference model can be very meaningful for both the parent and student.

Consider your worldview of teaching. Have your assumptions about curriculum planning, implementation, and assessment been altered or confirmed? The teaching qualities of diversity, authenticity, relationship, thoughtfulness, integrity, and knowledge will have an impact on the way you approach curriculum. You are entering an exciting career with no right answers, but with a great many possibilities.

One final word on this topic: Curriculum raises many questions and poses many challenges and opportunities for you to learn. Keep reading and thinking about this topic, and be open to possibilities that well-thought-out curriculum can open minds to inspire learners to achieve great things.

Key Terms

assessment 265
course integration 256
curriculum 250
educational philosophies 258
evaluation 266
formative assessment 265
hidden curriculum 250
inclusive education 259
measurement 267
null (empty) curriculum 251
performance-based assessment 265
planned curriculum 252
segregated education 259
standardized tests 266
student portfolio 265
student-led conferences 270
summative assessment 265

Suggested Further Reading

Resources

Provincial and Territorial Departments and Ministries Responsible for Education in Canada

Newfoundland and Labrador Department of Education
Confederation Building, West Block
St. John's, NL A1B 4J6
http://www.gov.nf.ca/edu

Nova Scotia Department of Education
Box 578 Halifax, NS B3J 2S9
http://www.ednet.ns.ca

Prince Edward Island Department of Education
Box 2000, 16 Fitzroy St.Charlottetown, PE C1A 7N8
http://www.gov.pe.ca/education

New Brunswick Department of Education
P.O. Box 6000
Fredericton, NB E3B 5H1
http://www.gov.nb.ca/education

Quebec Ministère de l'Education
Édifice Marie-Guyart
28e étage, 1035, rue de la Chevrotiere
Quebec, QC G1R 5A5
http://www.meq.gouv.qc.ca

Ontario Minister of Education
Mowat Block, 900 Bay Street
Toronto, ON M7A 1L2
http://edu.gov.on.ca

Manitoba Department of Education, Training and Youth
450 Broadway
Winnipeg, MB R3C 0V8
http://www.edu.gov.mb.ca

Saskatchewan Department of Education,
2220 College Avenue
Regina, SK S4P 3V7
http://www.sasked.gov.sk.ca

Alberta Learning
7th Floor, Commerce Place
10155 – 102 Street
Edmonton, AB T5J 4L5
http://www.learning.gov.ab.ca

British Columbia Ministry of Education
P. O. Box 9156, Stn. Prov. Govt.
Victoria, BC V8W 9H1
http://www.gov.bc.ca/bced

Nunavut Department of Education
P.O. Box 800
Government of Nunavut, Building 1099E
Iqaluit, NU X0A OHO
http://www.gov.nu.ca/education.htm

Northwest Territories Minister of Education, Culture and Employment
P.O. Box 1320
4501 – 50 Avenue,
Yellowknife, NT X1A 2L9
http://siksik.learnnet.nt.ca

Yukon Department of Education
P.O. Box 2703
Whitehorse, YK Y1A 2C6
http://www.gov.yk.ca/depts/education/

Standardized Testing

No More Tests: www.nomoretests.com

Fenwick, T. and Parsons, J. (2000). *The Art of Evaluation: A Handbook for Educators and Trainers.* Toronto: Thompson Educational Publishing.

Inclusive Education

Hutchinson, N. (2002). *Inclusion of exceptional learners in Canadian schools: A practical handbook for teachers.* Toronto: Prentice Hall.

Bunch, G. (1999). *Inclusion: How to: Essential classroom strategies*. Toronto: Inclusion Press.

Helmer, S. (1996). *Look at me when I talk to you: ESL learners in non-ESL classrooms.* Toronto: Pippin Publishing.

Bartlett, L. (2002). *Successful inclusion for educational leaders*. Upper Saddle River, NJ: Prentice Hall

Dyson, A. (2000). *Schools and special needs: Issues of innovation and inclusion*. London: P. Chapman.

Learning Disabilities Association of Canada: http://www.ldac-taac.ca/english/about.htm

Canadian Council for Exceptional Children: http://www.cec.sped.org

Council of Ministers of Education, Canada: http://www.cmec.ca

Schoolnet Project: http://www.schoolnet.ca/sne. A co-operative initiative of Canada's provincial, territorial, and federal governments, in consultation with educators, universities, colleges, and industry.

Chapter 12

Society, Culture, and Schooling

Sex, drugs, rock 'n' roll? Relax, mom and dad—today's teens are no wilder than you were.

—B. BERGMAN, "The Kids Are All Right," *Maclean's*, April 9, 2001

I do believe our culture is doing a bad job raising boys. The evidence is in the shocking violence.... It is in our overcrowded prisons and domestic violence shelters. It's in our adult bookstores and white supremacy groups. It's in our Ritalin controlled elementary schools and alcohol-soaked college campuses.

—WILLIAM POLLACK (1998), foreword to *Real Boys: Rescuing Our Sons from the Myths of Boyhood*

Let's decide who the prettiest girls in the world are.

—SIX GIRLS, AGED 6–9 (Author's Living Room, February 25, 2002)

Chapter Focus

This chapter is about understanding society, culture, and schools, particularly the influences of Canadian society on learners in Canadian schools. We begin the chapter with some commonly held assumptions and aims of schooling. We will consider how schools, teachers, and learners are influenced by societal issues such as divorce and violence, and what teachers can do and cannot do about those influences. We will also examine what role schools do and should play in Canadian society, and we will consider how schools help shape Canadian cultural values and attitudes. We will examine why schools are an important part of Canadian culture and why well-run and effective schools are important for the preservation of the Canadian way of life. We will describe what a well-run and effective school might look like in Canadian society.

Our goal in this chapter is for you to continue to develop your teaching worldview, to arrive at some fair and accurate conclusions about the most realistic and desirable relationship between Canadian schools and society. As we have done throughout this book with each of the other commonplaces (learners and learning; teachers and teaching; schools and classrooms; and curriculum and subject matter), we will ask you to integrate your conclusions, this time regarding schools and society, into your emerging teaching worldview. Societal trends in health, business, technology, values, and information deeply influence what is taught in schools. Societal issues such as divorce and violence also influence how well learners can learn what is taught in Canadian schools. You may, at this time in your teacher development, be tempted to conclude that schools should be concerned just with young people and teaching "the curriculum." We hope to stretch your understanding of teaching beyond just teaching the curriculum to include conclusions about how to deal with societal and cultural influences in schools. We expect that by the end of this chapter, you will recognize how mutually influential are schools, culture, and society. If a teacher ignores contemporary Canadian society and culture, and their influence in Canadian schools, the teacher ignores important conditions influencing what and how people can learn. As we discussed in Chapter 6, learners are active constructors of meaning, using their assumptions, values, theories, and ideas to make sense of new information. Society provides a wealth of assumptions, theories, values, and ideas that young people (and their parents) use to learn. New learning can be directed by societal learning; new learning can also be misdirected by societal learning. We invite you to give this chapter your careful attention, to consider the assumptions, theories, and values that shape the minds and behaviours of Canadian young people.

There are many complementary reasons for you to give special attention to this chapter. One reason is that parents and other school stakeholders call on professional educators to comment in informed and thoughtful ways on many issues in Canadian schools. These issues find their ways into a school's day-to-day life much as environmental influences find their way into ponds, streams, and rivers, and ultimately into us. As you may recall from Chapter 6, learners are part of an ecology (Bronfenbrenner, 1989).

Another reason is that a teacher's day-to-day experience is profoundly influenced by many of these issues. Children bring the effects of serious issues such as divorce, violence, and drugs into their classrooms. Other issues, impressive and sobering for their variety, also influence teachers. These include the current societal emphasis on standards, accountability of schools through academic achievement and grades, and the role and place of religion and other forms of spirituality in schools. Some influences affect many teachers directly, such as streaming special needs children in regular classrooms. Other influences are less immediate, but still of concern to many teachers. These include how schools can meaningfully connect with the "outside world" of business and the workplace, the place of charter and private schools within the larger public-school-based society, and how to deal with current values in society that conflict with the child's family and community values. Most teachers are understandably concerned with the pervasive and consciousness-shaping media, music, and violence in contemporary society and how best to help young people make good sense of it all. Within a comprehensive and critical worldview of society, teachers can make informed and thoughtful decisions on designing learning experiences that are most helpful for all their learners, including the learners who are most seriously affected by societal issues.

In this chapter, you can look forward to considering what are schools' responsibilities and aims in Canadian society. How do effective schools deal with social issues such as bullying and drug use? What social problems create the biggest day-to-day risks for learners in Canadian society?

Focus Questions

1. What responsibility should society place on schools to address social problems? What are reasonable expectations for schools in addressing societal issues?
2. In what ways should schools be social institutions, preserving the Canadian way of life? In what ways should schools be concerned only with their learners' academic success?
3. What are teacher responsibilities and rights in addressing social issues in their classrooms?
4. What social issues are most influential in a learner's ability to do well in school?
5. How should schools design their activities to help those learners most affected by social issues? Should schools use intervention programs and other innovations to help learners who have problems that originate in social issues?
6. Should teachers address social issues in their classrooms through religious and other values-based approaches?

Assumptions about Society, Culture, and Schools

The following assumptions invite you to reflect on your own assumptions, theories, and beliefs about society, culture, and schools. We invite you to begin building your own theory of schools and society, considering first what are the core issues facing both, and what might schools and teachers be reasonably expected to achieve.

Assumption 1: With the current emphasis in Canadian schools on grades and accountability, there is now widespread agreement in Canadian society about what schools should teach.

The debate over what schools should teach and emphasize has not ended with the current Canadian focus on accountability and student academic achievement. In

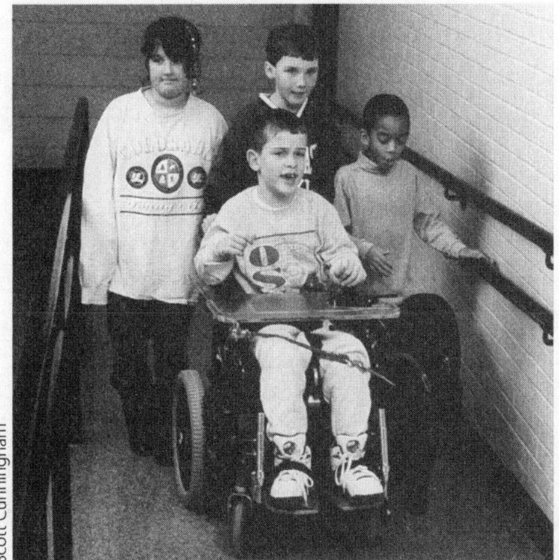

Scott Cunningham

Could the null curriculum be evident here?

some ways, the focus on grades and accountability has only heightened awareness of other issues that confound a school's ability to promote academic achievement for all learners. Today schools are asked to promote academic achievement among learners who may be experiencing the stresses of broken homes, violence, and little home support for academic achievement. Schools may be under funded and ill equipped to support **intervention programs,** which are ongoing and individualized approaches, such as peer tutoring, intended to prevent academic problems and help learners with special needs stay in regular classrooms. There is great pressure on teachers and schools to provide **compensatory education;** that is, additional support of materials, teacher aides, and individualized program planning that make up for specific special learning needs (e.g., where English is a second language), but which may take learners out of regular classrooms for some time. However, resources are hard to come by. It is no wonder teachers, as well as parents and other stakeholders, ask the question, What should schools be emphasizing?

Questions of emphasis and what schools should aim to accomplish create unique pressures for Canadian teachers. Canadian society is complex. It is a cultural mix of people who hold different ideas about what schools should do. This Canadian complexity is further enhanced by current workplace emphases on technology and computer use, the complexities of the workplace, and the uncertainties of the marketplace. Teachers also keenly feel the parents' desire to have schools address social issues such as violence. Many teachers wonder about the role and place of **values-based education,** formal school programming that emphasizes identification, assessment, and evaluation of specific pro-social ideas such as empathy, justice, and sharing. Some teachers believe that the way to improve society is through **character formation education,** a movement that emphasizes student development of specific values through critical thinking, formal instruction, or indoctrination. The rise in alternative delivery forms of education—charter schools, home schooling, and private schools—reflects many parents' desire to emphasize some particular aspect of schooling over another.

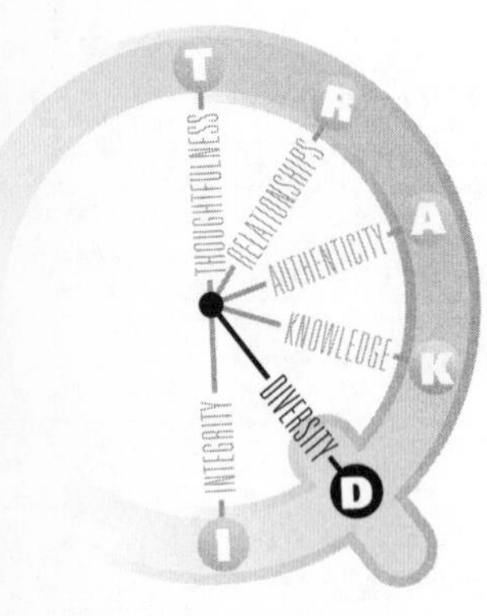

There is no widespread agreement about what should be taught in schools. Your entry into the profession of educator will include opportunities for you to participate in discussions about school emphases with parents, colleagues, and representatives of the Canadian workplace. As each generation of teachers has done before you, and each culture has done throughout history, you will have an opportunity to generate your own response to the question, What should schools emphasize?

Assumption 2: The values of Canadian society should determine what schools teach and what emphasis schools give to some topics over others.

We begin our discussion with this question, Who should lead whom in decision making regarding what schools teach—society and its values or schools and the values schools wish to emphasize? This question is an important one. Consider just a few aspects of this issue. In physical education should schools reflect and promote the community and professional sports emphasis on winning, competition, and choosing the best to be on the team? Should schools emphasize success on examinations through preparing-for-the examination approaches to standardized testing—commercially prepared and uniformly designed and administered tests? Should schools emphasize one theoretical perspective about human origins over another?

The idea that society should lead what is taught in schools is further complicated when we consider the complexity and **pluralism** of Canadian society. Canadian society is made of many cultures, systems of thought, and values. Many parents feel that schools should teach history, geography, basic mathematics, and content-based subjects. Others feel that an educated person needs to learn to be a critical thinker, a problem solver, and a synthesizer of knowledge, not just a consumer of knowledge. For supporters of education that promotes life-long learning and tools to help one be a life-long learner, fact-based education is no more than a form of elaborate trivia game for credit (Myers,1995).

At one time professional educators might have embraced the notion that what should be taught in school is what every educated person needs to know. Today we can find some, but not widespread, agreement about what it means to be an educated person. Perhaps you might choose to believe that the issue is not an either/or issue, but a both/and issue. Perhaps Canadian children can learn the facts of the cultural revolution in China and also study the historical and philosophical bases for the causes of the cultural revolution. Perhaps Canadian learners can memorize the facts of World War II or memorize the principles of citizenship in Canadian society. In addition, perhaps Canadian learners can study the historical values, theories of human development, theological and philosophical conceptions of human worth, and sociological principles of human organizations that help explain the causes of the second world war or Canadian citizenship practices. A.N. Whitehead (1929) said that education should be about teaching a few powerful ideas that explain and encompass all of human experience. That is a compelling position for some. Others believe that schools should teach as much as can be fit into a school curriculum, a view is that is represented by the analogy that if you scatter enough seeds on the ground, some of them are bound to take root. For some people, this is a compelling idea. Canadian society is so complex and its needs so varied that for some people, schools must provide as wide a variety of topics, issues, subjects, and concepts as possible. What assumptions do you hold about this issue of schools leading or following society?

Assumption 3: Religion needs to be kept out of Canadian schools. Canadian society is pluralistic, multicultural, and multi-faith; therefore, religion has no place in education.

If what we mean by religion is an individual's personal expression of spirituality and espousing of personal values, or a person's striving to meet deep needs of security and significance, then the question is, How can teachers possibly keep religion out of schools? Canadian culture is full of religious and spiritual beliefs about what brings meaning, purpose, and security. And all Canadians have some religious values, which their children carry with them into their daily discussions, thinking, and behaviour in schools. Sexual expression, consumerism, cars, hobbies, sports, music, beauty, work, and more have all taken on religious significance as they have replaced organized religion for many as the means of finding significance, security, and purpose in life.

Religion is already part of Canadian schools when schools emphasize values such as work, success, and achievement as ways to find personal meaning and purpose. When teachers comment affirmatively or negatively about music, sexual activity, or solutions to personal problems, teachers invariably make religious statements about personal meaning and purpose. Within this concept of religion then, neutrality is a myth, and each school day sees religion being taught—in the hidden curriculum, in the null curriculum, and even in the extracurricular program of a school. Religion can be taught within social studies classes on ethnocentrism, in language arts and literature classes with the great literature of our times. A more appropriate question to ask may be, What type of religion should be taught in schools?

Assumption 4: Advances in technology lead society; schools need to follow.

Technology has obviously revolutionized society. It has also raised many questions and posed many problems for teachers and schools. Teachers question how well prepared they are, for example, to use computers in their classrooms. Administrators complain about inadequate funding for purchasing computers, and for getting the resources necessary to integrate computers into school life. In faculties of education, training is often hit-and-miss for preparing teachers to use computers meaningfully in classrooms. Schools have more options for computer use than school resources, curriculum, and pedagogy can support. These include **computer-assisted instruction,** in which a teacher integrates computer technology into day-to-day programming (e.g., building Web pages or PowerPoint presentations as part of the regular curriculum and particular subjects in a classroom). Another option is **computer-based instruction,** in which the computer screen, and not the classroom, is the learning environment, and through which students can learn at a distance through three-way communication among teacher, text, and student. Another option is the **computer-mediated conference,** in which interactive, two-way communication, conducted synchronously or asynchronously, provides the instruction. These are just a few ways computers are being used in Canadian schools. Technology and the possible educational uses of technology are bewildering to some. We do know we can teach using computers. We don't know yet how well and in what ways computers can best be used in schools and curriculum.

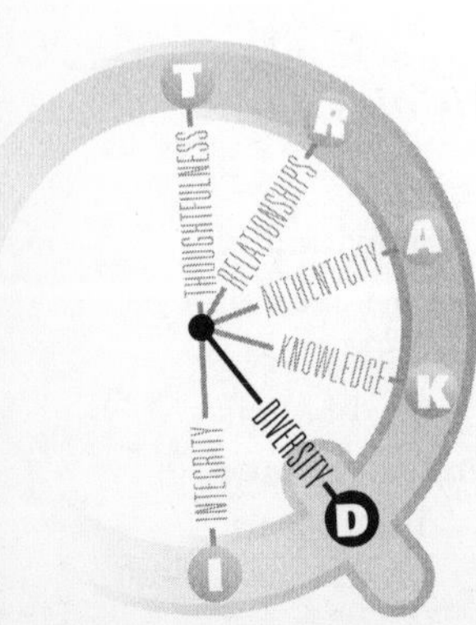

Technology might be about pushing the right buttons. Technology and its use does not necessarily include knowing how to speak, think, listen, or solve problems. As Michael Apple (1990) reminded us more than a decade ago, any teaching that pushes us away from relationship building should be questioned. To date, technology has not led schooling; technology has complicated schooling while creating many new possibilities for designing learning experiences for young people. How much schooling will be delivered through computer technology in the next ten years? How much has it changed education for you in the past ten years?

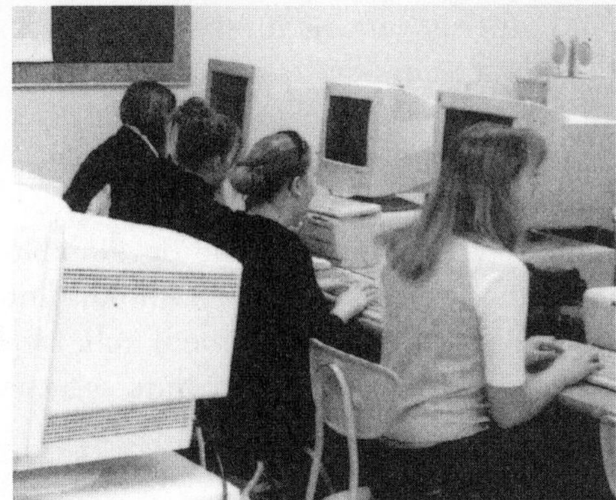

Should technology lead teaching?

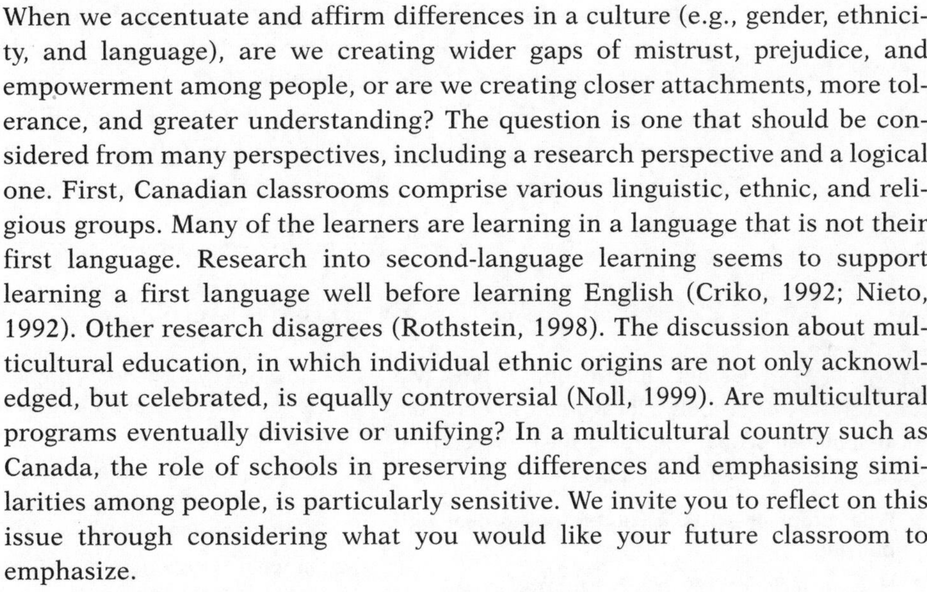

Assumption 5: Multiculturalism is about preserving people's way of life; schools need to create curriculum that honours differences in society.

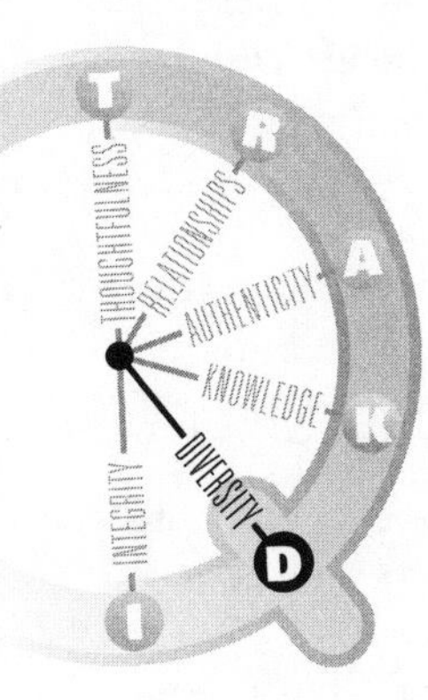

When we accentuate and affirm differences in a culture (e.g., gender, ethnicity, and language), are we creating wider gaps of mistrust, prejudice, and empowerment among people, or are we creating closer attachments, more tolerance, and greater understanding? The question is one that should be considered from many perspectives, including a research perspective and a logical one. First, Canadian classrooms comprise various linguistic, ethnic, and religious groups. Many of the learners are learning in a language that is not their first language. Research into second-language learning seems to support learning a first language well before learning English (Criko, 1992; Nieto, 1992). Other research disagrees (Rothstein, 1998). The discussion about multicultural education, in which individual ethnic origins are not only acknowledged, but celebrated, is equally controversial (Noll, 1999). Are multicultural programs eventually divisive or unifying? In a multicultural country such as Canada, the role of schools in preserving differences and emphasising similarities among people, is particularly sensitive. We invite you to reflect on this issue through considering what you would like your future classroom to emphasize.

Assumption 6: All children are born equal.

In your opinion, is this assumption true? Children's development is determined by the complex interaction of genes, environment, nutrition, community services, and neurological development. Children's development is a result of how well each developmental influence works with other influences. The social environment plays a particularly strong role in a child's development. We discussed in Chapter 6 how children are part of an ecology. They are born to a family—their immediate ecology. The influence of families in raising children has been well-documented (Baumrind, 1991). Families are part of a larger ecology—a neighbourhood, a workplace, a community, sometimes with agencies offering activities for children's recreation. The neighbourhood in turn is nested in an even larger ecology—a political system, a bureaucratic system, police services, and other government services that enhance or detract from a family's sense of security and significance. And further away from the child and family, but influential in every part of the ecology, is the ideology of the culture—the values and assumptions of the larger culture into which the child is born.

Each part of this ecology contributes to the development of the child. Together, all parts of the ecology make up society. All parts nurture the other parts. A child's development is influenced immediately by the family, but eventually by all parts of society. All parts contribute something to a child's development.

A child's development is dependent on how well and in what ways the child is provided for in each part of the ecology. All children are not equal, particularly when a society is unable to provide enabling and developmentally appropriate influences. Children will come into your classrooms with unequal financial opportunities, varying degrees of family support, different backgrounds of parenting styles, and, in some cases, few or no community activities and agencies to provide developmentally influential experiences.

Did a concern for children's development influence your choice of teaching as a profession? Is it reasonable to conclude that if we understand how to help children develop to their full potential within the ecology in which they find themselves, we will help them enjoy the one childhood they will ever have? Do you believe that you can help learners develop into full and productive citizens, parents, and participants in Canadian society and workplace?

12.1 FOR YOUR CONSIDERATION

Gather information from two schools, a local urban school and a local suburban school, regarding their approach to social issues. Use the following questions:

- What program exists in your school to deal with bullying?
- How are incidents of violence reported to parents? To the police?
- Does your staff have training to deal with violence and bullying?
- Are codes of discipline working in your school?
- Are social agencies involved in your school to help learners with special needs?
- How does your school's physical layout contribute to or hinder dealing with learners with special needs?
- What policies and practices characterize your approach to learners with varying religious and cultural requirements?
- In what ways does your school reflect the larger society? In what ways does your school contribute to the solutions of problems in Canadian society?
- Is social class an issue in your school?

At the end of your interviews, prepare two case studies to present to your colleagues in class.

Teacher Differences and Approaches to Teaching

The following scenario highlights how teachers see the world differently and therefore use different approaches to the teaching of controversial topics within a complex Canadian society.

Pardeep and Nicole were first in the staff room this Friday. Nicole asked Pardeep if he had read the latest Statistics Canada report, stating that one in three high school students have had sex.

Pardeep replied, "Well, we need a curriculum or program that helps these kids know how to handle the whole sex thing—contraception and condom use for sure."

"I don't see how you can say that," said Nicole. "For one thing, where are we going to fit that into our day? For another, sex is deeply tied to our personalities, to ourselves, and to our sense of who we are. What in the world, then, should we teach them? How to put on condoms? To teach about condoms and not teach about why sex can mess them up is to short-change these kids. We need to give them a moral basis for deciding how to behave before teaching them about the mechanics of sex."

"Oh, you're one of those save-it-for-marriage types, are you?" asked Pardeep. "Listen, kids are not saving it for marriage, so get real. We had better get off our high religious horse and teach these kids what they need to know to keep them from getting AIDS and other STDs. The wired-up religious zealots out there are not doing any good by telling kids not to have sex. They *are* having sex!"

"I know society is changing, and that kids are not going to make decisions like our parents did. But really, shouldn't we at least try to show kids why sex is full of complications, that sexual activity really doesn't serve them very well at the end of the day?" replied Nicole. "And I'm not on a religious high horse—I'm making good sense."

"Well, the issue is really one of helping these kids know how to be safe," said Pardeep. "The best sense we can make of all this sex stuff is to say, 'Here is how to use condoms, and there are options available if you do get an STD or if you want an abortion because you messed up."

Nicole relied, "I can't believe you believe what you just said. Sex is far too complex to throw a simple solution at, like putting on condoms properly, or getting an abortion. Besides, condoms don't offer any guarantee against STDs, and you know it."

"Where did you hear that?" asked Pardeep. "I guess I'm the one who had better teach these kids, not you. I think condoms are a hundred percent safe."

"Can anyone possibly believe that the solution to teenage sexual activity is somehow wrapped up in getting abortions or fixing up diseases? Come on, Pardeep, there is trail of broken hearts, dreams, and promises following sexual activity—that's why kids should 'keep it for marriage' if you want to put in that way. Listen, girls will use sex to get love, and boys will use love to get sex. It's all quite tragic."

"I think you're naïve, Nicole. Your head is in the sand," replied Pardeep. "I don't think that we should just let parents take on this issue. Over half of my kids live with only one parent. We have kids who have lousy home lives and little help there for making good choices. We have to teach these kids how to make good choices, no one else will it seems."

"I agree, Pardeep, we do have some responsibility to take on this sex issue with them; it's just that we should be thoughtful and take on the whole issue. But I come back to this problem of time—when can we possibly fit any more into our days? When can we do anything meaningful here?"

"Well, the kids can always come to me after school and I'll give them my advice, and that's probably all we can or maybe should do."

The conversation ended as the school buzzer sounded, signalling the start of the afternoon period. As far as anyone was able to determine, the school pregnancy rate remained the same, and no curriculum was ever introduced that addressed either condom use or the relationship of sex to morals, personal values, and personality.

Aims of Schooling

The conversation between Pardeep and Nicole reveals how **culture,** the ideas, assumptions, behaviours and attitudes of a particular group of people, daily confronts teachers and influences what happens in schools. Pardeep's and Nicole's worldviews are quite different. If you support Pardeep's position on the matter of how schools should deal with the societal issue of sexual activity and youth, you probably believe that schools should be pragmatic and should address problems with practical solutions. If you support Nicole's position, you probably believe that schools have a responsibility to deal with practical solutions within a larger conceptual and moral framework. Behind the scenes of this and most discussions you will participate in throughout your career are differing views about how schools should deal with society and culture, and what aims schools emphasize.

In the next few pages we will consider five commonly held aims of schooling in Canada and examine how societal and cultural realities influence how schools approach each aim.

Schooling to Prepare Tomorrow's Citizens

Today's children will become tomorrow's adults, raising their own families, leading and following others in the workplace, working in politics, voting, coaching teams in communities, working in social agencies to bring about quality policies and procedures in society. For some adults today, including teachers, this is a sobering thought. They believe that today's children are ill-equipped to take on responsibility and leadership roles in the future.

These adults often point to trends in society that reflect just how profoundly young people's lives have been transformed because the ecology they find themselves in has been transformed. Family size has steadily decreased, urbanization has increased, the proportion of children with mothers in the labour force has gone up, mother-only families have increased, and divorce rates are higher (Hernandez, 1994). Studies on the effects of divorce on children are quite unambiguous. Instability in husband's work, decline in family income, decreased quality of life, and a variety of psychological effects have all been well-documented (Conger et al., 1990; Elder, Conger, Foster, & Ardelt, 1992). If trends like these continue, will schools be able to adequately address the concomitant issues and strains produced in children?

Other adults remain quite positive about this generation's children and their potential to be productive and happy in the future. For these adults, "the kids are all right" (B. Bergman, 2001). Reginald Bibby's (2001) exhaustive survey of teens, dating back to 1975, looks at the entire range of adolescent issues, from sex, drugs, and violence to spirituality and sports preferences. Bibby concludes that today's adolescents are not much different than their parents were a generation or two before them.

Will the next generation of teenagers be viewed with equal affirmation? The question today for teachers is, How best to prepare today's young people for tomorrow's society?

> The children born in the year 2000 will vote for the first time in 2018. They will enter the labour force in full-time jobs in and about the year 2020. By then, Canada's working population will be required to generate enough Gross Domestic Product to support the post-war baby boom generation, all of whom will be over the age of 65, collecting public and private pensions, and in need of public and private services. When the children of 2000 reach working age, they will also make choices about partners and having children of their own. As they balance employment with their family responsibilities, they will determine how much time they can commit to civic life by participating in neighbourhood programs and projects and contributing to the creation of high quality community life. (Stroick & Jenson, 1999, p. 10)

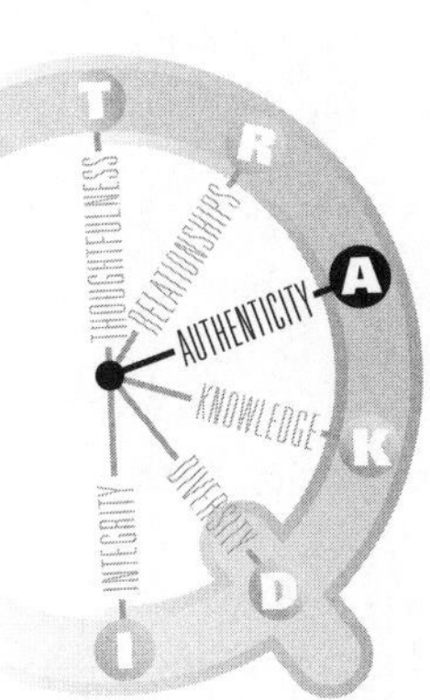

If schools are to adequately prepare tomorrow's citizens, they will need to prepare learners for a world that has not yet arrived. It is no wonder there exists among professional educators a range of opinions about exactly how to do this. Some teachers, perhaps like Pardeep in our previous scenario, might lean toward schools helping learners develop practical, applied skills that might be transferred to every aspect of life in society. You might infer, from Pardeep's line of reasoning and assumptions regarding sex education, that Pardeep wants schools to provide practical-service learning opportunities for young people. Preparation for the future is accomplished by today's practice, by schools providing services to society through young people being in direct workplace contact with the elderly, the sick, and those in our society who might be less fortunate, such as homeless individuals. On the other hand, you might infer from Nicole's line of reasoning that she wants to emphasize the development of prosocial values and character education. Each opinion carries with it a number of implications for how schools should be organized and run.

12.2 FOR YOUR CONSIDERATION

> Times are bad. Children no longer obey their parents, and everyone is writing a book.
>
> —MARCUS TULLIUS CICERO (106–43 BC)

This quotation implies that when it comes to adult views of young people, very little has changed. Research the various conceptions of childhood throughout history. Look for common themes. Also, look for differences in conceptions. Prepare a one-page report that identifies and analyzes the reasons that various societies at various times viewed young people differently.

Schooling for Socialization

Canadians want children to be socialized in particular ways. They want children to be responsible, honest, diligent, and prepared with the knowledge, skills, and attributes to handle technology, change, and the requirements of work and community life. Because family and community are still important values in Canadian society, Canadians want their children to grow up with the capacity to participate in family and community life and to have every opportunity to be successful in both. Many challenges face schools as they consider how best to socialize children into Canadian society.

Perhaps the biggest challenge is the nature of the Canadian society children are growing up into. That society is likely to look like the following (Stroick & Jenson, 1999):

> In the year 2000, between 400,000 and 500,000 children will be born across Canada. (p. 11)
>
> A large majority of these children will live in families with both parents in the labour force.... Regulated child care spaces will be available to an average of only 7.5 percent of children under age 12.... Uncounted numbers of school-aged children will spend time on their own as latchkey children.... (p. 11)
>
> The parents of these children will work longer hours and many young couples earn less than their parents did 20 years ago. Income polarization is increasing between a core group of older, highly skilled workers with good benefits and a group of mostly younger workers with low skills and precarious jobs. (p. 11)
>
> The "time crunch" parents experience will be severe as they struggle to balance employment with their family responsibilities. Despite the joys and rewards, having children is reported as the main reason for worsened relationship in the employment-family balance.... 50 percent of parents report difficulty in managing their family time. (p. 11)
>
> If current trends continue, many children born in the year 2000 are likely to experience economic vulnerability. Between 1989 and 1996, the total number of poor children in Canada (living in families whose total income before taxes falls below Statistics Canada's low income cut-off) increased by 60 percent, or 564,000 children. (p. 12)
>
> Children in poor and low-income families will be disadvantaged in multiple ways, such as being at risk from living in neighbourhoods that are unsafe, that have fewer resources and supports, and that have lower levels of community or social cohesion. (p. 12)
>
> [Many children] are likely to experience life in a variety of different kinds of families as a result of their parents' changing relationships. (p. 13)

(Source: From *What Is the Best Policy Mix for Canada's Young Children?* by Sharon M. Stroick and Jane Jenson, 1999, CPRN Study No. F/09, Ottawa: Renouf Publishing Co. Ltd. Reprinted with the permission of the Canadian Policy Research Network.)

The stresses faced by families cut across all economic levels. Parenting issues are not limited to poor families; all parents need help in socializing their children. Disadvantages in socialization can be partially offset by a combination of good parenting, adequate income, and supportive community programs (Stroick & Jenson, 1999). Some people argue for greater child tax benefits, universal health care, and increased tax reductions to help families improve their financial situation. This kind of discussion points to how the ecology may work in more helpful ways to support schools and their children and families. Others argue that much social assistance poses significant risks to the development and growth of children; they point to poor records of subsequent transition from low or no employment to greater workplace involvement.

Socializing children into a changing society is complicated further by the various ethnic, religious, and cultural backgrounds that schools are expected to incorporate. Sometimes the issues that arise from this extraordinary mix are simple and involve fairly straightforward decisions, such as whether to have a "Christian" Christmas celebration. Other times, the mix raises more profound questions and complex issues, such as parental styles of discipline or social engagement practices among peers and between students and teachers.

Schools are one place where young people are socialized. If you agree that schools should contribute to the socialization of Canadian youth, then what should schools do to preserve the individuality of learners while fostering the ideals of Canadian society, ideals that include democracy, fairness to all, and compassion for every person?

Schooling That Promotes Academic Achievement

Perhaps the aim that has the greatest support, historically and cross-culturally, is that schools should promote the acquisition of a body of skills and knowledge that will prepare learners for further education and for the workplace. The majority of parents polled support academic achievement as the top aim of schooling (L. Rose, Gallup, & Elan, 1997). However, achieving academic goals and success for all children is complicated again by societal issues. Some research indicates that a greater proportion of poor children experience developmental delays, that as many as twenty-five percent of children in low-income families may be developmentally delayed (Statistics Canada, 1999). These children begin behind the rest of children, thus compromising their potential for early academic success, a very important building block for future academic success. The influence of systematic, well-planned, early childhood learning experiences in promoting cognitive, social, and early academic development is widely accepted (Diamond, 1991). Yet many children do not have access to these early experiences. Societal problems are systemic, shaped by economic and societal factors, which in turn shape the opportunities children have to access **early intervention programs**—experiences in nurseries and play-schools where children are exposed to developmentally appropriate opportunities intended to help them start grade school on an equal basis with other children.

School-based issues also influence schools' ability to promote academic achievement. For example, school-based violence has caught most Canadians' attention over the past few years. Studies and surveys of studies have helped educators understand the nature of the school-based violence problem and how schools might respond to the problem (Day, Minevich, Hunt, & Hyrnkiw-Agimeri, 1994). School-based violence is associated with a range of risk factors that includes poverty, abuse, ineffective parenting, and academic failure (Offord, Boyle, & Racine, 1989). Schools have responded with a range of crisis management programs, bully-proofing programs, and training for teachers and parents to recognize risk factors and prevent trouble before it happens. There is tremendous interest in understanding the roots of violence and how schools can work with parents, learners, and community to deal with it. Some people claim that there has not been an increase in violence, simply that our culture's heightened sensitivity to violence has made us more aware of it. As Bala (1994) and others have noted, "Although one can ask how much of this increase is due to heightened sensitivity to violence and an increase in reporting rates, it is apparent that the public and professional community are increasingly concerned about youth violence" (p. 1).

Teachers are faced with perplexing societal issues when it comes to bullying and violence in schools. For example, now there is little doubt that television violence contributes to and encourages violent forms of behaviour. The undesirable effects of television have been confirmed in a series of three major studies conducted in 1972, 1982 and 1992 (American Psychological Association, 1993, p. 33). Together these and other studies led to the conclusion that viewing television violence increases violence in society (N. Anderson & Ventura 1993). Canadian television is awash in violence. Young people will likely not stop watching violent television shows and movies simply because they contribute to violence. How should teachers address violence and bullying in schools? The issue is complex. Television violence is not the sole contributor to societal and school-based violence. Biological factors (Lytton, 1990), familial factors, other contextual factors (Greenberg, Speltz, & Deklyn, 1993), and mental illness also contribute. For teachers to single out and deal with one cause only of violence would be wrongheaded. Most teachers will address the issue by encouraging in-class discussions of societal influences on violence (e.g., television), using school incidents of bullying and violence as opportunities to teach pro-social alternatives, or encouraging community-based interventions such as counselling for perpetrators and victims of violence.

Schools can play a crucial role in providing opportunities to develop pro-social behaviours, understand the cause and effects of violence, and provide for the basic needs of all children. In the story told earlier in this chapter, we might infer that Pardeep would approach the problem of school-and society-based violence perhaps by encouraging practical solutions, such as increased athletic and sports activity (to sublimate and direct aggression). He might suggest the use of bully proofing programs (which teach basic skills that bullied kids can use to thwart bullying), conflict resolution approaches (to know how to create win-win conflict-resolution solutions), and consequence-based discipline approaches. Pardeep's approach might be summarized as "acting and behaving into new ways of thinking."

Nicole, however, might emphasize the ideational, moral, and ethical dimensions of violence, perhaps pointing to the historical and societal pain caused by violence and guiding learners into increased empathy for victims of violence. She might show films such as *Schindler's List* in class to portray violence in its worst

Should schooling emphasize only academic achievement?

and most awful expression. Discussions in Nicole's class might centre on the root causes of violence, the Holocaust, and racism. Nicole's approach would be centred in the assumption that if root assumptions, theories, and ideas about life are changed, then behaviour can change. Nicole's approach might be summarized as "thinking into new ways of acting and behaving."

Contextual factors influence teachers' ability to promote academic achievement. If teachers are to promote academic achievement for all learners, they will have to adequately design learning experiences for different personality types and learning styles, for developmentally varied learners.

Schooling That Promotes Personal Growth and Development

Proponents of this aim want schools' emphasis to be on the child first and society second. Again, this aim is not easily achieved, and is therefore debated among educators. Proponents of this aim want children to develop positive self-concepts, healthy self-esteem, proper motivation for further pursuits of healthy activities, and full intellectual development (Gardner, 1993). You may wish to review Chapter 5 and our discussion about moral learning and empathy.

This aim places a great of deal of pressure on schools. Do a child's growth and development requirements ask more of a school than what a school can provide? A child's development requires a joint effort by all stakeholders in a child's life if there is to be any difference in a child's development. Tipper and Avard (1999) have identified the aspects that need to converge in contributing to child development. These include identification of what children should be expected to achieve by specific ages according to biological givens, what knowledge and skills are needed for the child to be considered contributory to society, and what social capacity is appropriate—the presence of empathy for family, self, and others in society. In order to contribute meaningfully to a child's growth and development, a school needs to find ways to share responsibility for children's well-being and work together with local social agencies.

Research emphasis seems to be shifting from preparing children for adulthood to determining children's health and well-being and promoting children's growth

12.3 FOR YOUR CONSIDERATION

Interview two teachers. Ask them to rank in order, according to the emphasis placed in their classroom, the following aspects of children's growth and development:

- emotional intelligence (self-awareness, empathy, handling emotions, and so on)
- self-concept formation (one's view of oneself physically, intellectually, socially)
- self-esteem (the value one places on self-concept)
- attitude toward the dignity and worth of people, regardless of race, ethnicity, or gender
- interpersonal skills (fair play, sharing, honesty)

Ask each teacher which approach he or she would recommend for teaching personal growth and development:

- indoctrination
- modelling
- problem-solving
- other?

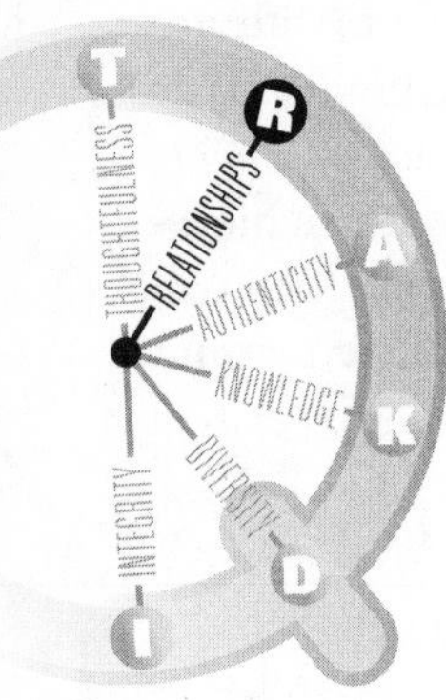

and development. In Canada, the National Longitudinal Survey of Canadian Children and Youth identifies factors that contribute to children's growth and development. These factors include family income, family composition, parenting practices, neighbourhood, and others. It is far too much to ask schools alone to be responsible for this. Again, schools need to be viewed as one part of the matrix of social services contributing to child growth and development.

Schooling to Promote Social Goals

Canadians today have options in schools. They can choose schools whose mission is to preserve a value system, a religious orientation, or to promote a particular branch of learning, such as arts or physical education. The rise of private, charter, and other forms of **alternative schools** reflects Canadian pluralism. The creation of schools based on the needs and interests of families has been, for some, one of the best developments within the Canadian school system. Edmonton has for years been viewed as a North American leader in offering parents choice (Nikoforuk, 2002). Others view the rise of alternative schools as a threat to a strong public school system. They claim that a **two-tiered school system**—a private or alternative system, provincially funded but accessible to parents with particular philosophical and academic interests, and a public one, provincially funded but accessed only by parents who are unable to access "better" schools because of geography or other reasons—would weaken the public system. "Funding of private schools diverts public money from an inclusive public purpose to an exclusive private purpose that may undermine the public purpose." (Edmonton Public Schools, 1997)

Some provinces, such as Alberta, appear to support independent schools by providing a percentage of per student funding to designated independent schools. Such schools receive partial provincial funding in part because they formally agree to follow an approved program of studies and hire certified teachers. In

1999 independent school funding levels were set at approximately sixty percent of the level for public schools ($2,544 per student in contrast to $4,239 per student). In Manitoba, for example, the climate seems less favourable to the growing number of private and independent schools. **Independent schools** may arrange formal partnerships with a public school district and offer the approved program of studies but with a particular philosophical or educational emphasis, such as fine arts. In Manitoba, funding for independent schools is at fifty percent of the level of funding for public schools. All Canadian provinces have either considered or have implemented **charter schools,** schools that are permitted to operate and offer special curricular emphases, such as computer-based instruction, but only as a result of applying under a special charter of a province's legislature.

The issue of public money supporting private and independent education is controversial. Proponents of **private schools** that promote a particular set of social goals or religious values claim, rightly, that their children are part of the "public" within a province and therefore deserve support for their education like any other child in the province. Opponents to public funding claim that the financial pie is only so big, and public funding to private schools depletes an already financially stressed public school system. Should all children in your province be funded the same way?

Alternative and private school curricula include fine arts, second-language, religious, work-based, and sports schools among others. Montessori schools offer child-centred, activity-based learning opportunities for younger children. Muslim schools, Waldorf schools, Christian schools, and other forms of values-based school provide choices for parents who want schools to promote character formation, the development of a particular set of values, assumptions, and beliefs. These schools preserve values and are intended to promote a specific social and personal growth and development agenda for their children.

On the other hand, some parents want children to be educated in schools that promote change. These parents want children to develop a critical consciousness, an awareness of social issues and how education might address these issues. While both sets of parents may wish to promote social goals and positive change, one set of parents wishes to preserve something in society, the other to change something in society.

Many schools in Canada include a mandatory service component, experiences planned by the school in which students serve in the community, helping people who are less fortunate. These schools bring young people into contact with life outside the school and are designed to promote chances to study and understand the root causes of social issues such as poverty and homelessness. Many of these schools, because they are private, are costly and out of reach for most parents. Should Canadian parents have the right to choose the type of school they want for their children, even if that choice is not available to all children within Canadian society?

School Responses to Social Issues

Schools in Canadian society are part of a larger context that includes school boards and parent councils that give schools broader opportunities to respond to

12.4 FOR YOUR CONSIDERATION

Identify what you would choose as the main aim of schooling. In making your choice, consider the following ten social issues:

- youth suicide
- teen pregnancies
- children in poverty
- family stress
- conflict and violence among youth
- uncertain job and career opportunities for youth
- media influence on youth social values
- reduction of extracurricular offerings in schools
- drug use
- depression among youth

Be prepared to defend your choice with a discussion among your classmates that includes each issue.

social issues. Schools can be organized to respond individually to social issues as well, and have traditionally attempted to respond to social issues through programs like bully proofing and zero tolerance to violence policies.

School Boards

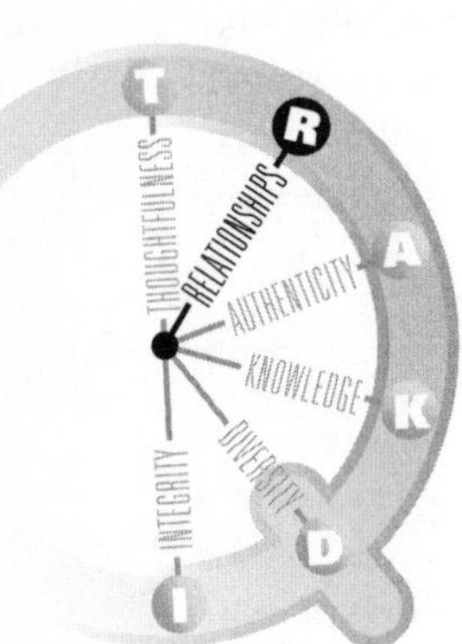

Schools as institutions—groups or bodies organized by a society to preserve and develop the Canadian way of life—have different means of responding to social issues. Schools are part of a larger network of groups and agencies that together make up a larger institutional structure. School boards, made up of elected officials charged with policy and governance responsibilities, including financial and legal ones, serve the larger public interest of ensuring that schools operate formally along legal lines. School boards address social issues through political means, by recommending programs that address bullying, for example.

Expanding Parental Involvement

By the mid-1990s, virtually all provinces and their departments of education had passed legislation approving parent councils. The goal was to give parents greater responsibility and authority in school decisions (McKenna & Willms, 1998). The establishment of parent councils is one means of expanding parental involvement in schools and their children's education and improving communication between parents and teachers. There are other dimensions of parental involvement in addition to formal decision making through schools councils. Epstein (1995) suggests five dimensions for meaningful parental involvement, including parenting and a home environment that encourages learning; effective two-way communication between parents and teachers, particularly regarding student progress; volunteerism; collaboration with the community; and home learning, in which parents are enabled in helping their children with homework.

Parental involvement may address social issues such as school dropout rates when they set high demands for mature behaviour and have high restrictiveness, high warmth, and high communication with children, producing instrumental competencies where children can set goals and put into action behaviours that help them achieve those goals (Baumrind, 1983). Some large-scale studies have found that parental involvement through volunteering and home learning that supported school-related activities had positive effects on academic achievement (Ho & Willms, 1996). Parental behaviour has been linked to school success when that involvement includes parents guiding and monitoring children's behaviour, helping children with school work, and discussing school practices and children's educational goals (P. Campbell & Mandel, 1990).

Parental involvement and support of their children's education gives professional educators opportunities to help shape parenting practices toward more effective outcomes. Parenting styles have an influence on school performance. Authoritative parenting has been found to produce competency in children (Baumrind,1991; L. Sternberg, Lamborn, Dornhbush, & Darling, 1992). Authoritative parents demand mature behaviour and are restrictive yet high in warmth and in communication. Teachers and parents working together may influence the design of both school and home activities that are authoritative in style and that promote competency in children.

Youth at Risk

A child's socio-economic status is a contributor to a child's school success. It is also an indicator of a child's risk for drug use, drop-out likelihood, and mental illness (Offord et al., 1989). The notion that schools can provide non-monetary forms of capital, such as social and cultural capital, has grown (Human Resources Development of Canada, 2000). **Social capital** includes the range of social relations that may prove to be an asset for the child; **cultural capital** includes aspects of high culture, such as attending opera and listening to classical music (Willms, 1999). If a child has high amounts of social capital, such as a network of relationships in the community—coaches, mentors, and positive adult role models—that child may stay in school longer and be more successful.

Risk factors, unfortunately, overlap. For example, psychological and conduct disorders that influence the development of children carry over into classrooms. The greatest overlap is reported to be between hyperactivity and conduct disorder (Offord et al., 1989). Living on welfare and living in subsidized housing were found to be related (Offord et al., 1989). However, other variables such as marital discord and low income were found to also have a relationship with conduct disorders in schools. The question is, What can schools do to address these issues?

Perhaps you believe that Canadian society is expecting too much from schools. It is clear that schools are experiencing an increase in the number of children growing up in less than ideal developmental conditions. Risk factors appear to be increasing. Funding and resources to support these children appear to be dwindling. The long-term solution would be to reduce the risk factors—to eliminate poverty, for example. However, schools and teachers are powerless to eliminate poverty, mental illness, and many other risk factors. What can teachers realistically be expected to do? Perhaps schools can increase opportunities for children to have greater social and cultural capital. For example, they may increase the number and range of programs that bring into the school caring and competent adults. Perhaps teachers can address more cogently other factors that may contribute to risk. This includes addressing with children the well-documented effects of television violence and how children might find alternative forms of recreation. Teachers may provide the best and most thoughtful information available regarding the deleterious effects of drug use. What are your solutions to this problem?

12.5 FOR YOUR CONSIDERATION

Is the idea of social and cultural capital—the idea that children and young people can have capital in the form of relationships, networks, and the best of culture (e.g., music)—appealing to you? If so, what forms of social capital do you think might contribute most to at-risk children's and youths' development?

School Organization

The organization and characteristics of a school have significant educative consequences for student outcomes for all students, but particularly at-risk students (Human Resources Development of Canada, 2000, p. 26; Bryk & Thum, 1989).

School characteristics that have been identified as associated with positive student outcomes include supportive and caring teachers; teachers with high but realistic expectations of student achievement; a stress on academic work; a quality curriculum; monitoring of student progress; time-on-tasks dedicated to active teaching and learning; fair and clear rules of conduct; co-operative decision making among teachers and students; principal's dedication to teaching and learning; and a commitment to helping students at risk from dropping out (Human Resources Development Canada, 2000, p. 26). Perhaps school characteristics increase student engagement with schools academically, socially, and athletically. Student engagement appears to reduce risk and promote achievement (Human Resources Development Canada, 2000).

Some critics of current school organization and characteristics suggest that schools do not do enough to assist youth through career planning and choices. Crites (1978) suggests that career choices begin at a young age and continue through adolescence. If young people do not have clear and sufficient career choice knowledge, the research indicates, they may have difficulty or be delayed in choosing a job or career (Hiebert, Magnusson, & Vesely, 1990). Perhaps schools might be organized around the aim of guiding young people into appropriate career choices. Do you agree? Some schools have required courses in career and life management, where students are given the knowledge and guidance required to make good career and job choices. Other schools have school-to-work relationships, where business and other workplace courses are taught within the school curriculum. What might schools do to help youth with career choices and school-to-job transition?

12.6 FOR YOUR CONSIDERATION

In your local school district, identify the school-approved programs that assist youth in transition from school to university and from school to jobs. What skills do these programs teach? How are schools organized to present these programs? How effective are these programs in assisting youth in transition?

Zero Tolerance and Other School Responses to Violence

There exists a good deal of debate regarding what zero tolerance to school violence should look like (Gabor, 1995). For some, zero tolerance means immediate and unqualified expulsion from schools. For others, it means immediate involvement of police and parents in serious acts of violence. For others, it means applying a range of consequences that are logical and immediate, connecting the punishment to the "crime."

Most people regard school violence as an extension of larger societal problems regarding violence. Society at large is responsible for violence, yet schools seem left to solve it, often again with little more than counselling by overworked teachers, bully-proofing programs, or expulsion of students.

Some school districts have created collaborative partnerships to develop ways of addressing school violence. The East York Board of Education and the Metropolitan Toronto Police Force provide one example. They have developed a protocol between police and school to deal with school violence, encouraging victims of violence to come forward and report violent incidents. Such partnerships are designed to increase public awareness of violence and its core issues. Some schools have created buddy systems, where younger children are partnered with older children. Bully-proofing programs are used to teach coping and resistance skills.

Whether violence has increased or we have all become more sensitized to it in our culture remains debatable. Your future role as a professional educator will include dealing with the issue of violence. What is your opinion about the solutions proposed in this section (zero tolerance, police–school partnerships, buddy systems, bully-proofing programs)?

Reflection and Perspective on the Chapter

The issues young people come up against every day in society have faces. Perhaps we need to conclude this somewhat sobering chapter with some hope. If societal issues have faces, and if the issues are among people, then they can be solved among people. Sometimes it seems as if adults in Canadian culture are teaching children to like all the wrong things: slasher movies, free and easy sex, MuchMusic, and narcissistic rock and movie stars. At other times, it seems that adults in Canadian culture are teaching children all the right things: sports skills and fine arts skills. Growing up in what many feel is a toxic culture, boys and girls face different issues. Boys are more likely to be shot; girls risk getting pregnant. Girls are more likely to have eating disorders, boys to be in principals' offices for discipline purposes (Pollack, 1998). Boys receive conflicting messages regarding "maleness," and may experience role confusion and ambiguity regarding what it means to be a man in today's western culture (Pollack, 1998). Many girls get lost to themselves, and to the rest of society, as they enter their teens and succumb to the "beauty and intelligence myths" that seduce girls into believing that to be worthy they must fit a beauty and intelligence stereotype (Pipher, 1994). Perhaps teachers and schools can address these issues more meaningfully through the use of positive role models—in real life, literature, and movies—or through stretching the worldview of students to include the cultural richness available in Canada, through music, the arts, and sports.

We invite you to consider the influences of society as possibilities to help each learner develop fully and progress toward the goal of being a healthy, happy worker, and citizen.

Key Terms

Suggested Further Reading

Sharpe, Denis B. (1992, Spring). Aspirations of youth: Job market reality versus the vocational career. *Canadian Vocational Journal*, *27*(4), 6–10. A study of more than 7 000 Newfoundland Grade 12 students in which the author examined job expectations, attitudes, and long-range plans of students. Gender bias and low hope for future career success were documented.

CHAPTER 13

The Evolution of Schooling in Canada—A Brief History

Chapter Focus

A study of the history of schooling helps us understand why schools were first established and how schooling evolved to become what it is today. Understanding the history of schooling is particularly important when dealing with change.

Since its inception, the practice of schooling has become institutionalized and politicized. These two conditions immediately introduce complexity into the operation and evolution of schooling. Institutions are among the most complex of entities to change (Sarason, 1990) and the political context in which the institution is cast renders this complexity even more intense. In the first section of this chapter we present a brief overview of the history of Canadian schooling to provide a context for issues and topics that will be discussed later in the chapter.

Of particular note is the matter of change in schooling. In earlier chapters we mentioned the complexity of today's society. Contemporary schooling must also be considered within the context of this complexity. There is a seeming paradox at work in discussions about schooling: in a time of rapid societal change and complexity, governments and interest groups tend to extol and practice traditional ways of working, consisting of rigid programs of study, uniforms, zero tolerance for certain behaviours, inflexible uses of time, one teacher for twenty-five to thirty students, and so on. We do not suggest that you criticize these practices per se, but rather that you question the adherence to traditional practices in a context of change.

Focus Questions

1. To what extent did the French culture exercise influence over schooling in New France?
2. In what ways was the British and Irish influence on schooling different from that of the French?

3. What were normal schools and what concerns about schooling caused them to be established in Canada?
4. How did the industrial organizational methods of the post-industrial revolution period influence schooling in Canada?
5. How have industrial organizational methods of the post-industrial revolution period become a possible source of concern in schooling?
6. To what extent and in what ways is schooling politicized?

Schooling in Canada Before Confederation

A Brief History of Schooling in French Canada

Assumption 1: Canadian public schools evolved from a common need to conform to a national agenda for schooling.

French colonists arrived in New France between 1608 and 1760. In 1760, the British commander James Wolfe defeated the forces of the French under Louis-Joseph de Montcalm, bringing New France under British control. The colonists from France were primarily uneducated people who had left their homeland for what they hoped would be a better life. These people did not possess knowledge from books, but they did possess a strong feeling for the culture of their mother country. They came to New France valuing hard work, common sense, good judgment, and the ability to organize for efficient labour. Underpinning these more secular values was a deeply held religious foundation contributing a strong moral code to the colonial society.

France had little interest in her North American colonies. New France was considered to be a veritable wasteland, good only for a meagre supply of pelts. Merchants earned little return for investments, and the mother country saw the colony only as a drain on financial and military resources required to defend its interests against hostile natives, foreign armies, and aggressive settlers from other lands. It was therefore left to the Roman Catholic Church, whose ministers were educated, to assume, along with parents, the main responsibility for education.

Before 1760, there were no laws governing education in Canada. The church was the *prima facie* authority for education, with support from the civil authorities: "The clergy founded the schools, the state encouraged them by its authority, its advice, and its funds" (Audet, 1970, p. 73).

Why were schools set up in New France? The answer lies in expedience. Colonists were largely uneducated and needed to devote their energies to the physical demands of survival. The clergy addressed the very strong moral and religious codes by which the colonists lived. It was to their charge that children were given for schooling. Through schools known as *petites écoles,* the clergy provided a curriculum of catechism, reading, writing, and arithmetic. The more able students learned the basics of Latin to set them up for later studies (Audet, 1970).

The religious orders were focused much of the time in seeking recruits for the clergy, in addition to providing the basic skills of learning. Toward the middle of the seventeenth century, trade schools, or schools of craftsmanship, were established to accommodate those who could not be persuaded toward the clerical life and to contribute to the commercial and industrial life of the colony.

The development and evolution of schooling in New France, then, must be understood through its involvement with the rest of society. New France was a homogeneous society with strong cultural ties to its mother country. Religion was a fundamental part of life. Families were establishing farms to feed themselves, and the church was seen as a safe and secure haven within which children could learn.

A Brief History of Schooling in English Canada

Just as schooling in New France was largely a reflection of schooling in the home country, so too was schooling in English Canada. Environment was also a dominant influence. The British Isles were a relatively compact settlement of people in a temperate climate. The skills people needed to survive were seldom impeded by a severe climate. Colonists arriving in the New World that is now Canada, however, were influenced by the interplay of inheritance and environment. Inheritance differed according to the colonists' home countries. British colonists came from England, Scotland, and Ireland, and each of these countries had strong traditions, customs, and rituals that contributed to a certain uniqueness in the settlements they established.

Settlers from the British Isles were more of an eclectic group than those from France. Their schooling experiences were not at all similar to those of the French. While French settlers were predominantly Roman Catholic, the religious background of the British colonists was more mixed but still with some Catholic influence.

Schooling in the British Isles, during the age of colonization from 1760 to 1840, tended to reflect societal attitudes and conditions of the times. Children from the upper classes were served by public schools (what we would consider private schools), or some form of elitist schools, endowed by benefactors. Children from the poorer masses were educated free of charge in schools provided by voluntary subscriptions and occasionally by legacies and endowments (Hamilton, 1970). In these schools, children were conditioned to become unskilled labouring people; there was a heavy emphasis on Bible reading and catechism study so that at least their destiny in the next life might be more promising. All in all, only a very basic education was provided.

One feature of English schooling that flourished was known as the monitorial system, a method of using student monitors for teaching large numbers of students. The teacher would instruct a number of brighter, more able students, who would then teach other groups of students. Monitors also were used to keep order, check attendance, and tend to other details of school routine (Hamilton, 1970). The great precision and heavy emphasis on control enabled the system to manage large numbers of students. This system also had a great impact on Canadian education; the one-room schools of an earlier era in Canada may have been beneficiaries of some aspects of its features. Indeed, vestiges may be seen even today in the form of peer tutoring and peer-helping strategies. In some elementary schools older children occasionally visit children in lower grades to help them with their learning.

Scottish education probably had a more direct influence on schooling in Canada. Scottish attitudes toward education generally were "almost reverential" (Hamilton, 1970, p. 39). Schooling was seen as a virtuous pursuit. Part of this virtue was a certain dedication to democratic practices and it was through this dedication that Scottish settlers were active in movements to reform education.

After about 1840 "traces of the British heritage are more difficult to identify" (Hamilton, 1970, p. 39). Influences from the countries of the British Isles certainly existed—the monitorial system, Scottish democratic beliefs, resources used in schools, teacher training by religious orders and denominational ministries—but it became clear that no colony and settlement would tolerate a system dictated by one particular persuasion. Colonists sought North American answers for North American issues; early signs of independence, perhaps?

Schooling in Canada Since Confederation

The British North America Act of 1867, in addition to giving the provinces sole responsibility for education, also formally established denominational schools in specific communities. Quebec, though primarily Catholic, allowed Protestant schools, and other provinces allowed denominational schools. Only Newfoundland has, in recent times, moved to establish denomination-free public schools.

The School Act directed schooling in Quebec from 1875. This Act did a number of things, but of particular note was the autonomy it bestowed on the Catholic and Protestant churches. Religious denominations have exercised a strong influence on schooling in French-speaking North America almost since colonization began. *Petit écoles*, vocational schools, residential schools, and later variations of colleges and private institutions all bear the influence of religious denominations. The Catholic Jesuit Order has a solid reputation for classical scholarship on a worldwide scale. A "good" education became almost synonymous with the terms *classical* and *traditional*, and to this day, especially at the secondary school level, such is often the case.

A typical one-room schoolhouse, teacher, and her pupils in the late nineteenth century in western Canada. (Glenbow Archives, Calgary, Alberta; NA 2568-1)

Control of Schooling in Quebec

Considerable debate took place in Quebec during the later years of the 1800s about uniformity in schooling. Topics under discussion included decision making, control of mandatory texts, and the merits of uniformity in schooling. Legislation enacted in 1899 ordered all Quebec school boards to use standard texts in all schools. A plethora of Legislative Acts concerning education —170 between 1875 and 1955—point to the relative instability of schooling in Quebec. Catholic and Protestant groups still tenaciously protected their autonomy; so legislation was difficult to enact smoothly. (Incidentally, the emergence of a strong Jewish lobby resulted in a 1903 Quebec Supreme Court decision to consider Jewish people as Protestants for education purposes.) Compulsory schooling was debated vigorously, along with compulsory texts, but each decision was laborious and fragile. One author of this book worked in Quebec during the mid-1960s when not only were texts prescribed, but teachers were expected to be on specific text pages by specific days. We are happy to say that the situation has changed considerably since then. Though Catholic and Protestant school jurisdictions still exercise strong influence in the province, schooling is less encumbered by intransigent behaviours of the past.

Control of Schooling in English Canada

Schooling in English Canada by the 1870s was somewhat less parochial than in French Canada. Fully graded elementary schools were common in the cities and this facilitated the schooling of large groups of children. Teaching methodology consisted mainly of memorizing facts, numbers, and verses. Grammatical and arithmetical rules were the stock of a teacher's trade. Teachers were the storehouses of knowledge, and children were seen as empty vessels to be filled. Creativity of action and thought was certainly not encouraged. Teachers in early rural schools operated in one-room schoolhouses and often lived in a room at the back of the school. Luckier teachers were provided with a special house called a *teacherage*. Local school boards monitored teachers' lives to the point where they were expected to adhere to strict ethical and moral codes of conduct. Courting and public drinking were frowned upon.

Normal Schools in Canada

Assumption 2: The first teacher preparation institutions in Canada were normal schools, which were the forerunners of today's universities.

Since the first grade schools appeared in Canada a great disparity has existed in the curriculum, administration, and staffing of the buildings. In the period prior to the British North America Act of 1867, as the colony matured and developed, debate about the need for regulation of schooling gained momentum. Tension

A nineteenth-century Normal School graduating class. (Glenbow Archives, Calgary, Alberta; NA 2332-1)

existed between those who favoured central bureaucratic authority and those who supported local community-based control. In Upper Canada in the early 1800s, for example, teacher performance was loosely monitored. Questions about selection and qualifications of teachers were left to parents to resolve. Titley (1990) details two options available to parents:

1. A group of parents could jointly engage a teacher and set up a classroom in a public structure, e.g., a community-built schoolhouse.
2. Parents could send children to people who gave lessons in their homes.

The loose monitoring of teacher selection, qualification, and performance led to many complaints about teachers. Local school boards, appointed from among reputable citizens of the communities in which the schools were located, examined teacher performance and issued reports. One report documenting complaints said that "many teachers were ... unfit for this responsible station, from their want either of literary or moral qualifications" (Titley, 1990, p. 38).

Egerton Ryerson, a government-appointed official with authority over school systems in Ontario, played a prominent role in establishing **centralized control of schooling.** He advocated the drawing up and overseeing of regulations by government officials. Ryerson received support for his ideas from Jean-Baptiste Meilleur of Quebec and Alexander Forrester of Nova Scotia, both of whom held positions similar to his in their respective governments. The overriding purpose of the move to centralize standards in schooling throughout the colonies in the early nineteenth century was to "elevate the tone of school teaching and to enhance its occupational credentials" (Axelrod, 1997, p. 46). The efforts to attain centralized control proved successful in 1843 when county superintendents were given responsibility for examining teachers, and the training of teachers was institutionalized. County superintendents toured schools, inspected teachers, and wrote reports "that often led, in some instances, to dismissal and recommendations for safety adjustments" (Titley, 1990, p. 39).

Model Schools

Model schools, formally endorsed in 1843, allowed prospective teachers to receive free instruction on subject matter and teaching methods from specially selected instructors in exemplary schools. These schools were often located close to where prospective teachers lived, and they provided a convenient form of teacher training. However, the teacher training was not very rigorous and these schools produced a great many teachers of dubious quality. Stamp (1982) reports that model schools, as they became widespread, "overstocked the market with poorly trained teachers" (p. 15).

Model schools were unregulated, and their lack of rigour contributed to the campaign of Ryerson and others for greater government regulation of teacher training.

Establishing Normal Schools

Normal schools originated in 1834 in France, where the *école normal* stressed the benefits of standardized teacher training. The concept quickly spread to other countries, notably Scotland, Ireland, and the United States. Ryerson, who was perhaps the leading advocate for centralized control of teacher training and certification, was impressed with the Irish approach exemplified by the Dublin Normal School. He was attracted to the standardized, non-denominational training and textbooks, both of which he imported into Upper Canada. He opened Canada's first normal school for elementary teachers with Thomas Robertson, who was associated with the Dublin Normal School, as its headmaster. Over the next decade normal schools were established in New Brunswick, Nova Scotia, Prince Edward Island, and Quebec.

Normal schools were "designed to raise beyond mere competence—or in some cases incompetence—the level of classroom instruction. Prospective teachers ideally would acquire habits, skills, and character structure appropriate to the morally forceful teacher" (Axelrod, 1997, p. 46). Programs in these schools, though varying from one part of the country to another, followed a curriculum that tended to stress rote learning and memorization. Behaviour expectations were strict to the point of being severe. Axelrod (1997) reports punctuality, compliance to authority, evening curfews, regular church attendance, and gender segregation as obligatory.

The rigorous regimes in normal schools during the years following their inception were influenced by the values and mores of the times. By 1850, Titley (1990) notes, it had become generally accepted in society that religious and moral education should not be left entirely to the church and the home, and that normal schools should provide well-rounded training to prospective teachers through instruction in these areas. "There were strict instructions regarding conduct and compulsory attendance at church and chapel, and rules against visiting any place of amusement without special permission" (Phillips, 1957, p. 535). The well-rounded training and strict instructions for prospective teachers were achieved through rigorous academic programs, full days of lectures, and a great deal of evening work. Repetition classes were offered during weekends.

A Typical Normal School Program

Axelrod (1997) describes a typical normal school program as follows:

- parsing (grammar)
- art of reading

- linear drawing
- mathematical, physical, and political geography
- history
- geometry
- algebra
- agricultural chemistry
- physics
- trigonometry

Miscellaneous subjects: music, composition, orthography (spelling) and philosophy of education were taken outside regular classroom hours.

Students may also have spent an hour a day at a model school observing or engaged in practice teaching. (pp. 46–47)

13.1 FOR YOUR CONSIDERATION

Do you consider your current teacher preparation program superior to the one described in Axelrod's description above? As you contemplate an answer to the question think about the entire discussion on normal schools, not only Axelrod's description. Discuss your reasons with others in the class. Are there similarities? Could your current program benefit from any aspects of the old normal school program? Why or why not?

Only a minority of Canadian teachers received professional instruction by the 1870s. Aspiring teachers were not required to attend normal schools. Model schools operated concurrently, and the unregulated standards of these schools continued to produce teachers of questionable quality.

Universities and Teacher Preparation

Normal schools continued to prosper through the beginning of the twentieth century with a continued focus on the preparation of elementary teachers. Secondary teachers attended university, gaining a baccalaureate degree in specific subjects as their primary qualification.

In the 1950s, normal schools became teachers' colleges with elementary preparation as their focus. After World War II a movement to recognize teaching as a profession started gaining momentum and it was considered desirable for all teachers to have a baccalaureate degree followed by one or two years of professional studies in education. This move toward **professionalizing teaching** led to the establishment of faculties of education in Alberta in 1945, Newfoundland in 1946, and British Columbia in 1956. The move to professionalize was impeded somewhat in the years after World War II by large numbers of children in schools, requiring large numbers of teachers to teach them. Moves to lengthen teacher preparation programs in university faculties were outweighed by the need to produce teachers as quickly as possible to teach children from the post-World War II baby boom. The pressure of numbers began to decrease in the early 1960s, and universities increasingly established professional faculties of education: Saskatchewan in 1964, Manitoba and Prince Edward Island in 1965, New Brunswick and Nova Scotia in 1969 (Sheffield, 1970). "Quebec was in the process of making the transfer, chiefly through the new Université du Québec, and Ontario had similar plans" (Sheffield, 1970, p. 432).

Canadian Education During the Twentieth Century

Assumption 3: The institution of public schooling developed in the early 1900s from research that defined knowledge about learning and teaching.

During the twentieth century Canada experienced a population growth of close to 400 percent (Parkay et al., 1996, p. 164). Immigrants from many parts of Europe, Asia, Africa, and the Middle East transformed the Canadian population into a markedly multicultural mosaic. The increase in population and the change in cultural complexion heralded a period of significant change in Canada.

In the early part of the century, schools in eastern Canada were organized into buildings containing a number of classes. The greater intensity and concentrations of people prompted this organization. However, the great expanses of the western part of the country meant that people were scattered in remote, isolated settlements. Smaller numbers of children were accommodated in one-room schoolhouses for Grades 1 through 12. We're sure you can see how the monitorial system could have possibilities in Western Canada.

Post–Industrial Revolution Effects on Schooling

The Industrial Revolution of nineteenth-century Europe spread into North America, bringing with it mass-production factory methods. Efficiency was the hallmark of these methods, and organizational development theorists of the early nineteenth century (Taylor, 1911) made significant contributions to the field. The industrial model of efficiency, assembly-line work, and mass production were elevated to high places on the economic altar. Schools, finding themselves with increasing numbers of children to deal with, also adopted the knowledge base of industrial efficiency. This is called the **industrial (factory) model of schooling.**

A further concern in schools was discipline. Controlling large numbers of children in places where learning was achieved through memorization, repetition, and regurgitation could be accomplished only by using firm authority. Industry provided a model for "producing" educated young people, but where to turn for a model for imposing authority? The military was a model of authority, discipline, and control, and to a certain degree military approaches to discipline were embraced as effective ways of controlling children in schools. Practices such as lining up in twos, marching forward on command, forming lines down the middle of hallways to separate movement of people in different directions, shouting to gain attention, strapping, rapping knuckles, and physically pulling and pushing children are some examples of military-influenced behaviour common in schools at that time. Physical "training," rather than the physical "education" of today, was practised in the gymnasium; manual training was provided instead of industrial education, and so on.

We expressed the view, in our earlier discussion of history, that schools reflected the societal conditions and mores of the times. Attitudes toward children were quite different in the nineteenth and earlier parts of the twentieth centuries. However, societal conditions and mores notwithstanding, a military-type regimen was easily adopted by an institution in which large numbers of young people were housed together. Are you able to identify any practices from your own schooling that might well be labelled militaristic and may have been influenced by this era?

13.2 FOR YOUR CONSIDERATION

Divide the class into groups of four. Establish the groups according to elementary, junior high, and high school, and allow people to choose their groups. Answer the following questions.

1. What aspects of schooling today reflect the industrial efficiency methods of the early 1900s?
2. Are you able to identify aspects of discipline reflecting the more militaristic approaches of the early 1900s?
3. Why are the aspects identified in numbers 1 and 2 above still evident in schools? Are they still appropriate? Why or why not?

Progressive Education in Schooling

Progressive education emerged during the 1930s and 1940s, largely in response to the autocratic methods just described. Dewey (1916) was the most notable proponent of progressive methods and his work is still acknowledged today. As a progressivist, Dewey recognized the individuality of children, resulting in learning that was child-focused: curriculum would consider student attitudes and involvement as much as the mandated programs of study. Progressivism was embraced with some enthusiasm, but it did not take root with any solidity. Implementation methods were loose at best. New ideas were promoted without the necessary attention to testing and teacher preparation. The result was that regular, previously tested ways of responding to children maintained their hold on schools.

Progressivism did not completely disappear, but it certainly assumed a low profile. Many teachers were older and did not embrace change enthusiastically. Other teachers were recruited reluctantly because of the economic conditions created by the Great Depression of the 1930s and the Second World War from 1939 to 1945. Even after the war, conditions in schools remained largely unchanged. Abbreviated training programs helped to meet teacher shortages. All in all, conditions in schools were such that the status quo was maintained, and the "regularized" (Sarason, 1990) ways of "doing" schooling prevailed.

The Post–World War II Period of Schooling in Canada

With the arrival of the 1950s, schooling began to embrace more student involvement and new approaches such as "enterprise" group work (students working in groups of four or five to find information on a topic, design a display, and present to the class). In the 1960s continuous progress (elementary children progressing through grade levels at their own rate of learning) and open-area schools were examples of efforts to escape regularized routines. However, conventions and orthodoxy are strong forces, and even today schooling tends to be drawn easily to regularized practices reflecting those of earlier years.

13.3 FOR YOUR CONSIDERATION

Refer to the section on Progressivism in Chapter 7 (p. 150) and then discuss the following questions as a whole class.

1. To what extent does progressivism embody knowledge about young people and how they learn best?
2. In what ways did you experience progressivist learning in secondary school? Why was it not more extensively used, or less, if that is your opinion?
3. How did you experience progressivist learning in elementary school? If you experienced it, was it widely used by all teachers?

Figure 13.1 offers a visual representation of the swings and trends in schools over the decades of the twentieth century for you to contemplate. We acknowledge that the representation is arguable, but suggest that powerful regularities that characterized the beginnings of mass schooling, certainly at the beginning of the twentieth century, are still detectable today.

Perhaps the strongest of these influences is the way that the delivery of learning is reminiscent of factory production methods—manageable numbers of students in separate classrooms with one teacher for specific time blocks during the school day moving from one classroom to another. Another early twentieth-century influence is progressive methods of learning, still observable in some elementary classrooms. Open curricula that provide teachers and students with opportunities to choose content and ways of learning—in social studies and language arts/English, for example—can still be found. Today's demand for results sees many jurisdictions reverting to measurable behavioural objectives, often considered questionable because they tend not to take into account the uniqueness of learners and the diversity of the learning process. It is not so much that schooling has not learned from educational discoveries, but rather that the dis-

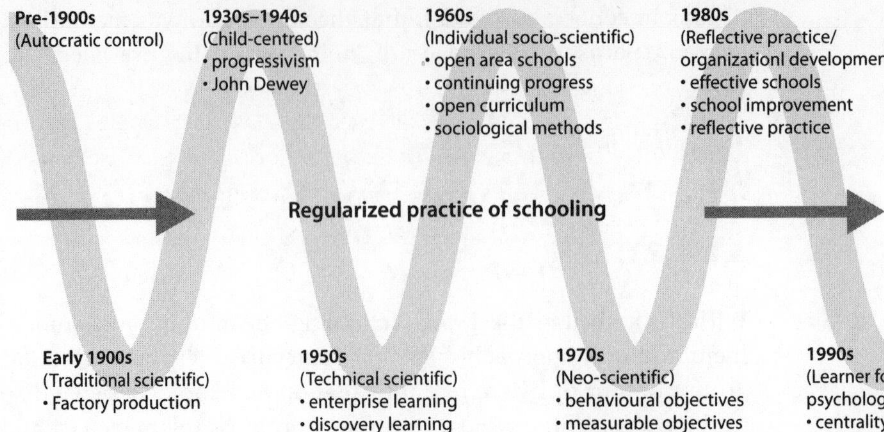

Figure 13.1 Broad Trends in Schooling During the 20th Century

13.4 FOR YOUR CONSIDERATION

1. How many of your classmates experienced an open-area learning environment in an elementary school where innovative cross-grade learning and teaching was practiced? Why was the experience successful? Why was it not successful? For either situation give your reasons.
2. How many attended a school built for open-area learning and teaching, in which teachers erected temporary walls with bookcases and screens to create conventional classroom spaces? Why do you think teachers divided the space in this way?

coveries seem to have been discounted almost by default. Admittedly this is arguable, but we invite you to contemplate the point.

What will happen during the twenty-first century? The story is unfolding. You, the readers, are the hope of schooling. We invite you to contemplate the brief history of schooling we have presented and seek to understand the old assumptions that still influence schooling today. To what extent should we strive to break the ties of convention and orthodoxy in ways that honour the value of tradition and worthy practice, while at the same time seeking fresh ways to understand schooling, that are sensitive to our changing world and the contemporary knowledge that informs us?

Organization of Provincial and Local Jurisdictions

Assumption 4: Schooling is essentially free from political interference and is unfettered in its attempts to accommodate progress and change.

Schools are influenced and shaped by many political forces in Canada. When you enter schools for the first time you may not be too aware of school politics. However, many interest groups, as well as elected bodies, have a special interest in schools and schooling. Those who are elected to bodies with defined responsibilities for schooling inevitably shape schools and exercise considerable influence on learning and teaching. Think about these influences and consider the information presented in Table 13.1, below:

Table 13.1 Elected Bodies with Responsibilities for Schooling

Elected Body	Responsibility and Influence
Provincial government	■ Provinces were given responsibility for education in Canada's founding constitution, Section 93 of the British North America (BNA) Act of 1867. The constitution was retained by Great Britain, through colonial precedent, until 1982, when it was repatriated to become the exclusive property of Canada. It is now called the Constitution Act of 1982. ■ The provinces administer education through departments and agencies that ■ allocate money for school districts ■ mandate and approve programs of study for all subjects in schools ■ set policies that govern school buildings, textbooks, support resources and accountability ■ solicit public opinion to guide legislation and policies ■ The provinces created school districts to be responsible for the day-to-day operation of public schools. School districts are guided by provincial legislation—school acts—that provide legal reference for their activities. The school acts provide for the election of local community members within each school district to provide governance for the system. Elected community members form a local school board.
Local school board	■ Designated local responsibility for schooling through the school acts of the respective provinces. ■ Elected by eligible voters in their respective jurisdictions to act on behalf of the province. ■ Typical responsibilities: ■ develop policies and regulations to direct schooling in their districts ■ hire superintendents to direct the administration of the district and to serve as liaison between the elected board and educational /administration facets of a board's operation ■ approve teachers, administrators, and other school personnel hired by the superintendent ■ establish policies and regulations to direct the operations of their school district respecting voters' wishes ■ set a school district budget ■ School boards raise money either through a combination of direct allocations from provincial/territorial governments and property taxes, or solely from provincial/territorial government allocations (Alberta, New Brunswick, Northwest Territories, and Prince Edward Island). (Note: The federal government has involvement in schooling through the allocation of certain funds and the administration of some special programs. The special programs are for adults or within federal institutions such as correction centres. Allocation of federal dollars for youth-related programs goes to provinces for their administration.)

We ask you to think about the nature of the political process. The same public that votes for representatives to provincial legislatures also votes for local school boards. You can see how the general public has a right to have their views on schooling heard, and this sometimes makes life in education quite interesting. The great variety of interest groups extant within communities, as well as elected representatives, all tend to have their own agendas for schools. Schools become the confluence of agendas, and it is often a complex matter with which to deal. Consider the various groups that influence schools. Below is a list to start you off (adapted from Parkay et al., 1996, p. 211), but try to think about others you could also add:

parents
students
teachers
provincial government
school board
administrators
taxpayers
businesses and corporations
alternative schooling proponents
minorities and women
educational theorists and researchers
private school proponents
religious adherents
religious opponents
traditionalists
progressivists

13.5 FOR YOUR CONSIDERATION

Divide your class into four groups representing the following:

- a Kindergarten–Grade 3 school
- a Grade 1–6 elementary school
- a Grade 5–8 middle school
- a Grade 9–12 high school

1. For each school consider the list of influences above and determine how those influences could affect your school.
2. Write the influences considered significant on a section of the board around your room.
3. As a whole group, look for those influences that appear to be common to all the schools in your discussion groups.

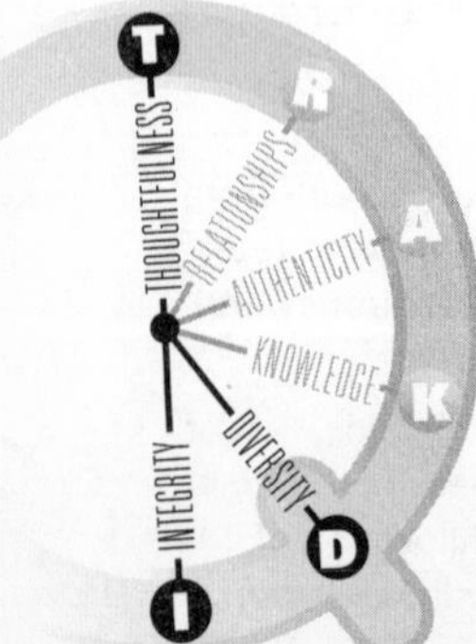

Can you imagine the complexity of debate about schooling with the agendas of all these groups swirling in the landscape? Fortunately, the debate is not constant, and schools are able to get on with learning and teaching with considerable success.

The many influences on schooling indicate that it is, after all, seen as a profoundly important institution. Children are our future, and society looks to them for its continued stability and prosperity. Schools are responsible for attending to the learning needs of children in ways that will establish them as stable and contributing members of society. As schools meet this responsibility they must, of course, work within the structures and procedures laid down by governing bodies, but in doing so they must strive to nurture and, if necessary, protect the welfare and prosperity of the young people with whom they work. The very public and political nature of schooling has resulted in many opinions about how schools should be organized. The needs of society (day-care, pre-school) along with special interest groups (religious schools, special needs schools, schools for high achievers) has resulted in many different expressions of schools in Canada. In the next section we provide a brief snapshot of these expressions.

Expressions of Schooling

Schooling is taking on a different complexion in Canada. Economic conditions fluctuate with the vagaries of a market economy, and prosperity is only as sustainable as the latest market celebration or crisis. Conservative political philosophies, strongly supportive of fiscal restraint and less government, encourage competition and free enterprise in areas where traditionally there have been high levels of government involvement. We see privatization encroaching into health care, social services, and criminal justice, as well as schooling. We provide you with succinct information about different expressions of schooling in Canadian society that reflect the changing complexion of society. Some expressions are established and others emerging. Early history has given us public schooling and some private schools. The later part of the twentieth century has seen new expressions of schooling enter the landscape of teaching.

Play School
- babies/infants to three or four years
- child care and babysitting, with some basic learning

Preschool
- children aged three to five years
- educational play
- socialization skills
- preparation for Kindergarten, depending on school's philosophy

Kindergarten/Early Childhood Education
- children aged four to six years
- heavy emphasis on learning through play
- socialization skills—sharing, co-operating, taking turns, etc.
- initiation to group learning and formal learning
- development of positive images of self

Primary/Elementary School
- Grades 1–3
- mandated provincial programs of study

Elementary School
- Grades 4–6/7
- mandated provincial programs of study

Middle School
- grades vary according to jurisdiction: Grades 5/6–8
- philosophy centred around needs of young adolescents
- mandated provincial programs of study

Junior High School
- usually Grades 7–9
- exist only in some provinces
- subject-centred approach
- high school model
- mandated provincial programs of study

High School

- Grades 8/9/10–12
- academic emphasis for post-secondary qualification
- some optional interest programs
- mandated provincial programs of study

Vocational High School

- Grades 9–12, as a rule
- emphasis on preparation for work force
- some academic work, usually modified programs
- mandated provincial programs of study

Alternative Schools

- exist within public school jurisdictions or may be private
- reflect particular philosophies of learning or special programs (e.g., fine arts, languages)
- if private, then fee-paying
- follow mandated provincial programs of study

Special Needs Schools

- exist within public jurisdictions or may be private
- serve children with identified unique learning difficulties or disabilities
- if private, then fee-paying
- may be excused from mandated provincial programs of study because of students' unique learning problems

Private Schools

- independent of public school jurisdiction
- follow mandated provincial programs of study
- fee-paying, though many receive some provincial support

Charter Schools

- arm's-length attachment to jurisdictions
- follow mandated provincial programs of study
- no fees
- available to all students
- set own operating procedures but are accountable to school board or provincial agency

Year-Round Schools

- instructional and vacation days divided more evenly over the whole year
- amount of instructional time remains the same
- follows mandated provincial programs of study

Modified Calendar Schools

- variation on year-round school, but summer vacation more closely approximates regular schools
- amount of instructional time remains the same
- follow mandated provincial programs of study

Home Schooling

- parent or tutor teaches students at home rather than sending them to school
- must follow mandated provincial programs of study
- accountable to local public school jurisdiction or provincial agency

Reflection and Perspective on the Chapter

History repeats itself! If this exclamation bears any truth, then what are the implications for schooling? Early colonists had to contend with problems of survival in a new and sometimes hostile environment. The fundamental place for education was the home. However, as Canada developed and immigrants continued to arrive, the complexion and complexity of society changed. Communities became more established. As the eighteenth century unfolded, agriculture and industry developed and the need for young people to receive an education became more acute. The response to this need was a somewhat random proliferation of schools with little or no guiding standards.

The cultural traditions of French and British settlers, embedded in the British North America Act of 1867; the work of Ryerson and others who fought for universality and diversity in Canada's schooling systems; and the general respect for diversity have evolved a country that embraces differences in schooling, respects cultural differences, and encourages immigrant peoples to preserve their indigenous cultures, traditions, and languages.

Moves to standardize schools and the training of teachers began to occur during the second half of the nineteenth century at a time when Canada was experiencing the effects of the post-industrial revolution era. This convergence of events is of some significance. The fledgling institution of public schooling became strongly influenced by management and control from the knowledge base of industry. Efficiency in factory production methods was embraced by schooling. This trend continued through the turn of the century to become established as the way to "do" schooling.

Political influence and control is a further consideration in schooling's growth and evolution. Schooling is society's way of preparing young people for life. As a public institution funded through tax dollars, schools are accountable to and controlled by government. We invite you to reflect upon the political nature of schooling with particular reference to the elected status of politicians. The traditional roots of schooling became established during the early 1900s and we have referred to the regularized practices of schooling. Politicians are elected for terms of three to five years, depending on the jurisdiction. To what extent do you think the political nature of schooling has affected its ability to respond to changes in society?

Teacher preparation moved from the more expedient normal schools to professional faculties of education in universities, resulting in greater rigour. Undoubtedly, many benefits accrued from this transition—rich research, more thoughtfulness and reflective practice, a thorough exposure to the professional knowledge base, and greater intellectual analysis of practice, for example. Has the thoroughness and rigour of university preparation had a significant impact on the practice of teaching and the way schooling is offered?

Moves to standardize public schooling during the late nineteenth and early twentieth centuries resulted in an identifiable approach to schooling becoming established: academic subjects, fine and practical arts, and physical education as the foundation, supplemented by extra-curricular sports and outdoor pursuits. To what extent does today's society tend to hold these traditional approaches to schooling as the most effective way to educate young people?

Key Terms

centralized control of schooling 300
industrialized (factory) model of schooling 303
normal schools 301
professionalizing teaching 302
progressive education 304

Suggested Further Reading

Young, J., & Levin, B. (2002). *Understanding Canadian schools: An introduction to educational administration*, 3rd ed., Scarborough, ON: Nelson/Thomson Canada Limited.

Chapter 14

Schooling in the Future: Adaptation and Change

> To think and investigate are now considered to be among the greatest glories of life. He who ascends the mountain steeps of thought, or plunges deepest into the ocean of unsolved doubt, is considered a benefactor of mankind. The intellect of the thinker, daring to seize the bolts of thought, is not impaled by a tyrannical Jupiter.
>
> Every phase of human economy has been investigated by the spirit of inquiry. This spirit is at the bottom of every progressive movement and is emblazoned on every landmark of civilization.
>
> It has supplanted doubt, uncertainty and superstition by promoting truth, knowledge and progress. The influence of this spirit has trained the statesman, guided the schoolmaster, and educated the masses.
>
> The spirit of inquiry should be made a subject of personal study. Our ability to learn and understand should be limited only by our power to acquire a greater fund of knowledge and skill. To be and to become—this is the tonic which should quicken the soul each new morning, the sparkling dew which should refresh the feet of those who tread the grassy sward. (Holst, 1911, p. 5)

The above quotation is interesting to think about in relation to the future of schooling. To what extent was the inquiry extolled in 1911 prominent in your school experience? When you were in school, did you experience "the tonic which should quicken the soul each new morning"? Now, you may feel that the use of a reference from 1911 is a rather weak attempt at drama, but we ask you to reflect on the meaning implicit in the above quotation. Consider its situation in history. During this time and some decades beyond, John Dewey was making powerful contributions to the knowledge base of schooling. In 1910, Dewey wrote:

> Surely if there is any knowledge that is of most worth it is knowledge of the ways by which anything is entitled to be called knowledge instead of being mere opinion or guess work or dogma.

> Such knowledge never can be learned by itself; it is not information, but a mode of intelligent practise, an habitual disposition of mind. Only by taking a hand in the making of knowledge, by transferring guess and opinion into belief authorized by inquiry, does one ever get a knowledge of the method of knowing. (In Archambault, 1964, p. 188)

The wisdom of Dewey and the imagery of Holst give us interesting insights into contemporary thinking at the beginning of the twentieth century. To what extent has schooling progressed from that period almost a century ago? To what extent have we achieved learning conditions that embrace understandings of knowledge and inquiry posited long ago? The swings and fluctuations evident in schooling in the years since the beginning of the twentieth century point to an institution that is susceptible to "outside" influences. It is, of course, debatable as to what these influences are and similarly debatable as to why the influences are allowed to affect schooling with such strength.

14.1 FOR YOUR CONSIDERATION

In Chapter 13, we used the term *confluence of agendas*. Refresh your memories as to what this term means. Engage in a whole-group discussion, addressing the following questions:

1. What are the five most dominant influences on schooling?
2. Discuss each influence and identify how it affects schools. Record group consensus on an organizing chart.
3. What is your opinion of these influences? Use the following Likert Scale to register the collective views of your group.

   Unsure None Insignificant Significant: tends to inhibit Significant: tends to promote

4. For the influences that tend to inhibit, what can be done? How can the promoting influences be encouraged?

As we consider the future of schooling, it is instructive to be cognizant of the past, to move forward with a clear knowledge of why we are where we are today. History, we are told, has a habit of repeating itself. If there is any truth to this adage, what are the implications for schooling, as we move into an uncertain future?

Chapter Focus

Schooling is entering an uncertain future. By this, we mean that the rapidity of change that is upon us is predicted to continue unabated. We invite you to think about how changes in ways of working, brought about by increasingly sophisticated technology and ways of accessing knowledge through ever-improving communications systems, have caused different forms of social and economic interactions. The cell phone alone has such incredible versatility that it may be called revolutionary.

Rapid changes in the world are causing economic fluctuations, such that provinces are taking stringent steps to eliminate deficits and debts. Sometimes dramatic budget cuts cause acute hardships for publicly funded schooling. On top of these funding reductions, there is a demand for accountability and results. Consider the impact on schooling of reduced support and resources, along with increased government testing in the quest for results to demonstrate cost effectiveness. How should schools respond to changes in a society that is increasingly knowledge driven? Can we continue to carry out schooling in much the same way as today?

The appearance of courses on topics such as wellness, self-renewal, getting in touch with nature, experiencing the arts, and seeking one's inner self are increasingly advertised in newspapers, magazines, and specialized publications. A visit to any bookstore will see extensive collections of books in the self-help, New Age, and spirituality sections. Even business sections include these themes in books on leadership. We will raise questions about the role of schooling in helping young people to search for meaning in life. The pressures on young people today are well known. The kind of future that they might reasonably anticipate will probably not see a decrease in the pressures. How can schooling help our youth find meaning in life from within themselves, as opposed to that meaning being imposed by seductive messages from without?

We will conclude the chapter by revisiting the themes of the book and attempting to enhance the coherency you bring to the qualities and commonplaces of teaching. Within this conclusion, complemented by the discussion in the chapter, we will invite you to think deeply about your worldview. "Your worldview is made up of your assumptions and understandings about the essential nature of the world" (Chapter 1, p. 6). Remember you *are* your assumptions; they are how you present yourself to the world. Discovering new assumptions, challenging the old, and uncovering those that are tacit is a life-long endeavour. Only in this way will your worldview be "unfenced."

Focus Questions

1. What role should schooling play in a "decent" society?
2. To what extent should schooling serve as an equalizer against inequities in a knowledge-driven economy?
3. Should schooling provide young people with balance in their lives, to counteract the stimulations of a complex, technological society?
4. How should schooling respond to a future of rapid change?

Some Assumptions About Schooling and the Future

Assumption 1: Public schools exist in a marketplace where it is appropriate that they compete with other forms of schooling; for example, private, charter, virtual, and home.

Politics and schooling are inseparable, if for no other reason than that jurisdiction for education is a constitutional right of provinces. In academic institutions of higher learning, the concept of public education is a matter for intelligent debate. Questions pertaining to equity, equality, egalitarianism, and individual and societal good are given honest airing and vigorous debate. The debate tends to focus on the general well-being of people and their society. Governments, we would argue, tend not to engage in such debate. Depending on the particular political persuasion of a party in power, the driving force will be political, ideological, and expedient. Market forces will prove dominant in more conservative political ideologies, and social concerns will prevail as a party leans toward the left of the political spectrum.

Political Influence on Schooling

Attitudes toward schooling, then, will be affected by the political winds. In Alberta, at the time of writing, a strongly conservative government is actively promoting and supporting the establishment of private schools. Ontario and British Columbia are on a similar path. Two conditions that affect admission to many private schools are 1) admission fees that tend to be prohibitive for many lower-income parents, and 2) testing to determine academic ability. One elementary school known to the authors claims to prepare children for university. Some private schools, particularly those with a religious orientation, and charter schools tend to be less discriminatory.

A tenet of political jurisdictions driven by market principles is that competition plays a pivotal role. Businesses expand constantly. Fast-food outlets, for example, replicate themselves to gain the most customers. Oil companies take over smaller competitors to improve their market share of profits. Governments establish regulatory bodies to guard against monopolies and cartels. The philosophy seems to be that competition ensures the highest quality of goods and services at the lowest prices. Through the dynamics of competition and entrepreneurial activity there seems to be an assumption that when economies flourish societies are well.

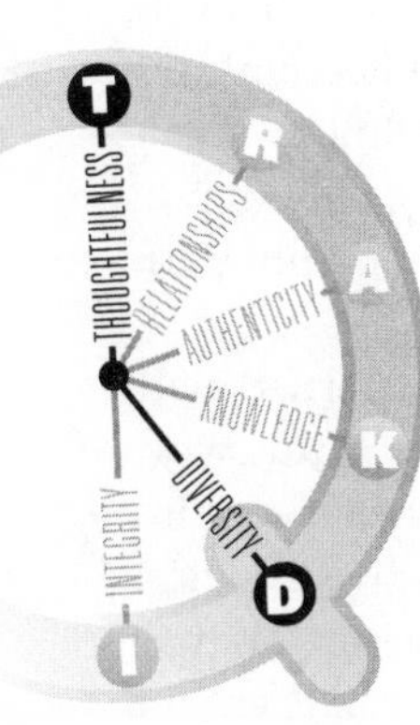

To what extent do competition and entrepreneurial activity contribute to the well-being of society in the social arena? What are the merits of a two-tiered health care system, for example? In the context of schooling, the larger question is about the role of schooling in society and the degree to which it contributes to the well-being of society. We acknowledge the similarity of this assumption to the one that follows, but we feel that it is useful to contemplate the concept of competition in schooling before moving to consider the idea of schooling as an equalizer. What is the role of public education in contributing to the well-being of people?

The essential issue, then, is the role of public education in society. Is vital public schooling—compulsory and equitable for all—an essential element of a fair and just society? In Chapter 8 (p. 195), we invited you to think about your personal philosophy of education and schooling. Your response to this assumption should be a fundamental part of your philosophy. Is public schooling merely utilitarian, preparing young people for the world of work or further study, or does it also have a more profound purpose? How does the role of public education fit in your worldview?

14.2 FOR YOUR CONSIDERATION

The central issue is what kind of society do we want to live in, in the future? If we segregate school children from each other on the basis of religion, race or wealth, we will ultimately end up with a society divided in this manner.... [I]t makes no sense to spend a great deal of time and money on commissions studying tolerance and understanding and then to use our tax dollars to segregate children and encourage social divisions.

—SHELDON CHUMIR, DECEASED SOCIAL ACTIVIST AND LAWYER (IN FORD, 1997)

"Well-meaning parents confuse basics with discipline."

—(FORD, 1997)

1. Explore the meaning of egalitarianism.
2. Consider the concept of egalitarianism in relation to Chumir's central issue of the kind of future society we want to live in. To what extent is Chumir adopting an egalitarian view toward public schooling? Do you support this position? Why, or why not?
3. What disposition on the political continuum (see For Your Consideration 14.3) would be most conducive to a vital approach to schooling?

Assumption 2: Public schooling is an equalizer that guards against the distortions of market forces.

This assumption is often a corollary to the previous one in that it sees the school as a guarantor of equal opportunity in the face of inequities that may be caused by conditions of a market economy. "Because schooling provides opportunities otherwise afforded only by family wealth and privilege, it is essential to the goal of democratic equality" (Feinberg, 1990, p. 163). We believe it is important to contemplate the school as an equalizer as you consider the future of schooling.

Children from families of lower socio-economic standing may experience disadvantages for a variety of reasons: poor nutrition, inability to access services demanding fees, home environments lacking in stimulation, parents who must work long hours in low-paying jobs to make ends meet. Schooling can be, to a considerable extent, a neutralizing force against these shortfalls, ensuring a childhood that is enriched through the stimulation of learning. When children encounter schooling that is not segregated, they are exposed to a richness of role models, possibilities, and self-affirming influences, all of which provide opportunities for developing knowledge, skills, abilities and attitudes for an optimistic future.

Political persuasions notwithstanding, teachers are always concerned with the welfare of young people. We cannot ensure equality of economic status within families and we cannot guarantee the physical, intellectual, and social equality of people. We can, however, ponder the moral question, To what degree should a society provide its young people with equal opportunity in schooling during their early formative years? Should there be a level playing field for all children and should compulsory public schooling be that equalizer?

Change in a Knowledge-Driven Society

Change is occurring with such rapidity that schools, in spite of their relative intransigence, will inevitably be affected. It is highly likely that technology will be

14.3 FOR YOUR CONSIDERATION

Consider this statement: The measure of a society is the degree to which it cares for the essential needs of its citizens, such that the citizens and their society flourish and prosper.

1. Using the continuum of political dispositions below, take a poll of your group and see how many would respond to this statement by leaning toward the conservative end of the continuum and how many would lean toward the social end. Divide the class along these lines.
2. Spend time with your respective group discussing the statement above, and clarify your reasons for your political disposition on the continuum.
3. Set up a group debate. Establish rules for the debate, and, with your instructor/leader as moderator, spend some time debating your respective views.

A more social disposition ________ A more conservative disposition

the strongest harbinger of change. Consider, then, the two most dominant influences on schooling for the future: privatization and technology. What do you see that the two have in common? Perhaps you see a number of things, but we are sure that prominent among them will be money. Private schooling usually involves high fees, and so does technology. Was this an issue in your group debate? We leave you to think about the above assumption with salient comments from Drucker (2001):

> The next society will be a knowledge society. Knowledge will be its key resource, and knowledge workers will be the dominant group in its workforce. Its three main characteristics will be:
>
> *Borderlessness, because knowledge travels even more effortlessly than money.*
>
> [Authors' note: Information technology, increasingly a part of school learning and a fundamental part of life in the future, is allowing knowledge to spread rapidly. Schools everywhere will have access to this knowledge and children, to be participants in society, should have access to it and know how to work with it for personal competence and prosperity.]
>
> *Upward mobility, available to everyone through easily acquired formal education.*
>
> [Authors' note: If children are to participate fully in society, then access to and facility with knowledge—so instantly available through information technology—must be an integral part of their school experience. To ensure that all children have this access and facility, society should embrace schooling in ways that are fair and equitable for all.]
>
> *The potential for failure as well as success. Anyone can acquire the "means of production," i.e., the knowledge required for the job, but not everyone can win.*
>
> [Authors' note: Clearly, not all young people will acquire a facility with knowledge that will allow them to access knowledge-related fields. Much like today, when some children have difficulty with typical school learning and find themselves more suited to service and manual occupations, so in the future children will likely find

themselves exploring similar options. They will, however, enter their future with knowledge of, and a facility with, technology that allows them to access knowledge.]

> Together, those three characteristics will make the knowledge society a highly competitive one, for organisations and individuals alike. Information technology, although only one of many new features of the next society, is already having one hugely important effect: it is allowing knowledge to spread near-instantly, and making it accessible to everyone." (Drucker, 2001, p. 4)

To what extent, then, should a society look to public schooling as an equalizer and guardian against possible distortions created by a future dependence upon knowledge?

The two assumptions we have invited you to consider so far are essentially political. We offer them because we believe the changing complexion of today's society is driven by the economy and its "means of production." The inequities often created by people's level of ability to access the economy, to be part of the "means of production," is always critical. In a knowledge-driven society, however, is it not fair to say that all should have equal access to the acquisition of knowledge?

Fair and equitable access to knowledge for a society's youth becomes a political issue. Is it acceptable to place public schooling in a competitive marketplace alongside private, fee-paying schools? Is competition among schools desirable? The debate likely comes down to a question of that which is best for children and, in turn, that which is best for the fabric of society. Schooling is a provincial responsibility and its future, therefore, lies squarely in the political arena.

Assumption 3: Schooling equips children with the knowledge, skills, competencies, and attitudes to cope with a rapidly changing and complex society.

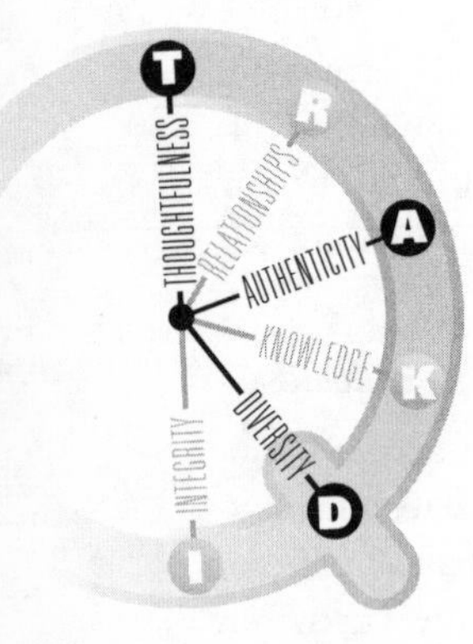

Time within school days is broken up into blocks during which children study various subjects. Do schools attempt to make explicit connections between these blocks? In most cases we suspect not. A better question might be, To what *extent* do schools make explicit attempts to understand the world of a child and organize learning in ways that help children understand their world more clearly? We have discussed the need for teachers to "understand the understanding of children" (Chapter 8). How important would it be to take cues from young people as a means of organizing learning time within a school day?

Coping in a Complex Society

Knowledge, skills, competencies, and attitudes to cope with a rapidly changing society may be understood in two ways:

1. those emanating from within subject areas, and therefore somewhat fragmented
2. those emanating from beyond subject areas and therefore more holistic

If the intention is to help a young person cope with a rapidly changing and complex society, then where do you think the primary source of inquiry should be? Good learning entails many things, but the ability to transfer learning, to make connections between learning and other aspects of life, is paramount (Chapter 8, pp. 188–191, and Chapter 11, p. 260). When learning is broken up, or fragmented, often the person who is expected to make connections is the one who is least able to do so—the learner. To address this matter, schools attempt to bring subject learning together through curriculum practices such as inter-disciplinary learning, integrative learning, humanities (combining language studies and social studies), and thematic learning (Chapter 11, pp. 255–258). How do you think schools should organize their time so that learning is facilitated most effectively?

Meaning in Life

Schooling is commonly seen as a preparation for life, but often this "preparation" is limited to subjects related to work or post-secondary education. As a result, some areas of study receive elevated status and others a less exalted level (see Assumption 2 in Chapter 11, p. 246). More "academic" subjects have their elevation manifested in provincial testing programs. "Important" areas of study are the ones used to determine the effectiveness of schooling systems. Fine arts pursuits and other areas of study deemed to be "of choice," including physical education in later years of high school, are not tested. What message does this communicate to young people and to society?

Helping Young People to Understand Themselves

At no time in history have human beings experienced change with today's intensity. Sometimes lost in this maelstrom of change is the impact it has on people at deeply personal levels. The proliferation of "wellness" services, exhortations for people to gain balance in their lives and a groundswell of interest in spirituality attest to the emerging need to rediscover our humanness. What is the essence of *being* human? Technology, materialism, consumerism, and incessant media messages—whether in advertising, news broadcasts showing the latest disasters, or questionable portrayals of society in film and television—all bombard people with pressures and images from a world beyond themselves. Do you think people are losing a sense of who they are? Are people responding to life through perceptions subliminally dictated by seductions in the world around them? What is the role of schooling in this context? To what extent might we anticipate that schooling can exercise a balancing influence for young people, such that they enter adulthood able to respond to the world through who they are, rather than what the world influences them to be?

A Curriculum for the Future

Fragmentation implies disconnected pieces. A fragmented curriculum, therefore, implies disconnected subject areas. Was there any connection between the learning you experienced in two subjects, say math and English, when you were in high school? If schooling is to help a young person understand and fathom her or his world, then how is fragmented, disconnected learning going to do this? Life is holistic, it is a series of involvements and interactions that, for our effective response, requires us to draw upon and apply knowledge and experience in seamless ways. Learning in school does not facilitate this kind of response. What do you see as a useful way of understanding a future curriculum?

Future teacher preparation studies will allow you to explore curriculum and its development, but we also ask you to reflect on the deeply human and spiritual needs of people, and on the way that the pressures of contemporary society cause notable imbalance in lives.

The Value of Creative and Emotional Expression

Subjects within current curricula that encourage young people to explore their creativity, inner feelings, and expressions of self are primarily within the fine arts. Interestingly, these areas of study, which contribute to quality of life and invite deeper expressions of creativity, emotions, and multi-sensory involvement, are deemed to be of less importance, and do not fall within a government's judgment of "core" subjects. They are not tested, and frequently they are the first to fall prey to funding cuts. What messages do we communicate when certain subjects receive a lower status than others? Society appears to value the arts privately but does not support them publicly as a priority in schooling. We would be wise to pay more attention to more holistic conceptions of curriculum as we ponder the role of schools in preparing young people for an increasingly complex and uncertain future.

Assumption 4: In the future, schooling will not be located in dedicated buildings as it is today.

Schooling today is unquestionably in a period of uncertainty. Demands for accountability and results (Chapter 12) are heard from many quarters, often with scant attention to the realities of life in school and the task of schooling. The nature of young people, their lives outside school, and the lack of "connectedness" between what the children are being asked to learn and the reality of their world present incredible complexity for educators. Gaskell (1995), in a signal report on Canadian secondary schools, states,

> The schools' efforts to cope with increasing demands to be more responsive, adaptive, rigorous, inclusive, and relevant are hampered by the problems of poverty, inequity, family distress, and social discord with which they must deal. Economic pressures are forcing families to relocate in search of work. Youth violence is a concern in many communities. "Traditional" families—a married couple with children—now account for fewer than 50% of Canadian families; divorces have increased dramatically, and almost 20% of children under 18 (1.2 million) were living in poverty in 1991. (p. 9)

Gaskell provides striking information for us to ponder. What implications does this have for schooling? More important, perhaps, are the implications for governments.

The previous assumptions invited you to reflect on political and philosophical aspects of schooling and its future. As we now wonder about the future manifestation of schools, government ideology and thoughts about schooling as an equalizer are more clearly in focus. With Gaskell's statement in mind, could parents' ability to pay be a factor influencing who gets a solid start in life? If schooling in the future will not be located in dedicated buildings, as our assumption posits, then where and how will our children be educated? Could these future schooling sites be in homes, workplaces, what we currently call post-secondary institutions, virtual classrooms/virtual schools, church-sponsored sites, business-sponsored sites, or simply a panoply of privately sponsored specialized sites to which children must apply for admission? Creative minds can, no doubt, imagine other possibilities. The following sections will provide information that will help you to contemplate these questions.

Schooling in the Future

Change is an inevitable part of the future. We have alluded elsewhere to the relative intransigence of schooling in response to the forces of change. We ask you to think about the propensity for people in schools to focus on tasks to be done and duties to be carried out. This is not intended to be a criticism; schools are busy places where it is necessary to be pragmatic. Again we raise the suggestion that pragmatism may be an impediment to growth, development, and change. The tendency to focus on tasks causes schooling to be susceptible to pendulum swings, current fads, and "latest trend" accusations.

Some Elements of Change for Future Schooling

A consideration of some generalized assumptions that have characterized schooling over past decades may give some insight into changes that schooling may

A school of the past (left) and a school for the future (right). (Photo on left, Glenbow Archives, Calgary, Alberta; NA 2664-2)

experience in the future. Control, for example, is a core element of likely changes. Have you noticed the degree to which students, especially in secondary schools, are given voice in their learning? Some might say that students are dependent on teachers and adults for being told what to do. This might be of little significance in a slow-to-change world where predictability was the norm. In a world of complexity and rapid change, young people must learn to be responsible, to become self-reliant, and to make decisions about their lives that enable them to know themselves and work effectively with others.

We also ask you to think about values. It would be easy to lapse into a litany of concerns about the world today. What could (should?) schools emphasize to contribute to a "decent" society, in which values such as compassion, caring, empathy, altruism, and honesty, for example, are honoured and embraced? Only in this way will young people be able to deal with life, rather than have life deal with them.

Young People's Involvement in Decision Making

How often were you able to make decisions about how you would learn when you were in high school? If you began a study of, say, World War I, would you have been consulted about how you would like to study the topic? Were you asked about your preferred ways of learning and how you would like to be assessed?

Another area of decision making is discipline and conduct. Did your school work with young people to determine policies and procedures for social conduct and protocol? Schools in the future will need to be clear on the skills and behaviours pertaining to the kind of learning young people will need to understand and live competently in a challenging world. Learning and learning environments will have to be flexible so that young people might experience the kind of personal growth necessary for success in life beyond school. A knowledge-based society will demand that youth be well-schooled in skills of metacognition. A knowledge-based society will require life-long learners, so it will be essential that young people learn how to learn. So, if we are to look to a fertile future for schooling, what is to be done differently?

An Orientation Toward Change

For many years schools have been advised to review their ways of working. Toward the end of the 1970s, schools were challenged to be more "effective" (Rutter, Maughtan, Mortimore, & Ouston, 1979; Edmunds & Fredericksen, 1979). As the next decade progressed, schools were encouraged to improve; "school improvement" emerged as the dominant credo (Creemers, Peters & Reynolds, 1989; Hopkins & Wideen, 1984). During the 1990s, schools were urged to "restructure" (Conley, 1993), "reframe" (Bolman & Deal, 1991), and engage in "renewal" (Goodlad, 1994). The early years of the twenty-first century have been marked by an emphasis on the need for change in schooling and a call for success to be demonstrated by results. This seemingly constant stream of advice was difficult for schools to deal with as they struggled to find the time and resources to give adequate attention to the demands.

Useful advice began to appear in the later part of the 1980s when Coombs (1988) suggested a consideration of change from a "things and people" perspective. Past practice, he opined, which had tended to concentrate on things rather than people, was often based on partly right assumptions, and tended to rely on prescribed solutions. A more productive way to proceed, he offered, was to concentrate on people rather than things, alter people's belief systems, encourage people to make decisions based upon contribution to beliefs and needs, and create open systems of thinking. Coombs urged schooling to take a different route. Legendary baseball player Yogi Berra suggested that when you come to a fork in the road, "Take it." We might do better to heed the example of poet Robert Frost and "take the road less travelled."

Some years after Coombs, Cuban (1991) introduced the idea of first-order and second-order change. He contends that first-order change tries to make what already exists more efficient and more effective. A basic belief of first-order change would be an acceptance that existing goals and structures are adequate and desirable. Second-order change seeks to alter the fundamental way in which the organization is put together. The basic belief would posit that existing goals and structure are inadequate and that change is desirable.

14.4 FOR YOUR CONSIDERATION

Contrast the positions described by Coombs and Cuban, illustrated below. Discuss the orientation to schooling that each position implies, and propose courses of action that you think might lead down a path less travelled.

POSITION A

COOMBS

- Concentration on things, rather than people
- Often based on partly right assumptions
- Tends to rely on prescribed solutions

CUBAN

First-order change:

- Try to make what already exists more efficient and more effective
- BASIC BELIEF: Existing goals and structure are adequate and desirable

POSITION B

COOMBS

- Concentration on people rather than things
- Alters people's belief systems
- People decide on things based on contribution to beliefs and needs
- Creates open systems of thinking

CUBAN

Second-order change:

- Seek to alter the fundamental way in which the organization is put together
- BASIC BELIEF: Existing goals and structure are inadequate and change is desirable

1. Typically, what is happening in schooling that would support the above contentions?
2. What changes need to occur to lead schooling down a "path less travelled"?

The Nature of Change: Change From Within

Change is personal; it represents a state of mind. Ways of knowing and behaving evolve from a patterning of previous experience that describes one's very being, or one's worldview. Our worldview is a collection of assumptions that, in effect, represent the way we present ourselves to the world. It is the way one is; the way one exists. The way a teacher approaches young people and deals with learning and teaching is dictated by that teacher's very being. The "being" that is a teacher will seldom change by decree, or fiat, or indeed by unsolicited pressure. Assumptions become patterned and entrenched within our being to the point of becoming tacit. They drive our actions and beliefs without our realizing that we hold them. The only way assumptions can be "updated" is by being challenged with new knowledge.

The most effective way for this challenge to occur is in social contexts. Professional discussion, dialogue, and conversation cause us to understand new knowledge through the questions and inquiry of others, as we collectively seek meaning and understanding. This is why teachers benefit from time together dealing with current knowledge about learning and teaching. Teachers, like principals, will seldom change through involvement in a new program or project. They will interpret the project through their being, through their current assumptions, and deal with it accordingly. For example, if a principal intends to introduce constructivist pedagogy into her school, she will be successful only to the extent that teachers

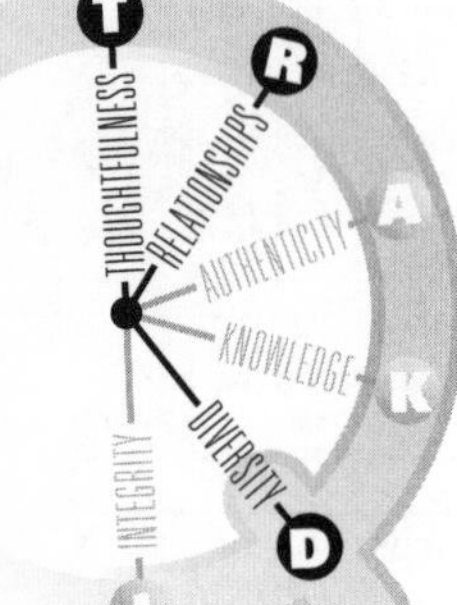

- understand it
- feel the need for it
- feel inclined to practice it

Constructivist learning pedagogy will be incorporated into a teacher's professional being only when the three conditions are present. Teachers may understand, see the need for, and feel inclined to practice it only if they have the opportunity to

- become aware
- engage in conversation with others
- reflect through social intercourse and solitude against the beliefs and assumptions that constitute their professional being and worldview

Allowing Time *for* Change; Allowing Time *to* Change

The time this change would take cannot be hurried. To disallow opportunities for teacher awareness, conversation, and reflection would mean to fall prey to prescribed solutions, and if anything has been learned over the last few decades in schooling it is that prescribed solutions seldom achieve the hoped-for results.

A typical example of this would be when a couple of enthusiastic teachers are sent to a workshop on some latest educational research. Manipulatives in math is a good example. The enthusiasts return to school genuinely excited about their new learning and immediately set about persuading other staff to adopt the pedagogy. Staff then, with varying degrees of enthusiasm, begin the task of implementing the innovation.

The inevitable pitfall is that would-be innovators have spent insufficient time clarifying the new assumptions required to bring adequate meaning and understanding to manipulative math pedagogy. The result is that old assumptions will likely drive the implementation. The use of manipulatives usually requires, to a considerable extent, children fathoming things out for themselves. Directing and telling from the front of a class, for example, does not honour the spirit of learning associated with the use of manipulatives.

Teachers tend to support what they have helped create. Only when beliefs and assumptions—the very being of a teacher—are accepting and understanding of proposed changes will effective change occur. Ultimately, change is personal, but it is becoming clear that environmental factors are germane. Our individual being functions best and flourishes in a social context. It follows that co-operation and collaboration would become not only fundamental elements of our professional environments, but essential for any school intent upon establishing common beliefs and values leading to change.

Fullan (1996), discussing moral purpose and change, stresses the importance of personal purpose and vision. He suggests that achieving personal vision is a much more open process than it sounds.

> Especially in moral occupations like teaching, the more one takes the risk to express personal purpose, the more kindred spirits one will find. A great deal of overlap will be experienced. Good ideas converge under conditions of communication and collaboration. Individuals will find that they can convert their own desires into social agendas with others. (p. 14)

Our teachers in the preceding example, who are intent on spreading the word about manipulatives, would do well to respect the value of "kindred spirits" and the creation of conditions needed for the convergence of good ideas. The environment in which teachers work should respect the notion that change is ultimately personal and must be embraced within one's personal vision to be understood.

And where do we stand when we revisit the imagery of Holst and the wisdom of Dewey with which we commenced this chapter? Do we find the conditions to which they allude extant in our schools? The dynamics that exist within schools, whether bureaucratic or otherwise, are often vexing, but always complex. It is really an understanding of these dynamics that will uncover a productive path for schools to follow as they respond to the rapidity of change in the future.

Reflection and Perspective on the Book

In the Preface we presented a message from Greene (1986) in which the expression, "breaking from anchorage" evoked understandings of preparing to be a teacher as a journey across a broad educational landscape. We offered you two "navigational" aids, or compass points, to provide guidance and sanctuary: six teaching qualities and five commonplaces of knowledge. The five commonplaces of knowledge functioned as an organizer, or framework, for the knowledge presented in the chapters. The six teaching qualities and references about the qualities a teacher would exhibit work together with the commonplaces to respond to the learning needs of children.

We remind you again about the importance of commonplaces as major influences on teachers and teaching. They serve as a reminder that teaching is a practical, social, and complex activity, the understanding of which entails thoughtfulness and perspective. The incredible number of professional judgments teachers make each day as they practice their profession are well informed by a thorough understanding of the commonplaces. When Shawn is misbehaving and not doing his math, what knowledge from each commonplace would we call upon to understand the situation?

The Importance of Being Thoughtful

Successful teaching recognizes, first and foremost, the learning needs of children on which preparations for teaching are based. Throughout the book we have encouraged thoughtfulness. In each chapter we posed questions inviting you to think about the knowledge presented and to come to your own conclusions. In short, this process has been designed to assist the diligent reader to formulate a personal philosophy of education. Chapter 8 provided specific information in that regard.

Knowing Your Assumptions

Each chapter has also invited you to think about your assumptions about learning, teaching, and schooling. We have presented many typically held assumptions and offered information on each for you to contemplate in relation to your personal beliefs. We *are* our assumptions; the composite of our assumptions represents how we present ourselves to the world, whether that presentation is in the classroom or beyond. A possible dilemma we pose to you is that frequently the assumptions we hold are tacit. As such, sometimes we may respond to new situations with assumptions that reside in old, inappropriate contexts. Perhaps this is why change in schooling has been so difficult to embrace.

Toward Expanding Our Worldview

Together, the beliefs and assumptions we hold form our worldview. In Chapter 1 we invited you to consider a worldview approach to understanding teaching through three related notions that may be expressed diagrammatically as follows:

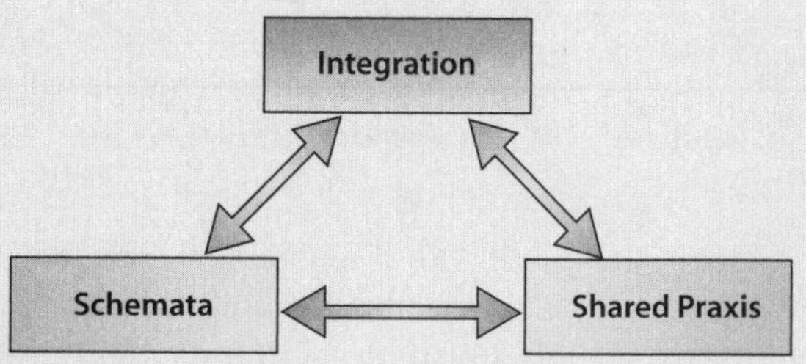

The understanding of, and the relationship between, these three notions is fundamental to a clear worldview—something we have encouraged throughout the book. Many stories in the book may be understood through the worldview held by the subjects: Teddy's teacher (Chapter 3), Melinda's teacher (Chapter 6), Jim Schmidt (Chapter 8), Lorenzo Sanchez (Chapter 8) and the principal at Grenfell School (Chapter 9) should prove interesting to revisit. We invite you to reflect upon their worldviews through the lens of the three notions expressed above and to contemplate their beliefs and assumptions. Which of their assumptions would receive support from the knowledge of the commonplaces presented in the book?

The Importance of Transfer of Learning

Our request for you to revisit the stories should not be interpreted as frivolous. One of the most tenuous links in new learning is the transfer of that learning to new and different contexts. We raised the importance of this need in Chapter 8 and invited you to think about conditions that must exist for transfer to be likely. We're sure you will see in the transfer process the looming presence of assumptions. Clearly a person's worldview is challenged by new knowledge, and the essence of the challenge is to the assumptions held. The significance of shared praxis in facilitating the process of transfer is apparent. Beliefs and assumptions receive the most rigorous review when they are exposed and analyzed in various social contexts. "We hope that you will uncover the assumptions you already have ... and will be prepared to engage in a shared praxis with your professor, your classmates, and your partner teachers and principals in the schools where you do your field experience" (Chapter 1). We hope this will extend to the rest of your career.

Toward a Safe and Prosperous Journey

Your journey into the teaching landscape is beginning and we wish you every success. In any journey one needs a sense of direction and purpose. An unknown wit was once heard to say of a group of people, "Unsure of where they were going, they redoubled their efforts." You would be wise to ponder this trite little aphorism. The teaching landscape is vast, and the journey never ending. It is thoughtfulness that will keep you on course. A successful teacher exhibits the very best of the teaching qualities, charting a course that visits the commonplaces of knowledge, which serve as sanctuaries throughout the landscape. Thoughtfulness and reflection will ensure that the course is true.

A safe and prosperous journey within the teaching landscape will be accomplished when the complexity of teaching is recognized. In Chapter 8 we alerted you to the dangers of "rendering the complex simple." The "safety" in the journey is in the knowledge that a teacher is "on course" and is, in thoughtful and informed ways, effectively responding to learning needs. "Prosperity" resides in the well being of learners. Thoughtful teachers recognize that success is determined through the ways they understand the learning needs of young people and apply that understanding to nurture growth and development in individuals.

A teacher has the task of discovering, within young people, those qualities that accentuate humanness, depth of possibilities and the unquenchable potential of the human spirit.

A daunting task? Somewhat romantic? Unrealistic? A moral responsibility?

We wish you well on your journey.

Suggested Further Reading

Fullan, M. and Stiegelbauer, S. (1991). *The new meaning of educational change,* 2nd ed. New York: Teachers College Press.

Brandt, R. (ed.) (2000). *Education in a new era*. Alexandria, VA: Association for Supervision and Curriculum Development.

Glossary

abstract thinking: the ability to form hypotheses and reason from premises that are not part of a learner's concrete experience.

abstraction: abstracting, or taking something away, from experience; a teacher might ask the learner to consider the main idea of a story, the problem to be solved in science, or the main question to ask of a social problem in social studies.

accommodation: changing schema to fit new realities. Learners' thinking accommodates to new information and to changes in their cognitive makeup.

accountability: the practice of holding people responsible for their behaviour and results.

action learning: learning through problem solving.

affective learning: learning that involves a learner's feelings of confidence, fear, expectancy of rewards, desire to please someone, and many other feelings intricately connected to learning.

alternative school: a publicly funded school that operates within a public school board but is organized around a particular philosophy.

assessment: the gathering of information about a learner's learning in order to make a judgment.

attention: the act of focusing one's mind; attention becomes more selective (able to block out what is irrelevant), more persistent (able to maintain itself for longer periods of time), and less "captured away" by discrepant stimuli such as noise or movement.

authenticity: professional behaviour in relationships, leadership, learning and teaching, curriculum, and assessment, that is genuine and sincere.

behaviourism: the belief that learning means a change in behaviour: if behaviour is caused to change then learning has occurred; it involves the use of reinforcers to deliberately control student behaviour.

cases: narrative accounts.

centralized control of schooling: the drawing up and overseeing of regulations by government officials of schools primarily at provincial and territorial levels, but also by local school jurisdictions.

cephalocaudal pattern: the growth proceeding from the head to the caudal, or tail, region of the body.

character formation education: a movement that emphasizes student development of specific values through critical thinking, formal instruction, or indoctrination.

charter school: a school that is permitted to operate and offer special curricular emphases, such as computer-based instruction and fine arts, but only after applying for a special charter within a provincial legislature. Charter schools must follow provincial programs of study.

classical conditioning: a process whereby responses, particularly physiological and emotional responses such as anxiety, fear, and excitement, can be drawn out of animals and people through a stimulus that would ordinarily not draw out that response.

classroom management: the techniques a teacher uses to create a positive learning environment, which include classroom control, discipline, and governance.

code of ethics: a set of guidelines that stipulates the minimum standards of professional conduct of teachers.

cognitive development: the orderly changes in the way learners think about their world. Cognition refers to knowledge, or to what learners think about.

cognitive learning theories: theories that posit that knowledge is constructed in the minds of learners, that knowledge acquisition, not a behaviour or response, is the goal of education.

collective identity: one's sense of what one's ethnic group is and what it stands for.

commonplaces of teaching: the common influences on every teacher's ability to teach effectively.

compensatory education: additional support of materials, teacher aides, and individualized program planning for specific special learning needs (e.g., where English is a second language) but which may take learners out of regular classrooms for some time.

computer-assisted instruction: teaching in which computer technology, e.g., building Web pages or PowerPoint presentations, is integrated into day-to-day programming, as part of the regular curriculum and particular subjects in a classroom.

computer-based instruction: education in which the computer screen, and not the classroom, is the learning environment; students can learn at a distance through three-way communication among teacher, text, and student.

computer-mediated conferences: a teaching method in which interactive, two-way communication, conducted synchronously or asynchronously, provides the instruction for students.

concept: a set of rules that a person uses to determine what something means and where it fits in a person's understanding.

connectedness: understanding relationships within a subject, between subjects, and between the subject and life itself. Connectedness in learning eliminates fragmentation, facilitates relevance and authenticity, and contributes to the meaningfulness of learning.

construction of meaning: meaning created in the mind of the learner, which occurs as a result of reflection on experience.

constructivism: an approach to learning and teaching that encourages learners to make sense of their world through taking an active role in acquiring, building, and understanding meaning and knowledge in social contexts.

contextual interference: the introduction of new skills and concepts in the midst of practising recently learned skills and concepts.

co-operative learning: a learner-focused instructional process in which small, selected groups of three to five individuals work together on a well-defined learning task for the purpose of increasing mastery and/or understanding of course content.

course integration: a teaching and learning practice that stresses organization that cuts across subject matter lines to bring various aspects of the student's learning into meaningful association.

cultural capital: the factors of personal or social background that help or hinder a child; includes aspects of high culture, such as attending opera or listening to classical music.

culture: the ideas, assumptions, behaviours, and attitudes of a particular group of people.

curriculum: programs of study, subject guides, and school-specific policy decisions that affect the ways of working and general conduct of a school; includes the goals of schooling, the outcomes intended or unintended, and all the experiences a learner has in school.

declarative knowledge: an idea or concept that corresponds to the real thing; specific knowledge regarding what a thing represents. Sometimes referred to as *semantic* knowledge, or what a thing means.

developmental delay: lagging behind similar-aged children in the orderly sequence of change, cognitively, physically, and psychologically.

direct teaching: a teaching approach in which a teacher responds to an entire class, usually from the front of a classroom, talking, explaining, showing, giving seat-work, and generally controlling the classroom activity. Relies heavily on explanations, examples, review, and practice.

discrepant stimuli: unusual or discordant stimuli, noise, or events that capture the visual and auditory attention of a learner (e.g., a loud noise).

diversity: variety in the backgrounds and learning abilities of people, and in approaches to learning and teaching.

domain-specific procedural knowledge: particular teaching skills, wisely applied through judgments made about particular situations.

early intervention program: experiences in nursery and play school where children are exposed to developmentally appropriate opportunities intended to help them start grade school on an equal basis with other children.

ecology of a school: the symbiotic relationship between functions and people toward the essential purpose of successfully meeting the learning needs of all people in the school's learning environment.

educational philosophies: curriculum theories concerning the relationship between a teacher's philosophy and the content and method she or he chooses to apply in the classroom.

elaboration: going beyond the event or experience; relating new information being taught to prior knowledge.

emancipatory constructivism: educational practices that help students become contributing members of a particular community of inquiry and active members of humanity's struggle for enlightenment and liberation.

emotional disability: a condition of unusual levels of psychological and physiological arousal.

emotional intelligence: the capacity for recognizing our own feelings and those of others, for motivating ourselves, for managing our own emotions and relationships.

empathy: the ability to respond positively to personal emotions and to understand and respond to the feelings of others in compassionate ways.

empowerment: to bestow power on others. Empowerment in education encourages learners to be active in and take responsibility for learning.

essentialism: a teaching orientation that believes that young people must be trained in basic skills in a traditional environment, to be good and useful members of society.

ethic of care: caring behaviour motivated out of love and natural inclination; judgments are not grounded in conformity to rules or principles; rather they are concerned with a relation itself; an obligation to stimulate natural caring. It differs significantly from the more conventional understanding of ethics in that it does not root itself in an emphasis on duty.

ethics: principles of conduct generally considered to be "good," "right," and "proper" for the welfare of both the individual and society.

ethnicity: the quality of being a member of an ethnic group.

evaluation: the judgment a teacher applies to the information gathered through assessment.

existentialism: the belief that people must confront the inevitability of death and that, preparatory to the event, they should be free to make choices and be clear about reasons for their existence.

external conditions for learning: the settings and atmosphere that are conducive to learning.

extrinsic motivation: external stimulations to attract learners to learning; this could include rewards that learners receive for work, such as a grade, a material object, avoidance of punishment, or parental approval.

fine-motor skills: flexibility in smaller regions of the body; fine-motor development comes after developing flexibility in large regions of the body.

formative assessment: the gathering of information on a learner, including testing, to inform the learner of ways to improve; the assessment does not lead to a mark or grade.

giftedness: above-average ability, creativity, or intelligence.

graded classroom: a classroom with children of similar ages.

hemisphere specialization: a theory of the structure and functions of the brain that suggests the two different sides of the human brain, right and left hemispheres, control two different "modes" of thinking.

hidden curriculum: unintended learning outcomes.

hierarchy: an organizational structure that typically sees increasing levels of power, with each level of the hierarchy having power over those below.

identity learning: a person's quest to achieve confidence, to feel a sense of well-being, through successful lifestyle decisions.

impediment of pragmatism: the hindrance that the practicality and pragmatism characteristic of life in school often causes by disallowing time for conversations needed to gain clarity about school-wide intentions. New knowledge and the challenging of assumptions may easily be relegated to a later time in favour of more immediate tasks that need to be done.

inclusive education: an approach that incorporates children with special learning or physical needs into regular, age-appropriate classrooms, and provides any support those children need to participate.

independent schools: schools that offer the approved program of studies of the provincial government, but have a particular philosophical or educational emphasis, such as fine arts. Independent schools do not receive full government financial support.

indirect teaching: a teaching approach in which a teacher establishes internal cognitive and psychological conditions within a learning environment to facilitate learning. Learners engage in a variety of learning experiences based on inquiry, problem solving, investigation, and discovery.

individual learning theories: theories that centre on individual changes in behaviour and on thinking through individual experience.

individualizing instruction: designing learning experiences that take into consideration that each learner is unique in areas such as personality and learning style.

industrial (factory) model of schooling: practices of schooling reminiscent of the early industrial model of efficiency, assembly-line work, and mass production methods on which schooling was based in the nineteenth century.

informal learning: learning that occurs informally through reflection with a coach or mentor on the day-to-day events of a school.

integrate: to combine different ideas into one whole, non-fragmented, and coherent idea.

integrated knowledge: combined knowledge from more than one source, for example intuition and empiricism.

integrity: a teaching quality; a word with ethical connotations that typically refers to doing what is right and good.

intelligence: a person's inherited and developed capacity for learning that is unique, as is one's fingerprint or personality.

intelligence quotient (IQ): a number denoting the ratio between mental age and chronological age.

internal conditions for learning: a psychological and emotional predisposition to learn, influenced by the situation and traits of a child, e.g., anxiety.

intervention programs: ongoing and individualized approaches, such as peer tutoring, intended to prevent academic problems and help learners with special needs stay in regular classrooms.

intrinsic motivation: the internal pleasure, enjoyment, and satisfaction a person derives from working on an activity.

kinesthetic learner: one who learns best through hands-on activity.

leadership disposition: the tendency to value and trust the competencies of people, working with and through their strengths and passions to effect a strong learning environment. Establishing conditions for teachers to work in collaboration—not in isolation—to foster the most successful learning possible for young people.

learned helplessness: the belief that events and circumstances in your life are uncontrollable.

learner-focused teaching: placing the nature and individual learning needs of learners foremost in the preparation and practice of teaching.

learning disability: a condition manifesting difficulties in acquiring knowledge.

learning style: the way individuals concentrate, process, internalize, and remember new and different material; a preferred way of perceiving and processing information.

macro-propositional knowledge: the gist of a thing, or what the essence is of an event, statement, or object. Alternative term for propositional knowledge.

magnet school: a school where the program focuses on a specific aspect of learning (e.g., fine and performing arts or programs for gifted and talented students), for which parents would choose to send their children there.

management disposition: the tendency to focus on completion of tasks and accomplishment of goals as ends in themselves, and using them as the internal standard by which role effectiveness is judged. Control is a characteristic of this disposition.

measurement: the standards teachers use to determine whether learners have learned and how much they have learned.

metacognitive: thinking about one's thinking.

mind-mapping: a technique used to "link memory" for the learner by representing thoughts with pictures and colours.

moral dilemmas: problems for which subjects must judge the best course of action by applying moral reasoning.

moral education: a process whereby principles for action on complex societal issues are formulated and applied through the development of thinking and action that reflects "right," "good," and "proper" ethical conduct.

moral learning: the learning process by which people acquire and practise principles of right, good, and proper ethical conduct.

morality of constraint: part of Piaget's model of children's moral development and thinking, often called moral realism. In this stage of morality children determine right action according to externally imposed rules.

motivation: the disposition or willingness of a person to engage in learning through a commitment to complete the learning task.

multi-age classroom: a classroom in which the developmental range is wider than that seen in a single-grade classroom in an attempt to break down the common categorization of students by not dividing them or the curriculum into steps through grade designation.

multiple intelligences: Gardner's theory of intelligence for nine forms of mental representation including musical, bodily–kinesthetic, logical–mathematical, verbal–linguistic, visual–spatial, interpersonal, intrapersonal, naturalistic, and spiritual intelligences.

narrative inquiry: telling and writing stories as a way to understand; capturing the experiences of people through asking questions about their personal stories. It seeks to explicate the past, explain the present, and anticipate the future through a respect for the knowledge contained in the storied lives of people.

negative reinforcement: the removal of a reinforcer as a consequence of a good behaviour.

non-graded classroom: a classroom that features the absence of grade labels and the use of competitive and comparative evaluation.

normal school: the institution for preparing teachers. It first started in France in 1834 as the *école normal.* Canadian normal schools, strongly influenced by the Irish model, stressed the benefits of standarized non-denominational teacher training and textbooks.

null curriculum: what is learned through what is not presented in schools.

open-area classroom: a classroom with multi-age grouping of students and teaming of teachers.

operant conditioning: a process in which it is held that learning has occurred when an emitted response is followed by a satisfying state of affairs, such as praise for work well done.

perennialism: a teaching orientation that views truth as constant and unchanging, or perennial. Perennialists believe that education should focus on the search for and dissemination of the unchanging truths and ideas contained in the great books from arts and science.

performance-based assessment: the gathering of information by inviting students to demonstrate their learning with a response, demonstration, performance, or product.

personal identity: one's sense of who one is and what one stands for.

planned curriculum: the expressed, or written, statement of goals and intended outcomes within a particular subject matter.

pluralism: a form of society comprising many cultures, systems of thought, and values.

private schools: schools that are separate from the public system and promote a particular set of social goals or religious values, but which may receive partial provincial funding. Private schools must agree to follow the approved provincial programs of study and hire certificated teachers.

professionalizing teaching: recognition of teaching as a profession, a view that gained momentum in the post-World War II years, when increasingly it was considered desirable for all teachers to have a baccalaureate degree followed by one or two years of professional studies in education.

progressive education: an educational approach that recognized the individuality of children, resulting in learning that was child-focused; curriculum would consider student attitudes and involvement as much as the mandated programs of study.

progressivism: a teaching orientation that views knowledge as somewhat tentative and incorporates change as a fundamental part of life.

propositional knowledge: the simplest knowledge representation, based on a simple, noun–verb relationship. For example, dogs bark or children play.

pro-social skills: skills that promote social and emotional growth and development in young people.

psychomotor learning: sequential development of understanding and skills in managing one's body and manipulating physical objects.

psychomotor skill: the ability to perceive and respond to environmental influences, such as the speed of a ball, and respond accordingly.

pull-out program: a program in which a teacher with special training withdraws a student from the regular classroom and works with the student in a separate room usually referred to as a resource room.

punishment: the application of some undesirable consequence to unfavourable behaviour.

reconstructionism: the belief that society needs to construct a new social order.

reductionism: the reduction of complex concepts and practices to simple understandings, largely because of insufficient time devoted to gaining meaning and understanding.

reflection: an active, persistent, and careful consideration of any belief or supposed form of knowledge, in light of the grounds supporting it.

reinforcement: using reinforcers to control student behaviour. When reinforcers are used and are contingent upon behaviours, they increase the likelihood that the behaviour will reoccur.

reinforcers: stimuli that follow behaviour.

relational ethics: the ethical orientation of caring, tied to experience. All questions and considerations focus on the human beings involved in the situations and their relations to each other.

relational stance: the position of wanting what is best for a learner and attempting to achieve what is best through a positive relationship with the learner.

scaffold: a piece of existing knowledge, similar to the new information and familiar to the learner, on which the learner can make personal meaning.

schema: a self-organized cluster of particular information, attitudes, and possible behaviours about a concept.

schemata: plural of schema.

school as an entity: a place with a unity of purpose where parents expect their children's learning needs to be met. A place where the functions and inter-relationships of a school's ecology combine with its character and moral nature to form a whole, an entity, focused to meet the learning needs of young people.

school as an organism: the synergistic relationship among all dimensions of a school's functioning. In a healthy school, all people who make up the school work and learn together to identify the school's dimensions, and define and describe the contribution of each dimension to learning in the school.

scripts: the steps of an activity, sequentially identifying what should be done first, second, and so on.

segregated education: an approach in which students identified as having special needs are taught in a segregated setting, a separate classroom or building, where they are set apart from their age peers.

self-concept: the self-portrait, the "picture" hung in the gallery of a learner's mind.

self-efficacy: confidence that a specific skill applied in a particular situation will produce results.

self-regulation: an individual's ability to make decisions about learning and life that will serve to enhance personal well being.

sensitive periods: times when a child is most susceptible to environment influences and when learning might best occur.

shared praxis: systematic, careful, and deliberate reflecting on the experiences that you and others have regarding teaching and learning.

situated performance: role-playing activities in which the learners participate by assuming specific subject positions, where the performed actions, motives, and circumstances are subject to critical reflection.

situational learning: learning that occurs informally through reflection with a coach or mentor within the day-to-day events.

social capital: the range of social relations that may prove to be an asset for the child.

social learning theories: theories that centre on learning through observing other people and acts, being influenced by what is seen more than by what is said.

standardized tests: commercially prepared and uniformly designed and administered tests, generally developed by provincial departments of education, given to students in pre-selected grades at pre-determined dates and times.

student portfolio: a collection of samples of a student's written work, graphs, charts, drawings, paintings, PowerPoint presentations, audio and video tapes, etc. to demonstrate the learning process and skill development.

student-led conferences: parent–teacher conferences that put the learner at the centre of the conference, encouraging the student to participate actively in the evaluation of his or her academic progress.

summative assessment: the gathering of information through testing to assign a mark or grade.

teacher-focused teaching: a teaching approach in which the teacher decides what is to be taught and what is to be learned by students. The teacher controls all classroom activities.

teaching for transfer: teaching so that learners apply new learning to what they have learned in different contexts. Transfer of learning involves prior learning affecting new learning or performance.

teaching portfolio: a document that details, in an organized manner, a teacher's efforts and accomplishments.

teaching qualities: qualities for effective teaching, such as knowledge, thoughtfulness, diversity, authenticity, integrity, and relationships.

team teaching: an approach to classroom instruction that involves two or more teachers who are responsible for co-operatively planning, teaching, and evaluating a group of students.

theory: a set of statements that describes and predicts aspects of some phenomenon.

thoughtfulness: engaging in reflection, inquiry, and conversation toward identifying, understanding, and challenging assumptions about learning and teaching.

tracking: the practice of separating students into different courses or course sequences.

transactional teaching: an active process in which information is transacted in free-flowing processes from teacher to students and among students, using mainly direct teaching and directed learning methods.

transformational teaching: teaching that emphasizes learning in the context of change within the learner. The teacher is facilitative and indirect, in the belief that learners should develop at their own rates in learning conditions that allow them to experience the freedom and enlightenment that will lead to responsibility and ownership.

transmissive teaching: teaching that transmits information from one source (the teacher) to another source (the student) in what is essentially a one-way process.

two-tiered school system: a private or alternative system, provincially funded but accessible to parents with particular philosophical and academic interests, and a public one, provincially funded but accessed only by parents who are unable to access "better" schools because of geography or other reasons.

values-based education: formal school programming that emphasizes identification, assessment, and evaluation of specific pro-social ideas such as empathy, justice, and sharing.

virtual instruction: instruction that takes place through computer-mediated communication, typically at a distance. Also called distance education.

worldview: a mental model, or inner representation, of the outer world, which is composed of the theories, beliefs, and assumptions we hold about the big issues of life.

zone of proximal development: the area of learning just beyond the learner's experience.

References

Aboriginal Education Directorate. (2002). *Aboriginal perspectives*. Retrieved July 7, 2002, from **http://www.edu.gov.mb.ca/ks4/abedu**

Adler, M. (1977). *Reforming education: The opening of the American mind*. New York: MacMillan Publishing Company.

Alberta Learning. (n.d.). *Facilitator's Training Manual* (Vol. 7). Edmonton, AB: Author.

Alberta Teachers' Association. (2002). *Code of professional conduct* [pamphlet]. Edmonton, AB. Retrieved from **www.teachers.ab.ca/professional/code.html**

The American School of Kuwait [advertisement]. Retrieved March 18, 2003, from **www.ask.edu.kw/jobs.html**

American Psychological Association. (1993). *Violence and youth: Psychology's response*. Cited in David M. Day, Carol A. Golench, Jyl MacDougall, Cheryl A. Beals-Gonzaléz, & Earlscourt Child and Family Centre, *School-based violence prevention in Canada: Results of a national survey of policies and programs* (1995). Corrections Branch, Ministry of the Solicitor General of Canada.

Anastasiow, N. (1993). *At-risk infants, interventions, families and research*. Baltimore, MD: Paul J. Brookes Publishing.

Anderson, J. (1990). *Cognitive psychology and its implications*. New York: W. Freeman and Company.

Andersen, N., & Ventura, G. (1994). Television and violence. *YTV News in Class,* 1–8. Cited in David M. Day, Carol A. Golench, Jyl MacDougall, Cheryl A. Beals-Gonzaléz, & Earlscourt Child and Family Centre, *School-based violence prevention in Canada: Results of a national survey of policies and programs* (1995). Corrections Branch, Ministry of the Solicitor General of Canada.

Anderson, R. (1989, February). The second wave of interest in team teaching. *Education Digest*, 18–21.

Anderson, R. (1992). *The nongraded elementary classroom: Lessons from history*. [Conference paper.] (ERIC Document Reproduction Service No. ED348161)

Aoki, T. (1990, January/February). Inspiriting the curriculum and pedagogy: Talks to teachers. *The ATA Magazine*, 37–42.

Apple, M.W. (1990). *Ideology and curriculum* (2nd ed.). New York: Routledge.

Arbaugh, J. (2000). Virtual classroom versus physical classroom: An exploratory study of class discussion patterns and student learning in an asynchronous internet-based MBA course. *Journal of Management Education, 24*(2), 213–233.

Archambault, R. (Ed.). (1964). *John Dewey on education: Selected writings*. New York: Random House.

Armstrong, D.G., Henson, K.T., & Savage, T.V. (1997). *Teaching today: An introduction to education* (5th ed.). Upper Saddle River, NJ: Prentice-Hall.

Athey, I., & Rubadeau, D. (1970). *Educational implications of Piaget's theory*. Waltham, MS: Xerox College Publishing.

Audet, L. (1970). Society and education in New France. In L. Audet, P. Stamp, & J. Wilson (Eds.), *Canadian education: A history*. Scarborough, ON: Prentice-Hall Canada.

Avramidis, E., Bayliss, P., & Burden, R. (2000). A survey into mainstream teachers' attitudes towards the inclusion of children with special educational needs in the ordinary school in one local education authority. *Educational Psychology, 20*(2), 191–211.

Axelrod, P. (1997). *The promise of schooling: Education in Canada, 1800–1914*. Toronto: University of Toronto Press.

Bagley, W. (1934). *Education and emergent man*. New York: Ronald Press.

Bala, N. (1994, February). *The legal response to youth violence.* Paper presented to National Conference on Youth Violence in Canada. Ottawa, ON.

Ballard, E. (1976, March). Letters from Teddy. *Home Life Magazine*, 34–35.

Ballard, E. (1995). Three Letters from Teddy. In J. Canfield and M. Hansen (Eds.), *The 2nd helping of chicken soup for the soul* (pp. 216–218). Deerfield Beach, FL: Health Communications, Inc.

Bandura, A. (1965). Vicarious processes: A case of no-trial learning. In L. Berkowitz (Ed.), *Advances in experimental social psychology*, Vol. 2 (pp. 1–55). New York: Academic Press.

Bandura A. (1977). *Social learning theory*. Englewood Cliffs, NJ: Prentice-Hall.

Bandura, A. (1989). Regulation of cognitive processes through perceived self-efficiency. *Developmental Psychology, 25*, 729–735.

Banks, J. (1993). Multicultural education: Characteristics and goals. In J. Banks and C. McGee-Banks (Eds.), *Multicultural education: Issues and perspectives.* (2nd ed.). (p. 3). Boston: Allyn and Bacon.

Barlow, C., Blythe, J., & Edmonds, M. (1999). *A handbook of interactive exercises for groups*. Needham Heights, MA: Allyn and Bacon, A Viacom Company.

Barrell, B. (1995). The texture of teaching. In D. Jones (Ed.), *The spirit of excellence* (pp. 13–29). Calgary, AB: Detselig Enterprises Ltd.

Barry, N., & Shannon, D. (1997, Summer). Portfolios in teacher education: A matter of perspective. *The Educational Forum, 61*, 320–328.

Barth, R. (2001, February). Teacher leader. *Phi Delta Kappan*, 443–449.

Bartlett, L. (2002). *Successful inclusion for educational leaders*. Upper Saddle River, NJ: Prentice Hall.

Baumrind, D. (1983). Rejoinder: Are authoritative families really harmonious? *Psychological Bulletin, 94*(1), 132–142.

Baumrind, D. (1991). The influence of parenting style on adolescent competence and substance abuse. *Journal of Early Adolescence, 11*, 56–95.

Beane, J. (1993, September). Problems and possibilities for an integrative curriculum. *Middle School Journal*, 18–23.

Beane, J. (1995, April). Curriculum integration and the discipline of knowledge. *Phi Delta Kappan*, 616–691.

Beane, J. (2001). Curriculum integration and the discipline of knowledge. In K. Ryan and J. Cooper (Eds.), *Kaleidoscope: Readings in education.* (9th ed.). (pp. 184–192). Boston: Houghton Mifflin.

Beggs, D. (1966). *Team teaching.* Bloomington: Indiana University Press.

Bender, P.E. (1997). *Leadership from within.* Toronto, ON: Stoddart Publishing.

Benedict, P. (2000, October). Feminization of education: The changing nature of teaching in Canada. *Canadian Teachers' Federation Conference Report*.

Bergman, B. (2001, April 9). The kids are all right. *Maclean's*, 47–51.

Bergman, E., Buergel, N., Enamuther, J., & Sanchez, A. (2000). Time spent by school children to eat lunch. *Journal of American Dietetic Association, 100*(6), 696–698.

Berk, L. (1994). *Child Development.* (3rd ed.). Boston: Allyn and Bacon.

Bibby, R. (2001). *Canada's teens: Today, yesterday and tomorrow*. Toronto: Stoddart.

Bloom, B. (1982). *All our children learning: A primer for parents, teachers, and other educators.* New York: McGraw-Hill.

Blum, Paul. (2001). *A teacher's guide to anger management.* London: Routledge Falmer.

Bochner, A. (2000). Criteria against ourselves. *Qualitative Inquiry, 6*(2), 266–272.

Bolman, L., & Deal, T. (1991). *Reframing organizations*. San Francisco: Jossey-Bass.

Borba, J., & Olvera, C. (2001, July/August). Student-led parent-teacher conferences. *The Clearing House*, 333–336.

Borich, G. (1992). *Effective teaching methods.* (3rd ed.). Englewood Cliffs, NJ: Merrill-Prentice Hall.

Brameld, T. (1956). *Toward a reconstructed philosophy of education*. New York: Holt, Rinehart and Winston.

Brandt, R.S. (1992). On building learning communities: A conversation with Hank Levin. *Educational Leadership, 50*(1), 19–23.

Brandt, R.S. (Ed.). (1992). *Performance assessment: Readings from educational leadership*. Alexandria, VA: Association for Supervision and Curriculum Development.

Bretherton, I. (1989). Pretense: The form and function of make-believe play. *Developmental Review, 9*, 383–401.

Brice, A., & Miller, R. (2000). Case studies in inclusion: What works, what doesn't. *Communication Disorder Quarterly, 21*(4), 237.

British Columbia Ministry of Education. (1996). *Gifted education: A resource guide for teachers*. Victoria, BC: Author.

British Columbia Teachers' Federation. (2001). *A handbook for new teachers*. Retrieved March, 2002, from **http://www.bctf.bc.ca/beginning/handbook**

Bronfenbrenner, U. (1989). Ecological systems theory. In R. Vasta (Ed.), *Annals of Child Development*, Vol. 6. Greenwich, CT: JAI Press.

Brookfield, Stephen D., & Preskill, S. (1999). *Discussion as a way of teaching: Tools and techniques for democratic classrooms*. San Francisco: Jossey-Bass.

Brooks G., & Brooks, M.G. (1993). *In search of understanding: The case for constructivist classrooms*. Alexandria, VA: Association for Supervision and Curriculum Development.

Brown, D. (1999, February). Promoting reflective thinking: Preservice teachers' literacy autobiographies as a common text. *Journal of Adolescent and Adult Literacy, 42*(5), 402–409.

Brown, J.S., Collins, A., & Duguid, P. (1989). Situated cognition and the culture of learning. *Educational Researcher, 18*(1), 32–42.

Brown, R. (1987, September). Who is accountable for thoughtfulness? *Phi Delta Kappan*, 49–52.

Brownlie, F., & King, J. (2000). *Learning in safe schools: Creating classrooms where all students belong*. Markham, ON: Pembroke Publishers.

Bruffee, K., Palmer, P., Gullette, M., Gillespie, D., et al. (1994). *Change, 26*(3), 38–44.

Bruner, J. (1971). *The relevance of education.* New York: Norton.

Bryk. A., & Thum, Y. (1989). *The effects of high school organization on dropping out: An exploratory investigation.* New Brunswick, NJ: Centre for Policy Research in Education.

Buzon, T., & Buzon, B. (1996). *The mind map book*. London: BBC Books.

Calgary Board of Education. (1993–94). *System report card: Assessment for learning*. Calgary, AB: Author.

Callender, W. Jr. (1994, October). Education and training in ABC Canada. *Literacy at Work, 7*.

Campbell, B. (1991). Multiple intelligences in the classroom. *Cooperative Learning, 12*(1), 24–25.

Campbell, B., Campbell, L., & Dickinson, D. (1992). *Teaching and learning through multiple intelligences.* Stanwood, WA: New Horizons for Learning.

Campbell, B. (1994). *Multiple intelligences handbook.* Stanwood, WA: Campbell & Associates.

Campbell, P., & Mandel, F. (1990). Connecting math achievement to parental influences. *Contemporary Educational Psychology*. In *Youth in transition survey—Project overview* (2001) (pp. i–70) (Cat. no. 81-588-XIE). Ottawa: Human Resources Development Canada.

Canadian Education Association. (1992). *Teacher recruitment and retention: How Canadian school boards attract teachers.* Toronto, ON: Author.

Canadian Teachers' Federation. (2000, October). Demographics of the teaching profession: The changing nature of teaching in Canada. *Canadian Teachers' Federation Conference Report*. Retrieved from **http://ctrf-face.ca/what/orther/report.htm#4**

Carroll, K. (1997). Providing meaningful learning through story and an inquiry approach to science education (2 pages). Retrieved from **http://www.newhorizons.org/arts_carroll.html**

Case, R. (1985). *Intellectual development: Birth to adulthood*. Orlando, FL: Academic Press.

Cassidy, K. (2001). Enhancing your experiential program with narrative theory. *The Journal of Experiential Education, 24*(1), 22–26.

Chapman, M. (1994). Active teaching for active learning in the primary classroom. *Prime Areas, 36*(3), 5.

Cheek, L. (2001). Pretty cool for a school. *Architecture, 90*(2), 39–42.

Chartock, R. (2000). *Educational foundations: An anthology*. Upper Saddle River, NJ: Merrill-Prentice Hall.

Clandinin, D.J., & Connelly, F.M. (1998). Personal experience methods. In N. Denzin and Y. Lincoln (Eds.), *Collecting and interpreting qualitative materials* (pp. 155–156). Thousand Oaks, CA: Sage.

Clarke, J., & Agne, R. (1997). *Interdisciplinary high school teaching: Strategies for integrated learning*. Boston: Allyn and Bacon.

Clemens, S. (1983). The sun's not broken, a cloud's just in the way: On child centered teaching. Mt. Rainer, MD: Gryphon House.

Conger, R., Elder, G., Lorenz, F., Conger, K., Simons, R., Whitbeck, L., Huck, J., & Melby, J. (1990). Linking economic hardship and marital quality and instability. *Journal of Marriage and the Family, 52*, 643–656.

Conle, C. (2000). Narrative inquiry: Research tool and medium for professional development. *European Journal of Teacher Education, 23*(1), 49–60.

Conley, D. (1993). *Roadmap to restructuring: Policies, practices and the emerging vision of schooling*. Eugene, OR: ERIC Clearinghouse on Educational Management.

Connelly, F.M., & Clandinin, D.J. (1988). *Teachers as curriculum planners: Narratives of experience*. New York: Teachers College Press.

Connelly, F.M., & Clandinin, D.J. (1990, June/July). Stories of experience and narrative inquiry. *Educational Researcher*, 2–4.

Coombs, A. (1988). New assumptions for educational reform. *Educational Leadership, 45*(5), 38–40.

Coppola, J., & Thomas, B. (2000). A model for e-classroom design beyond "chalk and talk." *T.H.E. Journal, 27*(6), 30–36.

Cousins, N. (1979). *Anatomy of an illness as perceived by the patient*. New York: Norton.

Covey, S. (1992). *Principle-centered leadership*. New York: Simon & Schuster.

Crabb, L. (1988). *Inside out*. Colorado Springs, CO: NavPress.

Creemers, B., Peters, T., & Reynolds, D. (Eds.). (1989). *School effectiveness and school improvement.* Proceedings of the Second International Congress, Rotterdam. Rockland, MA/Beroyn, PA: Swets and Zeitlinger, Inc.

Criko, G. (1992, March). The evaluation of bilingual education: From necessity and probability to possibility. *Educational Researcher*, 10–15.

Crites, J.O. (1978). *Theory and research handbook for career maturity inventory*. (2nd ed.). Monterey, CA: CTB/McGraw-Hill.

Cuban, L. (1991). A fundamental puzzle of school reform. *Phi Delta Kappan, 70*(5), 341–344.

Curtis, E. (1996). *Transformed thinking: Loving God with all your mind*. Franklin, TN: JKO Publishing.

Dale, E. (1969). *Audio-visual methods in learning*. (3rd ed.). New York: Dryden Press.

D'Arcangelo, M. (1998, November). The brains behind the brain. *Educational Leadership*, 20–25.

Darling-Hammond, L. (1997, September). Quality teaching: The critical key to teaching. *Principal*, 5–11.

Davis, B., Sumara, D., & Luce-Kapler, R. (2000). *Engaging minds: Learning and teaching in a complex world.* London: Lawrence Erlbaum & Associates.

Day, D., Minevich, A., Hunt, A., & Hyrnkiw-Agimeri, L. (1994, May). *Early detection of young offenders: Identification of risk and protective factors*. Paper presented at the Biannual University of Waterloo Conference on Child Development, Waterloo, ON.

Deaux, K. (1993). Commentary: Sorry wrong number: A reply to Gentile's call. *Psychological Science, 4*, 125–126.

Delisle, J. (1999). For gifted students, full inclusion is a partial solution. *Educational Leadership*, *57*(3), 80–83.

Devine, T.G. (1987). *Teaching study skills: A guide for teachers*. New York: Allyn and Bacon.

Dewey, J. (1915). *The school and society.* (Rev. ed.). Chicago, IL: University of Chicago Press.

Dewey, J. (1916). *Democracy and education: An introduction to the philosophy of education.* New York: Macmillan.

Dewey, J. (1964). Science as subject matter and as method. In R. Archambault (Ed.), *John Dewey on education: Selected writings* (pp. 182–192). New York: Random House.

Dewey, J. (1973). *Experience and education.* New York: Collier Books.

Diamond, M. (1991). Environmental influences on the young brain. In K.R. Gibson and A.C. Peterson (Eds.), *Brain maturation and cognitive development; comparative and cross cultural perspectives* (pp. 107–124). New York: Aldine de Gruyter.

Donaldson, E. (1995, May). Calgary's solution to the school-to-work transition. *Educational Leadership International*, 35–37.

Drucker, P. (2001). *The next society: A survey of the near future*. New York: The Economist Newspaper Group.

Druckman, D., & Bjork, R.A. (Eds.). (1991). *In the mind's eye: Enhancing human performance.* Washington, DC: Nahoval Academy Press.

Duckworth, E. (1996). *"The having of wonderful ideas" and other essays on teaching and learning*. New York: Teachers College Press.

Dunn, R. (1999). How do we teach them, if we don't know how they learn? *Teaching Pre K-8*, *29*(7), 50–52.

Dunn, R., & Dunn K. (1978). *Teaching students through their individual learning style*. Reston, VA: Reston Publishing Company, Inc.

Dunn, R., Dunn, K., & Price, G.E. (1990). *Learning styles inventory*. Lawrence, KS: Price Systems.

Dunsmuir, S. (2001, February). *The ideal teacher.* Handout presented at Westcast Conference, Calgary, AB.

Dyson, A. (2000). *Schools and special needs: issues of innovation and inclusion*. London: P. Chapman.

Edmonton Public Schools. (1997, November). *Position on funding of private schools*. Edmonton, AB: Author.

Edmunds, R., & Fredericksen, J. (1979). *Search for effective schools: The identification and analysis of city schools that are instructionally effective for poor children*. Cambridge, MA: Center for Urban Schools, Harvard University.

Edwards, B. (1999). *The new drawing on the right side of the brain*. New York: Jeremy P. Tarcher/Putnam.

Edwards, K. (2000). A fruitful approach to the integration of psychology and spirituality. *Journal of Psychology and Theology*, *28*(1), 66–72.

Egan, K. (1996). *The educated mind: How cognitive tools shape our understanding.* Chicago, IL: University of Chicago Press.

Eisner, E. (1991). Structure and magic in discipline-based art education. In D. Thistlewood (Ed.), *Critical studies in art and design education* (pp. 14–26). Portsmouth, NH: Heinemann.

Elder, G., Conger, R., Foster, E., & Ardelt, M. (1992). Families under economic pressure. *Journal of Family, 13*, 5–37.

Elementary Teachers' Federation of Ontario. (2000). Bill 81. The Safe Schools Act. Retrieved November 29, 2002, from **http://www.etfo.on.ca**

Elias, M.J., Zims, J.E., Weissberg, R.P., Frey, K.S., Greenberg, M.T., Haynes, M.M., et al. (1997). *Promoting social and emotional learning: Guidelines for educators*. Alexandria, VA: Association for Supervision and Curriculum Development.

Elkind, D. (1984). *All grown up and no place to go*. Reading, MA: Addison-Wesley.

Engebretson, K. (1997). The four point plan of the Melbrisu Guidelines and shared praxis: Two distinct and different methodologies. Retrieved January, 2001, from **http://www.acu.edu.au.fen/engebd03.htm**

Epstein, J. (1995). School/family/community partnerships—caring for the children we share. *Phi Delta Kappan, 76*(9), 701–712.

Erikson. E. (1968). *Identity, youth and crises*. New York: W.W. Norton.

Fahey, P., & Fingon, J. (1997, Summer). *Assessing oral presentations of student-teacher showcase portfolios, 61*, 354–359.

Feinberg, W. (1990). The moral responsibility of public schools. In J. Goodlad, R. Soder, & K. Sirotnik (Eds.), *The moral dimensions of teaching* (p. 163). San Francisco: Jossey-Bass.

Fenwick, T., & Parsons, J. (2000). *The art of evaluation: A handbook for educators and trainers*. Toronto: Thomson.

Feyten, C., & Nutta, J. (1999). *Virtual instruction issues and insights from an international perspective.* Englewood, CO: Libraries Unlimited, Inc.

Filipczak, B. (1995). Different strokes: Learning styles in the classroom. *Training, 32*(3), 43–49.

Finders, M., & Rose, S. (1999, April). If I were the teacher: Situated performances as pedagogical tools for teacher preparation. *English Education, 31*(3), 205–216.

Fine, S. (2001, February 5). Teachers drop out as stress takes it toll. *The Globe & Mail*, p. A3.

Fisher, B., & Cordeiro, P. (1994). Generating curriculum; building a shared curriculum. *Primary Voices, 2*(3), 2–7.

Fogarty, R. (1991, October). Ten ways to integrate curriculum. *Educational Leadership*, 61–65.

Ford, C. (1997, January 31). Well-meaning parents confuse basics with discipline. *The Calgary Herald*, p. A13.

Fowler, H., & Fowler, F. (Eds.). (1954). *The concise Oxford dictionary of current English*. London: Oxford University Press.

Foster, G., & Yesseldyke, J. (1978). Bias in teachers' observation of emotionally disturbed and learning disabled children. *Exceptional Children, 44*(8), 613–615.

Freire, P. (1988). *Pedagogy of the oppressed*. New York: Continuum.

Fullan, M. (1996). *Change forces: Probing the depths of educational reform*. New York: Falmer Press.

Fuller, C. (2001). Breathing, 'riting, and 'rithmetic: Fixing IAQ problems in school. *Engineered Systems, 18*(3), 64–67.

Fuller, F. (1969, March). Concerns of teachers: A developmental conceptualization. *American Educational Research Journal, 6*.

Fuller, F., & Brown, O. (1975). Becoming a teacher. In K. Ryan (Ed.), *Teacher education seventy-four yearbook of the National Society for the Study of Education*. Chicago: University of Chicago Press.

Futrell, M. (1999). Recruiting minority teachers. *Educational Leadership, 56*(8), 30–33.

Gabor, T. (1995). *School violence and the zero tolerance alternative: Some principles and policy prescriptions* (Cat. no., JS42-67/1995). Ottawa: Ministry of Supply and Services.

Gagne, F. (1991). Toward a differentiated model of giftedness and talent. In N. Calangelo and G.A. Davis (Eds.), *Handbook of gifted education* (pp. 65–80). Needham Heights, MA: Allyn and Bacon.

Gagne, F. (1995). Hidden meanings of the "talent development" concept. *The Education Forum, 59*, 350–362.

Gagne, R. (1985). *The condition of learning.* (3rd ed.). New York: Holt, Rinehart and Winston.

Gallo, D. (1989). Educating for empathy, reason and imagination. *The Journal of Creative Behavior, 23*(2), 98–115.

Ganzer, T. (2000, Winter). Teams of two: Insider ideas on building and supporting a mentor program. *Journal of Staff Development, 21*, 60–63.

Gardner, H. (1993). *Creating minds*. New York: Basic Books.

Gardner, H. (1995a). Multiple intelligence as a catalyst. *English Journal, 84*(8), 16–19.

Gardner, H. (1995b). Reflections on multiple intelligences: Myths and messages. *Phi Delta Kappan, 77*(3), 200–208.

Gardner, H. (1999). Who owns intelligence? *The Atlantic Monthly, 283*(2), 67–76.

Gaskell, J. (1995). *Secondary schools in Canada: The report of the exemplary schools project.* Toronto: Canadian Education Organization.

Gerein, C. (1997). *Portfolio checklist*. Unpublished classroom resource.

Gibson, E. (1991). *The odyssey in learning and perception*. Cambridge, MA: MIT Press.

Gibson, E.J. (1982). The concept of affordances in development of functionalism. In W.A. Collines (Ed.), *The concept of development: The Minnesota Symposium on Child Psychology,* Vol. 15 (pp. 55–81). Hillside, NJ: Erlbaum & Associates.

Gick, M.L., & Holyoak, K.J. (1980). Analogical problem solving. *Cognitive Psychology, 12*, 306–355.

Gick, M.L., & Holyoak, K.J. (1983). Schema induction and analogical transfer. *Cognitive Psychology, 15*, 1–38.

Glickman, C. (1990, September). Pushing school reform to a new edge: The seven ironies of school reform. *Phi Delta Kappan, 72*.

Gilligan, C. (1982). *In a different voice: Psychological theory and women's development.* Cambridge, MA: Harvard University Press.

Goleman, D. (1998). *Working with emotional intelligence*. New York: Bantam Books.

Good, T.L., & Brophy, J.E. (2000). *Looking in classrooms*. (8th ed.). New York: Addison-Wesley Longman.

Goodlad, J.I. (1984). *A place called school: Prospects for the future*. New York: McGraw-Hill.

Goodlad, J. (1994). *Educational renewal: Better teachers, better schools*. San Francisco: Jossey-Bass.

Gormlay, A.V., & Brodzinsky, D. (1989). *Lifespan human development.* Orlando, FL: Holt, Rinehart and Winston.

Graves, T. (1991, April). The controversy over group rewards in cooperative classrooms. *Educational Leadership*, 77–79.

Green, M. (1999). *The appropriate and effective use of security technologies in U.S. schools: A guide for schools and law enforcement agencies.* Los Alamos, NM: Sandia National Laboratories for the U.S. Department of Justice.

Greenberg, M., Speltz, M., & Deklyn, M. (1993). The role of attachment in the early development of disruptive behaviour problems. *Developmental Psychology, 5*, 191–213.

Greene, M. (1986). Landscapes and meanings. *Language Arts 63*(8), 783.

Gregorc, A. (1982). The razor's edge. *Challenge: Reaching and teaching the gifted child 1*(1), 37–40.

Groome, T. (1981). *Christian religious education.* San Francisco: Harper and Row.

Gross, R. (1991). *Peak learning: How to create your own lifelong education program for personal enlightenment and professional success*. New York: Jeremy P. Tarcher/Putnam.

Grudin, R. (1990). *The grace of great things: Creativity and innovations*. New York: Technor and Fields.

Guitieriez, G. (1973). *A theory of liberation*. Maryknot, NY: Orbis Press.

Guglielmi, R., & Tatrow, K. (1998). Occupational stress, burnout and health in teachers: A methodological and theoretical analysis. *Review of Educational Research 68*(1), 61–99.

Gupta, R., Derevensky, J., Tsanas, S.A., Klein, C., Bennet, A., & Kanevsky, L. (1995). A comparison of adolescent fears from Montreal to Vancouver. *Canadian Journal of School Psychology, 11*, 10–17.

Haberman, M. (1989). More minority teachers. *Phi Delta Kappan, 70*(10), 771–76.

Hamilton, W. (1970). The British heritage. In L. Audet, P. Stamp, & J. Wilson (Eds.),

Canadian education: A history (pp. 25–39). Scarborough, ON: Prentice Hall.

Harrow, A. (1972). *The taxonomy of the psychomotor domain: A guide for developing behavioral objectives*. New York: David McKay.

Hathaway, W. (1986, September). A study into the effects of light and color on pupil achievement, behavior and physiology. Paper presented at the CEFP 63rd Annual Conference. Nashville, TN.

Haury, D., & Milbourne, L. (1999, May). Should students be tracked in math or science? *ERIC Digest*, 1–4.

Haute, T., Heins, E., Tichenor, M., Coggins, C., & Hutchinson, C. (2000). Multiage classrooms: Putting theory into practice. *Contemporary Education, 71*(3), 30–35.

Heavey, B. (2000). Construction costs jump for wired schools. *Architecture, 89*(8), 48.

Henderson, B. (1992). Canada experientially: Every trail has a story. In G. Hanna (Ed.), *Celebrating our tradition, charting our future: Proceedings of the international conference of the Association for Experiential Education.* Banff, AB. (ERIC Document Reproduction Service No. ED353120)

Henderson, J., & Hawthorne, R. (1995). *Transformative curriculum leadership*. Englewood Cliffs, N J: Prentice-Hall.

Henry, T. (2001, March 22). Open up schools, let sunshine in; creature comforts can aid learning. *USA Today,* p. D08.

Herman, J., Aschbacker, P., & Winters, L. (1992). *A practical guide to alternative assessment*. Alexandria, VA: ASCD Association for Supervision and Curriculum Development.

Hernandez, D. (1994). Children's changing access to resources: A historical perspective. *Social Policy Report for Society for Research in Child Development,* Vol. III(1), 1–24.

Hiebert, B., Magnusson, K., & Vesely, M. (1990, January). *The effects of "moving on..." on the career maturity of grade 8 and 11 students.* Paper presented to the Sixteenth National Consultation on Vocational Counselling, Ottawa, ON.

Hicks, E.C. (1986). Museums and schools as partners. *ERIC Digest*, ED278380.

Ho, Sui-Chu E., & Willms, J.D. (1996). The effects of parental involvement on eighth grade achievement. *Sociology of Education, 69*, 126–141.

Hoerr, T. (1992, October). How our school applied multiple intelligences theory. *Educational Leadership,* 67–72.

Holst, P. (Ed.). (1911). *Practical home and school methods.* Chicago: The Holst Publishing Company.

Holstein, B. (1976). Irreversible, stepwise sequence in the development of moral judgement: A longitudinal study of males and females. In R.R. McCown, M. Driscoll, P. Roop, D.H. Saklofske, V.L. Schwean, I.W. Kelly, et al., *Educational psychology.* (2nd Cdn. Ed.). Scarborough, ON: Allyn and Bacon.

Hopkins, D., & Wideen, M. (1984). *Alternative perspectives on school improvement*. Philadelphia, PA: The Fulmet Press.

Hourcade, J., & Bauwens, J. (2001). Cooperative teaching: The renewal of teachers. *The Clearing House, 74*(5), 242–247.

Howard, G. (1996). Probing more deeply into the theory of multiple intelligences. National Association of Secondary School Principals. *NASSP Bulletin, 80*(583), 1–5.

Huffington, A. (1988). *Picasso: Creator and destroyer*. New York: Simon & Schuster.

Human Resources Development Canada. (2000). *Youth in transition survey: Project overview* (Catalogue no. 81-588-XIE). Ottawa, ON: Author.

Hunter, J., & Hatton, N. (1998). Approaches to the writing of cases: Experiences with pre-service Master of Teaching students. *Asia-Pacific Journal of Teacher Education, 26*(3), 235–245.

Hutchins, R. (1963). *A conversation on education.* Santa Barbara, CA: The Fund for the Republic.

Integrated Technologies, Inc., "Cone of Learning" [from Edgar Dale, Audio-Visual Methods in Technology, Holt Rinehart and Winston]. Retrieved August 1, 2002, from **www.intech.com/education**

Irwin, R. (1993). Art as discipline and art through integration. *The Journal*, CSEA, Canadian Society for Education through Art, *24*(1), 24–27.

Jacobs, H. (1989). *Interdisciplinary curriculum: Design and implementation.* Alexandria, VA: Association for Supervision and Curriculum Development.

Jaworski, J. (1998). *Synchronicity: The inner path of leadership*. San Francisco, CA: Barrett-Keohler Publishers.

Jenkins, D. (1996). Canadian women administrators share similar concerns: Results of the Senior Women Academic Administrators of Canada 1996 conference. *Women in Higher Education* (July).

Jensen, E. (1988). *Teaching with the brain in mind*. Alexandria, VA: Association for Supervision and Curriculum Development.

Johnson, D.W., & Johnson, R. (1987). *Learning together and alone: Cooperative, competitive, and individualistic learning.* Englewood Cliffs, NJ: Prentice-Hall.

Johnson, D.W., & Johnson, R. (1990). Successful skills for successful group work. In R.S. Brandt (Ed.), *Cooperative learning and the collaborative school* (pp. 51–54). Alexandria, VA: Association for Supervision and Curriculum Development.

Jones, D. (Ed.). (1995). *The spirit of teaching excellence*. Calgary, AB: Detselig Enterprises, Ltd.

Kamat, L. (1999). Mixed responses to standardized testing. *The Gazette: The Daily Student Newspaper at the University of Western Ontario*. Retrieved March 2000, from **http://www.gazette.uwo.ca/1999/march19/newst.htm**

Karre, I. (1994). *Busy, noisy and powerfully effective: Cooperative learning tools in the college classroom.* Greeley, CO: University of Northern Colorado.

Kessler, R. (2000). *The soul of education*. Alexandria, VA: Association for Supervision and Curriculum Development.

Kintsch, W. (1988). The role of knowledge in discourse comprehension: A construction integration model. *Psychological Review, 95*, 163–182.

Kirkpatrick, J. (1983). *Psychological seduction: The failure of modern psychology*. Nashville, TN: Thomas Nelson Inc.

Kirkwood, T. (2001, Winter) Preparing teachers to teach from a global perspective. *The Delta Kappa Gamma Bulletin*, 5–11.

Kluth, P. (2000). Community-references learning and the inclusive classroom. *Remedial and Special Education, 21*(1), 19.

Kochtanek, T., & Hein, K. (2000). Creating and nurturing distributed asynchronous learning environments. *Online Information Review, 24*(4), 280–93.

Kohlberg, L. (1969). Stage and sequence: The cognitive developmental approach to socialization. In D.A. Goslin (Ed.), *Handbook of socialization: Theory and research* (pp. 347–480). Chicago: Rand McNally.

Kohn, A. (1991). Caring kids: The role of the schools. *Phi Delta Kappan, 72*(7), 496–506.

Kohn, A. (1993). Choices for children: Why and how to let students decide. *Phi Delta Kappan*, *75*(1), 10.

Kohn, A. (1994, December). The truth about self-esteem. *Phi Delta Kappan,* 272–284.

Kouzes, J.M., & Posner, B.Z. (1999). *Encouraging the heart: A leader's guide to rewarding and reorganizing others*. San Francisco, CA: Jossey-Bass Publishers.

Kovalik, S., & Olsen, K. (1998). How emotions run in our students and our classroom. *National Association of Secondary School Principals Bulletin, 82*(598), 29–37.

Laminach, L., & Lawig, S. (1994). Building a generative curriculum. *Primary Voices K–6, 2*(3), 8–18.

LaRoque, L., & Downie, R. (1993). Staff collaboration. *Educator's Notebook, 4*(4), 1.

Learning Cone. (2000). Jiva Institute. Retrieved August 15, 2002, from **www.jivaworld.com/keys/learning_cone.htm.**

Le Francois, G. (2000). *Psychology for teaching*. (10th ed.). Belmont, CA: Wadsworth.

Lefton, L.A. (1994). *Psychology.* (5th ed.). Boston, MA: Allyn and Bacon.

Leinhardt, G. (1992). What research on learning tells us about teaching. *Educational Leadership, 49*(7) 20–25.

Levine, Mel. (2002). *A mind at a time*. Toronto: Simon and Schuster.

Lloyd, L. (1999). Multi-age classes and high ability students. *Review of Educational Research, 69*(2), 187–212.

Lucksinger, L. (2000). Teachers: Can we get them and keep them? *The Delta Kappa Gamma Bulletin, 67*(1), 11–15.

Lupart, J. (1995). Exceptional learners and teaching for transfer. In A. McKeough, J. Lupart, & A. Marini (Eds.), *Teaching for transfer: Fostering generalization in learning* (pp. 215–228). Mahwah, NJ: Lawrence Erlbaum Associates.

Lytton, H. (1990). Child and parent effects in boys' conduct disorder: A reinterpretation. *Developmental Psychology, 26*, 683–697.

Manafo, M. (2000, December). Reflections on field experience. *Phi Delta Kappan*, 307–309.

Matthews, W., & Kay, S. (2001). Rediscovering reality: Considering what works in the classroom. *School Psychology Quarterly, 16*(1), 113.

Margulies, N. (1995). *Learning & teaching mind mapping*. Tucson, AZ: Zepher Press.

Marini A., & Genereux, R. (1995). The challenge of teaching for transfer. In A. McKeough, J. Lupart, & A. Marini (Eds.), *Teaching for transfer: Fostering generalizations in learning* (pp. 1–17). Mahwah, NJ: Lawrence Erlbaum Associates.

Marsh, H.W., & Shavelson, R. (1985). Self-concept: Its multifaceted, hierarchical structure. *Educational Psychologist, 20*, 107–123.

Maslow, A. (1962). *Toward the psychology of being*. Princeton, NJ: Van Nostrand.

Maslow, A. (1970). *Motivation and personality*, 2nd ed. New York: Harper and Row.

Merkel, C. (1999). Folkloristics of educational spaces: Material lore in classroom with and without walls. *Library Trends, 47*(3), 417–438.

McCown, R., Driscoll, M., Schwean, V., Kelly, J., & Haines, L. (1999). *Educational psychology.* (2nd Cdn. ed.). Scarborough, ON: Allyn and Bacon.

McKenna, M., & Willms, J. (1998). The challenge facing parent councils in Canada. *Childhood Education, 74*(6), 378–383.

McMorrow, E. (2000). Good design, better scores. *Facilities Design and Management, 19*(9), 9.

McNeil, L.M. (1988). *Contradictions of control: School structure and school knowledge.* New York: Routledge, Chapman, and Hall.

Miller, J. (2000). *Education and the soul: Toward a spiritual curriculum.* Albany, NY: State University of New York Press.

Moffett, J. (1994). *The universal schoolhouse: Spiritual awakening through education*. San Francisco: Jossey-Bass.

Montagu, A. (1974). *Man's most dangerous myth: The fallacy of race*. (5th ed.). New York: Oxford University Press.

Mountcastle, V. (1998). Brain science at the century's ebb. *Daedolus, 127*(2), 1–36.

Mullins, B. (2000). The cultural repertoire of adult learning. *Adult Learning,* Vol. II (1), 3–5.

Myers, K. (1995). Waiting for wisdom. *Tabletalk, 19*(3), 58–60.

Naested, I. (1993). Educational innovations at Lester B. Pearson High School in Calgary, Alberta, Canada. Unpublished doctoral dissertation, Brigham Young University, Provo, UT.

Naested, I. (1998). *Art in the classroom: An integrated approach to teaching art in Canadian middle schools*. Toronto: Harcourt Brace.

Naested, I. (2000). *Lesson plans*. Mount Royal College student handout document.

National Post Survey. (2001, September). Second Quarterly Report, pp. 2–10.

National School Safety and Security Services. (2002). School safety and school security assessment. Retrieved July 16, 2002, from **http://www.schoolsecurity.org/consultants/security-assessments.html**

Newman, J.M. (1987, November). Learning to teach by uncovering our assumptions. *Language Arts, 67*(7), 727–737.

Nieto, S. (1992). *Affirming diversity: The sociopolitical context of multicultural education*. White Plains, NY: Longman.

Nicholls, J., & Hazzard, S.P. (1993). *Education as adventure: Lessons from the second grade*. New York: Teachers College Press.

Nikoforuk, A. (2002, March). Campus radical. *National Post*, Business supplement, 67–71.

Nist, S., Simpson, M., Olejnik, S., & Kealey, D. (1991). The relation between self-selected processes and test performance. *American Journal Research Journal, 28*, 849–874.

Noddings, N. (1988). *Caring: A feminine approach to ethics and moral education*. Berkeley, CA: University of California Press.

Noll, J. (Ed.). (1999). *Taking sides: Clashing views on controversial issues*. (10th ed.). Guilford, CT: McGraw-Hill.

Novak, M. (1975). "Story" and experience. In J.B. Wiggins (Ed.), *Religion as story* (pp. 175–200). Lanham, MD: University Press of America.

Nova Scotia Teachers Union. (2002, April). Tamarac students' anti-bullying program. *The Teacher,* 3.

Ontario English Catholic Teachers Association (OECTA). (2002, March). Weighing in: A discussion paper on provincial assessment policy. Retrieved from **www.oecta.on.ca**

O'Donnell, A. (1994, Winter). Facilitating scripted cooperation through the use of knowledge maps. *Cooperative Learning and College Teaching, 4*(2), 9–10.

Offord, D., Boyle, M., & Racine, J. (1989). *Ontario child health study: Children at risk*. Ottawa, ON: Queen's Printer.

Oliver, A. (1997). Plugging into multiple intelligences. *The Educational Digest, 62*(6), 61–64.

Oloroso, H. (1995). A work-based curriculum for cooperative education students. *Journal of Cooperative Education, 30*(2), 39–45.

Ontario College of Teachers. (2002). Ontario College of Teachers Act, 1996: Ontario Regulations 437197 Professional Misconduct. Retrieved June 22, 2002, from **http://www.oct.ca/english.html**

Owen, T. (2001, January). Learning with technology. *English Journal, 90*(3), 122–125.

Palloff, R., & Pratt, K. (1999). *Building learning communities in cyberspace: Effective strategies for the online classroom.* San Francisco, CA: Jossey-Bass Publishers.

Palmer, P. (1997, Nov/Dec.). The heart of a teacher. *Change, 29*(6), 14–21.

Palmer, P. (1998). *The courage to teach: Exploring the inner landscape of a teacher's life*. San Francisco, CA: Jossey-Bass Publishers.

Parkay, F., Hardcastle-Stanford, B., & Gougeon, T. (1996). *Becoming a teacher*. (Cdn. ed.). Scarborough, ON: Allyn and Bacon.

Parten, M. (1932). Social participation among preschool children. *Journal of Abnormal and Social Psychology, 27*, 243–269.

Paulson, F., Paulson, P, & Meyer, C. (1991, February). What makes a portfolio a portfolio? *Educational Leadership,* 60–64.

Pearce, K. (1999, Spring). Humor is leaven to the bread of teaching. *The Delta Kappa Gamma Bulletin, 65*(3), 46–50.

Percy, I. (1997). *Going deep: Exploring spirituality in life and leadership*. Toronto, ON: Macmillan Canada.

Perkins, D. (1999). The many faces of constructivism. *Educational Leadership, 57*(3), 6–11.

Peters, R. (1977). The place of Kohlberg's theory in moral education. In R.R. McCowan, M. Driscoll, P. Roop, D.H. Saklofske, V.L. Schwean, I.W. Kelly, et al., *Educational psychology.* (2nd Cdn. ed.). Scarborough, ON: Allyn and Bacon.

Phillips, C.E. (1957). *The development of education in Canada*. Toronto: WJ Gage and Company.

Phillips, D.C. (1995). The good, the bad and the ugly: The many faces of constructivism. *Educational Researcher, 24*(7), 5–12.

Piaget, J. (1963). *Origins of intelligence in children*. New York: Norton.

Piaget, J. (1983). Piaget's theory. In W. Kessen & P. Mussen (Eds.), *Handbook of child psychology,* Vol. 1: *History, theory and methods* (pp. 10–128). New York: John Wiley & Sons.

Pipher, M. (1994). *Reviving Ophelia*. New York: Grosset/Putnam.

Pollack, W. (1998). *Real boys: Rescuing our sons from the myths of boyhood.* New York: Henry Holt and Company.

Power, F., Higgins, A., & Kohlberg, L. (1989). *Lawrence Kohlberg's approach to moral education.* New York: Columbia University Press.

Prawat, R.S. (1992). Teachers' beliefs about teaching and learning: A constructivist perspective. *American Journal of Education, 100,* 354–395.

Preskill, S., & Jacobvitz, R. (2001). *Stories of teaching: A foundation for educational renewal.* Upper Saddle River, NJ: Prentice Hall.

Pressley, M. (1995). Comments on interpretation of results. *Reading Research Quarterly, 27,* p. 108.

Pressley, M., Borkowski, J.G., & Schneider, W. (1989). Good information processing: What it is and what education can do to promote it. *International Journal of Educational Research, 13,* 857–867.

Pressley, M., El-Dinary, P.B., & Brown, R. (1994). Transactional instruction of reading comprehension strategies. In J. Mangieri & C. Collins (Eds.), *Creating powerful thinking in teachers and students: Diverse perspectives* (pp. 112–139). Fort Worth, TX: Harcourt Brace.

Pressley, M., & Levin, J.R. (1977). Developmental differences in subjects' associative learning strategies and performance: Assessing a hypothesis. *Journal of Experimental Child Psychology, 24,* 53–59.

Pressley, M., & McCormick, C. (1995). *Advanced educational psychology for educators, researchers and policy makers.* New York: HarperCollins.

Rabinowitz, M., Freeman, K., & Cohen, S. (1992). Use and maintenance of strategies: The influence of accessibility on knowledge. *Journal of Educational Psychology, 84,* 211–218.

Reio, T.G. Jr., & Sanders-Reio, J.T. (2000). Combating workplace ageism. *Adult Learning, 11*(1), 10–13.

Renzulli, J. (1987). The three-ring conception of giftedness: a developmental model for creative productivity. In R. Sternberg and J. Davidson (Eds.), *Conceptions of giftedness* (pp. 53–92). New York: Cambridge University Press.

Renzulli, J. (1988). The multiple menu model for developing differentiated curriculum for the gifted and talented. *Gifted Child Quarterly, 32*(3), 298–309.

Rettig, P.R., & Khodavandi, M. (1998). Recruiting minority teachers: The UTOP program. *Phi Delta Kappa Fastbacks, 436,* 7–46.

Richardson, M., & Simmons, D. (1996, January). Recommended competencies for outdoor educators. *ERIC Digest,* 1–4.

Riley, P., & Gallo L. (2000). Electronic learning environments: Design considerations. *T.H.E. Journal, 27*(6), 50–54.

Rivkin, M. (2000). Outdoor experiences for young children. *ERIC Digest,* ED448013, 1–4.

Rogers, R., & Threatt, D. (2000). Peer assistance review: Lessons from Mt. Diablo. *Thrust for Educational Leadership, 29*(3), 14–16.

Rollans, M. (1992). *A handbook for teaching archaeology in Saskatchewan schools.* Saskatoon, SK: Western Heritage Services.

Rose, L., Gallup, A., & Elan, S. (1997, September). The 29th annual Phi Delta Gallup poll and other public attitudes toward public schools. *Phi Delta Kappan,* 41–56.

Rothstein, R. (1998). Bilingual education: The controversy. *Phi Delta Kappan, 79*(6), 462–466.

Rud, A., & Beck A. (2000). Kids and critters in class together. *Phi Delta Kappan, 82*(4), 313–315.

Rutter, M., Maughtan, B., Mortimore, P., & Ouston, J. (1979). *Fifteen thousand hours: Secondary schools and their effects on children.* London: Open Books Publishing Limited.

Samples, B. (1992, October). Using learning modalities to celebrate intelligence. *Educational Leadership*, 62–66.

Sarason, S. (1990). *The predictable failure of educational reform*. San Francisco: Jossey-Bass Publishers.

Sartre, J.P. (1972). Existentialism. In J. Rich (Ed.), *Readings in the philosophy of education*. Belmont, CA: Wadsworth.

Schamer, L., & Jackson, M. (1996). Coping with stress: Common sense about teacher burnout. *Education Canada, 36*(2), 28–31, 49.

Schneider, T., Walker, H., & Sprague, J. (2000). Applying the principles of crime prevention through environmental design. *Safe school design: A handbook for educational leaders:* Eugene, OR: ERIC Clearinghouse on Educational Management.

Schunk, D.H. (1991). Self-efficacy and academic motivation. *Educational Psychologist*, *26*, 207–232.

Schwab, J. (1973). The practical translation into curriculum. *School Review, 81*(4), 501–522.

Senge, P. (1990). *The fifth discipline: The art and practice of the learning organization*. New York: Doubleday.

Senge, P., Kleiner, A., Roberts, C., Ross, R., Roth, G., & Smith, B. (1999). *The dance of change: The challenges to sustaining momentum in learning organizations*. New York: Doubleday/Currency.

Secretan, L. (1997). *Reclaiming higher ground: Creating organizations that inspire the soul.* Toronto: Macmillan Publishing.

Sergiovanni, T. (1992). *Moral leadership: Getting to the heart of school improvement*. San Francisco, CA: Jossey-Bass.

Shack, S. (1973). *Women in Canadian education: The two-thirds minority*. Toronto: University of Toronto Faculty of Education, Guidance Centre.

Sharp, L. (1943). Outside the classroom. *The Educational Forum, 7*(4), 361–368.

Sheffield, E. (1970). The post-war surge in post-secondary education: 1945–1969. In L. Audet, R. Stamp, & J. Wilson (Eds.), *Canadian education: A history*. Scarborough, ON: Prentice Hall.

Shonkoff, J. (1984). The biological substrate and physical health in middle childhood. In W. Collins (Ed.), *Development during middle childhood: The years from six to twelve.* Washington, DC: National Academy Press.

Short, K., & Burke, C. (1996). Examining our beliefs and practices through inquiry. *Language Arts, 73*(2), 97–103.

Silver, H., Strong, R., & Perini, M. (2000). *So each may learn: Integrating learning styles and multiple intelligence*. Alexandria, VA: Association for Supervision and Curriculum Development.

Simmer, M. (2000). A joint position statement by the Canadian Psychological Association and the Canadian Association of School Psychologists on the Canadian press coverage of the province-wide achievement test results. Canadian Psychological Association. Retrieved from **http://www.cpa.ca/documents/joint_position.html**

Sizer, T. (1984). *Horace's compromise: The dilemma of the American high school*. Boston, MA: Houghton Mifflin.

Skinner, B. (1950). Are theories of learning necessary? *Psychological Review*, *57*, 193–216.

Slavin, R.E. (1987). Cooperative learning and the cooperative school. *Educational Leadership*, *45*, 7–13.

Smith, J. (1989). Don't go out of your way to integrate the arts. *Canadian Music Educator*, *30*(4), 423–45.

Smith J., & Raiford, R. (2000). Everything you ever wanted to know about lighting ... but were too afraid to ask. *Buildings, 94*(4), 79–93.

Smith, L., & Johnson, H. (1993). Control in the classroom: Listening to adolescent voices. *Language Arts*, *70*(1), 18–30.

Solomon, R. (1997). Race, role modeling and representation in teacher education and teaching. *Canadian Journal of Education, 22*(4), 395–410.

Soto, G., Muller E., Hunt, P., & Goetz, L. (2001). Critical issues in the inclusion of students who use augmentative and alternative communication: An education team perspective. *Augmentative and Alternative Communication, 17*(2), 62.

Sparkes, A., & Dickensen, B. (1987). Children's activity patterns: Treating the problem and not the symptom. *Health and Physical Education Project Newsletter, 9*, 1–3.

Springer, S. (1989, Spring). Educating the two sides of the brain: Separating fact from speculation. *American Educator*, 32–37.

Stamp, R. (1982). *The schools of Ontario 1976–1996*. Toronto: University of Toronto Press.

Statistics Canada. (1999). *Annual Demographic Statistics*, Cat. no. 71-005-XPB. Ottawa, ON: Statistics Canada.

Sternberg, L., Lamborn, S., Dornhbush, S., & Darling, N. (1992). The impact of parenting practices on adolescent achievement: Authoritative parenting, school involvement and encouragement of success. *Child Development*, p. 630.

Sternberg, R. (1989). *The triarchic mind: A new theory of human intelligence*. New York: Penguin Books.

Sternberg, R. (1991). Giftedness according to the triarchic theory of human intelligence. In N. Colangelo and G. Davis (Eds.), *Handbook of gifted education*. Needham Heights, MA: Allyn and Bacon.

Sternberg, R. (1995). *In search of the human mind*. Fort Worth, TX: Harcourt Brace.

Sternberg, R., & Williams W. (2002). *Educational psychology*. Boston, MA: Allyn and Bacon.

Stroick, S., & Jenson, J. (1999). *What is the best policy mix for young children?* CPRN Study No. F/09. Canadian Policy Research Networks, Inc. Ottawa, ON: Renouf Publishing.

Stuart, C., & Thurlow, D. (2000). Making it their own: Preservice teachers' experiences, beliefs and classroom practices. *Journal of Teacher Education, 51*(2), 113–121.

Sylwester, R. (1998, November). Art for the brain's sake. *Educational Leadership*, 31–33.

Tarr, P. (2001). Aesthetic codes in early childhood classrooms: What art educators can learn from Reggio Emilia. *Art Education, 54*(3), 33–39.

Taylor, F. (1911). *The principles of scientific management*. New York: W.W. Norton and Co.

Tice, T. (1999). Service learning. *The Education Digest, 64*(6), 38–39.

Tierno, M. (1996, Winter). Teaching as modeling: The impact of teacher behaviors upon student character formation. *The Educational Forum, 60*, 174–179.

Tipper, J., & Avard, D. (1999). *Building better outcomes for Canada's children.* Discussion paper No. F106. Ottawa, ON: Canadian Policy Research Networks.

Titley, E. (1990). *Canadian education: Historical themes and contemporary issues.* Calgary, AB: Detselig Enterprises.

Thelan, E., Ulrich, P., & Jensen, J. (1989). The developmental origins of locomotion. In M. Wollacott & A. Shumway-Cook (Eds.), *Development of posture and gait across the lifespan.* Columbia, SC: University of South Carolina Press.

Thiessen, D., Boscia, N., & Goodson, I. (1996). *Making a difference about differences: The lives and careers of racial minority immigrant teachers.* Toronto: Remitell/Garamond Press.

Thomas, B.R. (1990), in J. Goodlad, R. Soder, & K.A. Sirotnik (Eds.), *The school as a moral learning community: The moral dimensions of teaching*. San Francisco, CA: Jossey-Bass Publishers.

Thousand, J., & Willa, R. (1991, May). A futuristic view of the REI: A response to Jenkins, Poies, and Jewell. *Exceptional Children*, 556–560.

Travers, A., & Lalonde, D. (2000). *What's next? A job search guide for teachers.* (7th ed.). Kingston, ON: Lakeside Publishing.

Treffinger, D. (1991). Future goals and directions. In N. Colangelo & G. Davis (Eds.),

Handbook of gifted education. Needham Heights, MA: Allyn and Bacon.

Treffinger, D., & Sortore, M. (1992). *Programming for giftedness series.* Volumes 1–111. Sarasota, FL: Center for Creative Learning.

Trungpa, C. (1988). *Shambhala: The sacred path of the warrior*. Boston: Shambhala.

Tulving, E. (1983). *Elements of episodic memory.* Oxford, UK: Oxford University Press.

Trump, J. (1985). Team teaching. In T. Husen & T. Postethwaite (Eds.), *The international encyclopedia of education research and studies*, V8, T-2 (pp. 5158–5159). Oxford: Pergamon Press.

University of Calgary. (n.d.). *EDTS student handbook*. Calgary, AB: Author.

U.S. Schools continue to ban Halloween parties. (2000, October 26). *National Post*, p. SE2.

Vars, G. (1991, October). Integrated curriculum in historical perspective. *Education Leadership,* 14–15.

Viadero, D. (2001). Learning gap linked to LEP instruction. *Education Week*, *20*(32), 8.

Vygotsky, L.S. (1987). *Thinking and speech*. (N. Minick, Ed. & Trans.). New York: Plenum.

Waldron, P. (1996). Leadership and management: Contrasting dispositions. *The Canadian School Executive, 16*(3), 3–5.

Waldron, P., Collie, T., & Davies, C.M. (1999). *Telling stories about school: An invitation*. Upper Saddle River, NJ: Merrill/Prentice Hall.

Walker, L.J., DeVries, B., & Trevethan, S.D. (1987). Moral stages and moral orientations in real life and hypothetical dilemmas. *Child Development*, *58*, 842–858.

Wallerstein, J.S. (1991). The long-term effects of divorce on children: A review. *Journal of the American Academy of Child and Adolescent Psychiatry*, *30*, 349–360.

Wallis, J. (1981). *The call to conversion: Recovering the gospel for these times*. San Francisco: Harper & Row.

Watson, J. (1925). *Behaviorism*. (2nd ed.). New York: People's Institute.

Weiner, B. (1990). History of motivational research in education. *Journal of Education in Psychology*, *82*, 612–622.

Weiss, R. (2000). Memory and learning. *Training and Development, 54*(10), 46–50.

Western Canadian Protocol for Collaboration in Basic Education. *The common curriculum framework for K–12 mathematics*. Edmonton, AB: Alberta Education.

Whitehead, A.N. (1929). *The aims of education, and other essays*. New York: Macmillan.

Wiggins, G. (1987, Winter). Creating a thought-provoking curriculum. *American Educator*, 68–75.

Willms, J. (1999). *Effective strategies for dropout prevention of at-risk youth.* Gaitherberg, MD: Aspen Publishers, Inc.

Wilson, J. (1983, May). Reflections: A letter from Oxford. *Harvard Educational Review*, *53*(2), 188–193.

Winzer, M. (1995). *Educational psychology in the Canadian classroom.* (2nd ed.). Scarborough, ON: Allyn and Bacon Canada.

Woelders, A., & Moes, E. (2002). Testing undermines education in Korea. *Teacher: Newsmagazine for the B.C. Teachers Federation*, *14*(4), 20.

Woodhouse, J., & Knapp, C. (2000, December). Place-based curriculum and instruction: Outdoor and environmental education approaches. *ERIC Digest*, ED448012, 1–4.

Woolf, H. (Ed.). (1979). *Webster's new collegiate dictionary*. Toronto, ON: Thomas Allen and Sons, Ltd.

Woolfolk, A. (1998). *Educational psychology.* (7th ed.). Boston: Allyn and Bacon.

Woolfolk, A., Winne, P., & Perry, N. (1998). *Educational psychology*. Scarborough, ON: Allyn and Bacon Canada.

Yost, D., Sentner, S., & Forlenza-Bailey, A. (2000). An examination of the construct of critical reflection: Implications for teacher education programming in the 21st century. *Journal of Teacher Education*, *51*(1), 39–49.

Young, J., & Levin, B. (1998). *Understanding Canadian schools: An introduction to educational administration*, 2nd ed. Toronto: Harcourt Brace.

Zernike, K. (2001, August 5). The feng shui of schools. *New York Times,* N.Y. Late Edition (East Coast), p. 4A20.

Zimbardo, P., & Gerrig, R. (1996). *Psychology and life*. New York: HarperCollins College Publishers.

Zimmerman, B.J. (1990). Self-regulating academic learning and achievement: The emergence of a social-cognitive perspective. *Educational Psychology Review, 2,* 173–201.

Index